PEARSON   ALWAYS LEARNING

Kay L. Stewart • Marian Allen
Shelley Galliah

Forms of Writing
A Rhetoric and Handbook

Custom Edition for Athabasca University

Taken from:
Forms of Writing: A Rhetoric and Handbook, Sixth Edition
by Kay L. Stewart, Marian Allen,
and Shelley Galliah

Cover Art: Courtesy of PhotoDisc/Getty Images.

Taken from:

Forms of Writing: A Rhetoric and Handbook, Sixth Edition
by Kay L. Stewart, Marian Allen, and Shelley Galliah
Copyright © 2012, 2009, 2005, 2000 by Pearson Canada, Inc.
Published by Prentice Hall
Toronto, Ontario

This special edition published in cooperation with Pearson Learning Solutions.

Pearson Learning Solutions, 501 Boylston Street, Suite 900, Boston, MA 02116
A Pearson Education Company
www.pearsoned.com

Printed in Canada

19 XXXX 16 15

000200010270785403

MHB

ISBN 10: 1-256-35129-6
ISBN 13: 978-1-256-35129-0

CONTENTS

Preface to the Sixth Edition

The authors of *Forms of Writing* believe that good writing results when you consider your purpose, your audience, your subject, and your chosen form. Thus, these three main writing purposes are explored: sharing personal experience, explaining, and persuading. To demonstrate that these purposes can be used alone or combined with others, we explore them in both shorter and longer compositions. *Forms of Writing*, which covers paragraphs, personal writing, expository essays, summaries, reviews, interviews, and APA- and MLA-style research papers, is especially suitable for communication and introductory writing courses.

The modules on the writing process, ***Identifying Your Purpose and Audience*** and ***Gathering Material***, explain the steps in completing a writing assignment, from defining your purpose and audience to revising and proofreading. The modules on writing paragraphs and essays, ***Writing Better Paragraphs; The Key to Writing Essays; Sharing Personal Experience; Explaining One Subject; Explaining Two Subjects; Writing Summaries and Essays about Literature; Writing to Persuade;*** and ***Composing Research Papers*** discuss paragraph structure before exploring the general guidelines for writing essays, such as introductions, conclusions, essay body, and thesis statements. Then, these modules offer guidelines for building both paragraphs and longer compositions, which share personal experience, explain, and persuade. Two modules are dedicated to specific writing assignments: ***Writing Summaries and Essays about Literature,*** and ***Composing Research Papers***. The two modules on ***Revising Your Essay*** highlight methods for revising the structure, language, and style of your essay. The five modules on ***Proofreading*** define accepted practices in grammar, punctuation, and mechanics. The Appendix module, ***Essay and Citation Format***, covers the basics of APA and MLA format, such as guidelines for formatting, using quotations, and documenting sources. *Finally, the* ***Glossary of Grammatical Terms*** is a succinct list of key grammatical terms and their definitions.

New in the Sixth Edition:

- *Forms of Writing*, Sixth Edition, is offered in seventeen *self-contained modules*; that is, each module can be used alone or combined with others and/or selections from the *Canadian Mercury Writer* (http://www.pearsoncustom.com/custom-library/) to create an effective, personalized textbook that is tailored to your teaching strategies and your course's specific needs. Also, choose from over 1000 readings in the Custom Library to tailor the resource to your specific needs. (The *Canadian Mercury Writer* is available through the Pearson Custom

Library. Please see your Pearson Sales Representative for more information.)

- Answers for the Proofreading Exercises appear at the end of the relevant module.

- The content on modes of development is more substantial, demonstrating how each mode can sustain a paragraph or an essay, or be combined with others.

- Eighty percent of the student examples have been replaced. Accompanying fresh paragraph examples are these new essays: description, classification, comparison/contrast, and research (both APA and MLA styles).

- **Writing to Persuade** has been expanded to include a published opinion piece by Lianne George and an accompanying student position paper.

- The module **Composing Research Papers** has been extensively revised to include information on how students *actually* gather information. It contains advice on conducting online research, evaluating websites, and using (*and not using*) Wikipedia.

- The information in the Appendix module on both APA and MLA style has been updated.

Good writing!

Shelley Galliah

Identifying Your Purpose and Audience

For most writing tasks, you know the subject you are writing about, such as recycling or workplace injuries. You may also know the form your writing should take—a persuasive essay on recycling or a report on injuries. However, you may be less aware of the specific kinds of writing possible within these forms and the strategies for using them effectively.

Every piece of writing, whatever its subject and form, is shaped by its purpose and audience. The first question to ask concerns your purpose: What do I want this piece of writing to do? The second is about your audience: Who will read it?

1. DEFINING YOUR PURPOSE

This chapter will focus on three broad writing purposes: to share ideas and experiences, to explain, and to persuade. The first purpose leads to personal writing, the second to expository writing, and the third to persuasive writing. Your understanding of your purpose and audience will influence your choice of form and methods of development, your relationship to your readers, and your language and style.

In some writing situations, you may be free to choose your own purpose. If you wanted to write an article on grizzly bears for a general interest magazine, for instance, you could choose to share your own adventures in grizzly country, explain the grizzly's habits, or argue for better protection for this endangered species.

Writing to Share Personal Experience

Personal writing gives you the chance to explore what you think and how you feel about ideas and experiences and to share these discoveries with others; you may also write about your reactions to and perceptions of the world. However, personal writing does not always have to be the serious business of revealing your innermost thoughts and feelings. You, the writer, are on centre stage, and you may therefore choose to present yourself as comic or tragic, satiric or romantic, serious or slightly mad. In personal writing, the emphasis is on the writer's experience rather than the subject.

Sample Personal Writing—Purpose: To Share Personal Experience

I was thirteen at the time, in a new school, and desperate to make friends. For the first few weeks, everyone ignored me. Not that all my classmates were friends with each other. At lunch hour and after school, they divided into groups and alternately ignored and insulted each other. I was afraid that if I didn't make friends soon, they would stop ignoring and start insulting me. So one day, I followed a gang of five or six into the mall at lunch. As they straggled through The Bay, I kept several feet behind, stopping every now and then to gaze intently at leather brief-cases or umbrellas so they wouldn't think I was being pushy. When they clustered around the jewellery counter, I ducked down the next row. And there in front of me were bags and bags of candy, ready for Hallowe'en. Without thinking, I grabbed one and stuffed it under my jacket.

In this excerpt, the writer recounts a brief narrative that contextualizes the events, inviting us into the isolation, fear, and desire to belong that led to her shoplifting. We may disapprove of the theft, but we are drawn into the "I" and her subjective experience.

Writing to Explain

Your writing is expository whenever your main purpose is to provide information, to explain how something works or how something is done, or to explain the meaning of concepts, historical events, works of art, literary texts, etc. As the following example suggests, in expository writing, your emphasis is on your subject, rather than on your audience or on you. You and your readers have the same perspective—you are both peering through a microscope and trying to see the specimen on the glass slide.

Sample Expository Writing
Purpose: To Explain Behaviour

The most basic question about shoplifting is this one: Why do people steal? According to a security guard for Sears, the reason is not need: "In all the time I've worked here, and of all the arrests I've made, and I've made over 400 arrests, not once, not once was it out of need." Most shoplifters who are caught have more than enough money with them to pay for the item; many have credit cards as well. So why do they steal? According to Bill Cheung at The Bay, the peak seasons for shoplifting are September and January–February, when new school terms begin. Presumably, at the beginning of the term, students look at the clothes or toys their peers have and want them. Children and adolescents, it seems, shoplift to fit in.

—Amanda Thompson

This paragraph illustrates the principal features of much expository writing. The writer explains why some people shoplift without stating her opinion about the behaviour. She presents her information and analysis objectively, avoiding slanted language; she refers to shoplifters as *people* and *students*, not as *thieves* and *juvenile delinquents*. Thus, she keeps the focus on her subject, not on her opinions or on her own personality.

Writing to Persuade

There are many questions central to persuasive writing: What is good (for one person, a group, a nation, humanity, or the planet)? What is right? What should be done? What should be not done? In persuasive writing, you want to convince others to share your attitudes and beliefs, and, perhaps, to act on those beliefs. To accomplish your goal, you have to consider how to appeal to your audience. In the interplay among writer, subject, and audience, the emphasis in persuasive writing shifts toward the audience.

Sample Persuasive Writing
Purpose: To Change Opinion or Behaviour

Contrary to the popular view, most shoplifters do not steal because they are poor. A longtime security guard for Sears, who has arrested more than 400 shoplifters, points out that "not once" had the person stolen out of need. In fact, he stated that shoplifters usually have more than enough money with them to pay for the stolen goods, and they often have credit cards as well. They may tell themselves that the stores are so rich they will not miss this little eraser/tube of lipstick/makeup case/MP3 player/jacket. But it is not the stores that pay; honest customers pay through higher prices. Therefore, there is no reason to be lenient with shoplifters. Because they are as guilty of theft as the person who steals a wallet from a locker room or a CD player from a car, they should be similarly penalized. If we turn a blind eye to shoplifting, we are not only condoning a crime, but also sentencing ourselves and other consumers to pay the penalty.

Here the writer's purpose is not to explain some possible reasons for shoplifting, but to persuade readers to change their attitude, and possibly their behaviour, toward shoplifters. In contrast to the neutral language of the expository paragraph, the language here is emotionally charged: *honest, guilty, lenient, condoning, sentencing, penalized.* The writer also presents a cause-effect relationship that includes the readers: condoning shoplifting affects you. The language and approach focus attention on the attitude and action that the writer wants readers to adopt. Perhaps the reader who is persuaded by this argument might report a shoplifter the next time he or she sees one.

2. DEFINING YOUR AUDIENCE

In many school and work situations, however, your purpose will be given or implied. An assignment requiring that you write a persuasive essay on the positive effects of capital punishment defines your purpose. A manager who asks you to write a report on the success of the last marketing campaign assumes that you will explain such things as sales and profit, not air your frustrations about the workplace.

Thus, defining your purpose is the first step in writing; the second is defining your audience. Just as your style of speaking should change as you move from Facebook to the classroom, your style of writing should change with your audience. You will decide, for instance, how much background information to give and whether to use a formal or an informal style. To communicate your message and purpose effectively, you need to tailor both to the needs and expectations of your audience.

But what is an audience? The audience is the person or people who are reading your piece of writing.

In your writing and speaking, you probably address a number of audiences every day—those of your friends, your family, and your instructor. Even these categories can be further divided. If you were writing a letter to your six-year-old brother, you would address simpler topics and use uncomplicated language; if you were writing a letter to your mother, you would use higher language, discuss more difficult subject matter. Your purposes might also be different. Whereas you might be writing to *explain* college life to your fascinated younger brother—where and when you go to class, where and what you eat, and so on—you might be writing *to communicate personal experience* to your mother, such as your difficulties with the new college environment, your feelings of loneliness, and so on.

The writers most concerned about audience are those in the advertising business, who devote much time to analyzing their target audience—those who will be watching or reading the ad—in order to successfully persuade this audience to purchase this product or service.

Although you don't need to research your audience so intently, you should still consider it. Your audience might be your instructor, classmates, potential employer, or newspaper reader. Furthermore, your audience might be neutral, friendly, or hostile.

The two main audiences you will have are academic audiences and non-academic audiences. Your academic audience will be your instructors, who are grading your papers not according to their own tastes, but according to the standards and formats of writing in their professions and disciplines. For instance, a sociology instructor might want you to write in the first person, including your personal experiences and how they relate to your field of study, whereas a philosophy instructor might want you to adopt an objective tone, presenting a clear argument. An English instructor might want your thesis and main argument at the end of your introduction; however, your biology instructor might want a long summation of research before you state your main point. Although the advice offered here is useful across disciplines, pay attention to the expectations of your instructor, who represents a specific academic discipline and audience.

To determine the needs of your specific academic audience, study the assignment's instructions and the instructor's expectations. Is the instructor looking for a carefully balanced deductive argument? Is the writer allowed to include personal experience? How formal must the writing be? To determine the demands of your academic audience, ask questions, study the models and student examples, and read around in that discipline.

Non-Academic Audiences

Technically, non-academic audiences are the readers you imagine communicating to; they do not grade you. However, your instructor might ask you to imagine writing a paper for such an audience to test your adaptation of tone, style, and purpose. Your assignment would be graded according to how it met the needs of this specific audience. Here are some examples of assignments for a non-academic audience.

Write a letter to the editor stating your opinion about the "problem of graffiti" in cities. Here, your purpose is to persuade newspaper readers of your opinion of graffiti. To accommodate the varied education of your audience, you need to state your points using unpretentious language. To accommodate the form and purpose—a short persuasive letter—you need to state your opinion and your reasons immediately.

Write a humorous expository essay for Chatelaine. Here you are being asked to explain a subject to a presumed target audience of women. If you are unfamiliar with this magazine, you may want to pick up a copy in order to analyze its content, article length, and level of language. What subject do you choose? Do you write from a male or female standpoint? How would you go about making this article funny?

Write a review of a video game for Wired. To determine the audience for *Wired,* you will have to study the magazine to figure out the gender, level of education, interests, and so on of its readers; you might also read one of its reviews, noting the length and language.

Whatever audience you are writing for, whether it be academic or non-academic, there are general questions you can ask to determine your audience and construct a reader profile.

Making Reader Profiles

You can develop a clearer sense of your audience by asking these questions:

1. **Who** will read this piece? A specific person, such as a supervisor? A group of people with similar interests, such as *Avatar* fans? A group of people of varying ages and backgrounds, such as newspaper readers?

2. **Why** are they reading this piece? Are they looking for explanations? Are they looking for problems, solutions? Is my reader going to make a decision based on this piece? Or does my reader want another side or more information?

3. What **attitude** will my reader(s) probably bring to this piece of writing? Interest and enthusiasm? Hostility and defensiveness? Critical detachment?

4. How much **knowledge** will my reader(s) already have about my subject? What information do I need to provide? How much background information do I need to give? What terms, if any, do I need to define? What level of language or specialized terminology is appropriate to use? (You need to determine what your readers know so you can save your words to present new points and arguments.)

5. What **expectations** will my reader(s) have about the way this piece is written? Is there a specific format I should follow? (If unsure, look for *examples* of a similar piece in other publications, textbooks, or from your instructor.)

Answering these questions will give you a **reader profile**, a general sense of your audience's needs and expectations. Remembering this reader profile as you write or revise will help you communicate more effectively. If you consider what a potential employer looks for in a letter of application, for example, you can tailor your letter to match those expectations. Similarly, you can tailor any piece of writing to your audience.

Exercise 1

Choose two of the following subjects:

- destination weddings
- access to postsecondary education
- belly dancing
- women in reality TV
- geocaching
- extreme sports
- *The Lord of the Rings* (the books or the movies)

Using the example below as a guide, explain in a few words how each subject could be the basis for three pieces of writing with different purposes: one expository, one persuasive, and one personal.

Example: Article on the subject of bicycles.

Expository: to explain how to choose a bike *or* to compare/contrast mountain and road bikes
Persuasive: to persuade newspaper readers to wear helmets
Personal: to share your experience cycling from Jasper to Banff

Exercise 2

Choose one piece of writing from your response to Exercise 1; now, choose an audience from the following list:

- a magazine for elementary schoolchildren
- a newspaper
- an ezine devoted to that subject
- a television newscast
- an instructor
- an employer

Using the following example as a guide, create a reader profile. If you have difficulty filling in some of the profile, ask a classmate for his or her opinion.

Example: Letter to the editor in which you are arguing that adults should wear helmets when bicycling with children. You want to argue that adults should wear helmets so that they set good examples for their children, who will then wear helmets even when not under adult supervision. Ask yourself the following questions:

1. **Who** will read this piece?
   - A group of people of varying ages and backgrounds
   - Probably mostly adults

2. **Why** are they reading this piece?
   - People who read letters to the editor are probably interested in opinions, arguments, and local issues

3. What **attitude** will my reader(s) probably bring to this piece of writing?
   - Adults opposed to wearing helmets might be hostile. I might have to appease this audience by acknowledging their objections, by comparing helmets to seatbelts, and so on.
   - Parents with children might have a mixed attitude or be receptive.

4. How much **knowledge** will my reader(s) already have about the subject?
   - I might have to describe helmet laws for adults versus those for children, as well as the outcome of accidents for cyclists with and without helmets. I might have to stress the stats for children.
   - I might also have to iterate the commonly known but overlooked fact that children learn by example.

5. What **expectations** will my reader(s) have about the way this piece is written?
   - A letter to the editor must be short, persuasive, and in clear language. I might look at letter format as well as examine the letters published in that particular paper, looking at their length, tone, and so on.

Exercise 3

Using the same piece of writing you chose for Exercise 2 and choosing from the list in that exercise, make a reader profile for a different audience.

Exercise 4

Based on your reader profiles, briefly explain the major similarities and differences in the way you would write the piece for the two audiences you have chosen.

Checklist: Purpose and Audience

1. What is your **subject** for this piece of writing?

   _____

2. What is your **purpose**?

   To share personal experience about _____

   To explain what/how/why _____

   To change readers' opinions about _____

   To persuade readers to _____

3. Who is your **audience**?

   Are you writing for an academic audience? _____

   A non-academic audience? _____

4. What does your **reader profile** suggest about your audience's needs and expectations?

   _____

Gathering Material

Good writing, whether it's a letter to the editor or a term paper, begins with strong content focused on a central point. This chapter presents techniques to help you generate ideas, collect information, and find a focus. Feel free to change the order of these steps; for instance, you might prefer to narrow your topic before brainstorming or to outline before drafting.

1. BRAINSTORMING

When you **brainstorm**, you capture your spontaneous responses to your subject. Put a key word from your writing task in the centre of a blank page. Free associate by writing down ideas, examples, questions, memories, and feelings. Surround your key word with notes; do not reject or edit your thoughts, regardless of how strange or off-topic they seem. If you were preparing a report on the need for life skills courses in high school, for instance, you might end up with a brainstorming diagram like this:

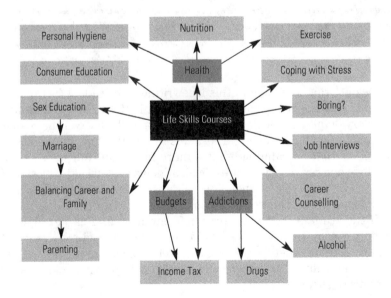

Because brainstorming gives you so many ideas to consider, you can find a fresh angle on your subject or choose material of special interest to your readers.

2. FREEWRITING

Many people disregard their most creative ideas, intuitions, and memories before they start. To avoid this internal censor, try **freewriting**, which is writing spontaneously and continuously about your subject for five or ten minutes. If you run out of material, jot down, "I can't think of anything to say." The key is to keep writing. Do not hesitate or worry about your words. After ten minutes, look over what you've written and sum it up in one sentence. If your summary suggests new ideas, freewrite for another ten minutes. Repeat this process until you have some worthwhile ideas.

Although freewriting is typically done with paper and pen, feel free to do it on a computer, but **do not stop** to use spell-check or edit yourself.

Here is a sample from a student, who, after being assigned an essay topic (Does Jessica Mitford present a convincing argument in "Behind the Formaldehyde Curtain?") decided to freewrite for ten minutes and had this to say:

Ick! I can't believe our crazy instructor made us read this essay. It was gross, yet I couldn't stop reading. It was like one of those disturbing programs on The Learning Channel, like Hoarding: Buried Alive. Mitford certainly turned me off embalming, with all her gorey details and explaination of the process. I don't don't want my lips pinned together. And I am pretty sure I don't want my relatives drowning in chemicals. The whole process seemed greasy and staged. I remember seeing Uncle Timmy in the casket last year. I was sad then, but now when I think about it, he had too much fake and bake on. The costs seems ridiculous. It was like 100 bucks to rent this nice fabric to drape over the coffen. Aunt Alice didn't even get to keep it. Still, this essay is old. There must be more enviromental friendly embalming now. But people want closure. Can you get closure with cremation?

Despite the confusion in this freewriting, the student has several workable ideas. On one hand, he thinks that Mitford, through her facts and gory details, connects to the emotions and the logic of the reader, making her case. However, he suspects that Mitford might be missing the point that embalming holds a more important purpose: saying goodbye and providing closure. He also seems somewhat interested in more environmentally friendly funeral rites, which might, in a research essay, lead to an exploration of and argument for green burials.

If the student did some further freewriting and gathered some evidence from the essay, he could better arrive at a rough idea to explore further, whether it was the need for embalming or the need to replace embalming with a procedure that still provides closure but perhaps does not harm the earth.

3. KEEPING A JOURNAL

Writing in a **journal**, whether in a scribbler or on a computer, can help you keep up with and remember your class reading as well as gather ideas and information for a long-term project. Use your journal entries to reflect on issues, respond to your reading, collect relevant newspaper or magazine items, jot down questions to pursue for class discussions and potential future essays, and record your progress. When you sit down to write your essay, you will have plenty of material. Journaling will also help you develop original thinking that goes beyond class discussion—what your instructor really wants to read.

Here are some journal entries from students, who, after reading "The Yellow Wallpaper," were told to focus on and respond to one character, and had these things to say:

Student #1:
March 4, 2011

I read "The Yellow Wallpaper" last night and am supposed to focus on a main character, so I decided upon John. He's the husband of Jane in the story. Doesn't seem like bad guy. Or is he? Hmm. He doesn't seem to be around much 'cause he's tending to other patients. Is he embarrassed of her? I found it odd that he's a doctor but that he couldn't find someone to diagnose his wife. Maybe he's afraid she will be seen as mad. Maybe he's hiding her in the country. Saving face. Maybe he's just like any other doctor from his day and age. They didn't know much about women, and many still don't. He reminds me of my grandfather who made my grandmother wait on him hand and foot, yet he called her his little dear, sweetums etc. Grandma never had a bank account or any independence. The names that John calls Jane are sooooo annoying—little goose, my child, etc. He doesn't seem to take his wife seriously. She is a child to him, not an equal. He laughs off her complaints.

Although this journal entry seems chaotic and disorganized, the student is arriving at some rough answers that might lead to a draft thesis. On one hand, she thinks that John shouldn't be blamed because he is a typical doctor of his time; on the other hand, she thinks that he might be at fault because he doesn't take his wife seriously and is perhaps more interested in his social status than her cure. This essay could be developed into a straight literary analysis essay with or without research.

Student #2:
March 4, 2011

Just finished reading "The Yellow Wallpaper." What a weird story. It took me forever to read, what with the choppy lines and the narrator's whacky images. I wasn't sure whether to laugh or cry at the end, with Jane crawling over and over her fainting husband. I am still not sure how crazy she was . . . or is at the end. She seemed bored but creative at the beginning, but also sad and with nothing to do. Maybe she needed a hobby. In psych class we were talking about modern cures for depression and the importance of mental and physical therapies, like art and rock-climbing. Anyway, Jane needs something to do to express herself so she wouldn't have to play with that ugly paper. Where is her baby? She might even be suffering from postpartum depression, which is sad, because this wasn't taken seriously until late. Even Tom Cruise once said that PPD was a joke and that meds were unnecessary, etc. Maybe that's why our instructor got us to read this crazy tale—cause it's still relevant.

The writer begins with Jane, but has a hard time focusing on the character because of a greater interest in the topicality of "The Yellow Wallpaper" and the commentary it makes on the treatment of mental illness, particularly depression and postpartum depression. The student, then, might channel this interest into a literary analysis essay supported by research.

Journal entries, on the surface, help you discover your ideas and learn about yourself. In the academic world, they also reveal what you find fascinating, odd, contradictory, or debatable about an idea or text, providing seeds for arguments and essays.

4. ASKING DISCOVERY QUESTIONS

Asking **discovery questions** is a focused way of gathering information on your topic. Discovery questions can help you narrow your topic and mode of development. There are three ways to use this technique.

1. ***Start with the journalist's five Ws and an H: Who, What, When, Where, Why, and How.*** Answering these questions will provide all the information that your reader might need. If you were writing a problem-solving report on theft from gym locker rooms, for instance, you might ask questions like these: Who reported the thefts? Who investigated? What was stolen? When? Where—men's or women's locker room or both? How did the thieves gain access to the articles? What changes would reduce the incidence of theft?

   If you are writing about an unfamiliar or complicated topic, such as global warming, you may need to do research to answer even these basic questions.

2. ***Ask questions based on methods of developing your ideas.*** That is, are you interested in telling a personal narrative, defining your subject, comparing and contrasting your subject with another, explaining a process, and so on? Or do you want to develop your ideas in a number of ways? To explore your topic and find out what truly interests you, pose questions. For an essay on alcoholism, for instance, you might ask the following:

   * How is alcoholism defined?
   * What are the types of alcoholism?
   * What other problems are associated with alcoholism?
   * What are the causes? The effects?
   * How does alcoholism compare with other kinds of addictions?
   * Is there a difference between alcoholism and alcohol abuse?

- Is there a story I could tell about alcoholism?
- What are the typical behaviours of alcoholics?
- How do social factors contribute to alcoholism?
- What are the strengths and weaknesses of current treatment programs?
- What analogy would help to explain the difficulties in overcoming alcoholism?
- What examples would support my points?

3. ***Ask questions specific to the appropriate academic discipline or area of inquiry.*** For instance, if you were writing an essay on the effects of alcoholism for a business course, you might be interested in the economic costs of this disease. Do alcoholics miss more work? Become ill more frequently? A paper for a social work course might ask the following: How does alcohol abuse affect family members and relationships? What are the main causes of addiction? If you were writing a paper for a psychology course, you might ask if an addictive personality profile can be defined. For a biology course, you might ask about the physical and psychological process of addiction. As you can see, to explore a topic, you must consider how to develop your ideas and what questions are relevant to your discipline.

Exercise 1

Make a brainstorming diagram for one of the following subjects:
- current trends in smart phones
- public figures you admire (or dislike)
- benefits of dog ownership
- the popularity of YouTube
- your favourite/least favourite type of movie
- North American funerals

Exercise 2

Choose a subject from the list above and generate material for an essay by freewriting or by asking discovery questions.

5. FINDING A FOCUS

After you have defined your purpose and audience and gathered ideas and information about your subject, you might be bewildered by the amount of information you have collected. To decide what to include and omit, you need a **focus.**

To find a focus, link your purpose and audience with one or more aspects of your subject. For a short piece, you might discuss one aspect in detail. For a longer piece, you may include several. Suppose, for example, that your subject is coyotes and that your purpose is to explain some aspect of this subject to newspaper readers. For a short piece, you might narrate an encounter with a coyote. For a longer piece, you might explain the presence of coyotes in urban areas or explain the difference between Eastern and Western coyotes.

Exercise 3

Using the material you have generated in Exercise 1 or 2, show how you could focus your material for five different purposes and audiences.

Example: Essay on the subject of life skills courses.

(see brainstorming diagram at the beginning of this chapter)

Purpose: to persuade teachers that preparing for job interviews by role-playing should be a part of every life skills course
Audience: teachers

6. FORMULATING A ROUGH THESIS STATEMENT

Some students discover their main point after drafting and outlining, whereas others prefer to begin with a main point. Although it is not advisable to begin an essay with a refined thesis (for you will limit and distort your subject), you might want to begin with a draft thesis or a rough idea of the main point that you intend to make.

After narrowing your focus, begin working on your thesis statement. If your focused subject is coyotes in urban areas, for instance, your thesis needs to make a point about these coyotes. Are they desirable? Problematic? A nuisance? A symptom of urban development? You also need to consider your audience and the length of your composition.

If this assignment is a research essay for an ecology course, for instance, you might decide to *explain* the reasons that coyotes are invading urban areas. Your rough thesis for this paper might be the following: "Coyotes are invading urban areas because of the destruction of traditional coyote habitat and reduced food sources." Because this is a rough thesis, you might discover, when writing your draft, that there are indeed other reasons coyotes are appearing in cities.

If you are writing a proposal for city council, on the other hand, you might briefly explain the effects of urban coyotes and try to *persuade your audience* to adopt a solution. Your thesis might be the following: "The city should have a plan to control the coyote population because coyotes are damaging property, preying on domestic pets, destroying livestock, and attacking people." If you were writing this essay in Western

Canada, you might discover that coyote attacks on people are rare and choose to omit this point. However, if you lived in Eastern Canada, where coyotes are larger and more aggressive, you might give this point more weight.

In general, then, a thesis has a subject, a main point (or opinion) about that subject (a *what*), and at least one reason for supporting this main point or for holding or stating that opinion (a *why* or a *how*). The *why* could be how you arrived at the opinion or why you think that point is relevant, depending on your essay type and purpose. In the example above, the subject is coyotes, the main point is that they need to be controlled, and the *why* consists of their effects.

Once you determine your rough thesis, you move on to the fast-drafting and outlining phases.

Exercise 4

To understand how thesis statements are structured, examine the sentences below, which have been dissected into the subject, the main point (or opinion) about the subject, and reasons for holding that main point (the *how* and/or the *why*). These examples are quite basic—remember that thesis statements can be structured in many ways.

Example: Eastern Canada is alienated from Western Canada because of geographical, political, and economic differences.

Subject = Eastern Canada
Main point about subject = is alienated from Western Canada
The *why* or reasons for this alienation = because of geographical, political, and economic differences

Example: "The Cask of Amontillado" uses irony and symbolism to express the theme that revenge is not always sweet.

Subject = "The Cask of Amontillado"
Main point about subject = has a theme that revenge is not always sweet
How this theme is demonstrated = uses irony and symbolism to express

Using the examples above as a guide, separate the following statements into the subject, main point, and the reasons for holding that main point (*how* or *why*).

- To help prevent their children from getting injured, parents should set an example by wearing helmets when bicycling.
- If you want to succeed at the marathon, your training program should include long runs, tempo workouts, and easy jogs.
- Training a puppy is like training a child; both require a sense of humour, patience, and discipline.
- To reduce taxes for the average Canadian, the Government of Canada should eliminate wasteful spending.

- Climbing a mountain last summer was a rewarding experience, which taught me about patience, discipline, and hard work.
- To put together Ikea furniture properly, you first need to take everything out of the box, organize the parts, and read the instructions.

7. DRAFTING, OUTLINING, AND REVISING

An outline shows you, at a glance, the main divisions of your paper and the relationships among major points, minor points, and details. Making an outline, then, helps you to classify your material and detect gaps in it. There are various ways of using fast-drafting and outlining; choose the method most suitable to your writing task and your work process. For instance, although we discuss making a preliminary outline first, you might draft before outlining.

Making a Preliminary Outline

Some writers are very organized from the beginning; they carefully plan what they want to say, either in their minds or in an outline, so that their first draft develops their rough thesis and a clear pattern of organization. If you are one of these writers, you might prefer to make a **preliminary outline** before fast-drafting. Using your focused subject or your rough thesis as a guide, jot down your main points and supporting details for each main point. After completing your preliminary outline, write a fast draft.

Fast-Drafting

If you decide to write a **fast draft** to flesh out your outline or help clarify your thinking, allot a fixed period—usually an hour or two. Using the material you have gathered through the previous stages— 1 to 5, and, if applicable, 6 and 7—allow yourself a specific amount of time to write a complete draft. Don't let yourself get bogged down. If you have trouble with the introduction, for example, either leave some space and return to it, or write your statement of focus and go on from there. If you didn't begin with a thesis, and you discovered your main point in the process of writing, go back and revise the introduction.

Making a Revision Outline

If you find that your fast draft is unbalanced and disorganized, you might want to make a **revision outline.** For each paragraph, write down the main points and supporting details. The outline will reveal problems in content and organization: paragraphs that need to be combined or divided, points that need further explanation, or topic sentences that need improvement. This step allows you to critically analyze your own work and take your reader's perspective.

To see which process works best for you, practise outlining and fast drafting an essay.

Exercise 5

Using material from Exercise 3, make a draft outline. Put your statement of focus at the top of the page as a guide to your main points. Under each main point, jot down necessary details. Then write a paragraph on the process. How well did making a draft outline work for you? Could you more easily see how to organize your material? Did the outline reveal areas where you needed more ideas or information? Or did the process seem mechanical and boring?

Exercise 6

Using your material from Exercises 1 or 2, fast-draft an essay. Then write a paragraph on the process. How well did fast-drafting work for you? Were you able to continue writing or did you get stuck? Did you begin with a thesis statement or did a main point emerge as you wrote? Did you come up with new ideas or examples?

8. MAKING A FORMAL OUTLINE

You can also make a **formal outline** of your final version to accompany a lengthy report or research paper. Some instructors, in fact, might ask you for a detailed formal outline before you submit a long essay, such as a research paper, so that they can evaluate your work and anticipate any problems in your thinking. Put your thesis—the main point of your piece—at the top of the page. List your major points with Roman numerals, your subpoints with capital letters, and details with Arabic numerals. The format of your outline should resemble the one below.

Sample Formal Outline

Thesis: Childhood obesity is a widespread but complicated problem, which has several causes and numerous short- and long-term physical effects.

   I. Extent of the problem

      A. Definition of obesity

      B. Percentage of obese children in Canada

      C. Comparing Canadian children to other children

II. Causes of childhood obesity

    A. Poor nutrition

        1. At home

        2. In schools

    B. Lack of exercise

        1. Statistics on lack of exercise

        2. Causes of lack of exercise

           a. More sedentary living than physical activity

           b. Physical education absent or reduced in schools

III. Effects of childhood obesity

    A. Associated physical problems (immediate effects)

        1. Early maturation

        2. High blood pressure

        3. Diabetes mellitus type 2

    B. Long-term effects

        1. Obese adults

        2. Physical problems of obese adults

IV. Solutions

    A. Educate parents

    B. Restore physical education in schools

    C. Early intervention

As you can see, each level of the outline (Roman numerals, capital letters, Arabic numerals) represents a division of the level above. For this reason, you should have at least two items at each level. (If you have an A, you must have a B; if you have a 1, you must have a 2.) Each item at a particular level must be an equivalent subdivision of the level above. For example, *Early maturation, High blood pressure,* and *Diabetes* are equivalent items under *Effects of childhood obesity.* This equivalence will be more obvious if you make items at each level grammatically parallel; for instance, these effects are all nouns. An outline will disclose whether you have adequately developed your ideas and sufficiently covered your subject.

Important Note: Although it is very important to generate ideas and to plan your essay, there is also the danger of overplanning. Whereas an unplanned essay might be disorganized or too short, not meeting the minimal assignment requirements, an overplanned essay also has its weaknesses.

If you spend too much time in the planning stage, you might not allot enough time to write enough drafts of the essay. As well, you might limit yourself too much, ignoring any new and exciting ideas that arise while you discover your topic. If you become too obsessed with organizing your material, you might forget what interested you about the topic in the first place; as a result, that vibrant idea becomes a boring one, the essay becomes a chore, and you write with a beleaguered and unspontaneous style. Also, if your outline is too detailed for the scope and length of your essay, you might create an argument that is too broad and not detailed enough. Your essay, then, might be undeveloped and unconvincing.

Remember that every student has a different process; discover the amount of planning and the strategies that work well for you. And don't forget this point: you also need time to revise and proofread your writing.

9. REVISING AND PROOFREADING

Revising and proofreading are two important, but separate, time-consuming steps of the composition process. Keep in mind, however, that strategies for revising and proofreading vary from form to form. For a brief letter, you may simply type out your request, proofread for mistakes, and seal it in the envelope. A letter of application, a report, or an essay will require a more careful consideration of content, organization, and style. Essays, of course, will require more time to both revise and proofread.

When you revise, you are looking at the big picture, gauging your piece of writing for appropriate content, organization, and tone. To revise, evaluate the content and organization of your draft according to the paragraph and essay checklist found below, and check the requirements of your composition or assignment. Make any necessary alterations.

If you are working on a computer and moving text around, you might make separate documents for your drafts. You can also work on your document in "markup," a view that is available under *Tools* on most Word programs. This view, among other things, allows you to insert commentary and see material you have deleted; it also allows you to have an interactive conversation with your draft and to anticipate the questions of your reader.

Next, read your work aloud to get a sense of its tone and how it sounds to another reader. If some sections seem wordy, monotonous, or stilted, revise them to the level of formality appropriate for the assignment.

After you have viewed your essay from this broad perspective, you need to examine it more closely. This is the proofreading stage. Read every sentence to seek out typos and errors in grammar and punctuation.

Finally, make sure that you have presented your work in the appropriate format.

Checklist: The Writing Process

1. a. Which method(s) of **gathering material** have you used?

   _____

   b. Do you have **enough material** to achieve your purpose?

   _____

2. What **focus** have you chosen for your subject?

_____

3. Have you written a **draft** to clarify your thoughts?

_____

4. Have you used an **outline** to organize your material?

_____

5. Have you **revised** your draft for content and organization?

_____

6. Have you **proofread** your writing to improve your style?

_____

7. Have you **proofread** your writing for careless errors?

_____

8. Have you presented your writing in an appropriate **format**?

_____

Weblinks

- York University Pre-writing Strategies Online Tutorial—an excellent resource that provides techniques and strategies for writing essays

  www.yorku.ca/tutorial/prewriting

- Drew University Writing Program Web Resources—good material on peer critiques as well as links to search engines, writing centres, and other resources

  www.users.drew.edu/~sjamieso/Webresources.html

- The Owl at Purdue University—one of the oldest, best, and most reliable sites for all kinds of information on composition

  owl.english.purdue.edu/owl/

- The University of Victoria Writer's Guide—one of the best sites for systematic coverage of the writing process

  web.uvic.ca/wguide/Pages/MasterToc.html

Writing Better Paragraphs

Paragraphs are the building blocks of writing. Introductory paragraphs lay the foundation; concluding paragraphs provide the capstone, or finishing touch. In between are the middle paragraphs, each one discussing one aspect of your subject (one point in an analysis, one step in a process, one event in a narrative, and so on). Each middle paragraph is thus both a self-contained piece of writing and a part of a larger structure. Here, we focus on general strategies for writing paragraphs, whether they be personal, expository, or persuasive.

1. TOPIC SENTENCES

The purpose of a topic sentence is to state the paragraph's main point. In essence, a topic sentence is a summary of that paragraph. You will, therefore, need to figure out exactly what idea you want to develop in each paragraph and clearly state that idea in a sentence. The topic sentence, then, controls the content of your paragraph, helping you decide which details to include and which to omit.

The paragraph below reveals what can go wrong if you don't have a topic sentence:

Some people regard physical fitness as a means to physical health and well-being. They believe that vigorous exercise strengthens the heart and lengthens life. Unfortunately, these exercise enthusiasts tend to monopolize all the equipment in a fitness centre. Other people exercise to make themselves more physically attractive. They want to reshape their bodies to fit the model that society presently holds as representative of physical perfection. I see both young and middle-aged women struggling to create a body that is genetically impossible for them. Still others are more interested in exercise clothes than in exercise itself. They wear the latest fashions in running shoes and yoga wear, but they would never work out for fear that sweat might ruin such expensive gear.

The writer's main point seems to be that people have various reasons for wanting to be part of the fitness scene, but the paragraph drifts into comments on the use of exercise equipment and on unrealistic goals for physical appearance. By beginning with a good topic sentence, the writer can stay on track and transform a jumbled paragraph into a stronger one describing the groups of people who exercise:

For various reasons, people want to be, or want to appear to be, part of the fitness scene. Some people regard physical fitness as a means to physical health and well-being. They believe that vigorous exercise strengthens the heart and lengthens life. Other people exercise to make themselves more physically attractive. That is, they want to reshape their bodies to fit society's present model of physical perfection. Still others are more interested in exercise clothes than in exercise itself. They are attracted to the latest fashions in running shoes and yoga wear, but they would never work out for fear that sweat might ruin such expensive gear.

Knowing your main idea will help you to determine which details are relevant.

However, not all writers are going to know their topic sentences immediately. In actual writing situations, you may need to begin with the details you have collected before determining your main point. Suppose, for example, that you were writing an essay on the popularity of online communities. One paragraph of this essay could focus on a particular one, such as Facebook. Your notes for such a paragraph might look like this:

- Facebook refers to itself as a "social utility" that brings people together.
- All you need to join Facebook is an existing email address and access to a computer.
- You set up an account with an email address and a profile, which can be as limited or as detailed as you want.
- With this account, you get a webpage, inbox, message board, and access to other friends.
- You can prevent strangers from seeing your profile.
- You can decide which information to share.
- You can join existing groups on Facebook or create your own.
- Facebook allows you to choose your friends and maintain the privacy of your information.
- You can communicate with individual people or with groups.
- You can upload and share photographs.
- You can create graffiti walls and movie lists.
- You invite friends to join, but they can refuse.

By reading through this list of details, you can see that it is somewhat disorganized and that it actually develops two points: one about the general process of joining and using Facebook and another about the privacy of this online community. After refining these main points into topic sentences, you might have paragraphs like those below.

Facebook, a popular online community that is easy to join, is stocked with tools that allow you to connect with other users while protecting your privacy. Using your email address and some select personal details, you follow the prompts and set up an account, which gives you a webpage, inbox, wall, and other amenities. Along with other activities, you can post messages, upload and share photographs, create albums, and join and create groups. You can build graffiti walls and *favourites* lists. Using the email addresses of people you know, you can invite them to join Facebook, assembling a group of friends.

This popular online community also has several privacy features. When asking friends to join, you can confirm how you know them. You also decide what information to share and who to share it with, deciding who is allowed to be your friend. Furthermore, you can create a limited profile, block your profile from strangers, and remove people from your friends list if they fail to act appropriately.

2. TYPES OF TOPIC SENTENCES

All topic sentences control the content of the paragraph and state the main idea, but they differ according to the purpose of the paragraph: to communicate personal experience or describe, to explain, or to persuade. Topic sentences will differ, then, in both tone and structure as demonstrated by the examples below:

PERSONAL EXPERIENCE	Although I was initially reluctant to join an online community, doing so made me feel more connected to other people.
EXPOSITORY (CLASSIFICATION)	There are three basic types of online communities: local communities, virtual communities of interest, and organizational communities.
EXPOSITORY (PROCESS)	If you follow these four steps, you can choose an online community that best suits your interests and lifestyle.
PERSUASION	Although people are hesitant about joining online communities because of privacy issues, the benefits of joining these communities far outweigh the risks.

Exercise 1

Read the following paragraph in which the writer attempts to pin down how his father influenced his life. Figure out the writer's main point and state it as clearly as you can in a topic sentence. Then rewrite the paragraph, eliminating any irrelevant details.

I must have gone out with Father many times: to the movies, to the pub (where I sat on the bench outside drinking pop), to football and hockey games. Always I had a sense of extreme pleasure and pride. Our dog Whiskers would sometimes tag along, and I enjoyed throwing sticks for him to retrieve. My father and I also had lots of personal fun and games. He would toss a football and I would pretend that I was the heroic receiver speeding away from fierce Argonaut defencemen. Or I would stand between two horse chestnut trees in the Crown Inn Gardens pretending that I was the Canadiens goalie waiting for Father's speeding puck, exulting in every spectacular save, every reckless plunge between flashing blades. "Great save, Lorenzo!" my father would shout. These trees have now been cut down to enlarge the parking lot. My fun was intensified by my father's own leaps of mind. He was never flamboyant in any of this; instead, he maintained a simple, involved plausibility.

3. THE BODY OF THE PARAGRAPH

Topic sentences make a point that is developed with more specific details. If your paragraph lacks these, you will have trouble explaining your ideas and convincing your readers of their validity. Consider the following example.

> **Cyclists who ignore the rules of the road are a danger to themselves and others.** Most motorists hate and fear cyclists just as most cyclists hate and fear motorists. When I see how cyclists ride anywhere and any way they want on the road, I wonder what they are protecting inside their helmets.

This paragraph consists of three generalizations making similar points, when it needs one topic sentence with a general statement followed by specific supporting details.

The topic sentence about cyclists, for example, suggests two subpoints to be explained further. Which rules of the road do cyclists ignore? How do they endanger themselves and others by ignoring these rules? You would develop the paragraph by using details to explain these subpoints: not wearing helmets, not signalling, riding on the wrong side of the road, and ignoring lights and signs. These details show the rules cyclists ignore as well as how they endanger both themselves and motorists.

If you have trouble developing your ideas, you may need to clarify your purpose: Is your aim to explain something? To persuade? To share your experiences? Once you decide on your main purpose, you will know what type of paragraph to write.

In the examples below, two paragraphs are broken down into their components: the first is an example paragraph whereas the second is a causal analysis paragraph from a persuasive essay on the effects of our fast-paced lifestyle.

Sample Paragraph

Cockroaches, members of the order Blattodea that have been around for some 300 million years, are surely one of the hardiest of insects.[1] They are able, with the exception of the polar

---

[1]This is the topic sentence, which focuses on the hardiness of the cockroach.

regions,[2] to live in a wide range of environments around the world. Mostly nocturnal, they know how to avoid their most dangerous predators—humans—living in households for an annoyingly long time. Cockroaches are **also** capable of surviving a month without food, and, as scavengers and omnivores, can eat anything. **For instance,** some have survived on the glue from postage stamps. **In addition,** these pests can hold their breath for forty-five minutes, lower their resting heart rate, and can withstand, per their body weight, six to fifteen times the radiation of humans.[3] Some science fiction writers **even** believe that after a nuclear blast, cockroaches will out-survive humans. The resilience of cockroaches, though amazing, makes them one of the most maligned group of insects.[4]

Sample Causal Analysis Paragraph

Finally, speeding up life causes health problems.[5] First, going too fast, combined with poor management skills, has made us reliant on fast food not only for its convenience, but also for its comfort. This fast-food addiction has helped to create an obese Canadian population. **In fact,** Statistics Canada (2004),[6] in its bulletin *The Daily*, reported that "5.5 million individuals were obese, and this statistic has increased substantially during the last twenty-five years" (para. 2). Obesity, which technically is defined as having a BMI of 30 or higher, can cause additional health problems, such as "high blood pressure, breathing problems, stroke, heart disease, diabetes, hyper-lipidemia, gall bladder disease, gout, and cancer" (*The Daily*, para. 5). Because people who don't eat properly often don't exercise regularly, the effects of poor eating are compounded. As these examples show, living too fast is bad for your physical health.[7]

Exercise 2

List several subpoints and examples to develop each of the following topic sentences:

1. Fast-food chains should help combat the rising levels of obesity.

2. Many drivers are too distracted.

3. There are several reasons that a lowly onion ring became more popular than Stephen Harper.

---

[2]Following this topic sentence are examples illustrating the hardiness of cockroaches. The transitional words linking sentences are bolded.

[3]The parallel structure of the sentences stresses the amazing physical qualities of this insect.

[4]This is the concluding sentence that brings the paragraph to a temporary close. This sentence stresses the hardiness of cockroaches by using the synonym *resilience*.

[5]This is the topic sentence for the third paragraph in a causal analysis paragraph on obesity. In this paragraph, the writer works on this chain of events: speeding up causes poor time management skills and anxiety. Rushed and anxious people avoid exercise and rely on fast food. This lifestyle leads to a host of other physical problems.

[6]In the examples, which are effects, the writer combines analysis with secondary sources. Here APA parenthetical citation format is used.

[7]This final sentence brings the paragraph to a temporary close.

4. PARAGRAPH STRUCTURE

There are two main ways of organizing information in a paragraph. You can begin, as in the above paragraphs, with your topic sentence and then fill in the reasons, examples, and other supporting details, or you can begin with these details and examples and gradually lead your reader to your main point. The first, which emphasizes your main point, is the structure for a *deductive paragraph*. The second, which emphasizes the process of thinking and leads to the main point, is the structure for an *inductive paragraph*.

Note: When writing a deductive paragraph, do not end it with the topic sentence for the next paragraph. Although your intention may be to provide a transition, you will actually confuse your readers about both your main point and paragraph structure.

The examples below reveal the differences between these paragraph structures.

Sample Paragraph: Topic-Sentence-First Arrangement (Deductive)

Zumba (pronounced *zoom-bah*), the workout program that is sweeping the world, transforms exercise into a party and packs a calorie-burning punch. The most important component of Zumba is the music, which consists of a catchy, if not hypnotic, mixture of slow and fast Latin rhythms. Added to this music are easy-to-follow dance moves that, after a few sessions, even beginners can easily master. Mixed in with this dancing are slow and fast intervals and jolts of resistance training. This combination of dancing and resistance can burn about 600 calories an hour. Because people are having a blast doing the Zumba program, they do not realize they are getting fit and burning calories.

Sample Paragraph: Details-First Arrangement (Inductive)

Because people are having a blast doing the Zumba program, they do not realize they are getting fit and burning calories. The most important component of Zumba is the music, which consists of a catchy, if not hypnotic, mixture of slow and fast Latin rhythms. Added to this music are easy-to-follow dance moves that, after a few sessions, even beginners can easily master. Mixed in with this dancing are slow and fast intervals and jolts of resistance training. This combination of dancing and resistance can burn about 600 calories an hour. Zumba, the workout program that is sweeping the world, definitely transforms exercise into a party and packs a calorie-burning punch.

Although the above is an example paragraph, inductive paragraphs are also effective in persuasive writing. For instance, if you are trying to convince a resistant or uninformed reader, or attempting to make an unpleasant proposal or a controversial point, consider presenting the details first. Organizing the paragraph this way will force the reader to consider your reasons and your argument. Consider the paragraph below, which was part of a speech delivered by a manager of a grocery store to his staff:

Recently, our overall profits have decreased by 10 percent. Additionally, our rate of sales per hour is down from $88 per employee to $74. We are also, because of increasing gas prices, produce scares, and crop shortages, experiencing a time when our costs are inordinately high. For every $1000 loss in each department, the store has had to cut twelve hours; for every $3000 loss, the store has cut the equivalent of one part-time employee. **Thus, in order to manage our losses, to prevent any future cuts in hours, and to avoid firing staff, management are urging part-time employees to take a temporary pay cut.**

Exercise 3

Write a paragraph on any subject that interests you. Begin with your topic sentence. Then rewrite the paragraph, putting the details first and ending with your topic sentence. Underline your topic sentence in each paragraph.

5. PARAGRAPH UNITY AND COHERENCE

Whether you are writing a descriptive, expository, or persuasive paragraph, it is essential that your paragraph be both **unified** and **coherent**. In a unified paragraph, every sentence develops the main idea of the topic sentence, by explaining, exemplifying, or expanding on this idea. A unified paragraph, then, contains no extraneous details.

Paragraph Unity

To check paragraph unity, test every sentence against the topic sentence. Sentences that don't develop the main idea should be removed or relocated. That is, move rather than delete particularly effective examples, for they may actually belong in another paragraph.

The best way to explain this concept is to examine a paragraph that is not unified. In the paragraph below on "blackouts," which sentences do not develop the main point?

To understand the dangers of blackouts, we first need to define them. A blackout is an alcohol-induced memory loss caused by a blockage of neurotransmitters that send memories from short-term memory to long-term memory. A blackout typically occurs when the blood alcohol level is over 0.15, far over the legal limit. It is commonly believed that only alcoholics get blackouts. People in blackouts appear to be functioning as a normal intoxicated person, having conversations, and so on. The actual blackout, or memory loss, which can last a few minutes to a few hours or more, does not appear until the next day. Blackouts should be distinguished from passing out or from drinking to the point of unconsciousness. Several college students have reported blackouts. At this point, the person usually fails to remember what happened after he or she left the bar.

The sentences that don't belong, and which could be incorporated into another paragraph discussing the common misconceptions of blackouts are these: "It is commonly believed . . ." and "Several college students . . ." As well, unless the person is going to give more information distinguishing blackouts from other alcohol-related episodes, the sentence "Blackouts . . . unconsconsciousness" should also be removed.

The revised paragraph would be as follows:

To understand the dangers of blackouts, people need to understand them. A blackout is an alcohol-induced memory loss caused by the blockage of neurotransmitters that send memories from short-term memory to long-term memory. A blackout typically occurs when the blood alcohol level is over 0.15, far over the legal limit. However, a person experiencing a blackout appears to be functioning as a normal intoxicated person, having conversations, and so on. The actual blackout, or memory loss, which can last a few minutes to a few hours or more, does not appear until the next day. At this point, the person usually fails to remember what happened after he or she left the bar.

Paragraph Coherence

Whereas unity is the development of one idea, coherence embodies those qualities of the paragraph that make that idea understandable. Coherent paragraphs, then, develop their main idea by presenting their information in the most effective and logical order, and by having smooth connections between their sentences. In other words, coherent paragraphs flow. If your instructor comments that your paragraphs are unified but not coherent, he or she is saying that though your paragraphs develop one idea, they lack flow. You probably need to reorder your sentences and add transitional words and expressions.

As you move from sentence to sentence and paragraph to paragraph, you constantly present your readers with a mixture of known information (terms and ideas you have already introduced) and new information. You can emphasize the continuity between known and new information and reinforce paragraph coherence (and flow) by using these stylistic devices. Transitional words not only order ideas and indicate relationships between them but also establish tone.

6. TRANSITIONS

1. *Use transitional words and phrases.*

The transitions in the list on the next page can clarify how you have organized your material, making it easier for your readers to move from one point to the next.

Transitions

	Informal	Formal
NARRATION	first, next, then, last, as soon as, early the following morning, later that day	in the beginning, in the end
DESCRIPTION	nearer, farther, on the right, on the left, at the top, at the bottom, to the east, beside, between, above	adjacent to
CLASSIFICATION	one group, another kind, a third type	one subcategory, moreover, furthermore
EXAMPLE	for example, for instance	to illustrate, a case in point
PROCESS ANALYSIS	first step, second step, next stage, final stage	
SYSTEMS ANALYSIS	one component, another part	the most important element
CAUSAL ANALYSIS	one reason, a final reason, the most important effect, although, because, despite, however	therefore, nevertheless, consequently, as a result, thus, if/then, provided that
DEFINITION	one meaning, another meaning, the most relevant meaning	primary meaning, secondary meaning
COMPARISON	and/also, but/too, in comparison, in contrast, similarly	just as/so too, not only/but also, neither/nor
EVALUATION		a practical advantage, a logical inconsistency, another legal aspect, from a moral perspective, an aesthetic weakness

A comparison of the following paragraphs reveals how transitions can dramatically increase the clarity of your ideas and the smoothness of your writing.

The paragraph below, which contextualizes the problem of graffiti, is choppy because of the short sentences and the missing transitions.

Sample Draft Paragraph without Transitions

Graffiti is a controversial topic that people have strong opinions about. Many people believe that graffiti is not art but vandalism. It damages private property and ruins communities. It increases crime. Tags allow gangs to mark their territory. Opponents of graffiti point to useless expressions painted on bridges and other pieces of private property. These markings seem to overshadow any works of art created by graffiti.

Sample Revised Paragraph with Added Transitions

Although graffiti is a controversial topic that people have strong opinions about, many believe that graffiti is not art but vandalism. These opponents argue that graffiti damages private property, ruins communities, and increases crime. Among other acts of graffiti, they point to tags, which allow gangs to mark their territory. As well, they mention all the useless expressions painted on bridges and other pieces of private property, which seem to overshadow any works of art created by graffiti.

2. ***Repeat key words or phrases.***

Don't be afraid of some repetition; reiterating a key word lets your readers know you are still talking about the same subject. If you introduce too many synonyms, readers may think you are offering new information. In the short paragraph below, the many synonyms for *bear* and *hunting partner* distract attention from the main subject, the father, and the act of surprising the wounded bear.

Dad was fearless. Once when he and a hunting partner were tracking deer in the foothills, they surprised a wounded bear in a thicket. When the maimed animal knocked his friend down, Dad struck the brute with an empty rifle, distracting the angry monster long enough for his companion to get up and shoot the beast.

The paragraph reads much more smoothly when fewer terms are introduced:

Dad was fearless. Once when he and a hunting partner were tracking deer in the foothills, they surprised a wounded bear in a thicket. When the bear knocked George down, Dad struck it with an empty rifle, distracting it long enough for George to get up and shoot it.

3. ***Use personal pronouns to refer to subjects previously named.***

Pronouns (*he, she, it, they*), like repeated terms, signal known information; in the example above, the pronoun *it*, which refers to the bear, is much clearer than *the brute* or *the beast*.

Below is an excerpt from Winston Churchill's speech on the evacuation at Dunkirk ("Wars Are Not Won by Evacuations"). Note the key words, phrases, and pronouns Churchill repeats. How do these repeated words and phrases affect the tone?

Even though large tracts of Europe and many old and famous states **have fallen** or **may fall** into the grip **of the Gestapo** and all the odious apparatus **of Nazi rule**, we shall not **flag** or **fail**. <u>**We shall go on to the end,** *we shall fight*</u> in France, *we shall fight* on the seas and oceans, *we shall fight* with growing confidence and strength in the air, we shall defend our island, whatever the cost may be, **we shall fight** on the beaches, **we shall fight** in the landing grounds, **we shall fight** in the fields and in the streets, **we shall fight** in the hills; <u>**we shall never surrender**</u>, and even if, which I do not for a moment believe, this island or a large part of it were **subjugated** and **starving**, then our Empire beyond the seas, **armed** and **guarded** by the British fleet, would <u>**carry on the struggle**</u>, until, in God's good time, the New World, with all its power and might, steps forth to the **rescue** and **liberation** of the old.

4. *Put the idea you plan to discuss next at the end of the sentence.*

   Link sentences by repeating the last word(s) of one sentence at the beginning of the next or by using a synonym and a demonstrative pronoun (*this, that, these, those*). Note the two examples below:

   British suffragettes challenged the existing system first through marches on Parliament, then through civil disobedience. When civil disobedience failed, they turned to property damage.

   British suffragettes challenged the existing system first through marches on Parliament, then through civil disobedience. When these measures failed, they turned to property damage.

5. *Use sentence structure to indicate logical relationships.*

   To show that two or more sentences contain equivalent points (as when you are giving a list of reasons, examples, or actions), use **parallel sentence structure**, expressing ideas of equal value in the same grammatical form.

FIRST SENTENCE	Slander may involve . . .
SECOND SENTENCE	It can also be . . .
THIRD SENTENCE	It is quite often . . .

   When you move from a general point to a specific detail, or vice versa, signal the shift by changing your sentence structure.

GENERAL POINT	Slander, in essence, is an ugly, malicious lie about someone. [The topic sentence is short and to the point, containing a short parenthetical expression "in essence."]
SPECIFIC EXAMPLE	It may involve . . . [The sentence begins with a subject and verb—change in sentence structure.]
SPECIFIC EXAMPLE	As well, slander can also be. . . . [The sentence begins with a transitional expression.]

   If you compare the following paragraphs, you will see how these devices achieve continuity and dramatically increase the flow of your writing. The material is from a personal essay on the writer's experiences with judo. The added transitional words indicate the process of bullying.

Sample Draft Paragraph

Bullies always have their little rituals. They go through a talking phase with a new kid who might be tough. If they aren't sure, they leave subtle threats and go away. After this little talk, they hammer an opponent who reveals a weakness. They try to make friends with the "mark" who appears too formidable. I was skinny and scared, and so bullies always beat me up.

Sample Revised Paragraph

When bullies encounter a "mark" who might be tough, they go through little rituals. First they talk to him. If this talk reveals a weakness in their opponent, they hammer him. If they still aren't sure, they leave subtle threats and go away. If he appears too formidable, they make friendship gestures. But when the new kid is skinny and scared, like me, there is no ritual. It's all fists.

—Dan Martin

Exercise 4

Write a descriptive paragraph on one of the items below. Use appropriate transitional devices that allow your reader to visualize spatial relationships among the things you describe.

- your bedroom
- a painting you admire
- a scene from your favourite movie
- the view from your living room window
- your favourite restaurant
- a specific behaviour of your dog or other pet

Exercise 5

Improve the following paragraph, which is somewhat choppy, by adding transitions and revising sentences to show the steps in the process and the details of these steps. You may need to combine or rewrite some sentences.

If you have a compact car, packing for a camping vacation, either for the weekend or for an entire week, requires a strategy. There are several procedures to take that will limit the stress of fitting all of the camping gear into a smaller vehicle. Pack one small bag of clothing for each family member. Take what is needed, not wanted "just in case." Bring only one bathing suit, one sleep toy for the children, and one pair of long pants. Arrange everything outside the car prior to loading. See how much is selected so that you can make a further re-evaluation. Place everything according to size and weight. The larger, heavier things should be at the bottom. Set them closest to the trunk. Meticulously pack everything into the car. Maximize the space you have. Utilize every available nook and cranny, especially that area between the two (often fighting) children. Follow these three easy steps. You will have a happy start to your family camping vacation.

Exercise 6

Improve the following paragraph by adding transitions and combining and revising sentences.

Greyhound adoption has become increasingly popular in recent years because of the suitability of these dogs as pets. They may take some time to adapt to life outside the kennel. They may attempt to walk through doors and windows. They may have difficulty going up and down stairs. They may be startled by loud noises. They have short coats and are excessively clean. They need mild to moderate exercise. They rarely bark. They can be quite gentle with other dogs. Especially smaller ones. Several are good to very good around cats and children. They become attached to their owners. They are often known affectionately as the "Velcro dog."

7. PARAGRAPH DIVISIONS

By dividing your material into paragraphs, you signal that all the information in a particular paragraph relates to one aspect of your subject. But paragraph division is also visual; you need to consider what your reader sees on the page. Paragraph length also affects the tempo of the piece as well as the engagement of the reader. Longer paragraphs, such as those in a persuasive paper, take a while to read and invite the reader to slow down, concentrate, and deeply engage with the subject, whereas short paragraphs, such as those often found in newspaper and magazine articles and much business writing, quicken the pace of reading and are appropriate for less weighty subjects.

Although the length of your paragraph depends on your subject matter and mode of development, in most college writing, your paragraphs should be neither too long nor too short.

Normally, you should be able to discuss one aspect of your subject adequately in about half a page. If you need more room to develop your ideas, or if your explanation is quite complicated, subdivide your paragraph. For example, instead of trying to discuss, in one paragraph, several effects of global warming, focus each paragraph on one effect, such as icecap melting or climate change.

If you are double-spacing and using a 10- to 12-point font, the ideal paragraph length is about $\frac{1}{2}$ to $\frac{2}{3}$ of a page long. Avoid paragraphs that are a page long.

Whereas long paragraphs bog the reader down, a series of too-short paragraphs not adequately developing points can create a fractured piece of writing. If several short paragraphs discuss only one aspect of your subject, such as how you get more exercise when you have a dog, combine them. If the paragraphs are too short but cannot be combined because they discuss different aspects of your subject, you may have to develop them with more examples and details or remove them altogether.

Similarly, random paragraph divisions—paragraphs that span for pages accompanied by ones that are only a few lines long—are visually unappealing and confusing. They also signal that your explanation or argument is not properly developed. If you want to vary your paragraph lengths, make sure there is a logical reason for doing so. Save your short paragraphs for emphasis, summaries, and transitions.

In the process analysis paragraph composition below, notice how the writer uses a combination of short and long paragraphs.

Although in my two years of employment as a bartender at Hazelmere Golf and Country Club I have come across a number of drinks including the Harvey Wallbanger and the infamous Rocky Mountain Bear, I was recently introduced to one of the finest shots this side of the border: the Flaming Lamborghini.

This drink, which gets it name from the way that it is prepared and the elements that it incorporates, is worth trying at home. To make it, you will need to acquire the following items: four 1 oz. shots of Kahlua, Sambuca, Blue Curaçao, and Baileys Irish Cream. Along with these, you require a chilled cocktail glass, matches, and one straw (colour is up to you). After gathering all the ingredients, begin by taking the 1 oz. shots of Kahlua and Sambuca and pouring them into the cocktail glass. When you have the two shots in the glass, set the mixture on fire and begin to "knock it back." As you reach the bottom of the glass, pour the two remaining shots into the glass to douse the flames. Faster than you can say the name of this drink, it should already be gone.

This flaming drink has its obvious advantages and disadvantages. Some appreciate being able to go from "0 to inebriated in under 5 seconds." Others scoff at the price. For $15.95, you can get your local bartender to whip up a Flaming Lamborghini, or you can invest your own money on the ingredients and make one yourself.

—*Adapted from a composition by Cody Heath*

Although effective paragraphs should have main points and vivid details, they don't all have to be the same length. Vary their length to create a more dynamic piece of writing.

Checklist: Paragraphs

	OK	NEEDS WORK
1. Is your purpose clear?	☐	☐
2. Have you chosen an appropriate method of development for your purpose and audience?	☐	☐
3. Does the topic sentence state the main point?	☐	☐
4. Are the details adequate?	☐	☐
5. Are the details relevant?	☐	☐
6. Is the paragraph a readable length (neither too long nor too short)?	☐	☐
7. Have you used effective transitions?	☐	☐
8. Have you chosen language appropriate to your purpose and audience?	☐	☐
9. Is your writing varied, concise, and stylistically interesting?	☐	☐

The Key to Writing Essays: The Thesis

1. WHAT IS AN ESSAY?

"Write an essay on euthanasia," one instructor says. Another asks you to write an essay about your first job interview or about the life cycle of the dragonfly. These instructions might make you ponder what, exactly, an essay is. The term *essay*, in fact, can be applied to a wide variety of nonfiction writing: light newspaper columns and impassioned letters to the editor; thoughtful magazine articles and scathing movie reviews; academic articles and research papers. Regardless of their different purposes and audiences, all these types of writing share a thesis, a main point about their subject.

2. WHAT IS A THESIS?

An opinion, which comes from the Latin stem *opinari* (to think or believe), is a view or judgment not necessarily supported by facts or knowledge. If you say, for instance, that the movie *The Lovely Bones* is not worth seeing, you are giving an opinion. However, if you say that the movie is not worth seeing because the overly complicated CGI effects overwhelm the beauty and simplicity of the original story, you are stating a thesis. You would then support this thesis with several concrete examples of these awkward special effects.

As the above example suggests, clearly stating your reasons controls the content of the essay and limits your discussion. You are not going to discuss all the reasons the movie should be avoided, but only those mentioned. Your thesis, then, is a sort of contract with your reader, telling him or her the material you will cover.

A thesis, in short, states an opinion that is supported by one or more valid reasons. There are three main types of thesis statements, which you will learn more about in the following sections.

In a **personal essay**, the thesis is a generalization based on your personal experience: "What this experience means to me is . . ."

EXAMPLE OF PERSONAL THESIS   Sleeping on the streets taught me about the humiliation and hopelessness that the homeless experience daily.

In an **expository essay**, the thesis is the overall point you want to explain: "What I am trying to explain is . . ."

From *Forms of Writing: A Rhetoric and Handbook*, Sixth Edition, Kay L. Stewart, Marian Allen, Shelley Galliah. Copyright © 2012 by Pearson Canada Inc. All rights reserved.

The four main causes of homelessness are the following: . . .

In a **persuasive essay**, the thesis presents the argument you want to convince your readers to accept: "What you should think (or do) is . . ." You can keep your persuasive thesis on track by including the word "should" in it.

EXAMPLE OF PERSUASIVE THESIS   Canadian cities should budget more time and money to eradicating homelessness.

Use these guidelines to formulate a better thesis, whatever the type:

- **State an opinion or a main point about your subject rather than merely rephrasing your subject or essay topic.** Suppose, for example, that your subject is *group homes for the mentally disabled* and you have narrowed this subject to the topic of *licensing regulations*. You will not have a thesis if you merely restate your subject: *This essay is about group homes for the mentally disabled*. Merely repeating your topic is no more useful: *This essay will discuss the licensing of group homes for the mentally disabled*. The wording and tone of your thesis will depend on what type of essay you are writing: personal, expository, or persuasive.

A thesis stating an opinion provides a much clearer focus for your essay:

PERSONAL THESIS   My experience working at a group home taught me the need for stricter licensing regulations. (Here, your opinion about your subject, the need for stricter licensing regulations, is based on your own personal experience.)

EXPOSITORY THESIS   Mandating the licensing of group homes is a difficult process because it involves the input of several organizations and governmental bodies. (The opinion that licensing is difficult will be supported by an analysis of the main organizations involved in decision-making.)

PERSUASIVE THESIS   Social services should tighten regulations governing the licensing of group homes for the mentally disabled, so that the mentally disabled get respect, not abuse or exploitation. (The opinion that regulations should be tightened is tied to a concrete effect: respect for the mentally disabled.)

- **State an opinion rather than a fact.** Factual statements don't suggest a topic for discussion. The thesis has to be a point that you are going to explain, illustrate, or prove in your entire essay, so facts are too specific; instead, facts are best for grabbing your reader's attention or proving your thesis. Let's say that in writing a letter to your local paper about encouraging greyhound rescue, you want to state that in the United States, thousands of ex-racing greyhounds are killed each year. Although this fact is shocking, it is too specific for a thesis, and could, instead, lead up to one. Your thesis might say, *To stop the killing of so many racing greyhounds, we should work to limit excessive breeding, ban greyhound racing, and encourage adoption.*

- **Make sure your thesis states *your* opinion, not the writer's.** When you are analyzing a piece of writing, such as an essay or a work of literature, you will include the writer's main point somewhere in your analysis, but it will not be your thesis. Your thesis will explain *your* interpretation of the piece or your evaluation of its strengths and weaknesses. In the above example, for instance, your thesis might be the following: *In the newspaper article "No Need to Kill Gracious Greyhounds" the writer presents a solid case for rescuing greyhounds by using a strong causal analysis argument, startling facts, and moving descriptions.*

- **Avoid generalizations and make the thesis as precise as possible.** If you state a well-defined opinion with one or more reasons to support it, as in the above example, you will know exactly what points to develop in your essay. Avoid generalizations: *These stories have a lot in common* or *The Second World War had a big impact on Canada.* Instead, state the most important similarities in the stories or the most important social, political, or economic effect(s) of the war: *The diversification of manufacturing caused by the Second World War transformed the Canadian economy.*

Important Note on the Thesis: As the above examples suggest, your thesis is shaped by your purpose, audience, essay structure, and methods of development. Also, because a thesis is based on your own unique perspective or opinion, there is no one correct thesis on a subject, but there are weak and unconvincing thesis statements. That is, even if you have a strong opinion, you must still support it with valid reasons. Without these reasons, your thesis will indeed be unsubstantiated and incomplete, which your instructor might mark as invalid or "wrong."

Exercise 1

Consider the following sentences as thesis statements for an essay. If you think the sentence makes a clear point that can control the content of the essay, write **C**. If it doesn't, explain how it could be improved and/or rewrite it.

1. Anabolic steroids can cause several physical problems.

2. Child-care workers don't get paid enough.

3. Certain cancer treatments are available in the United States but not in Canada.

4. Oil companies responsible for environmental disasters should face bigger fines.

5. The Internet has not lived up to its promise.

6. We should not allow our genetic information to be collected, for this information could be used against us.

7. The sequel to *Transformers* is worse than the original movie.

3. DISCOVERING YOUR THESIS

Although we have been talking about formulating your thesis, it is customary to gather some material or even write a first draft before determining your thesis. In fact, if you formulate a thesis first and then look for information to support it, you might develop a narrow-minded outlook, limiting your thinking and distorting your subject.

To figure out your thesis, follow these steps:

1. **Gather information about your subject.** Use one or more of these methods—brainstorming, freewriting, asking discovery questions, keeping a journal, conducting interviews, or doing research.

2. **Group this material into at least three or four categories.** These categories could be effects, causes, steps, types, parts, descriptions, events, and so on, depending on your essay. That is, if you were writing a personal essay on your experience in group homes, this material might be details of a few experiences; if you were writing an expository essay on the difficulty of regulating licensing, these categories might be the bodies responsible for this regulation (systems analysis/classification), the steps involved in regulating licensing (process analysis), or the reasons this regulation is so difficult (causal analysis).

3. **Formulate a thesis that focuses on the meaning of these broader categories.** Suppose, for example, that you have been asked to write an essay on your first job. If you have returned to school after a career as a nurse, you might write a personal essay on the satisfactions and frustrations of nursing when you began work twenty years ago; an expository essay comparing working conditions then and now; or a persuasive essay arguing that working conditions for nurses have hardly improved in twenty years. Whatever your focus, begin by jotting down information about various aspects of your job.

Nursing Twenty Years Ago
1. Earned $275/month with reasonable rates for room, board, and laundry in nurses' residence.
2. Advancement by seniority.

3. Good job security.

4. Not many chances to develop new skills.

5. Performed menial and routine tasks, no clinical specialization.

6. Worked 40-hour/five-day week; split shifts and short changes (e.g., worked 3:30 p.m.–midnight, then 7:30 a.m.–4 p.m.); understaffed.

7. Nurses supervised or administered; did little nurturing or ministering to patients.

8. Nurses expected to follow doctor's orders, not to make independent decisions.

9. Basic level of technology.

10. Doctors viewed nurses as subordinate.

11. Little interaction with management.

12. Education required: basic three-year diploma; training based on practice.

You would then group these aspects of nursing into more general categories:

- financial dimensions of employment (1, 2, 3, 6)
- professional responsibilities (4, 5, 8, 9, 12)
- possibilities for emotional satisfaction (7, 10, 11)

To work out a thesis, you would need to decide what point you could make about each of these dimensions of the job. You might choose the following points:

- Twenty years ago, nurses worked long hours with strenuous shift changes for low wages, but their jobs were relatively secure.
- In the past, opportunities for nurses to show initiative and develop new skills were quite limited.
- The emotional satisfactions of nursing were also limited by lack of direct contact with patients and nurses' subordinate position to doctors and hospital administration.

The main idea emerging is that twenty years ago nursing was a secure job, but one with limited opportunities for intellectual growth and emotional satisfaction.

The Personal Thesis

Whether a personal essay is narrative, descriptive, or reflective, the thesis should make a point about what the experience taught you about yourself, about others, or about life itself. The thesis, then, should still be relevant to your reader.

As a young woman seeking independence, I saw only the job security that nursing promised, not its limited opportunities for intellectual growth and personal satisfaction.

The Expository Thesis

The thesis for an expository essay is the generalization that grows out of the analysis of your material. The thesis explains the significance of the subject by telling the readers *what* its parts are, *how* it got that way, *why* it has the nature it has, or all three. This thesis explains *why* nursing twenty years ago was as it was.

> In the past, the relative abundance of health-care dollars meant that nursing jobs were secure; however, the hierarchical nature of the system meant that nursing provided limited opportunities for intellectual growth or emotional satisfaction.

The Persuasive Thesis

A persuasive thesis tells readers *what* they should think or do and *why*. Thus, a persuasive thesis often involves the word *should*.

One of the ways to reach this thesis is by evaluating the strengths and weaknesses of your subject. Your thesis may focus on strengths (*Nursing was a good career choice twenty years ago because of the job security it offered*) or weaknesses (*Nursing was a bad career choice because of the limited opportunities for intellectual growth and emotional satisfaction*). On most issues, however, readers are more likely to be convinced by a thesis that provides a balanced perspective—one that acknowledges the other point of view, as in the example below.

> Critics of today's nursing practitioners should not look to the past, idealizing the golden days of nursing. Although nursing jobs were more secure twenty years ago, the profession offered few opportunities for intellectual growth or emotional satisfaction.

The Comparative Thesis

When you are comparing, whether in a personal, expository, or persuasive essay, your thesis should do more than state the most important similarities or differences in your subjects. It should also explain how or why they are similar or different. If you were comparing working conditions in nursing twenty years ago and today, for instance, you might discover that opportunities for intellectual growth and personal satisfaction have increased, but job security has decreased. Your thesis might explain the reasons for these differences in this way:

> Changes in medical technology and in the structure of the health-care system make nursing more intellectually and emotionally satisfying than it was twenty years ago, but current cuts in health-care spending make jobs less secure.

4. ESSAY STRUCTURE

Although essays, like houses, come in a variety of shapes, they should all have a structure—a principle of organization binding the parts together. The structure generally has two functions: to show your readers how the parts of your essay relate to each other and to create interest. Your choice of structure for a particular piece of writing depends on your subject, purpose, and audience.

The overall structure of your essay is determined by where you put your thesis—near the beginning or near the end of the essay. Beginning with the thesis is effective for academic and persuasive essays, whereas ending with the thesis is most effective for some kinds of personal and persuasive essays. That is, if you were writing a persuasive letter to your newspaper about supporting the local SPCA, you might begin with a thesis stating the positive effects of such support; however, if you were writing a personal essay on owning a dog, you might end with what pet ownership taught you about dogs and yourself.

5. THE DEDUCTIVE ESSAY: BEGINNING WITH YOUR THESIS

Putting the thesis in your introduction provides a framework for the rest of the essay and emphasizes the results of your thinking. That is, you are essentially beginning with what you have already concluded after brainstorming, planning, and drafting your essay.

Advantages and Disadvantages

This method's main advantage is its clarity. By stating your main point first and then supporting it with evidence, you show your reader the relevance of your material. This method is particularly effective when discussing a complex or technical subject. Most readers will have trouble following several pages of specific detail if they don't know the main point. Thus, for most of the essays you write for academic courses, you will probably state your thesis first.

Beginning with your thesis may not be the best strategy, however, if you are writing about a controversial subject (the legalization of euthanasia) or on an unfamiliar topic (a comparison of Christian, Muslim, and Hindu funeral rites). You may alienate readers who feel forced to agree or disagree with your conclusions before they have had time to consider the controversy or understand the topic.

The Thesis

Your thesis, you will recall, gives your opinion about your subject and your reason(s) for holding that opinion. Some instructors may ask that you "blueprint" your thesis. Giving your reasons in the order you plan to discuss them provides a map for your readers. To show them where they are along the way, you use topic sentences to elaborate on the reasons, which are then developed in the body paragraphs.

In the following example, the thesis and topic sentences create a structure that focuses the reader's attention and controls the content of the essay.

Essay Topic: What are the effects of stress? Is any stress good? Incorporating research (at least four solid secondary sources), write a 1,500-word causal analysis essay on this topic.

Thesis: Although stress plays a crucial role in the survival of species, and some stress is actually beneficial, an overload of stress causes a wide variety of psychological and physical ailments.

The thesis answers *both* questions by saying that stress, though it once served a useful purpose, now has a number of harmful effects. Putting the benefits of stress in a subordinate clause (*Although stress plays a crucial role in the survival of species, and some stress is actually beneficial*) tells the reader that though this minor point will be discussed, probably near the beginning of this essay, the bulk of the essay will elaborate on the negative psychological and physical effects of stress. The causal analysis essay, then, moves toward the most important effect.

Possible Topic Sentences

—In the early history of humankind, stress was beneficial, for it ensured survival.

—Furthermore, some stress is actually beneficial to our health and well-being.

—Constant stress has been linked to several psychological problems.

—Constant stress also causes numerous short-term and long-term physical problems.

Giving an essay such a clearly defined structure is not easy; don't expect a perfectly worded thesis and matching topic sentences on the first attempt. Although you may discover a tentative thesis and major categories (such as physical and psychological effects), these categories—or the thesis—may change when you write an outline or a draft. When you revise, you can rewrite your thesis and topic sentences so that they provide a clear, logical framework.

The Introduction

In the deductive essay structure, the opening sentences define the range of material you will cover and provide a context for the thesis, which ends the introduction. The usual structure of the introduction for a deductive essay is the following: opening sentences, segue, and thesis. In an introduction, you want to lead the reader gently into the essay, moving from a controlled but general statement to a specific thesis.

Keep in mind, however, that some instructors, depending on the discipline, might prefer that the introduction be more abrupt or to the point; they might ask that you begin with the thesis or include a summary of the material to follow. Before beginning, ask your instructor about his or her preference and check the specific assignment format.

Your introduction can be based on several methods of developing ideas. In academic essays, for example, you may classify the material you plan to discuss (such as types of stress), define a key term from your thesis (such as *autism*), or sketch the development of a current situation (such as previous attempts to decriminalize marijuana). For a more personal essay or an essay for a more general audience, you may want to create interest by providing a vivid example, telling a relevant anecdote, or describing a detailed scene. You might begin an essay on stress, for instance, with a description of the typically harried, stressed individual.

Whatever method you choose, give your readers all the background information they need, including authors and titles of works, and dates and places of events.

Remember the following points when you are writing your introduction:

- **Avoid making large claims that the rest of your essay does not support.** Do not begin by saying *Since the beginning of time . . .* or *Throughout history . . .* or *Everyone suffers from stress . . .* unless you can (and will) provide hard evidence to support the generalization. Because you weren't there at time's beginning, because you won't be discussing all the stressed people throughout history, and because there are, indeed, some people who aren't stressed, these claims are both vague, impossible to prove, and, in fact, false; these openings will get a thumbs-down from your instructor.

- **State your thesis, not your topic.** Don't include a sentence that merely repeats the assigned topic, such as *In this essay I will discuss the dangerous effects of stress.* This thesis sounds too talky and doesn't clarify your topic.

- **Focus on the big picture, not the details.** You may choose to open with an example or incident that captures the essence of your argument. For instance, you might zoom in on the morning of a rushed businessman who is frantically commuting to work while checking his BlackBerry and eating his McBreakfast. Be wary, though, of including detailed information that belongs in the body of the essay.

Sample Introduction for an Expository Essay on Stress

(OPENING STATEMENT) Cell phones, BlackBerrys, drive-through takeouts, 24-hour grocery stores, all-night gyms, and microwaveable foods—these amenities feed our busy lives and our addiction to speed. The Internet, smart phones, and caffeine permit us to cram even more into every moment and to extend our waking hours into the wee hours of the night. **(SEGUE)** As a result, we are an underslept and overworked society. And the price we pay is stress—lots of it. **(THESIS)** Although stress once played a crucial role in survival, and some stress is indeed beneficial, an overload of stress causes a wide variety of psychological and physical ailments.

Sample Introduction for a Literary Analysis Essay

(OPENING STATEMENT) Customs can be traditions we adore, rules we blindly follow, and rituals we grudgingly accept. We may understand tradition without following it or follow tradition without understanding it. **(SEGUE)** These contradictory attitudes toward tradition and custom are illustrated in Shirley Jackson's "The Lottery," **(THESIS)** which, through its symbolism, setting, and characterization, illustrates this unsettling theme: traditions, even when violent and senseless, are difficult to change and harder to relinquish.

The Middle Paragraphs

Sometimes, such as when you are tracing the development of a concept or analyzing a chain of causes and effects, your material will determine the order of your middle paragraphs. That is, if you are explaining how to paint a room, instructions about taping would obviously comprise the first paragraph, edging the second, painting the third, and so on.

Usually, however, you will have to decide how to arrange your points and how to keep the reader intrigued. In an expository essay, to be organized and maintain interest, you might begin with the point that your readers will find easiest to understand and end with the most difficult. Alternatively, in a persuasive essay, you might build interest by beginning with your least important point and ending with the most important.

To see how you would determine the most important point, consider the structure of the essay on the effects of stress. The thesis and topic sentences suggest three blocks of material: the positive effects of stress, the negative psychological effects, and the negative physical effects. The writer has organized the material this way because she wants to move toward the more insidious, but least obvious, effect of stress—obesity—which is also her most significant point.

Remember that you can't always cover a block of material in a single paragraph. To support the point about *the negative psychological effects of stress*, for instance, you might need several paragraphs.

Whenever your discussion of a point takes up more than half a page (typed, double spaced), you need to use umbrella topic sentences—topic sentences that control the content of two or more paragraphs—and connecting topic sentences.

Sample Umbrella Topic Sentence That Could Control Three Paragraphs

Constant stress has been linked to minor psychological problems, several anxiety disorders, and depression.

Topic Sentence 1	Constant stress has been connected to minor psychological problems such as temporary insomnia and lack of libido. [Examples]
Topic Sentence 2	In addition, there is a connection between several anxiety disorders and high stress levels. [Examples]
Topic Sentence 3	Probably the least obvious but most common effect of stress is depression. [Examples]

The Conclusion

Your conclusion, which draws together the evidence and reinforces the main idea of the essay, has three basic components: a rephrasing of your thesis, a brief explanation of the significance of the major points, and a suggestion of the broader implications of the subject. In the conclusion, you are leaving the reader with some final thoughts; you might reveal how your essay or argument fits into a wider discussion or debate or encourage your reader to act. Whatever you decide, try to end with a bang, not a whimper.

The conclusion, in essence, has the opposite structure of the introduction: a restatement of thesis, followed by a segue, and then a statement pushing the thesis outward. Although you don't want to raise new issues or ask questions here, do explain how your essay fits into a wider context. Here are the three main ways to do so:

- Move from the specific to the general to suggest that the material you have covered is part of a larger issue.

  If we don't slow down now, we will pass down our fast-paced, super-stressed, unhealthy lifestyles to our children.

- Compare your subject with another subject with which your reader is likely to be familiar.

  Although medical professionals are worried about cancer, perhaps they should also be concerned about the effects of stress, which are also killing Canadians daily.

- Reinforce the significance of your subject by emphasizing its causes or effects.

  Because of the side effects of our fast-paced, super-stressed lives, we might want to consider a healthier option: losing our addiction to speed and slowing down.

Sample Conclusion

(THESIS) Although we still have the "fight-or-flight reaction," a primitive response left over from our cave-dwelling past, we must not let this reaction take over our lives. If we do, we risk developing a plethora of psychological and physical disorders and adding to the stress of our society. **(SEGUE)** Carl Honoré, founder of the Slow Movement, urges us to grasp "that middle point between fast and slow: going fast when it makes sense to be fast; going slow when it makes sense to be slow; and choosing the right speed, the right time for things" (359). **(CLOSING STATEMENT)** The solution, for all of us, lies in minor lifestyle changes, knowing when to stress and when to relax. We must all lose our addiction to speed and learn how to live a balanced, healthy life between fast and slow.

6. THE INDUCTIVE ESSAY: LEADING UP TO YOUR THESIS

If you choose the inductive method, your thesis may appear later on in your essay or at the end, or it may be implied rather than directly stated. This pattern emphasizes the process of your thinking rather than your conclusions. Before choosing this pattern, make sure that it is appropriate for your topic and that your instructor approves of it.

Advantages and Disadvantages

By delaying the presentation of your thesis, you can create suspense and interest. This approach is particularly effective in personal essays, in which you invite readers to share in the process of understanding your experience. Leading up to your thesis is also useful in persuasive essays in which you want readers to consider a potentially controversial point of view or to think in new ways about an old problem.

The danger with this method is that you may end up with many details but no main point. You can prevent this problem by structuring your essay according to one of the patterns discussed below.

Questions and Answers

In a question-and-answer pattern, your introduction poses a question that the essay answers. You may consider and reject possible answers before concluding with a satisfactory one, or you may give a series of partial answers that add up to a comprehensive one.

Introduction: The introduction sets out the problem or issue and asks the question to be answered. For instance, you might ask, "Why does Johnny, a six-year-old, have high blood pressure?" You would then rule out the typical answers before arriving at the real one.

Middle Paragraphs: The body of your essay presents possible answers in detail. Each answer forms a major section of the essay, composed of one or more paragraphs. You can help your readers follow the structure of your essay by repeating key terms and using parallel sentence structures. Arrange your paragraphs in a sequence such as simplest to most complex, or weakest answer to strongest answer. For instance, you might begin with the answer that Johnny is stressed, which is unlikely for most six-year-olds, and move to the answer that Johnny is overweight and underexercised.

Conclusion: The conclusion presents the best or most comprehensive answer as your thesis. Signal that you've reached your thesis by repeating the question from the introduction or by summarizing previous answers. Why does Johnny have high blood pressure? He has high blood pressure because at six years old, he is morbidly obese and severely unfit; Johnny is representative of the growing problem of childhood obesity in Canada.

The example below again demonstrates how the question-and-partial-answers pattern works.

Introduction [Question]	How can teachers help reduce violence in school?
Middle Paragraphs [Topic Sentences]	We can watch for signs . . .
	We can discuss the issue with students . . .
	We can also teach students ways of resolving arguments . . .
	Most important, we must model good problem-solving behaviour in our conflicts with students . . .
Conclusion [Thesis]	To reduce violence in schools, we must educate both ourselves and our students about the uses and misuses of power.

Specific Details to General Meaning

In the pattern of moving from the specific to the general, you begin with particular details and end with a thesis, either stated or implied, about the meaning of the experience as a whole.

Introduction: By using narrative or descriptive detail, you plunge your reader into the subject of your essay and arouse interest. You give a sense of structure by suggesting the final event of the narrative (*We wouldn't rest until we found the lost treasure of the Incas*) or the scope of the description (*The old neighbourhood was unrecognizable*).

Middle Paragraphs: In the body of the essay, fill in the specific details. As units of thought, your paragraphs will correspond to units of your narrative (*first week, next day, that afternoon, the moment had come*) or description (*the streets, the houses, our house*). Arrange your paragraphs in a chronological or spatial sequence that will lead naturally to your conclusion's generalization. Foreshadow this generalization by references to thoughts and feelings (*I wondered whether we were on a fool's errand*), or by choice of diction (*narrow streets, cracked sidewalks, shabby houses, our house shrunken and decayed*).

Conclusion: In the conclusion, sum up the meaning of the experience, either through explicit commentary (*The real treasures were those we had left behind: family, friends, and country*), or through an image that makes the point (*Staring back at me was the image of a white-haired old man, his face deeply creased by sorrow and worry. Several moments passed before I recognized my own reflection in the glass*).

Testing Your Inductive Structure

When you are using the inductive structure, use this test to determine whether the structure is working: Remove the thesis statement from the end of your essay; then, allow an astute reader, unfamiliar with the subject and your opinion of it, to read your essay. If the reader can approximately induce the thesis of your essay, putting it in his or her own words, than you have successfully led the reader to your main point. If the reader is confused, or does not know what point you are making, or thinks that the essay makes a number of diffuse or competing claims, your inductive structure probably needs some first aid. You may have to rethink the structure of your essay so that the thesis "matches" the paragraphs and evidence that have preceded it.

Checklist: Essays

	OK	NEEDS WORK
Thesis		
1. Does your thesis state a specific idea that the rest of the essay develops or proves?	☐	☐
Development		
2. Is all the material in the essay relevant to your thesis?	☐	☐
3. Are you satisfied that you have adequately supported your thesis?	☐	☐
4. Are the connections among your ideas stated as clearly as possible?	☐	☐
Essays That Begin with the Thesis (Deductive Essays)		
5. Does the introduction identify your subject and the range of material you will cover?	☐	☐
6. Does the introduction end with the thesis?	☐	☐

7. Do your paragraph divisions indicate the major sections of your essay?

8. Does each topic sentence clearly state the main point of the paragraph and show how the paragraph relates to or develops the thesis?

9. Do transitions help your reader to follow the connections among your ideas?

10. Does the conclusion return to the thesis, sum up the main points, and suggest a broader context or the implications of your subject?

Essays That Lead Up to the Thesis (Inductive Essays)

11. Does the introduction identify your subject, get the reader's interest, and suggest the structure of your essay?

12. Does the essay seem divided into the appropriate number of paragraphs?

13. Do transitions help your reader to follow the sequence of ideas, events, or details?

14. Does the conclusion sum up the ideas, events, or details by stating or clearly implying your thesis?

Sharing Personal Experience: Paragraphs and Essays

As newspapers, magazines, and television networks have discovered and, at times, exploited, readers and viewers have a seemingly insatiable interest in the personal lives of others. You too can enliven your writing by incorporating paragraphs about your own or someone else's experience. In this chapter, you will learn how to tell stories that illustrate your point; how to describe people, places, and things so that they come alive; and how to use analogies that convey your feelings and attitudes. Keep in mind that all of these methods of sharing personal experience can be developed into paragraphs and longer pieces. Alternatively, they can be incorporated into other essays.

1. TELLING A STORY

Telling stories is one of the main ways we make sense of our lives for ourselves and share our world with others. Funny, heroic, and romantic stories—they all have something to say about who we are. The stories we keep hidden—stories about our fears, our failures, our struggles—are often the ones that, when told, connect us to others.

Short personal narratives, composed of a paragraph or two, are often used to enliven other kinds of writing. An article criticizing cuts to health care, for instance, may begin with a story about a patient who died while waiting in the emergency room. These personal narratives will be our focus. You will also find narration combined with causal analysis and plot summaries.

Here are some suggestions for writing personal narratives.

- **Choose a single meaningful event with a definite beginning and end.** The event may be part of a larger story that you could write about in a personal essay. For instance, you might write a narrative paragraph about the last few miles of your first marathon, when, for many, the real pain begins. This paragraph could stand on its own or be part of a longer essay about training for a marathon.

- **Decide what point you want to make about this event.** Did your adventure, for example, teach you something about taking risks or about taking precautions? About trust or about self-reliance? About patience? Pain? You could state this point explicitly in a topic sentence, or you could allow it to emerge implicitly from the way you tell the story.

- **Decide how to organize your paragraph.** To heighten suspense, place the events in chronological order, with your main point emerging at the end. Or, if you want to emphasize your reflections on the incident, you could begin with your point and then tell the story.

- **Use transitions to help your reader follow the sequence of events.** Show how events are related in time by using terms such as *first, next, then, last, in the beginning, in the end, soon, later, as soon as, meanwhile,* and by referring to specific times, days, months, seasons, and dates.

- **Decide what information to include and exclude.** When composing personal paragraphs, writers are often tempted to include every detail, but doing so might make the paragraph bland, unfocused, or confusing. Choose the most vivid details to include. Even though you are writing a personal paragraph, every sentence must still contribute to and develop the topic sentence, whether it is stated or implied.

- **Select details that will create in readers a response similar to your own.** Recording small details can help to individualize your stories. In writing about a familiar situation, such as training your dog to sit, for example, you might make the experience fresh and humorous by describing all the scenarios you used to make Bella the beagle first learn this command.

- **Choose words that make the experience vivid for your reader and convey your attitude toward the event.** Use concrete language and imagery. Don't say the sky was blue; describe the sky as a deep azure. Instead of writing, at mile twenty of the marathon, that your legs hurt, say the following: *At mile twenty, every step felt like a milestone: my quads were lead, my calves were twisted into knots, and in place of my big toes were two bloody, throbbing stumps.*

- **Include your thoughts, feelings, and judgments about the event.** Direct statements about thoughts, feelings, and judgments help readers understand the significance of details. For example, you might begin or end a series of seemingly random and contradictory ideas with the statement *I was confused.*

Sample Personal Narrative

This narrative paragraph creates suspense through its precise details, expressions of feeling, and chronological arrangement of events. Because this is an inductive paragraph, the topic sentence is placed at the end. A paragraph such as this would make a good introduction to a personal essay.

In the sample below, notice how the writer uses spatial organization to organize the paragraph's details: she moves from the top to the bottom of her body to illustrate the physical pain experienced during the race. In this inductive composition, the writer presents the details first, leaving the main point until the end.

My eyes sting from the sweat constantly trickling into them, and my hot, crusty skin burns as it rubs against my sports bra. Blood, sweat, and salt mingle in the small of my back. My pelvis feels as if it has been squeezed into a too-small girdle and my running shorts, dripping wet, chafe my waist and thighs like a modern hair shirt. My bladder screams "go to the bathroom," but I won't satisfy it and lose one minute, even one second. My legs, two lead pipes welded awkwardly to my body, grow heavier and more and cumbersome with each step. My hip flexors move mechanically, almost robotically, and my quads have been tenderized by tiny meat hammers. The screams of my rock-hard calves won't let up, regardless of how I adjust my stride. The fat pads of my feet seem to have disappeared, my ankles are sore from pressing against wet laces, and through the white mesh of my shoes, I can see several bloody spots where my toenails used to be. I want to lie down by the side of the road, curl up, and sleep. Maybe die. But I must keep on trudging to stay on pace. I am at mile twenty of my very first marathon and I have six long and painful miles to go.

Exercise 1

Identify a quality you particularly like or dislike in yourself or someone else. Then write a narrative paragraph about an incident that reveals this quality.

Example: a roommate's stinginess—refusing to share nachos and pizza while we watched Team Canada play Team USA.

Exercise 2

Choose a significant experience in your life (such as a birth, death, marriage, divorce, move, accident, achievement, or failure). Use brainstorming to help you recall the small but meaningful incidents you associate with the experience (such as riding in an ambulance). Choose one of these incidents with a definite beginning and end, and write a narrative paragraph revealing its significance.

Example: *Experience*—the death of the family cat. *Event*—seeing the cat get run over and trying to hide its body from your sister. *Significance*—the need to protect fragile loved ones from pain or loss.

2. DESCRIBING A PERSON, PLACE, OR THING

When you describe people, places, or things, you attempt to translate into words how they look, sound, feel, smell, move, or taste. In description, then, your goal is not to tell but to show. Saying that Aunt Minnie's living room is horribly decorated is telling. Writing that Aunt Minnie's living room features greasy wood panelling left over from the seventies, a coffee-stained and cigarette-burned moss green loveseat, a selection of glaring neon-coloured macramé cushions, and a velvet Elvis overlooking a bedraggled wicker chair is showing. These details allow the reader to visualize Aunt Minnie's room, and, hopefully, agree with your opinion about her questionable decorating.

Although your goal is to connect to your reader's senses, there are, in fact, two kinds of description: objective and subjective. In objective description, such as in a scientific report, you are more concerned with stating facts or revealing a picture that can be seen and/or understood by most people; in subjective description, you choose details to create a snapshot that captures a certain mood, image, or dominant impression of your subject. Subjective description, then, is far more personal.

For instance, a geographer writing a scientific article about the Canadian Shield would probably use a lot of objective description, such as geographical coordinates, number of species, size of area, and so on: *The Canadian Shield, also known as the Laurentian Shield, is a massive U-shaped geological formation composed of exposed Precambrian rock, which extends from Western Canada to the Adirondack Mountains and from the Great Lakes to the Arctic Islands.*

However, a real estate agent selling holiday properties would no doubt rely more on subjective description: *What is Bliss? Bliss is hearing the waves tumble against the shore, wandering through quiet, lush, temperate forests, and watching raptors soar amidst the treetops. Bliss is not hearing the bustle and not feeling the tussle of the city. Bliss is here at Tofino Sands Beach Resort and Retirement Community. Call us today for a free brochure, and get one step closer to finding your own piece of heaven.*

In personal writing, in which you share experiences—such as your father's delight in reading bedtime stories, your fear as you walk down a deserted street at night, your love-hate relationship with an unreliable car—you will probably rely more on subjective description. You must decide which details to include and omit; if you try to describe everything, your reader will be confused and overwhelmed. As well, your main point will be unclear. If you wanted to show your father's delight in bedtime reading, for example, you would ignore the note of exasperation that crept into his voice if you interrupted too often, and instead describe his excitement as he "became" different characters in *Peter Pan*.

Although vivid descriptions of people, places, and things are central to most personal essays, they also make good introductions for expository and persuasive essays. For example, you might begin a persuasive essay on rescuing greyhounds by detailing how these racing dogs live in cramped kennels for most of the day before being summarily put down when their careers are over. A descriptive paragraph like this one adds human interest to discussions of general issues.

Follow these guidelines for writing descriptive paragraphs:

- **Choose a familiar subject or one you can observe while you write.** It can be surprisingly hard to remember the kinds of details to bring your paragraph to life—the colour of a friend's eyes, the sound of wind through trees, the smell of a schoolroom. If you choose to describe something from memory, try closing your eyes and putting yourself into the scene before you write about it.

- **Focus your paragraph.** To help you describe rather than give examples, focus on the details of your subject at a particular time or performing a particular action. For instance, you could vividly describe a kitten's playfulness—how it looks, moves, sounds—by taking one detail, such as how it acts in the mirror, and zeroing in on it. Without this focal point, you might end up giving many examples of a kitten's playful behaviour without adequately describing any of them.

- **Decide what dominant impression you want to convey about your subject.** A good description is not merely a catalogue of features: "Her house is a stucco bungalow from the fifties." Decide what dominant impression you want to create: a dog's silliness, an aunt's stubbornness, the peacefulness of a landscape.

- **Select details that contribute to your dominant impression.** Include a broad range of sensory details—not just how something looks, but also how it sounds, feels, tastes, smells, moves. You don't have to use all of these, however, for you don't want to overwhelm your reader's senses. If you were describing the atmosphere of a hockey playoff game, for example, you might want to focus on the sounds and the sights to convey the excitement.

- **Arrange the details in a spatial order, with the most important detail last.** Choose an arrangement that reflects how you, as an observer, would perceive your subject: in a panoramic sweep from left to right; from close up to farther away, or vice versa; or from the most obvious feature to the least obvious.

- **Show how objects are related in space.** Use transitional words such as *nearer, farther, on the right, on the left, at the top, at the bottom, to the east, to the west.* You want the reader to clearly see what you describe.

- **Begin or end with a point about the person, place, or thing.** *My cat is very playful* is a descriptive generalization, but it is not an interesting point about the kitten's behaviour. You could make a more interesting point about the transitory nature of youth and playfulness in a topic sentence: *Watching my kitten play, I remember how I used to make faces at myself in the mirror, not realizing that the scowls of childhood would settle into the lines of middle age.* Or you could let it emerge implicitly through your description: *Each day the kitten tires of the game more quickly, and soon we will both pass the mirror without a glance.*

In the following paragraph from a personal essay, the writer tells us almost nothing about the physical appearance of a teacher who "shocked me so much that I experienced a marked change in my attitude toward school and the subject of English." Instead, he chooses details that show how Mr. Wellington's surroundings reflect his vulnerability, and then makes this point in a topic sentence at the end.

Sample Personal Description

Mr. Wellington was neither neat nor tidy. The chaos of his room seemed to echo the sound of someone saying, "Hang on, it's in here somewhere. I just put it down yesterday. I'll find it." The walls were covered from top to bottom with posters, but not a single one was hung straight. His desk was inhabited by masses of paper that had somehow gathered there as if attracted by a "paper magnet." Surrounding his desk was a whole herd of dictionaries, including a condensed version of the Oxford English Dictionary, which required a magnifying glass to peer into the depths of its compiled wisdom. Mr. Wellington would frequently consult these books in efforts to stop the arguments waged against him about the meanings of words in the poems we analyzed in class. Throughout all this activity, his coffee cup was never to be seen detached from his hand. I cannot blame him for needing a cup of coffee to carry him through to the next period. It was his coffee cup that made him look human, vulnerable—not like the other teachers, who were not human but "teachers." Perhaps it was his vulnerability that inspired confidence, even though he was surrounded by what looked like ineptitude.

—Steve Marsh

Exercise 3

Make a list of the sensations you experience as you eat something, such as an ice cream cone or a slice of pizza. Use all of your senses. Arrange your list so that a point emerges from your description.

Exercise 4

Write a descriptive paragraph about one of the following: a person who has had an impact on your life, a place where you feel safe (or unsafe), or an object to which you have a strong attachment.

Exercise 5

Sit for half an hour in a public place—on a bus, in a mall, in church, at a hockey rink—and make notes about what you see, hear, and smell. If you have a MP3 player, consider dictating into it. Then write a descriptive paragraph about the place as a whole, one or more people in it, or a particular object. Be sure to select details that convey a dominant impression and make a point about your subject.

3. USING ANALOGIES

Attitudes and emotions are often difficult to describe without falling into clichés and generalities. Analogies, which are extended metaphors, allow you to translate inner experiences into vivid images that your reader can understand. They also grab your reader's attention, forcing him/her to see your subject in a new and startling light. Analogies, therefore, which make the abstract concrete, are effective in personal, expository, and persuasive writing. Consider, for example, the attitudes suggested by these metaphors:

Life is a highway. (Tom Cochrane)

Life is "a tale told by an idiot, full of sound and fury, signifying nothing." (*Macbeth*)

These metaphors could be developed into analogies by exploring, in a paragraph, the similarities they suggest. For the first, for instance, you might consider the attributes that both life and a highway share: distance, direction, destination, obstacles, detours, etc. These analogies would tell us much more about the writer (or character) than would statements such as "Life is full of challenges" or "Life sucks."

To write an effective analogy, follow these steps:

- **Make a list of metaphors or similes comparing your subject with a variety of things that are different in appearance, form, or kind, but are similar in behaviour.**

Overcoming an addiction is like

—salvaging a wrecked ship

—weaning a baby

—saying goodbye to an old friend

- **Choose the metaphor or simile that best suits the attitude or experience you want to convey.**

✗—salvaging a wrecked ship [does not acknowledge the pleasurable aspects of the addiction]

✗—weaning a baby [suggests we "grow out of" addictions]

✓—saying goodbye to an old, yet destructive friend [suggests that addictions, once pleasurable, must be forsaken]

- **Develop your metaphor or simile into a paragraph by exploring the similarities it suggests.**

What is it like to say goodbye to an old friend? There's the memory of good times and bad, the desire to hold on, and the need to let go. By emphasizing the positive aspects, the writer helps readers who do not share the addiction to understand why it is hard to abandon.

In the following example, the writer helps readers understand the debilitating effects of an unfamiliar health problem by comparing it to a more familiar condition.

Sample Analogy

Think back to the most persistent flu or cold you have ever had. Remember that day when the virus was at its worst, you know, around day two, three, or four. You wished you could remove your head from your body, and you were too exhausted to remove it even if you could have, and it was all you could do to get up and drink some juice and maybe take a cold tablet before you collapsed back into bed. Add to it: sides so tender and sore that when someone touches you, you yelp in pain; kidney infections so extreme you are doubled over as you walk and cannot right yourself. Add food allergies to most of the foods you used to eat with no problem, including a complete intolerance for sugar. Add chemical sensitivities so extreme that walking past a running vehicle, passing through a smoky room, or standing near an acquaintance wearing hairspray or perfume can result in muscle convulsions or an unexpected mood swing, severe headaches or more fatigue. Add seizures or blackouts. These are some of the physical symptoms experienced by the more than 250,000 people in Canada who suffer from Myalgic Encephalomyelitis, otherwise known as Chronic Fatigue Syndrome.

—Patti Skocdopole

Exercise 6

Complete each of the following similes.

1. Looking for a job is like _____.

2. Finding your way around an unfamiliar city is like _____.

3. Visiting the dentist is like _____.

4. Going on a blind date is like _____.

Exercise 7

Make a list of the similarities suggested by two of the similes in Exercise 6.

Review Exercise 8

Write a paragraph about a hard-to-communicate experience or feeling, using at least two of the methods discussed in this chapter: narration, description, and analogy. For example, you might convey the intensity of your feelings about your first car by both describing the car and developing an analogy with Aladdin's magic carpet.

4. PERSONAL ESSAYS

Although your main purpose when writing personal essays, just as in writing personal paragraphs, is to share your thoughts, feelings, and experiences, you must also explain what your experience means or why it is relevant. As we consider two kinds of personal essays (narrative and descriptive), we will discuss how to fulfill your readers' expectations. Most of your personal essays are likely to be based on events in your life, so we will examine narrative essays most closely.

Like other essays, narrative essays must have a point, a main idea. To see why a main idea is important, consider an example.

Suppose you decide to write about "My MS Bike Tour." The title, as you can see, doesn't suggest any point about the tour. It is unfocused. It offers no principle to help you select which events to include and which to omit, or how to arrange them effectively. So you might begin at the beginning, ramble on, go on to the end, talk about the middle, and stop. However, if you present the events in this manner, you will limit your audience; that is, a disorganized description might interest your mother or your best friend, someone who knows how you think and feel, but probably not your instructor, your desired reader, or someone considering completing the MS Bike Tour.

Imagine, then, that you will focus on one incident and title your essay "The Lesson of Suffering on My MS Bike Tour." You would now have a way of deciding what to include in your essay, and you might even think about how to present your material—such as describing your throbbing muscles as you pedalled up that long hill, battered by gusts of wind and driving rain.

Think about your physical struggle. What did you learn from it? There are many possible lessons that you might have learned—your ability to push against personal limits, for instance, or the power of nature, or empathy for those who encounter daily physical challenges. Most of us learn these lessons at some time. The deeper significance of your narrative will engage your readers. They will not only find out what happened, but also will discover the meaning of the experience, both for you and for their own lives. This meaning will be the thesis that you state or imply through your narrative.

However, what you have learned should not be a simple moral tacked on at the end (*From this incident I learned to appreciate my . . .*) Rather, the meaning should emerge from how you present the concrete details of the experience as well as your specific points. Instead of telling, show. Telling that this experience has changed your outlook is less effective than saying the following: *Whenever I feel not up to the challenge, I think of pedalling up that endless hill in the driving rain, my aches and pains reminding me of the joy of being alive and the healthy body that I will never again take for granted.*

Writing Narrative Essays: The Process

Follow these guidelines when writing a narrative essay:

1. Focus on a single experience, so that you can include a wealth of detail about it.

2. Make a central point about the meaning of this experience.

3. Put this central point (your thesis) at the beginning, at the end, or at the place in the narrative where the meaning of events becomes clear to you.

4. Arrange your material to create a specific effect, such as suspense, humour, or sorrow.

5. Include only events and details relevant to the central point.

6. Provide enough specific details about *who, what, when, where, why,* and *how,* so the reader understands how events and actions relate to the central point.

7. Make the sequence of events clear to readers by using transitional words and phrases to indicate time relationships (*the next morning, now that I look back*).

8. Create interest through diction, figurative language, and a good writing style.

5. SAMPLE NARRATIVE ESSAY

This personal essay, written by a university student, narrates the writer's early upbringing and experience with God before explaining his transition to atheism. Although O'Shaugnessy admits that "it is difficult to pinpoint the exact moment" he became an atheist, he details an event that made him question not only his own beliefs but also those of his fellow parishioners. There is, then, a definite turning point in this piece.

This is primarily a narrative essay, but other methods of development are effectively integrated: for instance, the writer incorporates several examples of how religion originally emotionally and intellectually challenged him, whereas he uses description to illustrate and to slow down the extremely uncomfortable moment at the Youth Encounter.

The tone of this piece is unique. Despite the provocative subject matter, the writer seems almost emotionally distant. He relies on neutral language, understatement, and negation. He disinterestedly debates the origin of his own morality. Also, much is left unsaid. That is, in the anointing with the Holy Oil, he focuses on what he *didn't* rather than what he *did* experience. As well, he reveals what being an atheist allows him to know rather than to feel and includes more questions than answers, before quietly suggesting, in the end, the connection between atheism and personal freedom.

Becoming an Atheist
by Michael O'Shaughnessy

It is difficult to pinpoint the exact moment when I became an atheist. I was raised Catholic, in a devout family environment. My father is Irish by descent—from the Catholic parts of the island, not the "occupied counties"—and a Quebecer by birth. My mother is an immigrant from the Philippines. My family not only attended weekly mass and all days of obligation, but also a lay prayer group affiliated with a group called Charismatic Catholics, which is Catholic in theology but borrows liberally from Protestant Pentecostal denominations (including an emphasis on the real presence of the Holy Spirit, lively music, and speaking in glossolalia).

I often got the chance to interact with my priest, a Jesuit and accomplished scholar who was working on his doctorate while in Canada. As such, not only was I emotionally enraptured by the religion, but intellectually engaged as well; I would often sit in on theological debates conducted by my priest—discussions ranging from the obstacles to ecumenical union with the Anglicans and Eastern Orthodox churches to the possible theological implications of Earth's being visited by extra-terrestrial creatures. (As a nine-year-old, guess which one I enjoyed more?)

At some point, however, it all began to ring hollow. My priest finished his doctorate and left for the Philippines. Meanwhile, the songs and glossolalia became familiar, and somehow less real.

I remember going to a Youth Encounter, which aimed to give adolescents an "encounter" with the Holy Spirit, and sitting through all the usual prayers and songs. At the end of the service came the anointing with Holy Oils. The aim of this consecration was to prepare one for their encounter with the Holy Spirit.

As in a scene out of a televangelist's infomercial, when the people in front of me in line were anointed, they lost strength in their bodies and had to be helped to the ground to lie down, so overwhelmed were they by the experience. So I waited with some degree of anxiety for my turn, and when it came? nothing. I felt nothing.

I searched for the sensation of oneness with the world, of the sagging of strength in my legs that I assumed would come, but nothing came. I simply had an oily forehead. A bit embarrassed, I faked the sagging of strength and lay down with the rest of the children, and then it occurred to me: Could all these people be faking too?

It was all downhill from there, as the saying goes. My parents had raised me as a devout Catholic, but they had also encouraged my intellectual curiosity. I was raised to question everything, and to argue well. (For as long as I can remember, if I could challenge a house rule and present a valid case for it being changed, it would be changed.) I had believed that it was impossible to know whether or not God is real, but had always accepted His existence on faith. Eventually, I came to abandon that, as I realized that the argument in favour of God was not particularly strong.

Though all good theoretically came from God, I didn't feel particularly evil now that I was denying his existence. Why did I not cheat on tests, skip class or lie to my parents if there was no God to watch over me and threaten me with punishment? Why did I bother being a good person at all? Though I wrestled with these questions, I never behaved in an amoral way. I concluded that my moral compass was not given to me by God but by my parents. I came to believe that "right" and "wrong" were based around the suffering of other people, and that morality can be summed up very succinctly in the words of Hippocrates: "First, do no harm."

I came to appreciate how the universe operates on its own, without any outside interference, and came to see how humanity evolved through a slow, incremental process over hundreds of millions of years, from the simplest single-celled organism, to the dinosaur, to the ape who carves great cities out of the earth. And eventually, in the midst of all this, I came to the conclusion that while there was nothing directly contradicting the existence of God—He could possibly be sitting in His divine director's chair watching this all happen—there was nothing to confirm it, either. So why believe it at all? And so I became an atheist.

It was lonely, at first. Even terrifying. But eventually I realized it meant I was free.

6. DESCRIPTIVE ESSAYS

If the unifying principle of narrative essays is what happened to me, the unifying principle of descriptive essays is what I experienced. Keep this distinction in mind because narrative essays may also include descriptions of people, places, and objects; as well, descriptive essays may include accounts of things happening. In description, however, your main focus is rendering your impressions of the world or of an experience.

Subjects

You can write descriptive essays about places, people, or other animate and inanimate things. You might write, for example, a brief essay about the habits of your next-door neighbour, a character sketch of a coach who taught you the importance of dedication, or a personal piece about a family heirloom to explain its meaning in your life.

Image and Meaning

Just as in narrative essays, concrete images create meaning more effectively than do direct statements. Specific images of people, places, and objects allow your reader to see through your eyes and thus to empathize with your thoughts, feelings, and judgments.

Organization

For short descriptive essays, you might allow the meaning of the whole to emerge gradually from the accumulation of details. However, in longer descriptive essays, you may need to state your main point near the beginning and bring in other methods of development—such as a comparison of one person with another or an analysis of the effects of a shifting population on a town.

Whatever overall structure you choose, you should arrange the parts of the essay by an appropriate principle of organization, usually spatial. This spatial organization may be literal (moving from one part of the town to the next) or figurative (moving from what is "easy to see" about a person to what is "hard to see"). Most important, your method of organization should culminate in an image conveying your dominant impression.

7. SAMPLE DESCRIPTIVE ESSAY

This short descriptive essay, written by a university student, artfully invokes the reader's senses to illustrate the atmosphere and to mark a shift in tone. First, the writer focuses on smell and sight to communicate the peacefulness and quiet of her grandmother's cheery kitchen before shifting to the horrible and unfamiliar noise that interrupted this blissful scene. From this point, the writer relies on several senses to stress the chaos of being shuffled into the bomb shelter. She also effectively uses several sentence fragments to mimic the mood of urgency and to reveal her own feelings of confusion and fear.

To build suspense, the writer uses an inductive structure, ending with a statement about the context, before relying on another fragment for the thesis: "And the Gulf War had just begun."

The writer's use of figures of speech is both skilled and inventive. For practice, see if you can find examples of metaphors, images, and personification.

Sugar Cookies and Bomb Shelters
by Judy Heilik

I'm sitting in my bubbe's kitchen, the cheery yellow walls enveloping me like one of her endless hugs. The smell of sugar cookies wafting from the oven mingles with the scent of the orange tree that I can see from the window. It's the tree that I pick a handful of oranges from each morning for our breakfast, and I notice that there is a marked empty space from my forages. If only I could reach a tiny bit further, I know that I would have an infinite supply, but my twelve-year-old arms can only stretch so far, even when I lean out the window standing on my tiptoes.

The breeze coming in from the window is gentle and warm, and when I tip back in my chair, I can feel the air dance around my body. Heaven. The oven timer beeps happily, and without opening my eyes, I can sense my bubbe walking her slow, lopsided walk to rescue the cookies. I know that they'll be too hot, just as I know that she'll turn a blind eye when I sneak one, the right corner of her mouth rising up in the sly conspiratory way that it does so very often.

I'm stuffing the piping hot cookie into my mouth, trying to suck air at the same time so as not to scald my tongue. I inadvertently choke on the crumbs as the shrillest sound I've ever heard shreds the peace and calm of the afternoon. Because I have never heard such a piercing noise, I'm convinced that my eardrums are going to explode. I look around in terror, and see the sly smile on my bubbe's face replaced with a hard twist to her mouth and a steely look in her eyes. She tells me to go and get the knapsack that's been sitting in the corner of my bedroom, unnoticed by me amid the magazines and books that are far more interesting.

When I come back into the kitchen, knapsack slung over my shoulder, my eyes tearing from the uncertainty of what's happening and my ears burning from the siren's scream, I see that my bubbe has two black, rubber, evil-looking things in her hands.

"Put this on" she tells me.

Mimicking her movements, I put the mask over my face and attach the elasticized strap behind my head. It's too loose, so she yanks it tighter, catching strands of hair as she does so. She grabs my hand, and with a speed that I've never before seen from her, pulls me through the apartment, down the stairs teeming with other panicked people, and onto the lawn surrounding the building. I get caught up in the wave of people streaming from the building, all heading towards a squat, grey, ugly structure. The bomb shelter. The place where my friends and I had snuck into just the day before to play Ping-Pong and make believe. The place where I was now choking on the hot stagnant air in my mask, staring at the other wide-eyed people who were staring back at me. I felt my bubbe press something into my hand. I felt the plastic of the handle crinkle as I gripped it, and felt its weight pulling on my fingers. In this moment of terror, I was still able to smell the comforting sweetness of the sugar cookies and oranges that she had hastily packed for me.

I was on vacation visiting my grandparents in Israel. And the Gulf War had just begun.

8. INTERVIEWS

When you are writing essays, interviews, which are a form of personal writing, can provide additional information and create interest. Conducting an interview, or a series of interviews, is useful for obtaining information about local people, issues, and events. If you were writing an essay on fetal alcohol syndrome, for instance, you might supplement your reading by speaking to teachers working with children who have FAS. Interviews are also interesting and self-contained pieces of writing that allow readers to enter into another person's world.

Here are some guidelines for conducting a good interview.

Preparing for the Interview

1. Choose your informant carefully. The most obvious choice is not always the best one. The drummer in a band, for instance, may have shrewder insights into the band's strengths and weaknesses than the lead singer.

2. Make a limited list of questions to gather the necessary information. Start the interview with straightforward questions. Alternate key questions with less relevant ones, so that you can finish your notes on important points while your informant answers the next question. Don't ask questions that can be answered with yes or no; ask open-ended questions that invite full responses.

3. Decide whether to take notes or to record the interview. Your choice depends on how comfortable you and your informant feel with each method and how you will use the material. If you plan to use only a few direct quotes, taking notes should be sufficient. However, tape the session if you want a lengthy first-hand account of the informant's experiences, if you plan to present your material in a question-and-answer format, or if misquoting your informant could cause problems.

4. When you request an interview, identify yourself and your project. Explain why the interview is important and how you will use the information. Give the person a sense of what you already know about the subject so that he or she will know how technical to be in response to your questions.

5. Arrange a convenient time and place for the interview and suggest how long you think the interview will take.

Conducting the Interview

1. Express appreciation for the interview. Then, tell the person again how you will use the information, assuring him or her of the confidentiality of his/her information.

2. Refer to, but don't be confined by, your list of questions.

3. Ask your informant to clarify, expand upon, or give examples of points. Specific details bring interviews to life.

4. If you are taking notes, don't write down everything; jot down facts and opinions, using key words to remember the context. Take down a few direct quotes to capture the informant's personality and view. Review your notes with your informant before leaving.

5. If appropriate, jot down details of the person's appearance, actions, manner of speaking, and the place, so that you can include them in your piece.

Writing Up the Interview

You can present interview material in a variety of ways. The question-and-answer format, which works like a dialogue, is effective when you want to probe some questions in detail. The edited transcript, in contrast, allows your informant to tell a story without interruption. Or, you can integrate your interview into an essay combining quotations, paraphrased material, background information, and a character description.
    Here are some guidelines for writing up the interview:

1. Use only the material that best suits the purpose of your piece.

2. Combine material from different parts of the interview to fully explain a point. Just make sure that you indicate that you are doing so.

3. Edit direct quotations to eliminate repetition, correct obvious mistakes, and so forth, but do not distort the meaning or tone of the original.

4. If you discover that you need to check facts or fill in missing information, make a list of questions and call your informant. Try to call only once.

5. After the interview, write a brief letter to the person you interviewed, expressing your thanks. If possible, send the person a courtesy copy of the piece.

9. SAMPLE INTERVIEW

Short excerpts from the interview below were integrated into a research essay on "The Yellow Wallpaper," a short story by Charlotte Perkins Gilman, which, among other things, deals with mental illness. Before the interview, the student asked the informant to read the story, comment on it, and think about her own experience with postpartum depression.

Q: What did you think of the story?

A: I thought it was terrifying, yet realistic and believable, but mostly I was really mad at John for not listening to his wife. I had to put the story down twice because I felt so frustrated for poor Jane. No one would take her seriously, listen to her.

Q: In what ways was your experience similar to Jane's?

A: I remember that after my second baby, I was so down, like the bottom had fallen out of me; I didn't want to do anything. I didn't even want to eat or brush my hair; all the little things were such a task, yet I was also supposed to be taking care of this helpless baby, who needed me. I wasn't up to it. Like Jane, I had mixed feelings about my baby. I wanted to see him, but he also made me nervous, and, I hate to say it, I was worried about hurting him; I could see myself . . . drowning him . . . smothering him . . . I was really, really scared. Jane never says it out loud, but the images of strangled heads must be her wish to strangle her baby. I didn't hallucinate, of course, but I was a little paranoid. I remember thinking that the Atco guy reading the meter was watching me, evaluating me as a mother, thinking I wasn't good enough.

Q: Did you talk to anyone about your feelings?

A: Not immediately . . . I had so much shame and uncertainty. I mean, how can you tell your husband that you can't look at your baby, that you are thinking about killing your own child, your own flesh and blood? And Philip, like John, was hardly home, so busy, and he has always been so rational—he only saw what he wanted to see.

Q: Then, how did you get help?

A: Believe it or not, I saw this special on PPD on TV, and there was this lady, this well-dressed professional, talking about the same feelings and how drugs helped her. She said she was thinking of committing suicide with her baby. Driving off a bridge one Sunday. Can you imagine? She was a CEO! But she looked so together right now—like a different lady. I didn't call my doctor right away, but soon afterwards.

Q: What did the doctor prescribe and how long did it take the drug to work?

A: I took antidepressants, for the first time in my life. It's hard to say how long it took me to feel better, but I remember that a week or so later . . . a cloud was lifted from me; I could think a lot more clearly and those dangerous thoughts went away. I still felt sad and tired but sane. It's too bad the narrator of the story didn't get the proper help.

Explaining One Subject

When your purpose is to explain, your focus is on your subject and what your readers need to know to understand your subject. In this chapter, we will discuss three ways of explaining one subject: **using examples**, **defining terms and concepts**, and **analyzing**.

This chapter will give you practice in using these methods to explain a subject within a single paragraph and within an essay. That is, expository paragraphs often appear within pieces of writing that persuade or share personal experience. If you were writing a persuasive essay about permitting gay marriage, for instance, you might devote a few paragraphs to explaining the definition of marriage in various cultures. On the other hand, you might choose to write an expository essay that develops one of these rhetorical modes.

1. USING EXAMPLES

Whenever you want to explain an idea or a concept, or prove an opinion, you need reasons and examples. Both help to answer these questions: *Why do you think so?* or *What is your proof?* Giving one or more reasons is the first step in explaining your generalization or proving your point; the next step is giving examples—specific instances that show your reason(s) to be valid. For your explanation to be strong, you need reasons and examples that readers can verify independently. Consider the following examples:

> This street is dangerous at night [opinion] because it is badly lit [verifiable reason]. In one four-block stretch, there is only one street lamp [verifiable example].

> This street is dangerous at night [opinion] because vampires gather here [reason not verifiable]. Drops of blood on the corner show where there was a vampire attack [example not verifiable].

Despite the popularity of books such as *Twilight*, vampires are still fictional entities, so using them as proof makes both your reasons and argument questionable.

Both reasons and examples, then, must have some basis in reality. And even if they do, not all readers will agree with your claim. They may not find your particular reasons convincing, or they may point to counter-examples. Nevertheless, by using sound reasons and good examples, you explain your point and demonstrate how you arrived at your opinion. These guidelines will help you use examples effectively.

Guidelines for Effective Use of Examples

- **Include an example to support any important general point.** Let's suppose you want to write a review of the movie *Avatar*, arguing that it doesn't deserve an Oscar—or, perhaps, your twelve dollars—for the following reasons: the story is unoriginal, the plot is non-existent, the acting is subpar, the characters are flat, and the effects are over-whelming. If you were going to discuss each of these reasons in one or two paragraphs, you would have to watch the movie again, analyzing it and choosing some concrete examples to support all of the above rea-sons. Examples will support your reasons and allow your reader to see how you arrived at this estimation.

- **Make sure your examples are typical.** Suppose, for instance, you are explaining that mandatory retirement is unfair. You might want to support your position by giving the example of your mother, who was not eligible for a full pension when she was forced to retire at sixty-five because she did not begin to work full-time until she was forty. If you used only this example to support your argument, readers might object, saying that your mother's case is atypical and therefore is poor evidence. This example would be effective, however, if you could show that many women are in the same situation. You would also want to use examples of people in different circumstances who also suffer because of mandatory retirement, such as those who change employers or careers.

- **Explain the meaning of your examples.** Don't expect an exam-ple to speak for itself; you must show its connection to the generality or point. Don't skip steps in your explanation.

  Online shopping can make your life easier. Solicited email advertisements can target your exact needs.

  Because the connection between online shopping and solicited email ads is unclear, the writer needs to add a few more sentences.
  Explain your point first with a reason and then give your example:

  Online shopping can make life easier. When people shop online, they are profiled and their product interests and hobbies are monitored. Instead of unsolicited email ads, people receive targeted messages for things that might interest them. For instance, people who buy running shoes will get emails announcing fitness equipment and vitamins, rather than Viagra, adult diapers, and quick-weight-loss aids. These consumer profiles, in fact, eliminate a lot of junk mail and also, in turn, make online shopping more efficient.

- **Integrate your examples smoothly.** If you haven't had much prac-tice using examples, you may be tempted to introduce them with awk-ward phrases such as *An example of this is when* . . . You can integrate your examples more smoothly by using constructions such as these: *for example, a further example, is exemplified by, for instance, an instance is, such as, this point is illustrated in, an illustration of this point is.*

This government's indifference to the needs of ordinary people is revealed in its plan to tax basic foods and children's clothing.

The adolescent's desire to conform is best exemplified by the popularity of the Xbox.

The half-hour line-ups in the cafeteria are further evidence of the need for more staff.

Sample Example Paragraphs (non-literary subject)

In the sample below, which is taken from an expository essay on passive-aggressive personality disorder, the first paragraph uses an extended illustration whereas the second offers several examples.

In passive-aggressive personality disorder, obstructionism or defiance is disguised as compliance. For instance, a person with passive-aggressive personality disorder will pretend to agree to another's requests and then do whatever he or she wants. The passive-aggressive, has, in fact, developed several strategies to avoid satisfying the demands of others. Here is one common scenario: Gina asks her husband, Bill, to go to the store to buy green onions, eggs, and mushrooms, which she needs for appetizers she is taking to a party that night. Bill hurriedly agrees to make a list, but he doesn't; he leaves work late, rushes to the store, doesn't answer Gina's text about the items, and returns home with celery, green peppers, and milk. Gina is unable to finish the recipe, so she sends Bill back to the store, and they end up arriving late to the party, which she has wanted to attend all week. In this sabotaging behaviour, Bill appears to be complying, but he is actually expressing his disapproval at both going to the store and attending the party. When these grocery store mishaps first occurred, Gina forgave Bill, attributing his behaviour to being tired, absent-minded, or perhaps even a bit stupid; she even believed that she was the one who was too demanding and unrelenting. However, after similar repeated episodes, Gina concluded that Bill was being intentionally obstinate. This pattern of behaviour began to threaten their relationship.

Here are some other common situations, in which disagreement is disguised as agreement, and their interpretations. Steve tells Amy that he will clean the garage later, but doesn't tell her when; this lack of specificity allows Steve to remain in control and Amy to feel powerless. Bethany tells her boss that the project isn't due until next week, causing her co-workers and boss to fret; delaying responsibilities until the last minute is another obstructionist tactic. That is, procrastination is a strategy that is often used to make others stressful. A tired Wanda, who has been cleaning all day, pops into the house to ask her daughter Sally to wash the dishes, and then returns to the yard work. Sally yells that she is doing the dishes, but works for only a few minutes before returning to check Facebook. Then, when Wanda returns after working in the garden for another hour, and she is somewhat upset that the dishes aren't done, Sally replies, "I'll get to the dishes when I have time." Sally uses another obstructionist tactic to deflect from the original denied request. In the mind of the passive-aggressive, there are always more important activities that take priority over the simple requests of others, resulting in stress in, if not dissolution of, both interpersonal and work relationships.

Sample Example Paragraphs (literary subject)

The selection below is taken from a literary analysis essay on Joseph Conrad's seethingly ironic story "An Outpost of Progress." To support the topic sentence, the writer uses several examples in the first paragraph and one longer example in the second.

In "An Outpost of Progress," Joseph Conrad uses irony to demonstrate Kayerts and Carlier's ignorance of their real roles and duties at the trading station. For instance, these two men believe their mission is enlightening the "savages" and furthering civilization; however, they spend their days being idle, dreaming of the steamer's return, and reading sappy adventure stories. They, in fact, see themselves as "heroes" when they are mere babysitters of an unproductive station. Likewise, they are thrilled by the danger in these tales without realizing the precariousness of their own situation: there is a neighbouring warlike tribe, their food rations are extremely low, and they are susceptible to several tropical diseases. And their choice of non-fiction also reveals their naïveté; that is, their wholehearted agreement with the article "Our Colonial Expansion" proves that they, too, are brainwashed by the imperialist propaganda. They are consoled by the idea that they are bringing light to this dark place, when they, and others like them, are really robbing the country blind.

Furthermore their misinterpretation of Makola and his role provides another ironic twist. Kayerts and Carlier believe that they are in charge of Makola and the station, but Makola proves that he is, in fact, the real boss when he exchanges the inefficient, sick workers for ivory, acting as the loyal imperialist. This trading of the workers causes Kayerts and Carlier to reject (temporarily, of course) the tainted ivory exclaiming, self-righteously, that "slavery is an awful thing" (Conrad 895). This statement reveals how Kayerts and Carlier are in denial that they are just overpaid overseers and that the workers have, in fact, been enslaved all along. The layers of irony also act as foreshadowing; Conrad hints that these two men, who are completely out of touch with reality, are obviously ill-equipped to survive if the steamer is delayed. These inept men become symbols of imperialism's ironies and abuses.

—Adapted from a literary analysis essay written by Jocelynn Malinowski

Exercise 1

Choose one of the opinions below and give two or three reasons for agreeing or disagreeing. Support your reasons with examples.

1. *Maclean's* rankings of universities are useful (not useful).

2. The movie *In Bruges*, despite its violent plot, makes several statements against violence.

3. There are many reasons why people gain weight over Christmas.

4. The federal government should (should not) require labelling of all genetically modified foods.

2. DEFINING TERMS AND CONCEPTS

"There's glory for you!"

"I don't know what you mean by 'glory,'" Alice said.

Humpty Dumpty smiled contemptuously. "Of course you don't—till I tell you. I meant 'there's a nice knock-down argument for you!'"

"But 'glory' doesn't mean 'a nice knock-down argument,'" Alice objected.

"When I use a word," Humpty Dumpty said in a rather scornful tone, "it means just what I choose it to mean—neither more nor less."

—From *Through the Looking Glass* by Lewis Carroll

Humpty Dumpty may get away with arbitrarily deciding what words mean, but most of us cannot. If we want to communicate successfully, we have to use words in ways that others will understand. Thus, when you use words unfamiliar to your readers, or use familiar words in an unfamiliar way, you must provide **definitions**.

In exams and other kinds of academic writing, you may be asked to define terms to show that you know what they mean. In most writing, however, you provide definitions not to demonstrate your own knowledge but to help your reader understand what you are talking about. Depending on what kind of information your reader needs, you may use a synonym, a class definition, an extended definition, or a restrictive definition.

Synonyms

A **synonym** is a word that means the same, or nearly the same, as another word. Use synonyms, set off by commas or enclosed in parentheses, to define slang expressions, specialized terms of trades and professions, regional and dialect usages, and foreign words and phrases. This example illustrates how to integrate synonyms smoothly:

> Psychologists might argue that much of the comedy of *Curb Your Enthusiasm* comes from *Schadenfreude* (joy from the suffering of others).

Class Definitions

A **class definition** explains a term by saying what kind of thing it is (its class) and how it is different from other members of its class. CDs, for instance, are in the class of recorded music, but so are vinyl albums, cassettes, and music files.

This is the standard form of the class definition:

> An *X* is a member of the class *Y* with the characteristics *A, B, C*. . . .
>
> A bailiff [term to be defined] is a person [class] who performs limited functions within a judicial system, such as having custody of prisoners in court, serving warrants, or serving as magistrate for minor offences [distinguishing characteristics].

Extended Definitions

When a synonym or class definition does not offer enough explanation, you will need an **extended definition**. Some writers take a paragraph, even a whole essay, to define a term. In a persuasive essay, for example, you might give an extended definition of the word *violence* to show that the term also applies to the destruction of the environment.

Don't insult your readers by defining words they know, but never assume your subject is as familiar to them as it is to you. Remember who you are writing for. For an audience of young people, for instance, you might need to define *avatar*, but probably not *social networking*. However, for an older audience, you might need to define *online community* but probably not *Internet*.

Here are three ways to expand definitions:

1. Add examples.
2. Give negative examples—that is, refine your term by giving words or things that might seem to be included in the class but actually are not.
3. Use an analogy to compare your term with something familiar. For instance, if you wanted to explain random sampling to readers who were not social scientists, you might use the analogy of pulling a handful of assorted candies from a jar.

Restrictive Definitions

Our understanding of words, especially of abstract terms such as *violence, loyalty, pornography,* and *censorship,* is shaped by our own experiences, and we bring these personal connotations to our reading. You can make sure that you and your readers are talking the same language by using a **restrictive definition**.

Because a restrictive definition specifies which meaning, from a range of possible meanings, you are using, it allows you to limit your treatment of your subject. For instance, you might first consider various meanings of the word *censorship* before specifying that you will use the word formally to mean the passage of laws designed to prevent the publication of certain material. Accordingly, your readers cannot expect you to discuss other actions that they might consider censorship, such as the withdrawing of books from libraries or the banning of T-shirt slogans. As this example suggests, restrictive definitions are particularly necessary when the meaning of a term is controversial.

Because they establish common ground with readers and mark out the territory to discuss, restrictive definitions also make good introductions. If you were writing a research paper on the debate over family values, you might begin by defining the term so that your readers understand your main purpose: to replace the current restrictive definition with a more inclusive one.

Sample Restrictive Definition Paragraph

Conservative thinkers often attack social policies they perceive to be harmful to "family values," and yet they seldom define what they mean by *family* or *values.* Before the Industrial

Revolution, most of Europe's population lived in extended families consisting of assorted grandparents, parents, children, and other adults, related or unrelated, for this extended family was the most efficient economic unit. After the expansion of the middle classes in the early nineteenth century, more couples could afford to establish their own households, which usually consisted of parents and children (and perhaps a servant or two). This family unit evolved into the North American ideal nuclear family, in which the father provided the income, the mother stayed home and looked after the children, and the children obeyed their parents. It is this ideal that conservative thinkers generally have in mind when they defend "family values." However, this family, in many ways, is a very Western institution. In addition, economic pressures created by divorce, unemployment, and the changing role of women are again forcing us to redefine what we mean by *family* and to recognize the diversity in family values.

Sources of Definitions

When you need to define a word, begin with a standard dictionary such as those published by Gage, Random House, Oxford, and Webster. For more detailed information about specialized meanings, changes in meaning over time, and current usage, consult works such as the following, found in the reference section of your library:

- **Unabridged dictionaries.** The *Oxford English Dictionary* provides a history of each word's use and changes in meaning. Schools often have the OED online; the OED is also available as a CD-ROM that you can download onto your desktop.

- **Specialized dictionaries.** These are available for many professions and academic disciplines. Some examples are the *Dictionary of Business and Economics*, *Dictionary of Philosophy*, *Dictionary of Symbolism*, and the *Oxford Dictionary of Twentieth-Century World History*.

Exercise 2

Give a synonym or class definition that would explain each of these terms to readers unfamiliar with your subject:

1. avatar (or other term from popular culture)

2. quasar (or other scientific term)

3. the 'hood (or other slang expression)

4. halfpipe (or other sports term)

5. *joie de vivre* (or other non-English expression)

6. profit margin (or other business term)

Exercise 3

Write an extended definition of one of the following terms:

- sweat lodge
- bodybuilding (or other physical pursuit)
- Tai Chi (or other martial art)
- pysanka (or other cultural artifact)
- reiki (or other alternative health technique)

Exercise 4

Write a paragraph of restrictive definition for one of the following terms:

- patriotism
- equal opportunity
- intelligence
- justice
- euthanasia
- fascism

3. ANALYZING: DIVIDING YOUR SUBJECT INTO PARTS

Analysis is a way of explaining a subject by dividing it into its parts and showing how the parts relate to the whole. Here, three types of analysis are discussed: **systems analysis**, which shows the relation of parts in space; **process analysis**, which shows the sequence of parts in time; and **causal analysis**, which shows the relationship between causes and effects.

By dividing up a complex or unfamiliar task, situation, or idea into smaller units, you can often make it easier for readers to understand your subject. For particular writing assignments, you may use these three types of analysis alone or in combination. In writing a how-to article on gardening, for example, you would use process analysis to develop your material. But in writing a more generic expository essay on gardening, you might include sections on the various processes, on the types of plants suitable for Canadian climates, and on the effects of too much or too little watering.

Explaining Systems

We tend to think of a system as a physical object with working parts, such as a computer or the body's digestive system. However, you can also explain how abstract systems, such as governments or ideologies, "work" by showing how the parts are related to the whole. Aesthetic objects—such as music, dance, drama, film, video games, and literary works—can likewise be considered as systems in which parts work together to create a whole. For instance, you might find that a certain movie communicates the theme of despair. To explain how the movie creates this theme, you would consider elements such as lighting, pacing, dialogue, characters, costume, setting, shots, etc.

A systems analysis is like a blueprint providing an objective general description of your subject rather than a subjective particular description. If you were analyzing the functions of the federal cabinet, for instance, you would discuss the role of the minister of the environment, not his or her personality or height.

Begin with a topic sentence that identifies the system and explains its purpose. Next, describe the most obvious or most important part of the system, such as the prime minister, and show how other parts function in relation to it. Then, using appropriate transitions, explain the function of each part in relation to the whole.

Sample Systems Analysis Paragraph: Abstract System

In this example, the writer shows how the parts of an abstract system—the Hollywood movie studios of the early twentieth century—worked together to create a film industry that continues to dominate world markets.

The Hollywood studio system, which dominated the production of American movies from the 1920s to the 1950s, was essentially a system for efficiently mass-producing movies. At the head of the major studios (such as Columbia, MGM, Paramount, RKO, and Warner Brothers) were the movie producers. Like the heads of factories, movie producers controlled the financing of their products and exercised considerable control over how the products were made. The producers hired actors and approved script choices and script writers. They also hired the director for each film, and thus influenced how the action was staged and photographed. Movies were shot under tightly controlled conditions in the huge holdings of land, buildings, and sound stages that constituted the studio lot. The staples of the Hollywood system—westerns, thrillers, science fiction, and horror movies—could thus be shot quickly on ready-made sets. In addition, each studio had all the departments necessary to make a movie, including publicity, costuming, set design, story production, and makeup. Like the personnel of these departments, actors were constantly available on low-salary, long-term contract, such as Humphrey Bogart, Joan Crawford, Bette Davis, Clark Gable, and John Wayne. These low-cost production methods enabled the studios to produce hundreds of films a year and thus laid the groundwork for Hollywood's continuing dominance of the world film industry.

Exercise 5

Write a paragraph explaining the parts of a physical object with which you are familiar, showing how these parts function as a whole. Here are some possible subjects:

- a snowboard
- an iPod, BlackBerry, or iPhone
- a home entertainment system

- a full-suspension mountain bike
- a fish tank filter

Exercise 6

Write a paragraph explaining the parts of an abstract system with which you are familiar, showing how the system functions as a whole. Here are some possible subjects:

- an organization you belong to
- a band, choir, or similar musical group
- a particular ecosystem, such as your backyard
- a video game
- an ad or a commercial

Explaining Processes

Process analysis is of two types: **informational**, which explains how something happens ("How Airplanes Fly"); and **instructional**, which explains how to do something ("How to Fly an Airplane"). In each case, you emphasize what happens (or should happen) every time the process is repeated ("How to Sew from a Pattern"), rather than what happened during one particular instance ("How My Bad Sewing Ruined My Prom Dress").

The amount of detail you include depends on your purpose and audience. When you are writing informational process analysis or explaining how a process unfolds, focus on the major stages so that your readers get a sense of the whole process. However, when you are writing instructional process analysis or giving readers directions to follow, discuss each step in detail, allowing your reader to imagine the process and to see any potential problems. In informational process analysis, then, you want the reader to understand the process, whereas in instructional analysis, you want the reader to see, feel, and replicate the process.

For both types of process analysis, begin with a topic sentence identifying the process and its major stages. Then discuss the stages, and the steps within each stage, in the order they occur. Use transitions indicating time relationships (*next, after, then*) or enumeration (*first, second, third*) to signal movement from one stage or step to the next.

In instructional process analysis, also known as the how-to essay, the writer addresses the reader as "you."

Below is an instructional process paragraph on the process of painting a wall, followed by an informational process paragraph on getting injured while running. The first paragraph is deductive (beginning with its topic sentence), whereas the second is inductive (ending with its main point.)

Although both paragraphs use a lot of transitional words and expressions to guide the reader, they have a few differences. See if you can pick these out.

For an example of more detailed instructions, see the Sample Instructional Process Analysis Essay in Part 6 of this chapter.

Sample Instructional Process Analysis Paragraph

If you want a neat and thorough job, you should follow these six major stages when painting a wall: testing, trimming, taping, edging, filling, and finishing. First, test the paint on the wall to make sure you have the correct colour. Put a few coats of paint on a small section and wait a few days for the colour to settle. If the colour is off or too bright, you might want to return to the store to darken the paint or, if necessary, select a new colour. Next, you must trim. If your room has doors or window ledges, you should paint these first, usually in a white or off-white colour with an eggshell to semigloss finish. After the trim is dry, tape it, along with the ceiling, making sure you use the medium green painter's tape. Then, do the edging, which means using a fine brush or trim roller to paint a 3–4 inch swath around the room, taking special care around doors and windows. Make sure you have at least two coats of edging; you may need more with watery or red-tinted paints. When the edging is complete, you are ready for the final step: painting the interior of the wall. Start rolling in a V formation, using large clean strokes. Keep in mind that if you are using a paint in the red family, you may need many coats, whereas you will need fewer coats with paints containing a lot of brown or black. When you are done, use an artist's brush to fill in minor mistakes before removing the tape. Following these steps will ensure a neat and thorough painting job.

Sample Informational Process Analysis Paragraph

Believe it or not, there is a process by which beginning runners get injured. First, beginning runners often go to their local box store and casually purchase the cheapest shoe available. Then, they end up exercising in footwear that doesn't suit their feet, pronation style, or required level of cushioning. Secondly, novices often become addicted to both the "runner's high" and the weight loss effects of running. As a result, they increase their mileage too quickly, leading to early overuse injuries. Thirdly, because every new activity involves a certain amount of discomfort, new runners often ignore the aches and pains that could be early tell-tale signs of injuries, such as chondromalacia patella. Lastly, new runners, in their excitement and gung-ho attitude, often forget that exercise involves balance; thus, they don't strengthen the muscles that running might weaken (the quadriceps, for instance), and they likewise don't stretch the tissues that running might tighten (the hamstrings and the iliotibial band). To avoid getting injured, then, people should have their feet and stride evaluated, buy their shoes at a technical running store, increase their mileage by no more than 10 percent per week, carefully evaluate their new aches and pains, and begin or continue with a regimented weight-training and stretching program.

Exercise 7

Write a paragraph explaining a process. Choose your own topic or one of the following:

- how to operate a piece of equipment
- how to teach a child a particular skill, such as tying shoelaces

- how to settle disputes with a partner or roommate
- how to take blood pressure
- how to train a dog to heel

Explaining Causes and Effects: Causal Analysis

Whereas process analysis explains *how something happens* or *how to do something*, causal analysis explains *why something happens*. Thus, analyzing causes and effects is central to much of the writing you will do in school or at work. You may write a research paper for a history course on the causes of the War of 1812, a report on how the threat of terrorism has affected the travel industry, or a letter to your insurance agent on the causes of a traffic accident. Keep in mind that most interesting and complex subjects have multiple causes and effects. Brainstorming, asking discovery questions, and researching will help you avoid an oversimplified analysis.

For a research paper on the effects of cutbacks in government spending on education, for instance, your first response might be to focus on the financial strain students are under because of higher tuition fees. You would gain a broader perspective, however, by brainstorming about other effects on students and reading about the effects on schools and postsecondary institutions. Your final essay might examine the effects of funding cuts on students, teachers, and institutions.

If you are explaining independent causes or effects, arrange your material in an order that suits your audience. You might discover, for example, that the three main causes of traffic accidents are poor road conditions, impaired driving, and mechanical failure. There is no causal connection among these three factors. (Drinking too much doesn't cause icy roads or malfunctioning cars.) If you were writing an essay, you would decide which cause to emphasize, and discuss it last. However, if you were writing a report for the city transportation department, you would discuss the main factor first.

When discussing a chain of causes and effects (A causes B, B causes C, C causes D), make sure that your topic sentence focuses on the most significant cause(s) and effect(s). Arrange your material in chronological order, but, to clarify that you are writing a causal analysis rather than a narrative, choose words and expressions that emphasize causal connections (*a major effect, a second cause, one consequence; caused, resulted, affected; as a result, because, consequently, therefore, thus*). An essay on the effects of the Riel Rebellion on federal politics might have these notes:

1. Riel's execution **caused** a renewed demand for rights by the French Québécois.
2. These demands alarmed the federal government, which **consequently** abolished French language rights in Manitoba.

3. This action **resulted** in loss of support for the Conservative Party in Quebec.

4. This decline in support **caused** the party to lose the next federal election.

5. Quebec's pivotal role in federal politics is a continuing **effect** of its position as the sole defender of the rights of French-speaking Canadians.

In writing your paragraph, you would add a topic sentence emphasizing the most significant effect (Quebec's increased power). You would also fill in additional details while keeping the focus on the chain of causes and effects, as in the paragraph below.

Sample Causal Analysis Paragraph

Although the failure of the Riel Rebellion weakened the position of French-speaking Canadians in Manitoba, it had the enormously significant effect of strengthening the power of French-speaking Canadians in Quebec. Before Riel was executed in 1885, Quebec had ignored the struggle of the French-speaking Manitobans to maintain their cultural identity. As a result of his execution, Riel became a martyr to the cause of rights for all French Canadians and the focus for a renewed demand for French rights in Quebec. Alarmed, the federal government abolished French education rights in Manitoba in 1890; Quebec thus became the only province where provincial rights guaranteed the survival of French culture in Canada. The consequence of this action, it soon became obvious, was that no federal government could remain in power if it lacked Quebec's support. The Conservative Party, weakened by Macdonald's death in 1891, lost the election of 1896 mostly because it had offended Quebec by abolishing French rights in Manitoba; the Liberals, led by Wilfrid Laurier, gained power by securing a large majority in Quebec. Since that time, no federal government has been able to ignore the province.

Exercise 8

Write two separate lists of causes explaining why you were (or were not) successful in your last job (or job search). Make one a list of independent causes; present the second list as a chain of causes and effects.

4. WRITING EXPOSITORY ESSAYS: THE PROCESS

In expository essays, just as in expository paragraphs, you explain a subject, which might be a short story, a problem, an historical event, a current situation, or a theory, to a particular audience. Expository paragraphs can, with the addition of details, be developed into longer essays. For instance, the previous paragraph on Louis Riel could easily be broken down into, at least, a five-paragraph essay. Indeed, whole dissertations have been written on the very complicated subject of Louis Riel and what he symbolizes to various parts of Canada.

Regardless of the subject of your expository essay, you use the same steps in formulating your thesis and organizing your material.

Choosing a Primary Method of Development and a Focus

Some essay assignments state or imply a primary method of development and a focus. For instance, if you were asked to analyze the causes and/or effects of childhood obesity, you would probably choose causal analysis, but if you were asked to explain how a prime minister is chosen, you would use informational process analysis. Often, you will simply get a topic from your instructor, so you will have to decide upon an expository method. If you have a singular subject, and a primary method of development is not given or implied, make notes on what each method of exposition could contribute to your essay.

You might begin work on an expository essay on childhood obesity by making this list:

Method of Development	Possible Material
PROCESS ANALYSIS	The process of overweight children turning into obese adults *or* how malnourished babies turn into overweight children.
SYSTEMS ANALYSIS	How schools dealing with unfit children fit into the system of health supports. How popular culture can be seen as a system that promotes obesity.
CAUSAL ANALYSIS	What causes obesity among children? Poverty? Lack of exercise? Too much fast food? Too much time on the computer?
DEFINITION	Definitions of obesity, BMI, etc. and how they have changed throughout history. Also, how different nations define obesity.

From a list of possibilities, you choose a focus and a method of development, remembering your audience. If you are writing for a newspaper or a magazine, your interests and your assumptions of those of your readers will guide you. If you are writing on child obesity for *Chatelaine,* most of your readers will be middle-class women with children. To appeal to them and make them connected to this problem, you might explain how childhood obesity is not just a personal but a national issue.

However, if you are writing for a satirical magazine that often criticizes the excesses and biases of the media, you might want to expose how fast food and technological ads are contributing to obesity in young people.

When you are writing an essay for a course, you will probably choose a focus reflecting the concerns, objectives, or methodology of that discipline. Sociologists, for example, study the relationships between groups and society. For a sociology course, you might focus on the responsibility of the school system in handling the problem of childhood obesity or how peer groups affect healthy lifestyle choices.

Gathering Material

There are many sources of material for expository essays. For subjects you are familiar with, brainstorming about your personal knowledge and experience will often provide enough information. From your own experience working with people with food addictions, for example, you could write a process analysis essay explaining the struggle with weight loss.

Sometimes, though, you may have to gather information from other sources. You can conduct interviews, do field research, or consult other published materials.

However you gather material, keep your focus and method of development in mind. These will help you decide what information is relevant to your essay.

Formulating a Thesis

After gathering various bits of information, you need to ask yourself what they add up to. This process of synthesizing your material will lead you to a main idea, a thesis. A good thesis for an expository essay should state an opinion about your subject and give reasons that set the limits of your discussion: why one definition of a controversial term is better than another; how the setting in a short story contributes to the theme; what causes abusive relationships among family members. A statement such as *Obesity has many causes* does neither.

In contrast, the following thesis states an opinion and clearly defines the scope of the essay. *Although obesity is a complicated problem, it has three identifiable causes that can be amended: lack of physical activity; an overabundance of cheap, unhealthy food; and poverty coupled with inadequate education about nutrition.*

Including Other Methods of Development

Write your first draft using only your primary method of development (process, causal analysis, and so on). When you revise, however, you may discover that to explain the meaning of your subject clearly, you need to add definitions of terms (*nutrition*), comparisons (*money budgeted to food in middle-class families and in poor families*). You might create interest by using the methods for sharing personal experience.

Organizing Your Essay

Expository essays written for college and university courses are usually organized deductively with the thesis in the introduction, topic sentences

showing how each middle paragraph relates to the thesis, and a restatement and extension of the thesis in the conclusion. This method of organization contains a well-defined framework, keeping both the writer and
the reader on track.

5. THE INSTRUCTIONAL PROCESS ANALYSIS ESSAY

Probably the most prevalent form of expository writing is the how-to
article or the instructional process essay. If you browse your local book-
store or your favourite magazine, you will find instructional books and
articles on several topics: managing your money or your children, choosing a doctor or a spouse, dealing with anger or the plumbing. Because
you probably have skills to teach other people, you too can write how-to
articles.

Writing How-To Articles: The Process

Follow these steps:

1. Choose a procedure that you know well and that you can explain
   in five to ten steps. Making a sandwich is too simple; building a
   spacecraft is too complex.

2. Decide how much explanation and what level of language is
   appropriate for your intended audience. If you were telling children
   how to make cookies, for instance, you might say, *Put the mixing
   bowl in the refrigerator for an hour. Then take small pieces
   of dough and form them into balls about half the size of your
   fist.* For experienced cooks, you would say, *Chill the dough
   and form into balls.*

3. Write a short introduction pointing out the benefits of learning the
   procedure. Include a list of tools or materials required and where
   to obtain them, if appropriate.

4. Describe the steps for your procedure in the order in which your
   reader should follow them. Number the steps or use transitional
   phrases clearly identifying them (*the first step*, *the next step*, *the
   third step*). Explain the purpose or reason for each step. Don't be
   vague; provide enough detail for the reader to visualize and carry
   out the process.

5. Throughout the process, use a familiar tone, addressing the reader
   as "you." Doing so helps the reader understand and replicate the
   process.

6. Anticipate any problems that your reader might have and suggest
   solutions.

7. Write a short conclusion emphasizing the desirable qualities of the
   finished product or the benefits of learning the procedure.

6. SAMPLE OF AN INSTRUCTIONAL PROCESS ANALYSIS ESSAY

The essay below was a process analysis essay written for a first-year composition course. Because the student was stumped, the instructor asked her to write about a process she performed recently.

Fast Relief for You and Your Dog

Dogs live for the moment; they play roughly, eat anything, and will roll in things that would bring a tear to a skunk's eye. These beloved members of our families will even bring home new-found friends, such as lice. Have no fear: the canine louse is one of the most easily managed parasites that you can encounter. With a proper diagnosis, the careful and repeated use of topical treatments, and a thorough cleaning of your home and dog, you can easily expel these pests from your home.

The first sign that something is wrong with Rover is intense itching and a general feeling of doggie discomfort. Call the veterinarian and make an appointment to get the appropriate diagnosis of your mutt's malaise. The vet will probably inform you that your dog is providing a warm and hairy home to hundreds, perhaps thousands, of little lice. He will tell you not to be so upset, for lice cannot move as fast as mites and they certainly cannot jump like fleas; he will also inform you that lice will not cause any serious ailments and they can live only on their canine host, preferring to remain where they are, sucking, biting, and laying eggs throughout their short lifespan. Then he will tell you to find them. Lice are tiny brownish-red specks attached to the skin, and their eggs are tiny white bits attached to the hair shaft, close to the scalp. If you see them, you must begin dealing with the situation immediately.

Your first step in eliminating the lice is purchasing some commonly used delousing items and getting your tub ready. You will need a three-month topical flea and tick treatment, a flea comb, and a good quality hypoallergenic shampoo. Next, in the bathtub, you should start the delousing process; make sure you have a rubber mat in the tub and several towels around the tub. Then, try to remove as many of the lice as possible, using the flea comb to loosen the lice and eggs from the skin and fur. To wash them off, wet the dog down and then apply shampoo liberally. It is important to get your fingers down to the scalp and rub the skin, for you are trying to detach the lice so that they will be washed down the drain. Do not worry if you cannot get all of the eggs or lice, as this process will be ongoing.

Once the dog is bathed and thoroughly dried, carefully apply the topical treatment. It is extremely important to follow the instructions included in the package. You will apply this treatment to five different locations from the base of the tail to the bottom of the neck, making sure to part the fur and apply it to the skin. Don't apply too much in one spot because you do not want it running off the dog. This product will kill almost all of the lice and eggs that did not get washed off in the bath. Do not bathe the dog for at least a week afterward because you do not want to wash the product off the dog. The topical treatment should be applied once a month for three months to ensure complete annihilation of the unwanted guests.

During the next few months, you must clean your house and maintain your dog so that neither is infested again. You must regularly vacuum all floors, carpets, and furniture, paying special attention to the dog's sleeping quarters. It is important to routinely inspect and clean your dog as well to make sure that any remaining eggs have not hatched. From one week after the first application until the second application, you can bathe your dog as much as is necessary. The more you comb and bathe Rover, the more pests you will wash off him. Bathing must be done at home and not at the groomer's unless you would like to share your problem with his other canine friends.

Discovering lice on your dog, then, need not be a stressful experience. Once diagnosed, this problem can be eliminated without too much disruption of your daily routine. Of all the external parasites a dog can pick up, lice are the easiest to get rid of. If lice ever infest your dog, have faith that if you follow the process outlined above, you can turn your walking louse house back into the faithful companion you know and love.

—*Erin Zier*

7. CAUSAL ANALYSIS ESSAYS: THE PROCESS

1. Choose an event, problem, or phenomenon that interests you and that is suitable for your essay length. For a 1000-word essay, you might discuss some of the causes of the decline in reading in North America but *not* the declining literacy rates in the world.

2. Decide whether you want to focus on *causes* or *effects* or both.

3. Brainstorm about potential causes and effects of your phenomenon or event before deciding on a few on which to focus.

4. Try not to oversimplify your subject, recognizing that most complicated phenomena have several causes and effects.

5. Avoid committing the flaw of post-hoc reasoning, which is confusing coincidence with causation. For instance, you walked into class late, your teacher scowled at you, and you failed your exam. You would be guilty of post-hoc reasoning if you blamed your bad grade on your lateness or teacher's disapproval. In reality, these events were coincidental; that is, the real reason you failed your exam was lack of preparation.

6. Decide on a principle of organization. Do you present your causes from most obvious to least obvious? Or least important to most important?

7. When writing, try to dedicate at least one paragraph to each cause or effect, making sure that you use enough examples and illustrations to support your reasoning.

8. EXAMPLE OF A CAUSAL ANALYSIS ESSAY

This essay below, which was written for a first-year university composition course, is a short paper that uses causal analysis to explain some of the points for and against legalizing marijuana. The author sheds light on some of the falsehoods associated with this drug while explaining its medicinal benefits. Notice how the writer uses primary analysis and secondary sources to explain the real effects of marijuana. Also note that the writer has chosen APA style for his system of referencing.

Cush Should Not Be Crushed

In William Bennett's persuasive essay "Should Drugs Be Legalized?," originally printed in *The Reader's Digest* in 1990, the author argues against the legalization of drugs, stating, "I find no merit in the legalizers' case. The simple fact is that drug use is wrong" (p. 204). Understandably, all drugs should not be legalized because drug use, for the most part, is wrong, but it is unfair for Bennett and for others to group marijuana with other monstrous killers, such as crystal meth, crack cocaine, and heroin. Although governments and various medical associations have focused on proving the negative side effects of marijuana, in the process, these agencies have misunderstood the herb and damaged its reputation. *Although marijuana is an illegal drug, and overusing it can cause harm, people need to appreciate its positive medicinal effects and also understand the myths associated with its use.*

Indeed, excessive use of marijuana is connected to a very specific health risk: respiratory disease due to smoking. A survey by Kaiser Permanente concluded that "daily marijuana-only smokers have a 19% higher rate of respiratory complaints than non-smokers" (Polen, 1993, p. 596). Also, according to Dr. Donald Tashkin of UCLA (1993), "Although more information is certainly needed, sufficient data have been accumulated concerning the health effects of marijuana to warrant counselling by physicians against the smoking of marijuana" (p. 653). Yes, marijuana, if smoked in excess, will negatively affect one's health. Common sense, though, tells us to expect harmful effects when smoke of *any* sort is inhaled into the lungs, whether it's from cigarettes, cannabis, or even campfires. In fact, inhaling the air in overpopulated industrial cities could actually be more harmful than inhaling the smoke from marijuana, especially when a person is exposed to this polluted air since birth.

Even if marijuana is harmful to the lungs, there are various ways that a person can experience its benefits while reducing the impact of the hazardous smoke. Using a water-filtration system, such as a water bong, a person can decrease smoke levels while increasing the levels of tetrahydrocannabinol (THC) and cannabidiol (CBD), the chemicals generating the effect. More efficient yet are vaporizers, which use a slow building heat, instead of a flame, to allow a person to inhale THC and CBD in a potent, gentle mist. Higher-strength cannabis in either system will also reduce the quantity that needs to be used as well as the amount of smoke produced. And if the user doesn't feel comfortable inhaling smoke, marijuana can be ingested orally, resulting in similar and often prolonged effects. In fact, this method is becoming increasingly popular in patients who are prescribed medicinal marijuana.

Marijuana, especially when the smoke level is reduced, is a powerful and multipurpose medicine. It is gaining popularity and respect, especially with patients suffering from multiple sclerosis, cancer, glaucoma, HIV/AIDS, and hepatitis C. In fact, a recent study has concluded that "a standardized Cannabis sativa plant extract might lower spasm frequency and increase mobility with tolerable side effects in MS patients not responding to other drugs" (*Multiple Sclerosis*, 2004, p. 417). In other words, the THC from marijuana has been found to increase the pain tolerance of a major side effect of MS: muscle spasms. Cancer patients, too, often turn to marijuana to cope with pain and increase their appetites, especially if chemotherapy has destroyed the latter. (Marijuana is notorious for causing the munchies). In response to these effects, officials have made medicinal marijuana available to registered patients across Canada and in fourteen US states. According to Mirken (2007), this movement is the beginning of "a thundering rejection of the unscientific policies of the last 10 years" (p.163).

Marijuana not only helps sufferers of chronic and debilitating diseases, but also helps people afflicted with pain disorders and minor ailments, that is, marijuana also has promise as a casual medicine. According to research from the University of California (Casida, 2008), "Marijuana calms people down and relieves pain . . . scientists in California have found a way to boost the positive effects associated with cannabis use" (p. 4). Lester Grinspoon, MD, (2007) adds that "marijuana is effective at relieving nausea and vomiting, spasticity, appetite loss, certain types of pain, and other debilitating symptoms" (para. 6). Most of these symptoms are regularly experienced by the general public, whether due to the common flu or even a hangover. Marijuana, then, could help healthy members of the population. Responding to its wide range of uses, scientists are currently attempting to alter the chemical composition of the plant so that they can isolate and increase the drug's medicinal value.

Marijuana, then, should not be labelled such a horrific drug, nor should it be categorized with harder illicit substances, such as cocaine or ecstacy. Robert Volkmann, MD, (2004) states that "there are NO REPORTED DEATHS from [marijuana] use" (para. 8). Though marijuana is mentioned in medical examiners' reports, it is usually referenced in combination with alcohol or other drugs. In the United States, in fact, deaths caused by legalized cigarettes (five million annually) are much higher than those caused by illegal hard drugs (roughly 223 000 annually). Also, other drugs, such as ecstasy, are far more lethal than weed. This past year in Edmonton, there have been numerous newspaper headlines about ecstasy-related deaths. Perhaps the most disturbing story yet was that of the 14-year-old girl at Galaxyland's Rock N' Ride, who died after she overdosed on six pills. She would most likely still be alive today if it were only six joints that she had smoked, although smoking six joints is highly unlikely. Furthermore, studies have shown that in order to overdose on cannabis, a person must use 40 000 times his/her usual dosage, another impossible feat. And marijuana also has reverse tolerance, which means that the more one uses, the less one needs to use. The public is often unaware of these facts about marijuana's dosage and addictiveness, resulting in the drug getting an unnecessarily terrible reputation.

Furthermore, marijuana has not been shown to increase the number of vehicular accidents. During a presentation in class, one student labelled marijuana as the second leading cause of car accidents, next to alcohol. The truth, according to the data provided by the Canadian Automobile Association in 2008, is that the main cause of car accidents is actually cell phone use. Next to phones is eating while driving; then, there is finally alcohol at number five. Drug use is listed directly *after* alcohol. One might argue that there would be more drug-related accidents recorded if there were a marijuana testing unit similar to a Breathalyzer. Well, there is. Roadside drug testing, established by the Government of Canada in 2006, consists of licking the pad of a special device that reports the detection of cannabis, methamphetamine, or ecstasy within five minutes. If the result is positive, the driver is detained and further testing is administered. Driving under the influence is definitely a serious issue, but people must get the facts straight before connecting marijuana use and vehicular accidents.

As the poster child for the war against drugs, marijuana is too often blamed for its negative effects, whereas it is not commended for its benefits. This skewed public image prevents marijuana from assisting the people who need it the most. For example, my mother, who suffers from MS, is a non-user of marijuana. And as a non-user, she experiences excruciating pain during her unrelenting, uncontrollable spasms. Although marijuana could help ease the agony of my mother and that of fellow chronic disease sufferers, the stigma attached to this drug prevents her and others from ingesting it and feeling its powerful medicinal effects. The myths surrounding marijuana need to be dispelled so that *we can all* reap the rewards of this amazing 5000-year-old drug.

—*Nick Marks*

Explaining Two Subjects

When your purpose is to explain two or more subjects, you will use either comparison/contrast or classification/division. This chapter will give you practice in using these methods to explain two or more subjects within a single paragraph and within an essay. That is, expository paragraphs often appear both alone and within pieces of writing that persuade or share personal experience. If you were writing a persuasive essay about permitting gay marriage, you might compare religious attitudes toward homosexuality. On the other hand, you might write an entire comparison/contrast essay on the differing attitudes and political reactions to same-sex partnerships in the United States and Canada.

1. COMPARING

When you compare, you match similarities and differences in two or more subjects. **Comparison** may be your primary method of development in a piece of writing, or you may combine comparison with other methods of development.

To compare subjects effectively, you need a basis of comparison, which tells you on which similarities and differences to focus. For example, if you are asked on a biology exam to compare the fertilization process in mammals and amphibians, you are given a basis of comparison.

When you aren't given a topic, your purpose and audience may suggest a basis of comparison. If you are comparing two computers, your basis of comparison will be determined by whether your reader is a college instructor, a graphic designer, or a gamer. If your reader is a gamer, you might compare the multimedia options of two computers.

In other writing situations, the basis of your comparison may not be so obvious. Suppose you were writing an essay comparing attitudes toward immigrants in Canada and the United States. You would need to consider many facts and opinions before deciding on a general similarity or difference to use as a basis of comparison.

When your basis of comparison is not obvious, follow these steps:

List Similarities and Differences

Although making lists seems time-consuming, it serves three purposes: it ensures that you have lots of material, that you compare equivalent aspects of your subjects, and that you provide the same information about both. Let's take an example.

In writing about the differences between First Nations storytelling and Western storytelling, for instance, one student wanted to reinforce her point by comparing similar folk tales, "The Ghost Owl" and "The Three Bears." She compiled these lists:

"The Ghost Owl"

—The main character is a small girl who brings trouble on herself by crying when she doesn't get what she wants.

—She is put outside the lodge, carried away by an owl, rescued by a hawk, and restored to her home when she has killed the owl and has "grown up" enough to follow Grandfather Hawk's instructions.

—Animal figures are distinct from humans but equal to humans and part of the same world.

"The Three Bears"

—The main character is Goldilocks, who brings trouble on herself by following her impulses (sampling the bears' food, chairs, and beds) instead of completing her errand.

—She is frightened and jumps out of the window when the bears discover her wrongdoing, but her fate is uncertain.

—Animal figures are symbols of human society (the bears live and act like "civilized" humans, not bears).

These lists provide more than enough material for a paragraph, so the student would need to select the most appropriate material for her purpose.

Choose a Basis of Comparison

The next step is to decide on a *basis of comparison*—the general characteristic that will be the focus of your discussion of similarities and/or differences. The lists above suggest two main possibilities: the fate of the main character and the role of animal figures. The student chose the fate of the main character as her basis of comparison because that difference would best support her thesis (see below).

Formulate a Main Idea

Then you must decide what point to make about your basis of comparison and put it in a topic sentence. Do not merely say something like *The main characters come to different ends in "The Ghost Owl" and "The Three Bears"* or *Differences between First Nations storytelling and Western storytelling are evident in folk tales such as "The Ghost Owl" and "The Three Bears."* If you are writing a self-contained comparison paragraph, think about the general meaning you can draw from the specific details.

Suppose, for instance, that you were comparing the endings of the two folk tales in response to a short-answer exam question. You know that in "The Ghost Owl," the main character, now a young woman, passes a final test of obedience and returns to her village, where no one recognizes her because Grandfather Hawk has dressed her as a warrior. After she admits she is the girl whose mother put her out for the owls for being naughty, her mother cries and pleads for forgiveness. The young men ask if they can wear warrior clothes like hers, thus giving her a role in creating the Cheyenne soldier societies. You might conclude that this story's ending emphasizes the reintegration of the girl into the community and the valuable contributions of her personal experience. In "The Three Bears," in contrast, the bears never see Goldilocks again and her fate is uncertain: she might have broken her neck in jumping from the window; she might have become lost in the woods; or she might have gone home to be reprimanded. The ending thus focuses on Goldilocks' punishment and banishment from the "civilized" society of the bears. You could combine these ideas about the fates of the two characters in this topic sentence:

> The fate of the main character in "The Ghost Owl" emphasizes the benefits of reintegrating troublesome individuals into the community, whereas the fate of Goldilocks in "The Three Bears" emphasizes the dangers of defying authority.

If you are writing a comparison paragraph as part of an essay, you must figure out a main idea that both explains the specific details relevant to your basis of comparison and shows how those details support your thesis. The student's thesis is that First Nations storytelling reflects the cultural belief in a universe in which all life is equal and in balance, whereas Western storytelling reflects the cultural belief in a hierarchical order in which humankind is separate from and superior to the natural world. To connect her paragraph on the two stories with this thesis, she might write this topic sentence:

> The fate of the main character in the folk tale "The Ghost Owl" reflects Native beliefs about equality and balance in the universe, whereas the fate of Goldilocks in "The Three Bears" reflects Western society's emphasis on hierarchy and separation from nature.

To clarify the connection between her topic sentence and the details about the stories, she would explain that in Native culture, reintegrating troublesome individuals is necessary to restore equality and balance, whereas in Western culture, punishing transgressors or exiling them to a threatening natural world is necessary to maintain hierarchical authority.

Organize Your Comparison

Block Method
The **block method** is the simplest way of organizing a brief comparison. In this method, you mention both subjects in your topic sentence.

Then, in the paragraph, you say everything about one subject before moving on to the other. When you are ready to discuss the second subject, you signal the shift by a transitional word or phrase. Organizing the comparison of the two folk tales by the block method might give you the following paragraph:

Sample Block Method

The fate of the main character in "The Ghost Owl" emphasizes the benefits of reintegrating troublesome individuals into the community, whereas the fate of Goldilocks in "The Three Bears" emphasizes the dangers of defying authority. In "The Ghost Owl," the main character is reunited with her community only when she has "grown up" enough to want to do so and has successfully passed a final test of obedience. Because Grandfather Hawk has dressed her as a warrior, no one in the village recognizes her until she humbly admits she is the naughty girl whose mother put her out for the owls. The responses of her mother and the young warriors signal her reintegration into the community. Her mother cries and pleads for forgiveness, and the young men ask if they can wear warrior clothes like hers. The warrior clothes represent the strength, courage, and cunning she has learned through following the teachings of Grandfather Hawk. The ending thus emphasizes not only her reintegration into the community but also the valuable contribution she can make: her instructions to the young men lead to the creation of the Cheyenne soldier societies. In "The Three Bears," however, Goldilocks' fate is uncertain: she might have broken her neck in jumping from the window; she might have become lost in the woods; or she might have found her way home and been whipped for being naughty. The ending thus focuses on Goldilocks' banishment from the "civilized" society the bears represent and her possible punishments for disobeying her mother and flouting social conventions. Unlike the girl of "The Ghost Owl," she is not given the chance to learn valuable lessons from her experience or to contribute to the good of her community.

If the material is too long for one paragraph, you can easily start a new paragraph when you shift to your second subject.

Point-by-Point Method

The **point-by-point method**, in which you shift back and forth between subjects, is sometimes more effective than the block method when you are organizing a longer piece of writing, such as a comparison essay. If you have several points you want to make in a paragraph, however, shifting between subjects can produce an annoying or confusing Ping-Pong effect, as in this revised version of the previous example:

Sample Point-by-Point Method

The fate of the main character in "The Ghost Owl" emphasizes the benefits of reintegrating troublesome individuals into the community, whereas the fate of Goldilocks in "The Three Bears" emphasizes the dangers of defying authority. In "The Ghost Owl," the main character is reunited with her community only when she has "grown up" enough to want to do so and has successfully passed a final test of obedience. In "The Three Bears," in contrast, Goldilocks' fate is uncertain: she might have broken her neck in jumping from the window; she might have become lost in the woods; or she might have found her way home and been whipped for being naughty. When the girl in "The Ghost Owl" returns to her village, she is dressed as a warrior, and so no one recognizes her until she humbly admits she is the naughty girl whose mother put her out for the owls. Her mother cries and pleads for forgiveness, and the young men ask if they can wear warrior clothes like hers. In contrast, the bears never see Goldilocks again; if she has made her way back to her home, her mother would have been angry and whipped her. The responses of the mother and the young men in. . . .

Exercice 1

Choose two topics from the following and list the similarities and differences between the subjects being compared.

- golf and hockey (or two other sports)
- love and infatuation
- watching TV and reading
- assertiveness and aggressiveness
- high school and university
- the cleaning habits of you and your roommate
- the climates in two places you have lived
- two funerals or burial rites you have attended

Exercice 2

Find a basis of comparison for each of the two topics that you chose in Exercise 1 above. Then decide what point you would make about each topic. For example, what would you compare/contrast about high school and university? Assignments? Exams? Students? Environment? Instructors? Comparing/contrasting one of these would be appropriate for a paragraph; comparing/contrasting several would be appropriate for an essay.

Exercice 3

Select a method of organization (block or point-by-point) and write a comparison paragraph based on one topic that you selected in Exercise 1. Keep in mind that your purpose is to explain, not to persuade or to share personal experience (though of course you may draw on your experience).

2. PATTERNS FOR COMPARISON ESSAYS

Just as you can use either the block or the point-by-point method to develop comparison paragraphs, you can use these methods to develop comparison essays. Both methods have their advantages and disadvantages.

Block Method

When you use the block method, you cover all the aspects of one subject before you discuss the other.

Advantages: Clarity and Simplicity

The block method allows you to develop the points about one subject before you turn to the other. That is, you might discuss setting, structure, and characterization in story A before comparing or contrasting these three elements in story B. It is, therefore, simple to work with when you don't have much time to organize an essay, such as in an exam. The block method can work well for short essays on familiar subjects. It is also effective when you are using a brief treatment of one subject as a basis for a more lengthy treatment of another. Finally, if you are comparing more than two subjects, you will probably need to use the block method to avoid fragmenting your material.

In the block method, you are less likely to distort your material by trying too hard to find similarities or by exaggerating the importance of one aspect of a subject. The drawbacks of one cancer treatment, for instance, may outweigh those of another.

Disadvantages: Repetition and Loss of Focus

One disadvantage of the block method is that readers may forget what you have said about your first subject by the time they read about your second subject. For this reason, you may have to repeat certain points. Another danger is that you may dilute or lose the basis of your comparison: the common element you are discussing (such as the training of child-care workers versus babysitters or the economic effects of two policies). As a result, your reader may decide that you have discussed both subjects but not compared them. To avoid this problem, make tight comparisons and contrasts.

Sample Outline: Block Method

If you were using the block method to organize an essay comparing your experiences of city life and small-town life, your outline might look like this.

I. Small-town life
    A. Lack of amenities and poor infrastructure
    B. Absence of culture/entertainment
    C. Lack of crime
    D. Quiet, friendly atmosphere
II. City life
    A. Wealth of amenities and solid infrastructure
    B. Plenty of entertainment, nightlife, and cultural activities
    C. More crime
    D. Noisy, impersonal atmosphere

Notice that this structure leads naturally to putting your thesis at the end, where you draw together your comparisons. In this case, you might argue that although the advantages of city life are access to amenities and entertainment, the disadvantages are its higher crime rate and its atmosphere. You conclude that you prefer small-town life.

Point-by-Point Method

When you use the point-by-point method, you consider one aspect of both subjects before moving on to another aspect of both subjects.

Advantages: Focus and Conciseness

An important advantage of the point-by-point method is that, by bringing specific points about your subjects closer together, you help your reader to grasp the most important similarities and differences. This method, then, avoids one of the main disadvantages of the block method: repetition. This emphasis on points of similarity and difference also keeps you focused on the task of comparing. For these reasons, this method is often better for organizing a lengthy and complex comparison.

Disadvantages: Complexity and Fragmentation

Because you have to identify all the points of similarity and difference you plan to discuss before you begin writing, this method is time-consuming and difficult to use for in-class essays. Another disadvantage is that if you don't have much to say about each point, your essay may Ping-Pong rapidly from one subject to the other. You can correct this problem by brainstorming to gather a lot of material, by refining your points, or by combining subpoints so that you write separate paragraphs on each aspect of each subject, as illustrated in the outline below.

Sample Outline: Point-by-Point Method

Chemotherapy vs. Radiotherapy:

    I. Introduction

    II. Definition of both treatments
       A. Definition of chemotherapy
          1. Main kinds of drugs
          2. Nanoparticles and other experimental approaches
       B. Definition of radiotherapy
          1. Internal radiotherapy
          2. External radiotherapy

    III. Treatment plan
       A. When and why chemotherapy is used
       B. When and why radiotherapy is used

    IV. Side effects
       A. Side effects of chemotherapy drugs
       B. Side effects of radiotherapy

V. Effectiveness of both treatments
   A. Effectiveness of chemotherapy alone
   B. Effectiveness of radiotherapy alone
   C. Effectiveness of these treatments combined
VI. Conclusion

3. EXAMPLE OF A COMPARISON ESSAY

The essay below, which compares/contrasts rap music and country music, was written for a first-year college course. Notice how the opening uses a quote from a major country artist to get the reader's attention and how the thesis includes a counter-argument. By structuring the thesis this way, the writer informs the reader that she is first going to acknowledge the differences of these genres before explaining their similarities, which, to her, are more important. The writer develops her argument by using several examples from both genres of music.

The immortal man in black, Johnny Cash, was once quoted as saying that "rap is crap." Indeed Cash's controversial statement has been used, for years, as proof of the questionable worth of much urban music. What Cash failed to realize in this statement, however, is that rap is not so different from country, after all. Although on the surface, rap and country music artists have different origins and looks, both musical genres share similar diversity, popularity, and heroes.

Country music and rap music have very different origins. Although the roots of country music are in the banjo and fiddle tunes of the British Isles, American country originated in the deep South, where these traditional sounds were mixed with ethnic and African rhythms and instruments. The first "country" song was supposedly played by fiddler Eck Robertson. However, the genre of country, which in its early days was referred to as Western music or cowboy songs, wasn't recognized until between 1930 and 1940. In country's early inception, music from stringed instruments, usually guitars and banjos, was accompanied by stories often celebrating the simple, rustic life. With the exception of figures like Marty Robertson and Charlie Pride, it was white artists who played and sang most of these tunes.

Although rap obviously has its roots in early African-American music, its official debut was not until the 70s, when it was suddenly blaring out of blasters in urban areas, especially the ghettoes of New York and LA. The first recorded rap recording is considered the Sugar Hill Gang's "Rapper's Delight" (1979). Instead of being strummed on guitars, rap songs were created by DJs, turn tables, and MCs. Rappers also incorporated scratching, beatboxing, and looping, either memorizing their lyrics or making them up on the spot. In fact, the term *rap*, slang for *conversation* or *discussion*, is appropriate for the lyrics of this music, which consists of observations, slang, jargon, and commentary on urban living. Unlike country, rap started as the music of urban black America.

Nelly and Tim McGraw dueted on "Country Grammar," but most rap artists wouldn't be caught within ten feet of a cowboy hat and most country artists wouldn't be caught within ten feet of gold teeth or bling. Although there are exceptions, most rap and country artists have their typical and distinctive uniforms. The country look is about blending in and being the down-home guy or gal: the tight denim tuxedo (jean jackets and jeans), Stetson hat, rugged cowboy boots, and simple T-shirt are often worn. The more exotic and retro country stars might wear black, but if they wear bling, it is usually in the form of a shiny belt buckle or exotic-skin cowboy boots. All in all, the look pays homage to country's rural roots.

Rap, on the other hand, seems to prioritize the glitzy, the baggy, and the bling. Whereas Tim McGraw might not be able to breathe in his jeans, Nellie and 50 Cent swim inside theirs. Typical rap uniforms include the shiny (often white) gym suit, baggy denim pants, hoodies with logos, Adidas shoes, and bulky (often ridiculous) neck pieces, such as hood ornaments. (Flavor Flav, from Public Enemy, mocked this trend by wearing a giant clock dangling from his neck; fortunately or unfortunately, this timepiece is now inseparable from him.) Whereas Country artists often celebrate rural culture, however, rappers, such as Snoop Dogg, glamorize pimp culture, wearing zoot suits, fedoras, fur coats, and, of course, surrounding themselves with scantily clad (or undressed) women, whom they treat as accessories. Both uniforms, though, are about fantasies of America: one about the purity of the untouched rural United States and the other about the dangerous get-rich-quick urban America.

Despite these superficial differences, and the stereotypes associated with each, both rap and country are incredibly diverse musical genres. Presently, rap music can be divided into the following subgenres: political, old school, gangsta, revolutionary, hardcore, horrorcore, G-funk, East Coast, West Coast, Dirty South, hyphy, abstract, pop, and religious. These subgenres speak of the variety of lyrics and the size and demographic variation of rap's audiences. Country music, though not as diverse, can also be subdivided. There is the honky-tonk sound, the Western sound, the rockabilly sound, the outlaw sound, and, the most popular, the Nashville sound. Country music is also categorized by traditional, bluegrass, alternative, pop, folk, and fusion. Like rap, there is much controversy over what is the original and the best, truest country.

Both genres are also popular in the Unites States, often trading top-ten spots on the Billboards. For instance, at the time of the essay's writing, the number-one song in the US is by rapper Ludacris, whereas the number-two song is by folksy alt-country act Lady Antebellum. Although rap currently hogs more of the top-ten spots, one of the top selling acts right now is new country songstress Taylor Swift. In fact, 2009's two biggest Grammy award winners are from the worlds of rap and country: Taylor Swift and Beyoncé Knowles. Taylor Swift, who recently sold 10 million records, is ready to become the top-selling country artist of all time. Relative old-timer Garth Brooks has topped both the Country Albums chart and Billboards top 200 list several times. And rap music also has its top sellers. According to *Times Online,* Eminem has sold at least 80 million albums since 1995; Jay-Z has sold 50 million since 1996; and Tupac, who has been dead since 1996, has sold upwards of 75 million albums to date. Although rap, which shares just 10% of North American record sales, is probably less popular than country on the continent, it may be more popular outside of it. It is clear that despite the mocking of country by rappers and of rap by country artists, both genres, perhaps because of their adaptability and diversity, are here to stay.

Lastly, both genres were condemned in their early stages and share outlaw heroes. Because some country music had its roots in gospel and early rock and roll, it was often regarded as devilish and sinful, shocking both churchgoers and concerned parents. And some of the heroes of country music are also less than angelic: Johnny Cash, for instance, was a notorious abuser of alcohol and drugs, and several of his songs are about violence, especially murder. Although there were no East Coast–West Coast gang wars in country music, country music has often heroized dark villains and outlaws, as in the music of Johnny Cash, Waylon Jennings, Kris Kristofferson, and Willie Nelson. There are many genres of rap, but some of the most popular, such as gangsta and political, have glorified thug life, gang violence, drug use, and pimp culture. Rap heroes and outlaws are varied: Tupac, Biggie, 50 Cent, Dr. Dre, and Eminem. In his early songs and interviews, 50 Cent used to prove his street cred by bragging about the times he had been shot. Tupac and Biggie, still heroes to this day, were gunned down in episodes of rap/gang war violence. Snoop Dogg's early videos show him parading as a pimp. But it is Eminem who most solidifies the rap/country connection. With his harsh upbringing, his poverty, his battles with addiction, and troubled relationships, some see him as the urban version of Johnny Cash.

Country and rap, then, though they come from slightly different backgrounds and court very different looks, share similar diversity, popularity, and heroes. Johnny Cash experimented with several types of music, such as rock, country, rockabilly, and alt-country. It is unfortunate that he died before, say, making a duet with Eminem, and ultimately discovering that rap, perhaps, is *not* crap.

4. CLASSIFYING

Classifying and **dividing** are similar processes that organize facts. When you classify, you begin with many items and group them into categories. For instance, if you were organizing an online website in which people could download MP3s, you might classify your musical genres into country, rock, pop, alternative, urban, classical, folk, and electronic. Of course, within these categories, there would be further division.

For most paragraphs and essays, though, you will have fewer categories to work with. For instance, if you were writing an essay on the effects of unemployment, and your brainstorming gave you a long list of effects, you might decide to classify these effects into economic, social, and psychological. When you divide, then, you start with a general category, such as *effects of unemployment*, and break this category into specific types or kinds of effects. In classification, you move from details to generalizations, whereas in division, you move from generalizations to details. You will move between both of these processes when writing, but, for the purpose of clarity, we will refer to these as classification paragraphs.

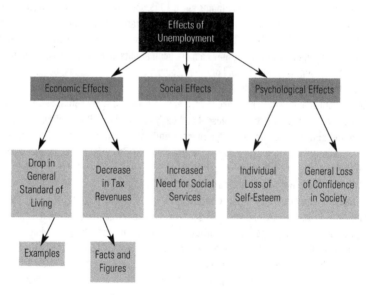

Both types of classification paragraphs could be expanded into essays, in which you would dedicate a paragraph or more to developing each of your subcategories.

For this reason, classification/division paragraphs make good overviews of material you will then explain further, and good summaries of material you have already covered. And, as the example below shows, they are also ideal for making humorous points.

Sample Classification/Division Paragraph

Homo Camperus, an abundant and diverse species of nomadic wanderers, can be divided into three subspecies according to their differing modes of shelter: Homo Camperus Motorhomeous, Homo Camperus Fanaticus, and Homo Camperus Miscellaneous. The Motorhomeous subspecies is easily recognizable by the giant, house-like structures its members inhabit, variously known as *motorhomes, Winnebagos, camper-trailers,* and last but not least, *highway menaces.* While members of this subspecies enjoy the campground's version of nature as much as the other Camperus groups, they also need the security of sturdy walls, real beds, and their own porta-potties. Fanaticus, in contrast, does not believe in sleeping under anything but a nylon roof. While Motorhomeous lurks within the relative safety of the forest, Fanaticus braves the windy, treeless beachfront, relishing the challenge of having to extra-stake a tent. For Fanaticus, the tent is the ultimate sign of high status and economic/social well-being, and so the more tents one has, the better. Usually, there are two colossal ones: one tent for sleeping and the other for meals and for planning the daily outings to climb mountains or kayak raging rivers. The third and most abundant subspecies, Miscellaneous, is made up of members of the abnormal and unconventional Camperus who wander into the campground for the first time. Miscellaneous groups never have more than one tent, a small, inferior one that they don't know how to erect. They always forget some key piece of equipment, such as tent pegs, which they end up borrowing from the smug Fanaticus. In windy, rainy, or otherwise inclement weather, they abandon their flimsy shelter and retreat to their cars, to the delight of the cozy Motorhomeous and intrepid Fanaticus.

—*James Stevenson*

Here are suggestions for writing classification paragraphs:

- **Choose a general category that you know enough about to divide into two to four subcategories** (for example: customers at your workplace, types of running shoes, Stephen King novels).

- **Decide on a principle of classification, and state this principle at the beginning of your paragraph.** A principle of classification tells you how to divide things into groups. In the above example, campers are divided according to their preferred mode of shelter. Likewise, you could divide running-shoe–store customers according to attitudes toward staff, dedication to running, or spending habits. Each of these is a principle of classification.

- **Make a list of the types represented by your principle of classification.** If you chose *dedication to running* as your principle of classification, you might come up with types such as these: the recreational runner, the weekend warrior, the beginning runner, the fitness runner, the treadmill addict, and the amateur athlete.

- **Describe two to four types, depending upon how much you need to say to explain each type.** Use actual examples (Billy the ultra runner who gets out three times a day) or hypothetical examples (the kinds of running shoes the weekend warrior usually buys).

- **To signal your shift from one subcategory to another, use parallel sentence structure and/or transitions that indicate enumeration** (*first, second, next, finally*).

- **Begin or end your paragraph with the point you want to make.** For example, *As you snicker at recreational runners, remember you were once one of them.*

Exercise 4

Complete the following diagrams with appropriate categories and examples. Notice that police dramas can be classified in at least **two** different ways. Can you figure out two other principles of classification for this subject?

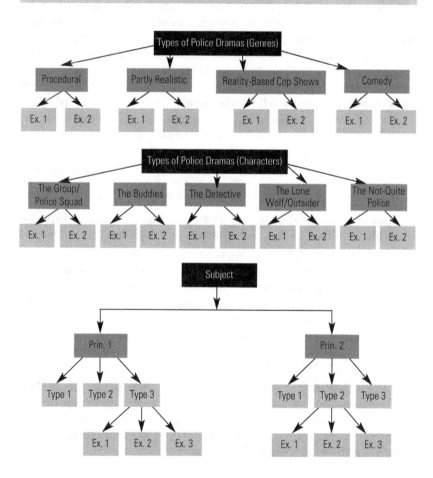

5. SAMPLE OF A CLASSIFICATION ESSAY

In the following light-hearted essay, the writer, a first-year college student and mother, attempts to classify her daughter's friends. Notice how the student goes beyond the three-paragraph model to include both categories and subcategories.

Playing Parental Scientist: Classifying My Daughter's Friends

Parenthood is like an unstable science experiment. The profession is not only plagued with variables that defy control, but also riddled with contradictory results. The same procedures that prove successful today may, in fact, fail tomorrow. Thus, ineffective parental scientists, such as I, cling to those practices that are actually *within* their control, such as classifying their children's friends. My three older sons have provided a variety of species for me to catalogue; however, it has been my youngest bait, Vanessa, who has lured the most diverse group of 17- to 20-year-olds to my laboratory (house). Based on the behaviours, motivations, and some unique appearance traits, Vanessa's friends can be divided into three main groups: the sinceres, the suitors, and the searchers.

The group called "the sinceres" consists of members who come in a wide range of shapes, ages, gender, and maturity. Physical appearance is not a factor here. These individuals frequent our household simply because they like being with Vanessa and they want to nurture their friendship with her. They have no false pretences, no hidden agendas. Their behaviour is characterized by child-like play, crafts, and bouts of drama. Observing their typical interactions of laughter, mess, movie-making, and sleepovers is definitely entertaining.

In contrast to the sinceres, "the suitors" are an all-male group, who are classified according to three criteria. As the title implies, their motivation is to rent space in Vanessa's heart or at least get a date or two for their efforts. This group requires division into two, very distinct, subcategories: the spindly, mop-haired musicians and the mature musclemen.

The first subcategory of suitors, the spindly, mop-haired musicians, is truly the most obscure group of young adults, with uncanny resemblances in appearance and behaviour.

That is, each of the five men in this group has exactly the same body structure: they all resemble toothpick men. Neither an ounce of fat nor an ounce of muscle exists on the frames of these ectomorphs. These individuals also all sport the same hairdo, or lack thereof, which consists of long, messy strands obstructing their vision. As if in consensus, they all dress in a remarkably similar fashion, wearing skin-tight jeans and dark T-shirts. Another mysterious commonality within this group of nonconformists is that all are gifted musicians. All sing; in addition, four play the guitar and one plays the drums. Their musical ability has offered an inspiring diversion for the analyst; however, at this time, their primary goal remains unaccomplished.

The second subcategory of suitors is the mature musclemen. This is the smallest group in quantity, but what they lack in numbers, they definitely make up for in brute size! These three accomplished sportsmen each stand over six feet tall. The members of this group are educated, well kept, and neatly dressed; also, these gentlemen adhere to social norms. Although their motivation resembles that of the mop-haired musicians, their behaviour could not be more opposite. These individuals can quote Shakespeare, engage in games of chess, and share their travel and work experiences with flair. Portraying perfect manners, these suitors, sadly, have not managed to take up residence in Vanessa's heart. These musclemen do, however, make striking backdrops as escorts, especially in graduation and wedding photos.

The third main category of Vanessa's friends, "the searchers," is by far the largest in number. These individuals initially cross over the threshold under the guise of sincere friends, but when their intentions are examined under the microscope, their hidden agendas can be discerned. They are *all* searching for a specific reason; that is, why they are searching determines what subcategory they belong to. For example, if they are hunting for food, they are placed with the hungry-searchers; if they are looking for guidance, they are classified with the hurting-searchers; and if they are questing for closeness with one of Vanessa's brothers, they are grouped with the hormonally charged—searchers.

The hungry-searchers are identified mainly by their behaviours. They show up precisely at meal times, spouting copious compliments pertaining to delicious aromas. Other times, they rummage around like scavengers through the cookie jar, the cupboards, the fridge, and the freezer. Leaving no crumb unturned, this group is annoyingly hungry and even more persistent. If there happens to be homemade baking in the oven, they can smell it a mile off, packing together like wolves, circling around, waiting impatiently for their prey to emerge. Even when the analyst is off-shift, and the hungry-searchers have paid a visit in her absence, the evidence is undeniable. A trail of empty cartons, containers, packages, and cans litters the area. This group can empty the storeroom faster than a cyclone and has made this scientist consider cupboard locks. . . several of them.

The hurting-searchers, in contrast, are slow moving and despondent. They are typically preoccupied, appearing concerned and loitering close to the analyst. They are looking for guidance, advice, or perhaps some parental company. Session openers, such as, "just between you and me. . ." are dead give-aways that one is conversing with a member of this group. Heavy-hearted, they often blurt out their problems without any encouragement. On other occasions, probing and prodding may be needed to coax out their concerns. Still, at other times, especially if alcohol is part of the equation, they wait in line, as if to confess their sins, looking for absolution. The listener may emerge with sore facial muscles and a multi-pierced tongue because of her effort to restrain expressions of shock.

Finally, there is the last, but certainly not least interesting, subgroup of searchers: the once sincere friends who have mutated to join the hormonally charged. The exact number in this dangerous group of females cannot be verified, for subjects tend to migrate, randomly and with no apparent warning. This group's members are characterized by their ulterior motives, strange behaviours, and attempts to be provocative. Suddenly, these young child-like friends are trying desperately to display their feminine wiles. Everything about them has changed! The pitch in their voice, their laugh, their walk, and their whole persona is loaded with the loud message: "Hey! Look at me. I am sexy! I have matured overnight, and I can prove it!" These hormonally charged chicks do not hang around Vanessa, nor are they interested in what is happening in the kitchen. No, they are highly territorial and intensely focused not on her, but on one of her brothers. This group provides the observer with many excuses to raise her eyebrows and discreetly chuckle.

Although I don't condone stereotyping, I must admit that classifying my daughter's friends was an interesting, eye-opening process, which strikingly revealed how similar seemingly disparate individuals actually are. By establishing the criteria for categorization as motivations, behaviours, and appearances, you, too, can classify people. For me, this activity has become an entertaining pastime, which has allowed an escape from the unpredictability of parenthood along with the welcome, though temporary, illusion of control.

—*S. Lyons*

Writing Summaries and Essays about Literature

1. SUMMARIES OF NONFICTION BOOKS AND ARTICLES

Summarizing a nonfiction book or an article from a newspaper, magazine, or scholarly journal means briefly explaining the work's content, not analyzing its meaning. Self-contained summaries appear in annotated bibliographies, abstracts accompanying research papers, formal reports, and proposals. You will most likely integrate your summary into a review, position paper, or research paper. Follow the steps below when summarizing nonfiction works.

Steps for Summarizing Nonfiction Works

1. Write down complete bibliographical information for the article, chapter, or book, using the appropriate format (MLA, APA, or other) for your audience.

2. Identify the thesis, which is most likely in the introduction or conclusion, and restate it in your own words. If no thesis is stated, as is usually the case in more personal and less formal essays, determine what the thesis is and formulate it in your own words.

3. Identify the main sections. Look for guideposts: Does the thesis outline the structure of the piece? Do topic sentences or transitions indicate stages in development? Do headings or other typographical devices suggest the main divisions? For instance, a classification essay on sight hounds might be broken down into easily distinguishable sections.

4. State the main idea of each section in your own words.

5. Locate and record subpoints and examples for the main idea of each section. Using point form will remind you not to merely paraphrase every sentence. Include brief quotations when the author's own words seem particularly important. Put quotation marks around any quoted material and include the page reference.

6. Define all important key terms in your own words and include them in your summary. Pay special attention to words in italics or boldface. Look up unfamiliar words.

Writing the Summary

1. Give complete bibliographical information (author, title, place of publication, publisher, date) either as a heading or in the first sentence of your summary.

2. First, state your summing up and the writer's thesis in a sentence or two. Then, in a few paragraphs, explain the main idea of each section, using enough subpoints and examples to clarify it. Show how these points are connected by emphasizing the writer's purpose or method of development, such as comparison or classification.

3. Keep the material approximately in the same order and proportion as in the original. Do not exaggerate the importance of an interesting point or ignore a particularly confusing one.

4. Use denotative (emotionally neutral) language, and focus on the article or chapter itself rather than your responses to it. Mention the writer's name or refer to the writer frequently to clarify that you are presenting his or her opinions on the subject, not your own. Remember to use quotation marks and to give page references for all quotations.

5. If you have been asked to include an evaluation of either the content or the style of the original, put your evaluation, clearly indicated as such, in a separate paragraph. In your evaluation, do not provide personal opinion but refer to the strengths and weaknesses of the original.

2. SAMPLE SUMMARY OF AN EXPOSITORY ESSAY

A sample summary of John Intini's expository essay, "Look at Us: Suddenly We're All Celebrities," can be found at the end of the essay.

Look at Us: Suddenly We're All Celebrities
by John Intini

Michael Tyas's Hollywood experiment lasted eight long months. "I was an intern on a reality TV show in LA, and was hating it with a passion because it wasn't reality," says Tyas, who prefers not to reveal the name of the show. "I logged all of the original footage—about 500 hours—so I saw the real story, and then I saw the fantasy story they made out of it." So the 23-year-old freelance photographer, now back in his parents' Shelburne, Ontario, home, did what thousands from his generation have done: he turned the camera on himself.

Tyas began a vlog—an online video diary of his life. "I always thought it would be cool to get my face in front of hundreds of people." He's unapologetic about building a site around his remarkably ordinary existence—his first post was a six-minute tour of his filthy LA apartment; more recently he's included a clip of his trip to the Ontario

Science Centre, and another just hanging out at a friend's apartment. "I make narcissism look good," says Tyas, who has made $8.49 in ad sales on his site since April 2005. "It's a very positive thing to like yourself and think you're marketable enough to put your face out there."

His confidence, cultural observers point out, is not an anomaly. "This is the Barney Generation," says Alison Hearn, an assistant professor of information and media studies at the University of Western Ontario. "These kids have grown up in a world in which they've constantly been told they're special." This age of narcissism has spawned an industry that's all about you and me. And now, a few years into the Me Media revolution, an array of professional-grade vanity products and services have cropped up to meet the new narcissists' needs. "They're all ways of defining yourself," says Hearn, "creating an image of yourself and then falling in love with it."

Anyone interested in a bit of immortality? No problem. For a fee ranging from $15,000 to $80,000, London, England–based eDv, which bills itself as the "personal motion picture company," gets professional filmmakers to sort through your old home videos, conduct and tape interviews with your family, and edit together a high-quality biography. If that seems too commercial or too much work, try buying your way into the pages of a book by a favourite author. This is often done through charity auctions. Last September, John Grisham, Dave Eggers, and Stephen King put the names of upcoming characters on the block (a Florida woman paid US$25,100 for the right to put her brother's name to a character in King's new book).

There are many other ways of making yourself a star. One website, based in the Netherlands, allows users to create their own soap opera by posting messages, pictures, and video from their own lives. While it doesn't much resemble your typical mid-afternoon guilty pleasure, that hasn't stopped people from posting and visitors from checking in and voting for their favourites. The highest-ranking "stars" can win prizes, including a celebrity magazine feature (the site is run by a magazine publisher). Then there's Playstation 2's EyeToy—a digital camera that literally places gamers within a video game. In *Kung Fu*, users can show off their martial arts skills by taking on the bad guys with their very own digitized hands and feet.

Technology is in part to blame. It's helped us meet these needs—and create them. The affordability of digital cameras, for instance, has sparked a surge in the popularity of self-portraits. Most young people are perfectly comfortable taking their own pictures—a key part of their Internet egos on MySpace and the like. Some change their photo almost every day. "It's an image economy," says Hearn. "It's all about branding yourself."

Some, like Erica Morgan, have devoted entire websites to self-portraiture—a form in which one can be a star on *both* sides of the camera. Since February 2003, Morgan, who was born in South Carolina and now lives in Sydney, Australia, takes a photo of herself every day and posts it on her site (1,111 at last count). "At first I was a little concerned about obsessive strangers," says the 27-year-old photographer. "And a little self-conscious about pulling out my camera and turning it in my direction." Apparently, she got over it.

These days—again, thanks to technology—you can pretty much get your likeness plastered on anything. This business niche hearkens back to those booths at shopping malls that would print your picture on a coffee mug or a T-shirt. By contemporary standards, that old personalized fare appears like cave art. Today, fond parents can get a replica doll made of their children for US$139. To create a 23-inch Mini Me, parents can go on mytwinn.com and build the doll themselves, or send in a photo of junior and have the toy specialists do the legwork. The doll is an exact likeness; freckles and birthmarks are hand-painted at no additional cost. A couple of years ago, a California-based firm started selling personalized confetti—your digital images were turned into tiny paper scraps. Before they shut down, the company had sold 30,000 bags—starting at US$17 each—to people who wanted to be the life of the party.

Our look-at-me industry has even found its way into the art world. Send about $400 and a saliva sample to Ottawa-based DNA 11, and you'll receive an 18 × 24-inch portrait (available in one of eight colours) of your very own personal genetic code. "Before we started, we thought that everyone with a big ego would want one of these hanging in their offices—and we have lots of CEOs, power-brokers, investment brokers and venture capitalists that own our artwork," says co-founder Adrian Salamunovic, whose company has shipped art to thirty countries and sold more than 1,000 prints since last July. "But moms and grandmas have done it too. For most, ego doesn't play a factor." In celebration of its one-year anniversary, the company is unveiling this week a new twist on the original: fingerprint portraits. "What we do is not in-your-face narcissistic—like say an oil painting of my face over the fireplace," says Salamunovic, 30. "This is highly personal art—it's one of one. And you're a collaborator."

The proliferation of personalized services may just be a logical next step for a society in which everything—from weddings to funerals—is hyper-personalized. For several years now, thanks in large part to the reality TV craze, we've been told that we can be stars. Now we're starting to act like it. At the extreme end of the spectrum, people, desperate for the rock-star treatment, can hire an entourage—complete with a bodyguard, faux-friends and paparazzi photographers to greet them climbing out of a limo at the hottest club.

An effect of all this is the elevation of the completely ordinary. The clearest model may be YouTube, the video-sharing website with the narcissistic "Broadcast Yourself" tag line, which is getting 70 million video views a day. YouTube has hundreds of thousands of clips from rock concerts and old TV shows, but the very random—and sometimes humorous—videos of regular people doing boring stuff have also played an integral role in the site's success. We're not just finding ways to share our very mundane lives, we're also tuning in to watch other people's. One recent trend involved users posting videos of themselves watching other youtubers watching YouTube.

Or consider the six-month-old vlog of Dan O'Rourke, a provincial government policy worker in Halifax, who says that making himself the star is simply a product of necessity. "I'm the only actor I can afford," says the 26-year-old, who spends as many as ten hours a week working on his vlog. "I just do things that I think will turn out interesting without a target audience in mind." Road trips, he says, usually make for the best posts, but, much to his own surprise, his most popular clip so far—which has attracted more than 1,000 views—was a 30-second spot during which he pours out a container of spoiled chocolate milk.

People seem to be going to greater heights in the pursuit of real reality—and they aren't exactly succeeding. "Authenticity is a very hazy construct," says Marc Ouellette, who teaches English and cultural studies at McMaster University. "In the race for distinction, everyone ends up ultimately looking the same." And often, he suggests, we end up using the modes of mainstream and celebrity culture, even when we think we're being original. "I'd like to think that it's totally their voice, but I don't," he says. "There are so many forces. It's not purely narcissistic since it's almost always attached to some pre-existing cultural and celebrity icon."

In fact, more than narcissism, Ouellette believes many of us today suffer from solipsism—the inability to recognize the existence of another viewpoint. "Solipsism is supposed to end by mid-adolescence, but I don't think it's disappearing at the same stage in the cognitive process that it used to," he says. "Most people get to a point in their lives when they recognize that others have a viewpoint that is just as valid as their own. With adolescence starting earlier and ending later, some never get to that stage. It ultimately comes down to always thinking, 'what's in it for me?'"

Sample Summary of Expository Essay

John Intini's article "Look at Us: Suddenly We're All Celebrities," published in *Maclean's* magazine in November 2006, uses causal analysis and examples to support its thesis: that the "Me Media" generation, which is both a product of technology and an instigator of further technological innovations, is both narcissistic and solipsistic.

Intini begins his article with a typical example of what Alison Hearn terms the "Barney Generation" (par. 3): Michael Tyas, who creates a blog of his daily existence. In subsequent paragraphs, Intini explains how technology allows people to immortalize themselves or transform into celebrities. He mentions a company that makes personal home movies (eDv), websites allowing "users to create their own soap operas by posting messages, pictures and video from their own lives" (par. 5), and a video camera that places gamers in the game. Even your genetic code, Intini says, can be transformed into a unique piece of art.

Intini blames technology and media trends for causing and perpetuating this narcissism. Firstly, the digital camera made it easy to take pictures and post them on the web. Secondly, the media, first through reality TV and now through YouTube, has glorified the hyper-personalized and elevated the ordinary.

In the end, Intini points out the effects, some ironic, of people expressing their individuality. Because people are modelling their behaviour after celebrity culture and other bloggers, they end up being more similar than unique. Also, according to cultural studies professor Marc Ouellette, openly sharing actually creates an adolescent solipsism for a whole culture continually preoccupied with "What's in it for me?" (par. 11).

3. PLOT SUMMARIES

Plot summaries, which condense what happens in novels, films, and similar narratives, are useful when you write reviews, essays, or research papers analyzing narrative works. Whereas the summary of a nonfiction work explains what the article, essay, or book says, that of a fictional work relates what happens. Although they can vary in length, most plot summaries are a paragraph or two long, depending on the amount of detail appropriate for your purpose and audience.

Follow these steps when writing a plot summary:

1. Analyze the work to determine its main issue: Is it the conflict between good and evil? Or the horrors of war? State this issue in

your topic sentence, along with the author or director and title of the work.

2. In the body of the paragraph, describe the plot's main events. Clarify the causal connections among these events by emphasizing why an event occurred and by explaining its effects. If you are summarizing a long or complex work, you might need to classify the events in the main plot and those in the subplot. Present events in the same order as in the original unless you need to modify this order to fit your classification. Include other elements, such as characterization and setting, if necessary to explain the plot.

3. End your summary with the last major event. Your concluding sentence should return to the main point about the work stated in your topic sentence.

4. SAMPLE PLOT SUMMARY OF A NOVEL

Margaret Atwood's dystopian novel *Oryx and Crake* is summarized below.

In *Oryx and Crake*, Margaret Atwood creates a disturbing but accurate dystopian world of unethical science, omnipotent corporations, and environmental devastation. In the beginning of the book, the reader is introduced to Snowman, a vermin-infested, sheet-wearing creature huddling in a tree. Through a series of flashbacks, the reader learns the story of Snowman and the world he once inhabited. Snowman, a.k.a. Jimmy, and his academic elite parents once lived in one of the compounds, a gated world run by a biotech corporation. His father worked in eugenics, but his mother, disgusted by her world, left the family to become an environmental terrorist. As an adolescent, Jimmie meets Glenn, a.k.a. Crake, a genius haunted by his father's mysterious death. The two spend their adolescence playing violent video games and exploring their eroded world. After graduating, they go their separate ways— one to a high-end science university and the other to a decaying arts academy—until Crake hires Jimmy to work on the BlyssPluss pill, and Paradice, a project creating model humans. At Paradice, Jimmy meets Oryx, whom he believes is a young girl from a porn site he once viewed. After working at Paradice for some time, Crake disperses the BlyssPluss pill, enacting his apocalyptic plan and leaving Jimmie as guardian of these strange green-eyed beings called the Crakers. At the end of the novel, Snowman is about to encounter some strangers; the reader is left wondering whether he will make human contact, whether the Crakers will continue to evolve, and whether Crake's "utopia" will devolve.

5. ESSAYS ANALYZING LITERATURE
Purpose and Audience

Some students confuse writing a summary with writing a literary analysis essay; however, these are definitely separate tasks with different goals. In a summary of a literary text, your main goal is to **synthesize**, or put together, the events of the text in order to describe what happened. In literary analysis, on the other hand, your purpose is to **analyze**, or take the text apart, in order to describe some aspect of the text's meaning. In a summary, you state the facts; in an analysis essay, you study the significance of textual details to arrive at its deeper meanings and possible themes.

By reading the text carefully, you develop a sense of its ideas, such as the idea that "choices have consequences" running through the novels of David Adams Richards. Then you analyze the work, or a portion of it, such as a play's scene or a novel's setting, by asking discovery questions. After this analysis, you refine your sense of theme, showing how you arrived at your interpretation.

Because you are writing primarily for an instructor familiar with the work, you may be unsure of how much to say. You don't need to provide all the details you would for someone who has never read the text—that is, you don't need to summarize the plot—but you do need to set up quotations and examples, which you use as evidence of your claims. These quotations and examples prove your reasoning, reveal how you developed your interpretation, and allow the reader to engage with your discussion.

Writing about Literature: The Process

When you analyze works of nonfiction, such as essays, research articles, and proposals, you focus more on the validity of their arguments. Contrarily, when you analyze works of imaginative literature—novels, stories, plays, and poems—you concentrate on their aesthetic qualities and moral implications.

You can write a more effective essay on literature by following these steps:

1. **Decide on a focus and a method of development.** Most assignments in introductory literature courses give you a focus, such as explaining how one or more elements—the setting, characterization, or style—relate to the theme of the work as a whole.

   The method of development for this type of exposition is **analysis**, the division of something into its parts (your chosen elements) in order to explain the whole (the theme) more clearly. Some instructors might specify which elements to focus on, whereas others will let you choose the elements that best contribute to the theme.

   In addition to analysis, some topics require **comparison or the discussion of two subjects**: *Compare the theme of initiation in stories X and Y.* For other topics, you may be asked to assess the strengths and weaknesses of a work: *Which film version of* Hamlet *better interprets Hamlet's difficulties in avenging his father's death?* For this topic, in addition to analysis and comparison, you would also use **persuasion**.

If your topic is more general, such as *Discuss three poems by Margaret Atwood*, you will have to brainstorm first to narrow your topic. By doing so, you will decide which poems to discuss based on what elements they have in common.

2. **Analyze the relevant element(s) or section(s) of the work.** Using the discovery questions for imaginative literature in the next section, take notes on each of the literary elements to determine which ones you will use in your analysis. If you are writing a compare/contrast essay on two literary works, divide your page into two columns, systematically taking notes on each element as you proceed. By doing so, you can easily see which elements can best be compared/contrasted in your essay.

3. **Formulate a thesis.** The thesis should make a point about the theme of the work and how each element contributes to that theme. Be sure that you have not merely restated the essay topic (*This essay will analyze the use of landscape in a poem by Margaret Atwood*) or made a vague generalization (*Many poets use landscape to express their moods*). To direct your reader to the relevance of the use of landscape, you would need a thesis such as this one: *In Margaret Atwood's poem "Journey to the Interior," landscape mirrors the struggle against depression.*

4. **Organize your essay.** In your introduction, give the authors and titles of the works you plan to discuss and establish your essay's **focus**. *Put your thesis at the end of your introduction.* In the body of your essay, keep your reader's attention on your subject by beginning each paragraph with a topic sentence identifying one aspect of your subject. If you were writing an essay on the symbolism in William Faulkner's "A Rose for Emily," each sentence might state the significance of one symbol.

The decaying Grierson mansion symbolizes how Miss Emily is caught between the past and the present.

Miss Emily's parlour represents her mental disorder and her continued subservience to her father.

Being trapped in time is revealed by Miss Emily's physical description.

These topic sentences all address symbols, but their different structures give the essay variety. In these paragraphs, you would give reasons, details, examples, and quotations to support each interpretative point, making sure to clearly link the point to the supporting evidence. For instance, you would discuss how certain features of the house, its rotting exteriority, proximity to gas pumps, physical darkness, etc., reveal how Emily is caught between the two time periods.

In the conclusion of your essay, restate your thesis and summarize your important points. If appropriate, suggest a broader context into which your interpretation fits.

6. SAMPLE LITERARY ANALYSIS PARAGRAPH

Dramatic irony is used in Kate Chopin's "A Story of an Hour" to demonstrate the secret long-ings behind the façade of the content nineteenth century wife.[1] After she is told of her hus-band's death, Mrs. Mallard retires to her bedroom. Although her friends believe she is mourning her husband's death, the reader sees her sitting in her room feeling the first hints of joy.[2] The reader spies on Louise as she sees[3] "in the open square before her house the tops of trees that were all aquiver with the new spring life. The delicious breath of rain was in the air" (66). The irony in this moment is obvious. Instead of feeling the despair and loss that society expects, Louise feels hope and bliss because she is now not a widow who has lost her husband but a woman who, like the reawakening trees, is reborn and "aquiver" with passion, life, and freedom.[4] Though she acts, just as she has always acted, like the dutiful mourn-ing wife, newly widowed Louise reveals her passion, relief, and joy to both herself and to the readers.[5]

DISCOVERY QUESTIONS: IMAGINATIVE LITERATURE

Subject What is this work about?

Genre What kind of work is this (detective story, revenge tragedy, dramatic monologue)? What are the characteristics of this genre?

Setting What is the time, place, and social environment in which the work is set? (Alice Munro's *Lives of Girls and Women* is set among the working poor in rural Ontario in the late 1940s and 1950s.) What effect does the setting have on characters' lives?

What values are associated with different times, places, or social environments? In drama and film, what do costumes, lighting, sets, and music contribute to the setting?

Structure How is the work put together?

Narrative/Dramatic Structure: What sets the plot in motion? What are the main events? Does the plot reach a crisis? How are the events arranged (chronologically, from present to past, from main plot to subplots)? What is the underlying issue or purpose that connects the events (a spiritual quest, a critique of society, a revelation of the main character's true nature)?

Poetic Structure: How are the thoughts and feelings organized? Why does the poem begin and end as it does? Does the structure

---

[1] This is the topic sentence.

[2] This sentence summarizes an event from the text and contextualizes a quote.

[3] Notice how the quote is grammatically integrated into the sentence and how the parenthetical citation, in MLA format, follows the quote but precedes the period.

[4] These two sentences elaborate on the significance of the quote and connect the quote to the main idea in the topic sentence.

[5] This sentence brings the discussion to a temporary close.

follow the conventions of a particular kind of poem (an Italian sonnet, for example)?

Characterization What are the characters like? Is there a broad range of characters? How would you classify them? Are the characters given depth and complexity (are they developed?) or are they stereotypes? Are the characters symbolic? What techniques are used to portray them (appearance, characteristic actions, speech, opinions of others, self-revelation)? Do characters change? What do we learn about the workings of race, class, gender, or other factors from the way characters live their lives? What do their names reveal about them?

Point of View Whose eyes do we see through? Whose voice do we hear? In stories and novels, this voice is referred to as the narrator. Because you cannot be sure that the voice you hear in a poem is the poet's, it is customary to use the term *speaker* when you refer to the point of view in a poem.

Is the narrator (stories, novels) or the speaker (poetry) a participant, referring to himself or herself as "I"? How reliable is this narrator or speaker? Does he or she seem to be telling the whole truth?

Is the narrator or speaker a non-participant, referring to the characters as *he, she,* or *they*? Is the narrator/speaker omniscient, seeing into the minds of all the characters? Does the narrator/speaker comment directly on the characters or the action?

Style (Diction and Sentence Structure) What are the effects of language level (formal, standard, informal) and word choice? Are there any unusual or especially effective words? Is slang used? Specialized language? In poetry, what effects are achieved through the sounds of words? How does word choice contribute to the characterization, setting, and theme? What are the effects of sentence patterns? Does the writer favour long, complex sentences or short, simple ones? Are sentence fragments used to create emphasis, excitement, informality? Is parallelism used distinctively? In poetry, how are lines and stanzas used? In films and plays, what are the effects of the pacing of dialogue and action? How does language contribute to characterization, setting, and theme?

Style (Imagery and Symbolism) Does the writer use any significant figures of speech (similes, metaphors, personification)? Do images and symbols create patterns of meaning? How do imagery and symbolism contribute to the characterization, setting, and theme?

Theme What is the central idea of the work?

Integrating Secondary Sources

If you wish to integrate other critics' interpretations into your essay, it's important that you cite your sources carefully.

That is, if you use outside material, whether it is from a book, article, or the Internet, you must cite, in the body of the essay, exactly where you retrieved this material. This internal reference must be matched with a full bibliographical citation in a Works Cited or References list. In the essay below, the writer uses parenthetical citations to reference the poem's lines and then includes a full citation at the end.

7. SAMPLE ESSAY ANALYZING LITERATURE: ESSAY ON POETRY

The following sample essay demonstrates how you can analyze a piece of writing to explain its theme. Here is the poem the essay analyzes:

Warren Pryor

When every pencil meant a sacrifice
his parents boarded him in town
slaving to free him from the stony fields
the meager acreage that bore them down.

They blushed with pride when, at his graduation,
they watched him picking up the slender scroll,
his passport from the years of brutal toil
and lonely patience in a barren hole.

When he went in the Bank their cups ran over.
They marvelled how he wore a milk-white shirt
work days and jeans on Sundays. He was saved
from their thistle-strewn farm and its red dirt.

And he said nothing. Hard and serious
like a young bear inside his teller's cage,
his axe-hewn hands upon the paper bills
aching with empty strength and throttled rage.

—Alden Nowlan

Reprinted by permission of Claudine Nowlan.

Wasted Sacrifices in "Warren Pryor"

In his poem "Warren Pryor," Alden Nowlan explores the sad consequences of good intentions. Like most parents, Warren's parents want the best for him. Their vision of a good life for their son, however, is based on what they imagine he wants, not what he really wants. For this reason, their sacrifices create a trap of duty from which Warren cannot escape. Every element in this poem—structure, sound patterns, rhythm, diction, and imagery—reinforces the central irony: children who are forced to fulfill their parents' dreams end up with lives as imprisoning as those their parents dreamed of escaping.

Nowlan develops the contrast between what Warren wants and what his parents want for him through the sequence of events and shift in point of view that create the structure of the poem. The poem begins with Warren's parents painfully scraping together the money for their son to live in town and complete high school. The second stanza is devoted to their enormous pleasure and pride when he graduates and gains "his passport from the years of brutal toil" (line 7). In the third stanza, when Warren gets a job in a bank, his parents "marvel" that he now wears his good clothes every day but Sunday. The final lines of this stanza, which describe the parents' triumph at rescuing their son from "their thistle-strewn farm," mark the turning point of the poem.

In the fourth stanza, Nowlan abruptly shifts the point of view and at last we see Warren himself: caged, miserable, strangled by his parents' sacrifices. The rigid structure of the poem emphasizes the imprisonment Warren feels as he paces in his teller's cage. Most of the lines have ten syllables. Every stanza has four lines and the same rhyme scheme: abcb. The rhythm of the lines, especially in the first two stanzas, is mostly regular iambic pentameter:

When every pencil meant a sacrifice
his parents boarded him in town

When the point of view shifts in the fourth stanza, so does the rhythm: "And he said nothing." (line 13). The extra stressed syllables and the dramatic pause within the line give us a vivid sense of Warren's agony.

Both the diction and imagery of "Warren Pryor" emphasize the theme of wasted sacrifices. The words describing the farm—"stony fields," "meager acreage," "barren hole," "thistle-strewn"—make it easy for us to see the hardships his parents have endured. Surely his assistance would have made their lives easier; instead, they "slaved" in "lonely patience" to "free" their son. The allusion to the Twenty-Third Psalm in the comment "their cups ran over" suggests their complete happiness when Warren secures a job in a bank. Indeed, the cup of their contentment spills over the "milk-white shirt" he wears to work.

By comparing Warren to a "young bear," Nowlan suggests that the son is by nature unsuited for the job his parents delight in. The simile stresses his youth, power, wildness. He is both literally in a cage—the barred cubicle bank tellers used to work in—and figuratively imprisoned by his parents' expectations. The idea that Warren is trapped in a bank seems especially apt, for he will spend his life paying for the sacrifices his parents have made for him. The metaphors describing Warren's hands emphasize his sacrifices. His hands are "axe-hewn" (strong and roughly made), suggesting that he is better suited to wielding an axe than handling paper bills. His hands are "aching with empty strength" because, in the irony that concludes the poem, he longs to do exactly the work his parents' sacrifices have kept him from. As he strangles his frustration, he sacrifices his own desires so that his parents can keep their illusions.

Nowlan develops the real sadness of wasted sacrifices through every element of "Warren Pryor." Through the first three stanzas, we share the parents' pleasure in their own accomplishments. The central irony of the poem, of course, is that they have gained their happiness at the expense of their son's. Throughout the poem, Nowlan's skillful diction and imagery emphasize the sad reality of what their sacrifices have actually accomplished. While they congratulate themselves on rescuing him, Warren paces within the cage his parents' sacrifices have created for him. In a few short lines, Nowlan vividly captures the all-too-common conflict between parents' expectations and their child's fulfillment.

Works Cited

Nowlan, Alden. "Warren Prior." *Canadian Literature in English: Texts and Contexts,* Vol. 2. Ed. Laura Moss and Cynthia Sugars. Toronto: Pearson Education Canada, 2008. 351-352. Print.

8. SAMPLE ESSAY ANALYZING A POPULAR SONG

If your instructor asks you to analyze a popular song, use the same techniques and terminology that you would use to analyze a poem. Rap songs, for instance, are often carefully written, using words with complicated connotations, several kinds of rhymes, and assonance and alliteration.

Below is an essay analyzing Eminem's Oscar-winning song, "Lose Yourself." The complete and correct lyrics to this song can be located at several websites, such as this one: http://www.azlyrics.com/lyrics/eminem/loseyourself.html

Despite being plagued by controversy during his career, Eminem transformed his adversity into inspiration through his song "Lose Yourself." In this song, Eminem uses his rap music to motivate youths to pursue their dreams regardless of mental obstacles and the barriers of class and race. The powerful message of "Lose Yourself" speaks to every underdog: seize the day, for this life is the only shot you'll get. In his song "Lose Yourself," Eminem uses structure, diction, and figurative language to develop his urgent message of seizing the moment.

The narrative structure of "Lose Yourself" is organized to tell of Eminem's frantic fight to change his life. In the first verse, as Eminem describes himself as a struggling rapper, the mood is very tense. Because he has stage fright, he cannot perform. But he does not give up; he goes "back to the lab" and continues composing and practising his rhymes. In the second verse, the tone is skeptical as Eminem contemplates the pros and cons of stardom. The speaker concludes that although there are negative aspects to stardom, it is better than his current life. If he does not take the chance to succeed, he knows that somebody else will, for there are a limited number of stars made each year. In the third verse, the mood is darker and more intense as Eminem describes his life-and-death situation. When he realizes that he is going to end up in jail or dead, just another unfortunate working-class failure, he becomes determined to positively change his life in Nowheresville. Although the song ends with us not knowing how his narrative concludes, the reader senses that the speaker must continue striving; he does not have the option of relinquishing his struggle because if he gives up, he is spiritually, mentally, and physically dead.

Eminem further develops his urgent rhythm and message in "Lose Yourself" through the use of diction, particularly words connoting violence and oppression. To relate to his youthful audience, Eminem, of course, uses slang words that carry additional meanings. For example, the slang words *drop bombs* mean not only to rhyme but also to target and destroy your opponent, which gives the impression Eminem is in a battle. The slang word *dope* implies that Eminem is calm and focused even when he is up against the odds. Also in the first verse, Eminem mimics the struggle and imprisonment in his life through assonance with *sweaty, weak,* and *heavy.* As the song progresses, the tempo increases with the use of feminine (double syllable) and masculine (single syllable) rhyme. The jabbing rhythm created by the feminine rhyme *mama, drama,* and *wanna* as well as the hard masculine rhyme created by words like *shot, not,* and *got* gives the impression of someone who is trapped by the decisions he has made and is in a fight against time. As a result, the urgent, frantic tone created by the rhythm and diction expresses that Eminem has only one chance to prove himself.

Similes, metaphors, and allusions vividly express the *carpe diem* theme in "Lose Yourself." First, animal imagery amplifies who the speaker is—victimized and, at times, powerless. Because he feels trapped "like two dogs caged" (line 45), Eminem is determined to make a positive change in his life. He is unwilling to be "like a snail," under his shell, hiding from possible pain, risk, and opportunity. In fact, Eminem's careful use of metaphors describes a person who has been a victim of circumstance but who is determined to make his own destiny. For instance, the name "Rabbit" suggests a victim who has no control over the experiment of his own life. However, the phrase "his whole back's to the ropes" (line 15) describes the victim fighting back. First, the double meaning of the phrase "back to the lab again" (line 19) implies that the "rabbit" or victim must go back to reality and continue living out his drudgery. Second, the phrase implies that he is not going to let his disappointments discourage him from his goal; the rabbit will continue to create (procreate) in the lab or compose more rhymes. Through the ciphers he writes, the rabbit will duplicate himself and ensure his survival.

There is also, of course, with the name "Rabbit," the connection to going down the rabbit hole, or entering a strange and confusing world that doesn't make sense—a journey perhaps aided by marijuana. However, there are more obvious allusions that the speaker uses to get his message across to the audience. The allusion to "the Pied Piper" (line 49) implies that Eminem has paid his dues in life, and it is now time for him to strike out on his own and to be a leader not a follower. Eminem reiterates the message that life is about struggle and taking chances by alluding to "Mekhi Phifer." Life is not like the movies; there is no happy ending unless you stand up and take action. Comparing his present life in the trailer park to hell with the words "Salem's lot," the speaker is desperate that he make his shot count. Therefore, the figurative language reflects the importance of seizing opportunities and making a change in your life.

Violence, poverty, and hopelessness are the reality for many young people. "Lose Yourself" is Eminem's anthem for all youths to seize the moment and to make their own opportunities with perseverance and passion. Through "Lose Yourself," Eminem encourages youths not to let society and the harsh realities of life oppress them and define who they are and what they become. After all, "You can do anything you set your mind to, man" (line 71).

—*Jocelynnn Malinowski*

9. SAMPLE ESSAY ANALYZING LITERATURE: COMPARATIVE ESSAY ON FICTION

The Ties That Bind in MacLeod's "The Boat" and Grove's "Snow"
by Toni Williams

Both "The Boat" written by Alistair MacLeod and "Snow" by Frederick Philip Grove depict lives of struggle and hardship in the unforgiving and harsh Canadian landscape. In both stories, the land seems to preordain the destiny of one or more characters, both in life as well as in death. In these tales of Canadian lives, MacLeod and Grove employ different points of view, descriptions of setting, and character development to depict the struggle of human beings bound both to the land and to the emotional ties of tradition and culture.

Grove and MacLeod use point of view to demonstrate their main characters' struggle with the harsh environment and the rigid expectations of culture. In "Snow," Grove employs a limited omniscient point of view to describe the setting, characters, and action. Grove only enters the consciousness of one character very briefly when, halfway through the story, the men enter the squalor of a sparsely furnished farmhouse and discover the wife of the missing farmer. She is resolutely awaiting news of her husband's demise. The author provides a glimpse into the emotions of one of the characters, Abe, a stoic, capable neighbour whose thoughts display empathy for the woman: "He would have liked to say a word of comfort, of hope. What was to be said?" (370). This limited insight into the character's thoughts and feelings reflects the settlers' acceptance of their lot in life: Their life is to be hard and there is no use in thinking about it or talking about it. This approach also focuses the reader on the harshness of the landscape and its menacing personality rather than on the specific identities of the characters.

In "The Boat," MacLeod uses the first person point of view to display the narrator's connection to family and to a mariner's way of life. The narrator, the son of the story, looks back into the past to recall how he displaced himself from the landscape and his father's chosen profession. The "I" reinforces the need for individuality in this world; not all characters should follow the call of the sea. But the "I" of the story also enforces the narrator's feelings of guilt about finishing his education and becoming a fisherman: "And I felt that I had been very small in a little secret place within me and that even the completion of high school was for me a silly shallow selfish dream" (460). The "I" of the narrator is contrasted with the "we" of the family and the "we" of the community of fishermen: "And so we fished through the heat of August and into the cooler days of September" (461) and "we fished on into October when it began to roughen" (461). Through the feelings and observations of the narrator, the reader is able to relate to his struggle between the emotional and cultural ties of his family and his yearning for another identity and another world entirely.

Through the descriptions of setting, the authors demonstrate the connection their respective characters have with their seemingly preordained way of life. The author of "The Boat" uses rich description and attention to detail to describe the family's home, the boat, the people, and the community. The description of the home depicts a lifestyle almost completely centred on a livelihood connected to the sea. In this house, two rooms are focused on: the kitchen, which is the locus of the family and "a buffer zone between the immaculate order of ten other rooms" and the "disruptive chaos of the single room that was my father's" (453). The books of this room are described in great detail: they "covered the bureau," "overburdened the heroic little table," "filled a baffling and unknowable cave," and "spilled from the walls and grew up from the floor" (453). The personification of these books represents how reading and a desire for a life beyond fishing make the father's life bearable. His passion for reading reflects his interior life, his yearning for something other than the role dictated by circumstance of geography. It is also in this room that the father shares with his children his interest in the world beyond the tiny fishing community. "Shortly after my sisters began to read the books, they grew restless and lost interest in darning socks and baking bread . . ." (455), wanting to leave the small fishing community. This room, then, is both the father's sanctuary and a doorway to other possible lives. Despite the mother's constant protests about reading "trash" and her arguments "against what she had discovered but could not understand" (455), the father continues to share the outside world through books and conversation, giving the children permission to break tradition and to follow their own dreams.

Whereas MacLeod develops a cultural setting by describing the family home and by focusing on the thoughts and interactions of his characters, Grove's setting is more minimalist. The narrator is more interested in describing the harsh climate and the environmental challenges of a prairie settler's lifestyle. The narrator describes a beautiful but menacing land: "Stars without number blazed in the dark blue sky which presented that brilliant and uncompromising appearance always characterizing, on the northern plains of America, those nights in the dead of winter when the thermometer dips to its lowest levels" (367). Through his limited description and interaction of people in the story and the stark, cold description of the land, Grove paints a picture of a matter-of-fact, unquestioning people, struggling to survive in an unrelenting battle against the elements. Although MacLeod vividly describes the home of the family in his story, Grove pays little attention to the details of the two homes in "Snow"; the houses are not seen as homes but as shelters. How they are decorated is inconsequential to people who live in this spare, limited environment and who are at the mercy of the land. Grove's detailed description of the harsh climate and the daunting landscape create a sense that the land is bigger than the people and, as such, in control of their fate.

Grove and MacLeod approach character development quite differently as they portray the struggle of human beings against the environment and the expectations of tradition and culture. Grove's sparse character descriptions reinforce the harshness of the prairie landscape and the isolation of the settlers. The characters in "Snow" also interact very little, again demonstrating their seclusion and, perhaps, stoicism. The author also uses labels such as "the newcomer" (368) and "the home owner" (367) to describe the men in the story; they are not people so much as they are types. Their lives and fates have been played out before. Likewise, the narrator does not give the young woman in the story a name, nor does he describe her children. Character development in this story comes not through illustrations of the people themselves, but rather through the language used to capture the rugged and hazardous landscape they inhabit—the most important character and the most daunting antagonist. The reader gets a sense of a resolute people, determined to relinquish their selfishness and even their identities to thrive in a harsh and unforgiving land.

MacLeod, on the other hand, provides rich detail when describing the characters in "The Boat," especially the attributes of the narrator's father. Much attention is paid to describing his appearance, his interests, and his interactions with others, therein portraying his attitude towards the maritime way of life. The reader easily realizes that the man has never really accepted his lot in life and probably shouldn't be at sea. "My father did not tan—he never tanned—because of his reddish complexion, the salt water irritated his skin as it had for sixty years" (460). And in that summer, the narrator realizes that "perhaps my father had never been intended for a fisherman either physically or mentally" (460). The father's inability to tolerate the salt water and his body's unending reaction to and rejection of the elements display his resistance to the lifestyle forced upon him. In the end, the father succumbs to the ravages of the sea, as does Grove's Redcliffe, the missing man, to the prairie snowstorm.

Whereas both stories focus on human beings' indelible ties to the land and to culture, they illustrate these ties by describing very different landscapes and by employing different points of view and character development. The narrator of "The Boat" leaves his home to pursue his academic interests, forever haunted by the expectations of his mother and the undeniable pull of the mariner's lifestyle. Though many of the characters in "The Boat" leave their home community, in "Snow," they seem resolved to (perhaps foolishly) stay on and continue to struggle against the land. This sentiment is evident in the comment made by Redcliffe's mother-in-law, who, upon realizing that the death of her son-in-law means that they will lose their farm, replies, "God's will be done!" (373). Her statement exemplifies the acknowledgement of a fate ordained not by choice, but by nature, tradition, culture, and God, forces still haunting the lives of Canadian farmers and fishermen.

Works Cited

Grove, Frederick Philip. "Snow." *The Nelson Introduction to Literature.* Ed. Al Valleau and Jack Finnbogason. Toronto: Thomson Nelson, 2004. 366-373. Print.

MacLeod, Alistair. "The Boat." *The Nelson Introduction to Literature.* Ed. Al Valleau and Jack Finnbogason. Toronto: Thomson Nelson, 2004. 450-462. Print.

Writing to Persuade

1. PERSUASIVE WRITING

In any form of persuasive writing, your purpose is to change or reinforce your readers' opinions and, in some cases, encourage those readers to act. Persuasion rests on three principal kinds of appeals to readers: logical, ethical, and emotional.

Logical appeals are the reasons and evidence supporting your position. Through logical appeals, you demonstrate your ability to think critically about an issue, to evaluate other points of view, to see connections between general principles and particular facts. **Ethical appeals** are the direct and indirect ways you connect to your readers' morals and beliefs. You build a bridge to your readers by connecting to their beliefs, appearing fair, and considering counter-arguments. **Emotional appeals** are the direct and indirect ways you engage readers' feelings, usually through language. You create emotional appeals by considering the denotations and connotations of words, using sharp anecdotes, images, and analogies, and using forceful language. Although it is sometimes difficult to distinguish these three appeals, they are all part of a successful persuasive argument.

Consider the passage below. What appeals are most obvious?

Our oceans are in serious crisis. It is tragic that we know more about Mars than we know about deep ocean life, yet we are destroying the ocean floor with pollution, oil spills, and seabed trawling. "Dead zones" of lifelessness, fishing stocks decimated, coral reefs destroyed, and whales hunted to extinction: is this the future of our oceans? Not if we act now. They are our oceans and it is our choice. We must save our seas.

This passage, through its use of highly charged negative words (*crisis, tragic, destroying, dead, lifelessness, decimated, destroyed,* and *extinction*) and its imagery of the devastation of our oceans, is obviously appealing to the readers' emotions. Yet it also uses the second person (*we, our, us*) several times to build a bridge to readers. Just as *we* have created this problem, *we* must also find a solution. For this proposal to be successful, however, it would have to incorporate some concrete facts about the problem as well as solutions to it.

To choose an effective combination of appeals for a particular piece, you must decide whether you are addressing a friendly, hostile, or neutral audience.

From *Forms of Writing: A Rhetoric and Handbook*, Sixth Edition, Kay L. Stewart, Marian Allen, Shelley Galliah. Copyright © 2012 by Pearson Canada Inc. All rights reserved.

A friendly audience shares your basic concerns, but needs to be roused to action or renewed commitment. A parent speaking to community league members about building a new playground would be addressing a friendly audience, who, though receptive to the idea, needs to be convinced of its practicality. For reviews, letters to the editor, or opinion pieces on noncontroversial topics, you can usually assume a friendly audience.

At the other extreme is the hostile audience, actively opposed to your position. An employer trying to persuade workers to accept wage cutbacks would face such an audience. For a hostile audience, you need to consider using all three appeals. Workers, for example, might be more willing to accept lower wages from an employer who argued that "we're all in this together" (ethical appeal) than from one who seemed overly logical and unconcerned about their welfare. When you write essays on controversial subjects, such as abortion or euthanasia, you need to not alienate readers. Your goal is to win over a hostile audience, transforming it into a neutral or even friendly one.

Most of the essays you write for courses are directed to neutral readers who expect a carefully reasoned argument without too many emotional appeals. These readers will pay more attention to persuasive pieces that do not take extreme positions, that consider the merits of different points of view, that present extensive evidence to support their position, and that contain few logical flaws.

Organizing Persuasive Writing

How you arrange the parts of your essay will be determined by what your readers need to know and what you think they will find most convincing.

When you are writing for a neutral audience, state your position in the introduction. Your readers will appreciate a clearly defined thesis, topic sentences indicating the stages of your argument, substantial paragraphs showing clear reasoning and supporting evidence, and a conclusion summarizing and extending your argument.

If you expect strong opposition, either because you are writing for a hostile audience or taking an unpopular stand on a controversial issue, you may want to anticipate your readers' objections by first discussing the merits and drawbacks of the counter-arguments before presenting your thesis and reasoning. When you reach your conclusion, your opponents may be more willing to acknowledge your position than they would have been if you had abruptly stated it in your introduction.

This type of organization also works well for a friendly but perhaps complacent audience. To encourage readers to think more carefully about a position they take for granted, you might begin with arguments upon which there is widespread agreement, such as the problem with the GST, and then raise the question of whether the situation is really as simplistic or as satisfactory as it appears. You might begin by agreeing that the GST is not perfect and that there are valid arguments for eliminating it, but that removing this tax could have several negative effects.

In this chapter, you will find some basic guidelines for four types of persuasive writing: reviews, letters to the editor, opinion pieces, and position papers.

2. REVIEWS

You are probably most familiar with the brief reviews of books, films, television programs, and eating places printed in newspapers and general-interest magazines, such as *Maclean's* and *Time*. These reviews intend to give casual readers some sense of whether a new movie is worth seeing or a new restaurant is worth visiting.

Longer reviews—often called **review articles** or **review essays**—are designed for readers with some knowledge of the subject. Gamers, for example, might read the reviews of all the new videogames in *Electronic Gaming Monthly*. Academic journals often carry review articles on research in specific areas, such as new treatments for diseases. Because these reviews provide substantial background information and extensive commentary, they are very useful sources for research papers.

We will focus on guidelines for writing brief reviews for a general audience. To expand the treatment of your subject into a review essay, consult appropriate sources of information: other reviews, other works by the same person or group, articles relevant to your subject, biographical dictionaries, newspaper files, and so forth.

Follow these guidelines when writing a brief review:

1. **In your review, include identifying information.** This information (determined by your intended audience and type of publication) usually appears in a separate heading before your review or in your introduction. Here is what you should include:

   Book review: author, title, publisher, price, type, length, hardcover or paperback. As applicable: name of editor, translator, or other contributors; supplementary material provided (such as maps, illustrations, appendix, index); date of publication; edition.

   Computer software review: product, manufacturer, price, system requirements. As applicable: other products in category, ordering information.

   Film review: title, director, distributor, type, principal actors. As applicable: date of release; length; suitability rating; other contributors (music, special effects, etc.).

   Live performance review (as applicable): title, name of person or group, place, date(s), type, price.

   Product review: manufacturer, model, price, availability, warranty, service record.

Recorded music review: title, person or group, type, label, price.

Restaurant review: name, address, type of food, business hours, price range, credit cards accepted, availability of alcoholic beverages, decor, service. If applicable, include reservation requirements and dress code.

2. **Try for a lively introduction**, one that will catch your readers' interest and convey your general opinion of what you are reviewing.

3. **Give readers a sense of the whole through a brief summary or description.** Don't include so many details that there is nothing left for readers to discover. Never give away surprise effects or the endings of films, plays, or novels. (Remember that a review of a work includes much less plot detail than a summary of a work.)

4. **Using specific examples, discuss what you liked and disliked about what you are reviewing.** Be balanced, for even the aspects you like the most may appeal only to certain people.

5. **End with a snappy summary of your overall judgment.**

3. SAMPLE MOVIE REVIEW

Here is a sample movie review, written for a newspaper.

Stranger Than Fiction: One Odd but Delightful Movie

After all the hype given to *Borat,* Bond, and the other summer blockbusters, it was refreshing to see a movie that quietly lived up to its expectations: *Stranger Than Fiction.* Starring Will Ferrell as Harold Frick, an unassuming tax fraud investigator who discovers that he may, in fact, be a fictional character, this charming movie explores the tenuous boundary between reality and fiction. After hearing someone narrating his every move, Harold decides to explore the origin and meaning of this voice, ending up in the office of literature professor Dr. Jules Hilbert, played by a quirky, coffee-swilling Dustin Hoffman. With humorous results, Harold investigates the type of book he is in so he can figure out his ending, eventually meeting up with his nemesis and creator, chain-smoking, obsessive-compulsive author Karen Eiffel (Emma Thompson). Harold's charm and his pathetic dilemma forces the author to question her genre of tragicomedy as well as her dismal, uneventful life. This movie also features Maggie Gyllenhaal, perfectly cast as Ana Pascal, the tax-evading baker who becomes Frick's unexpected love interest. *Stranger Than Fiction,* which is indeed a movie stranger than most of the recent fare, is bursting with literary allusions, subtle ironies, stunning moments, and unconventional relationships. If nothing else, this movie will make you appreciate the written word. Go see it.

4. LETTERS TO THE EDITOR

Most letters to the editor are intended to persuade readers that something is good or bad: the premier is doing a good or a lousy job, park trails should or should not be paved, nurses should or should not have the right to strike. They are generally short, about 250 to 500 words. Paragraphs within the letter are also short because they are usually printed in narrow columns. The following guidelines will help you make your point quickly and effectively:

1. **Focus on a particular issue of interest to a number of readers, and, if possible, link that issue to a current situation.** A general plea for world peace, for example, is less likely to hold your readers' attention than an argument against selling arms to warring countries. Identify the issue in your first paragraph.

2. **Explain why the issue concerns you.** Are you writing as a spokesperson for a relief organization? As a pacifist? As a citizen upholding the ideal of Canada as a peacekeeping nation?

3. **Briefly state your own position and your reasons for holding it.**

4. **Instead of condemning people who hold other views, try to establish common ground with them.** Summarize their positions accurately, acknowledging their point of view. You might acknowledge a country's need to defend itself but point out that access to more powerful weapons increases the likelihood of bloodshed.

5. **If possible, suggest a practical action that readers can take.** They can't ensure world peace, but they can write a letter to a local politician.

5. SAMPLE LETTER TO THE EDITOR

In this letter, the writer focuses on the uproar caused by Prime Minister's Stephen Harper's controversial G8 child and maternal health care initiative.

Dear Editor and readers,

As a feminist and a humanist interested in the rights of all people, especially those in the undeveloped world, I am disturbed by Stephen Harper's decision that the new G8 child and maternal health care initiative not include abortions.

Harper defends his decision by arguing that he wants a G8 policy that does not divide Canadians. In the House of Commons, during question period on Tuesday, April 27, he explained, "Canadians want to see the foreign aid money used for things to help save the lives of women and children in ways that unite the Canadian people."

However, our prime minister fails to see how divisive this policy actually is. Although abortion is a controversial issue, Canadians of all political stamps are upset that Harper has reversed a twenty-five-year-old policy. Secondly, this policy divides Canada from the US and makes us seem more right-wing than our southernly neighbour. Almost immediately after entering office, Barack Obama revised Bush's G8 maternal health care initiative, so it included abortions.

Thirdly, the policy separates Canada from the rest of the world, effectively saying that it is okay for an unprepared Canadian woman to terminate a pregnancy but not acceptable for a Congolese woman, gang-raped in an atrocious war crime, to get a needed abortion. Fourthly, the prime minister is alienating himself from progressive female voters and women's groups, who argue that omitting abortion is a travesty that sets women's reproductive rights back decades.

Harper's decision, unfortunately, is not surprising. Throughout his leadership, he has either acted in secrecy or acted as a dictator, often making overly right-wing decisions that oppose public opinion and what Canada supposedly stands for: an unjudgmental, open-minded, progressive country.

We need to reclaim Canada from Harper and his conservative morality before it's too late. Speak up and write your MP. If Harper can so cavalierly take away the reproductive rights of global women, what will he attempt to take away from women residing on his own turf?

—Monica Raley

6. OPINION PIECES

Using your own knowledge and experience, you can write opinion pieces: short persuasive essays about topical issues. Columnists such as Heather Mallick, Allan Fotheringham, and Margaret Wente write opinion pieces for newspapers and magazines.

Many opinion pieces often begin with a personal anecdote and then employ the strategy of giving reasons with examples as supporting evidence.

Why Are We Dressing Our Daughters Like This?
by Lianne George

In his most recent visual tome, *Katlick School,* the famed American fashion photographer Sante D'Orazio examines the titillating power of the Catholic schoolgirl uniform—a fetish, his publishers write, "as psychosexually resonant as the black motorcycle jacket or the nurse's uniform." The book chronicles the coming of age of Kat, a "beautiful Latina schoolgirl," whose sexual curiosity grows increasingly outsized for her pleated skirt and bobby socks. (It's not the most original idea, maybe, but it's a crowd-pleaser.) Kat's unraveling begins with flashes of Snoopy underwear. In a matter of pages, she's traded in her pressed plaid uniform for nothing but a pair of thigh-high spike-heeled boots. "I was experimenting with a symbol of virginity, the untouched, the ideal, the romantic notion of the pure," says D'Orazio, who famously enshrined Pamela Anderson in the canon of erotic coffee-table literature in 2005 with *Pam: American Icon.* "That is what the uniform signifies."

The book also signifies something rather less high-minded—it's a lascivious ode to the cultural muse of the moment, the Lolita. Shortly after it was launched last month, the Catholic League for Religious and Civil Rights registered its disgust in the *New York Post* (after which, not coincidentally, sales of *Katlick School* spiked). And yet, the response was not entirely honest. Because if there is one iconic symbol of the girl-about-to-go-wild, it's the schoolgirl uniform—and the Catholic community is well aware of it.

Even before Britney Spears paired a kilt with pigtails and a midriff-baring blouse in the 1998 video that launched her career, the kilt was a source of deep discomfort for Catholic schoolteachers, administrators and parents. Rules evolved to control its power: it should be three inches from the knee—no higher—and one Canadian uniform manufacturer even patented the X-Kilt, with built-in shorts to prevent girls from transforming them into miniskirts. So far, in Ontario alone, at least seven Catholic schools have voted to phase out the garment altogether. "It always has been an issue," says Ron Crocco, principal of St. Augustine Catholic High School in Markham, Ont., where the kilt was banned in 2003. "As a male, it's difficult to enforce, to say: your kilt is too short. Because then, why am I looking there?" In a post-Britney era, it seems, the kilt is just too sexy for school.

How, then, to explain the low-slung jeans, sequined halter tops and lacy miniskirts that so many young girls are wearing to class? In fact, in the broader universe of children's clothing, "Why am I looking there?" has become an increasingly pressing question. Streetwear for little girls has never been more overtly provocative. Girls as young as 6 are adopting the external cues of womanhood, adorning themselves not only with lip gloss and nail polish, but also body sprays, skin glitters and spa lotions. Club Libby Lu, a Saks Fifth Avenue spinoff with 62 outlets across the United States, invites "super fabulous girls" ages 6 and up to book "sparkle spa" makeover parties for their friends.

North American retailers like La Senza Girl, Abercrombie & Fitch and Limited Too sell fishnet stockings, skinny jeans, message panties and padded "bralettes" in micro-sizes. In 2002, Abercrombie & Fitch launched its infamous kiddie thong collection, arguing that girls as young as 10 "are style-conscious and want underwear that doesn't produce a Visible Panty Line." (They have since dropped the line.) Earlier this month, the New York designer Marc Jacobs, having his pick of every grown-up bombshell in Hollywood, tapped 12-year-old Dakota Fanning, star of the newly released *Charlotte's Web*, to be the face of his latest womenswear collection.

Meanwhile, in an odd inversion of the Lolita trend, women old enough to vote are embracing the trappings of girlhood, with varying degrees of tongue-in-cheek. Victoria's Secret's lingerie collections have innocent, girlie names like "Angels" and "Pink." Starlets such as Paris Hilton and Britney Spears tote around miniature dogs in tutus—called Tinkerbell and Bit Bit—as though they were cuddly stuffed animals. In her latest video, "Fergalicious," the musician Fergie is dressed in a sexed-up Brownie uniform, surrounded by a troupe of bootie-popping Brownie dancers. Last month, the British retailer Tesco landed in hot water over a pole-dancing kit for sale on its website. The kit, packaged in a pink plastic tube, featured an illustrated Barbie-type character and bubble letters that read: "Unleash the sex kitten inside." It was inadvertently placed on the site's children's toy section, where it looked so entirely at home that none of the Web designers questioned it. Perhaps most creepily, we're in a moment when one of the latest celebrity "trends"—exemplified by Spears and Lindsay Lohan—is to expose one's privates, completely waxed to look like a 10-year-old's, from the backseat of a car.

The eroticization of girlhood—once the stuff of Russian literature, Atom Egoyan films, Japanese comic books and good old-fashioned American porn—has been seeping ever more into the larger culture. Now it is one of our dominant aesthetics. In a Lolita-tinged culture, whether the sell is "my body is underdeveloped, but I am precocious" or "my brain is underdeveloped, but I am stacked," the message is the same: exploit me. "For adult women, that notion of being kind of girlie and innocent and sexually pure, as well as very sexy, has been in men's magazines forever," says Lyn Mikel Brown, co-author of *Packaging Girlhood: Rescuing Our Daughters from Marketers' Schemes*. But whether it's because of the pornification of culture or the extreme worship of youth, the trend has migrated to ever younger age groups. Add this to the fact that the physiological onset of puberty itself keeps inching downward, and the definitions of "girl" and "women" have become moving targets. Which raises the question: what does it mean for little girls when the very things of their lives—kilts, puppies, angels, pink, princesses—become fetishized to the point of rendering them obscene?

In stores marketing to young girls, a phenomenon that the authors of *Packaging Girlhood* have termed "the pink wars" is easy to discern. There's the sweet, innocent "princess" girl (baby pink) and the saucy, naughty "diva" girl (hot pink). The two aesthetics are clearly delineated in the selection of novelty T-shirts on offer. A "princess," for instance, would wear one of these scrawled across her chest: *Sweet Treats, Angel, Daddy's Girl, Official Cheer Bunny*. While a "diva" would gravitate toward: *Trouble-maker, Drama Queen, You Will Do What I Say*, and of course, Paris Hilton's idiotic tag line, *That's Hot*. But T-shirts are just the beginning. It is the "total girl" marketers are after, write Brown and Sharon Lamb in *Packaging Girlhood*. "'xTotal girl' to marketers means finding every inch of their body to adorn," they write. "Expanding one's market means not just reaching down to the lower ages for products introduced to the older ages, but finding new parts of their bodies to colonize or own. The tiniest parts, the forgotten parts, such as nails, which should be dirty after a day of play." Implicit in the various products available is a sexy wink that has never before been associated with children so young.

Or so we think. The idea of children as innocent is a relatively modern one. "Children are the great vessels of fantasy," says Anne Hollander, a New York-based clothing historian and author of the classic 1978 text *Seeing Through Clothes*. Historically, a mother saw a little girl as a smaller, unspoiled version of herself, and so a daughter should be formed in her mother's image—and through most of history, she was. Up until the late 18th century, children, both male and female, were outfitted like little adults. Labourers' children dressed like labourers, and society children dressed like their elders, in garments designed for their pomp and rigidity to encourage socially appropriate behaviour. Moreover, says Hollander, royal children were dressed to look sexually attractive so that heads of state in other countries might look at their portraits and think, hmm, maybe I'd like to marry that sweet thing. "Girls of 6 wore low-cut dresses and very fetching hairdos," she says. "You can see it in the paintings, all meant to be sent off to Louis XV or some such. They don't have any breasts yet, but never mind."

It was only with the advent of the Romantic period in the late 1700s that modern notions of childhood arose, inspired largely by the sentimental writings of the Swiss-born philosopher Jean-Jacques Rousseau. "As the 18th century took on its second half," says Hollander, "you have an idea that children are a separate marvellous, terribly fragile, impressionable, innocent kind of creature that needs freedom and liberty of all kinds. There was the sense of nature infusing everything. They get to play and have a wonderful time and move all of their parts." And so, for the first time, girls were dressed differently from their adult counterparts—in a simple chemise with a sash.

As the Victorian age crept in, there was a stiffening of everybody's clothing, but girls and women remained sartorially distinct. "It was very, very important that the girls wore short dresses and the ladies wore long dresses," says Hollander. "Girls wore their hair down in curls or braids and put their hair up at the time they got long dresses—whenever they were supposed to be marriageable. The idea was that children are innocent. They don't have any sexuality, so don't worry."

What we're seeing now, she says, is a reversion to pre-Enlightenment days, a time before children were innocent, when they were nothing but smaller versions of ourselves in every way. "We are back in the 17th century," she says. "We're dressing little kids like adults and adults are dressing like little children. There is no distinction once again. A girl is a woman by the time she's 8 and a woman remains a girl until she's 80."

For many parents, there's nothing wrong with this. Kids are always trying to be more like teenagers, and the precocious fashions are kind of sweet and funny in the way those Anne Geddes photos of kids kissing are. "There is a mistaken sense that kids don't get the joke or the meaning so it's okay for them to wear sexualized slogans," says Susan Linn, an instructor in psychiatry at Harvard Medical School and a co-founder of the coalition Campaign for a Commercial-Free Childhood.

But even for parents who do have a problem with these off-the-rack identities, there is tremendous pressure to buy in. For one thing, they are susceptible to the "everyone is doing it" argument, and they don't want their kid to be ostracized. For another, it's often the least of their concerns. "They are in the middle of numerous commercially created battles with their children," says Linn. "Battles about junk food, violent media, expensive brands and all sorts of things. It's hard, if not impossible, to say no all of the time."

The popular marketing spin—which, incidentally, is supposed to reassure parents in some way—is that it is kids who are "getting older younger," a theory called age compression, brought on by the fact that young people have never had access to so much information. But what we're really seeing, says Linn, is marketers exploiting the natural tendency of young girls to want to emulate older girls, who appear to them to have more independence and social prestige.

In the end, then, it's not really a kid problem, but a grown-up problem. Because girls, looking the way they look, are only aping grown women, which serves to remind us of the turmoil and confusion surrounding what we currently believe a woman should be. The New York-based writer Ariel Levy documented this phenomenon, which she dubbed "raunch culture," in her 2006 book *Female Chauvinist Pigs*. The idea is that, in a post-feminist universe, a woman can be the agent of her own objectification and still be empowered. And so we see a boom in trends inspired by porn culture: pole-dancing and striptease lessons, boob jobs and Brazilian waxes. "A tawdry, tarty, cartoonlike version of female sexuality has become so ubiquitous, it no longer seems particular," writes Levy. "What we once regarded as a kind of sexual expression, we now view as sexuality." More recently, the *New York Times* columnist Bob Herbert, inspired by an Abercrombie & Fitch T-shirt he came across that read *Who Needs A Brain When I Have These?*, addressed what he calls a "disrespectful, degrading, contemptuous treatment of women" that has become "so pervasive and so mainstream that it has just about lost its ability to shock."

"This is some sort of response to the feminist movement," says Hollander. In fact, it's part of a trial-and-error continuum. In the '70s, as women prepared to invade the workplace en masse, the most overt manifestation of this new societal phase was sartorial. "It meant throwing out the skirts and certainly girdles and dressing so that you couldn't tell the difference between a man and a woman, except very small things," she says. "The masculine wardrobe was entirely co-opted by women. Suits and shoulder pads denied curves. Breasts and behinds and hips were not in fashion."

The current hyper-feminine aesthetic, one could argue, is an over-correction of this correction—an almost fanatical reclaiming of pink and frilly. But what may have been born of a spirit of defiance has lost its revolutionary edge, and now young girls are learning the not-so-progressive lesson that their primary value lies in their worth as sex objects. "Just because we are post doesn't mean we are feminists," writes Levy. "There is a widespread assumption that simply because my generation of women has the good fortune to live in a world touched by the feminist movement, that means everything we do is magically imbued with its agenda."

The trickle-down effect we're now seeing among very young girls has resulted in a Junior Miss version of raunch culture. Watching kids adopt these same behaviours is like looking at the larger culture through a funhouse mirror. On the body of a six-year-old, the diminishing aspect of an *Eye Candy* T-shirt is amplified and twisted—and entirely devoid of any of the irony that makes it pseudo-radical coming from a twentysomething pop star. "The problem is that girls are acquiring the trappings of maturity," Linn says, "but there's no indication that their social or emotional development is keeping pace." In fact, the aspiring-up trend preys upon and heightens the particular insecurities of kids in this age group. "Will she be popular? Will she be invited somewhere? With what group does she belong?" write Brown and Lamb. "Before a girl has half a chance to reflect on issues of belonging and desirability, she is being confronted with a market that tells her she should be concerned about this—even when she's as young as 8."

We tell girls that, in wearing these things, they are somehow expressing themselves in an essential way. "If Ts expressed who a girl is," write Brown and Sharon Lamb, "you'd think she'd be wearing the T she got at the summer camp she went to, the music festival she attended or the Humane Society where she volunteers to walk the dogs. But instead they express 'attitude' rather than interests, skills, concerns, and hobbies." Worse still, in their very construction, these clothes prescribe behaviours that are hard to describe as empowering. A micro-mini, for instance, is a great disincentive to playing on the monkey bars. A halter top and tight, low-rise jeans make it rather more challenging to run and jump. "Every message to a preteen girl," write Brown and Lamb, "says that it's preferable to pose on the beach rather than surf, to shop rather than play, to decorate rather than invent."

But for marketers, it's not about grooming girls to be the next generation's cast of *Girls Gone Wild*. It has much more to do with grooming them to be promiscuous consumers. "Marketers are not setting out to sexualize little girls," says

Susan Linn. "They are setting out to make a profit selling clothes to and for children and don't care what the consequences are." Girls themselves don't necessarily understand the clothing as sexual, she says, but "what they do comprehend is that they get a lot of attention by dressing in a particular way."

Female power has always been inextricably linked to ornamentation. When a woman comes of age, the convention is that she takes on a series of external cues to indicate sexual readiness: bright red lips that signal arousal, high heels that show off shapely legs, clothing that hugs fertile curves. This is what it means to be a sophisticated, mature and, to some extent, a powerful woman. But these things no longer correspond to any sort of biological turning point. Instead, they signify a claiming of personal economic autonomy. Call it consumer readiness. And as far as marketers are concerned, girls are never too young to be ready.

In fact, the most important identity of all for girls to cultivate is their identity as shoppers. For example, the educational toy brand International Playthings has a product called My First Purse, marketed to girls two years old and up. It's pink, purple and plush, and it includes play accessories, among them a wallet, debit card, lipstick, keys, mirror, and cellphone. (No, they don't make oversized baby-blue billfolds for boys to wedge in the back of their diapers.) Likewise, Mattel's Barbie Bank-with-ME ATM machine for girls 3 and up that takes bills and coins and displays their balance on the screen. The debit card activates sound effects and banking commands from Barbie. Anyone for a game of "Transfer funds"?

Ultimately, it is the "play" aspect of aspirational products that seems to have evaporated. Young girls have always loved to play dress-up—to trip around the house in their mother's heels and pearls. Playing mom, playing house, playing glamour girl or doctor was about little girls creating safe spaces for themselves in which to experiment with grown-up female identities. The difference is you can turn play off. Play time is confined and varied. Whereas now, taking on a womanly identity is incorporated into girls' everyday lives. They don't see it as a pretend purse, it's *their* purse. Wearing a halter top is not for dress-up, it's for show. "There's a seriousness to it that there wasn't," says Brown. "Now, it's really not about fantasy play. It's about adopting something that's out there for them. It's like practice for something very specific, to be like Jessica Simpson."

The latest dolls for girls offer not-so-subtle reinforcement of the same ideas. Twenty years ago, popular collections including Cabbage Patch Kids and Strawberry Shortcake had big floppy hats, pudgy limbs, and silly clothing. They were cartoonish—with bright colours and scents created to appeal to kids' imaginations. In 2001, MGA Entertainment launched the Bratz dolls with the tag line: "The girls with a passion for fashion." These toys, says Linn, are a "ratcheted up male fantasy of what women should look like—big eyes, big lips, big breasts, an anorexic waistline and very long legs." Soon, the Bratz dolls—who do nothing but shop and socialize—were outselling even Barbie, grossing roughly US$2 billion per year. Mattel fought back with a sluttier, more urban line of Barbie dolls called the My Scene collection. "That kind of plastic sexuality seems to be normalized for younger and younger kids," says Linn. We used to worry about Barbie, with her improbable proportions and dismal math skills. Now we long for Barbie. Not the new Bling Bling Barbie, but the old one with the job. At least she tried to do math.

It is no coincidence that the Lolita moment is surfacing now, at a time when boys are supposedly in crisis, says Brown. "Twenty years ago, we were talking about girls and loss of voice and self-esteem and there were all these empowerment programs," says Brown. "Now we have girls and women more likely to go to college, getting better grades, being really out there and claiming more power. What women are doing is challenging the status quo, and when that happens, things tighten up. It's an anxiety, a collective response."

And so, while adults try to navigate all of these complicated, fragmented ideals about gender, childhood, empowerment and sexuality, girls have become our ideological guinea pigs. And they're being taught some pretty unappealing lessons. "You can learn a whole lot of very serious narcissism by being brought up to be looked at constantly," says Hollander. "That was Marie Antoinette's upbringing, who was scheduled to be the queen of France since she was born." And we all know how that one turned out.

Unless we are prepared to see six-year-olds in garters, then it would seem we're ready for another backlash. Already, the boundaries of what the public will put up with are beginning to constrict. Religious and family groups, media critics, feminists and other concerned citizens have teamed up to halt production of certain products deemed too outrageous—including a line of Bratz bras for little girls, and a line of Hasbro dolls aimed at six-year-olds based on the Pussycat Dolls, a burlesque troupe turned singing group. Now, advocacy groups have their sights set on a new line of clothing for babies called Pimpfants. "It's a kid thang," the company's slogan says. But when you see a six-month-old child in a *M.I.L.F.* onesie, even the most permissive grown-up has to stop and ask herself, whom is this really about?

7. POSITION PAPERS

The purpose of a position paper is to present reasons explaining why you agree or disagree with an argument. Writing this kind of essay will help you develop your critical thinking skills, for it requires you to analyze, evaluate, and formulate your own opinion.

Writing Position Papers: The Process

Here are the main steps for writing a position paper:

1. **Briefly summarize the piece you are responding to.** State the article's subject, thesis, organization of ideas, and most important points. Summarizing the article is a useful first step because it helps you to understand the author's ideas. Include a brief version of your summary in your position paper to help your readers understand your response.

2. **Analyze and evaluate the author's three appeals** (see the chart "Evaluating Logical, Ethical, and Emotional Appeals" that follows this section). To analyze the logical appeal and decide your

position, whether you agree or disagree with the writer's argument, make a list of points you agree and disagree with. Make a list of potential counter-arguments and evidence. After evaluating the argument, analyze the emotional and ethical appeals.

3. **Identify the writer's basis of evaluation.** Is the writer's position based on moral, practical, logical, or aesthetic criteria, or a combination of these perspectives?

4. **Clarify your own basis of evaluation.** Do the points you agree with reflect your moral position on the subject? Do you doubt the practicality of the author's position?

5. **Formulate your thesis.** It should present both your evaluation of the writer's point of view and your own opinion.

6. **Organize your response to include opposing arguments.** In persuasive writing, it is wise to address counter-arguments, or arguments opposing your position. Doing so demonstrates your credibility, showing you have considered both sides of the issue before arriving at an informed decision. When addressing counter-arguments, be considerate yet firm; do not use rude or deprecating language or personal attacks.

One approach is to take up an opposing argument point by point, examining its strengths and weaknesses and pointing out alternatives. You might adopt this method if you wanted to argue directly against a series of proposals contained in a document.

Another way to introduce counter-arguments is to briefly summarize other views about your subject, indicate why you agree or disagree, and then state your thesis. You might use this method if you wanted to argue that positions X, Y, and Z were all based on self-interest whereas your position is based on the common good. These two methods are examples of an evaluative or "pro-con" structure—an organization based on arguments for (*pro*) and arguments against (*con*) your position.

Below, the writer contends and dismantles the argument that the media is responsible for violent behaviour.

There is no denying that television has an effect on its viewers. And thanks to shows like *CSI* and *Criminal Minds*, which weekly feature atrocious crimes and decomposing bodies, programs are far more gory today than they were even twenty-five years ago, when the most gratuitously violent shows on television were the relatively tame *Hill Street Blues* and *Miami Vice*. Accompanying these contemporary programs are videos, video games, and even the nightly news, which all contain smatterings of death and destruction. The media is definitely becoming increasingly obsessed with violent imagery.

However, there is also no denying that as long as television has been around, society has scapegoated it, blaming it for society's bad decisions and deviant behaviour. And long before television, other forms of media were censored, such as the radio and its lascivious teen-destroying rock and roll. Elvis, tame when compared to today's gangsta rappers, was once even considered dangerous, if not demonic. Blaming the media, then, is nothing new. And doing so not only oversimplifies the extremely complicated problem of and solutions for aggressive and inappropriate behaviour, but also misleads the public. That is, the causal relationship between violent media and violent behaviour, as this essay will show, is very suspect.

Evaluating Logical, Ethical, and Emotional Appeals

Logical Appeals First, evaluate the evidence.

- Do all the points support the thesis?
- Are key terms defined?
- Do comparisons proceed from a common basis?
- Are examples used appropriately? That is, has the writer chosen the most effective examples to prove or support the point?
- Is there enough evidence to support the main points?
- Are facts and figures accurate, up to date, and taken from reliable and identified sources? Are they used appropriately? (That is, if you are arguing about child obesity in Canada, using American statistics is inappropriate.)

Next, look for logical fallacies.

Logical fallacies, which are flaws in reasoning leading to illogical claims, are either unintentional or intentional; that is, they are caused by either errors in the writer's reasoning process or by the writer's attempt to manipulate readers. Test the validity of the author's reasoning and evidence by searching for these logical fallacies. And when you write your own persuasive papers, make sure you also avoid these errors. (This list is by no means extensive, but is an introduction to the most common logical fallacies.)

- Does the author assume the truth of a conclusion that actually needs to be argued (begging the question)?
- Does the author intentionally omit points that could weaken the argument (fallacy of exclusion)?
- Does the author jump to conclusions based on too little evidence or too small a sample size (hasty generalization)?
- Does the author make generalizations about a group of people (stereotyping)?
- Does the author oversimplify an issue by reducing it to two extreme alternatives (either/or fallacy)?
- Does the author claim that two things are alike when they are more different than similar (misplaced analogy)?
- Does the author make faulty causal connections? Watch for these problems with causal reasoning: (1) claiming that what is true in some instances is true in all instances; (2) claiming that something happening after an event was caused by it; (3) claiming a single cause or effect of something that may have multiple causes or effects; (4) claiming unlikely or exaggerated predicted effects; and (5) claiming that one event will cause a domino effect or a series of uncontrollable consequences (slippery-slope reasoning).
- Does the author sidetrack the reader by bringing up unrelated matters that distract the audience (red herring)?

- Does the author cite authorities cited within their field of expertise? Or are the authors cited not experts (*argumentum ad verecundiam*)?
- Does the author trivialize or distort opposing points of view?
- Does the author attack the person making the argument instead of the argument (*ad hominem* argument)?

Ethical Appeals These questions help you define the author's values and attitudes.

- Does the author appeal to values he or she believes readers share (such as patriotism, family values, concern for the environment)? Sometimes the author will appeal to these values if he or she assumes a friendly audience or if he or she is trying to convert a hostile audience.
- Does the author establish a relationship with readers through direct comments, choice of personal pronouns (I, we), or emotional appeals (see section 1)? Is this relationship friendly? Hostile? Does the author sound like an expert?
- Does the author present a balanced perspective? Address counter-arguments?
- Does the author use evidence responsibly?
- Does the author make personal attacks on those who hold different opinions or appeal to readers' prejudices against certain groups?

Emotional Appeals
- What attitude toward the subject (such as anger, concern, sadness) does the writer convey through choices in diction, sentence structure, and other stylistic devices? What uses, if any, does the writer make of humour, wit, irony?
- Does the writer use appropriate emotional appeals for the audience?
- How does the author's personality, as reflected in the piece, affect your response?
- Does the writer use too much slanted or emotional language? (Keep in mind that emotional appeals, when they *substitute for or warp logic*, are a logical flaw.)

Steps in Preparing Your Position Paper

1. Briefly, in the first paragraph of your paper, **summarize the article you are responding to**.
2. **Analyze and evaluate the author's logical, ethical, and emotional appeals.**

Strengths

- George's logical appeal is fairly strong; she uses several points and examples from popular culture and the retail world to support her point about the eroticization of girlhood.
- The author appropriately uses causal analysis to explore this trend.

- The author contextualizes her argument by showing how children have been viewed throughout history.

- George connects to the reader and reveals her credibility (ethos and logos) by bringing in expert secondary sources to help substantiate her reasoning, such as Lyn Mikel Brown, author of *Packaging Girlhood: Rescuing Our Daughters from Marketers' Schemes;* Anne Hollander, author of *Seeing Through Clothes*; Susan Linn, an instructor in psychiatry at Harvard Medical School; and Ariel Levi, expert in raunch culture and author of *Female Chauvinist Pigs*.

- The author's emotional appeals are fairly strong; she grabs the reader's attention in the opening by mentioning the controversial Catholic schoolgirl uniform; she provides examples of several shocking toys and trends; and she injects humour into her essay in several places.

Weaknesses

- George's audience is unclear; although she uses mostly Western examples, it is unclear whether she is talking about all girls, or just those in North America.

- Her argument is based on the unproven assumption (begging the question) that most girls dress in inappropriate and erotic ways. She fails to mention girls and parents who may be rejecting this trend.

- There are other weaknesses connected to the essay's logical appeal, structure, and organization of evidence: the author fails to limit her thesis, provide a counter-argument, or suggest concrete solutions to the problem. She also gives so many causes of the erotization of girlhood that her argument is often difficult to follow.

3. **Identify the writer's basis of evaluation.**

George's argument is mostly based on moral grounds. She argues that women's confusion about childhood, sexuality, femininity, etc., is turning their children into ideological guinea pigs. She asks that parents be aware of the attitudes they are promulgating and that they not give in to the demands of the marketers, who turn a profit by eroticizing girls. She mentions what children lose when they become more interested in how they look than in how they play. She wants readers to help stop the manufacturing of products that are too outrageous.

4. **Clarify the basis of your evaluation.**

Agree with George's position on moral grounds.

5. **Formulate your rough thesis statement.**

Although Lianne George's argument is somewhat unfocused and undecided on one cause of the eroticization of girlhood, she depicts the complexity of the problem while skillfully using ethical and emotional appeals.

By putting the weaknesses of the essay in a subordinate clause (*Although . . . appeals*), you are telling the reader that you will discuss the weaknesses but that the main part of your essay will be dedicated to the article's strengths.

6. **Organize your essay to include opposing arguments.** You could begin by writing a paragraph or two taking up all the arguments against your position or you can address these arguments one by one throughout your essay. Use strong topic sentences, which make the main points in the body of your essay much more obvious. In each topic sentence, make a point about some aspect of the writer's logic, evidence, or use of emotional appeals.

8. SAMPLE POSITION PAPER

In the short position paper below, the writer fairly analyzes the strengths and weaknesses of George's argument.

Lianne George's "Why Are We Dressing Our Daughters Like This?" originally printed in *Maclean's* magazine, is a causal analysis essay discussing the reasons for and effects of the eroticization of girlhood. George uses several examples from popular culture, marketing, and the media to demonstrate how all combine to promote the sexualization of little girls. George's audience seems to be primarily women, whom she urges to question their own conflicts about sexuality and girlhood so that they don't affect their daughters. Although George overly generalizes about the sexualization of little girls, and has an argument that is at times disorganized and unfocused, she depicts the complexity of this problem while skilfully using ethical and emotional appeals. She thoroughly explains that this trend, which involves both girls and women, needs to be halted before there is no such thing as childhood.

One of the logical weaknesses of George's essay is the writer's vagueness about her subject and audience. Although George uses Western examples, it is unclear whether she is talking about all girls, or solely those in North America. She also begs the question, for her argument is based on the unproven assumption that most girls dress in this sexualized fashion and that their parents condone this attire and its associated behaviour. That is, she fails to mention, either in her introduction or a counter-argument, that there may be young girls and parents who are bucking this trend.

Another one of the weaknesses of George's essay is its organization. The argument is hard to follow and presents too many causes of this sexualization. For instance, in the opening of the essay, the writer begins with the controversial Catholic school girl uniform, which was popularized by Britney Spears. Then, she criticizes stores that eroticize girlhood before explaining how the idea of children as innocent is a relatively new one. Next, she discusses parents' involvement in this conspicuous consumption, the eroticization of both girls and women as a backlash against feminism, and more examples of toys that enforce precocious sexuality, gender roles, and the loss of childhood. It is not always clear, then, where the argument is heading and what, if any, is the main cause of the sexualization of children. Her approach and organization can leave the reader feeling disoriented. George attempts to discuss too much in the confines of this essay and should have considered reorganizing or limiting her argument.

However, what can be viewed as a weakness can also be counted as a strength. That is, perhaps George cannot commit to one cause because of how complicated the problem is. The author is writing, after all, from the position of a concerned citizen, woman, and perhaps parent, and not from the specialized perspective of an anthropologist or sociologist. The scope of her argument represents how she and other women or parents might be so overwhelmed by the problem that a solution seems impossible.

Although the essay's organization threatens George's logical appeal, the amount of evidence certainly compensates. The writer has thoroughly researched the problem, incorporating solid primary evidence and secondary sources. To support her claims about the media's role in eroticizing girlhood, she mentions Britney Spears, Paris Hilton, and Fergie. To indict name-brand stores, she reveals how chains like La Senza Girl, Abercrombie & Fitch, and Limited Too marketed or market inappropriate products to girls such as "fishnet stockings, skinny jeans, message panties, and padded 'bralettes' in micro sizes" (par. 5). To explore the causes of this paradigm shift, which are indeed complicated, she has these experts weigh in: Lyn Mikel Brown, author of *Packaging Girlhood: Rescuing Our Daughters from Marketers' Schemes*; Anne Hollander, author of *Seeing Through Clothes*; Susan Linn, an instructor in psychiatry at Harvard Medical School; and Ariel Levi, expert in raunch culture and author of *Female Chauvinist Pigs*. Whereas all contribute different perspectives on the problem, most agree or allude to the point that this sexualization is being targeted at younger and younger age groups and that the pornification of culture, as seen in "pole-dancing and striptease lessons, boob jobs and Brazilian waxes" has unfortunately become mainstream (par. 16). The trend of eroticizing both women and girls seems virtually impossible to curtail, let alone stop.

Also, through these examples, George appeals to the morals and beliefs of her female readers, so that they closely examine their own attitudes before infecting/affecting their children or the girls who view them as role models. She asks that her readers not confuse sexual empowerment with sexual objectification and exploitation and that they not pass these confused attitudes on to their children. Women, argues George, have to be aware that this return to the pink and the frilly might indeed be a reinstatement of firm gender roles and an unfortunate, yet disguised, backlash against the feminist movement.

In her strong ethical appeal, she also connects to the parents' fears and anxieties about raising their children. Firstly, she sympathizes with the difficulties parents face, understanding that they "are in the middle of numerous commercially created battles with their children . . . Battles about junk food, violent media, expensive brands and all sorts of things. It's hard, if not impossible, to say no all of the time" (Linn qtd. in George, par. 14). George may indict marketers and the media, but she does not blindly blame parents, who must struggle against all these seemingly insurmountable forces. She also alludes to the parental concern that kids, who already seem to grow up too quickly, are maturing even faster now. George suggests that girls wearing low-slung pants, mini-skirts, and plush purses are going to miss out on the chance of playing, getting dirty, and being a child. No parent wants to see his or her little girl mature too quickly.

One of George's other strengths is her emotional appeals: her shocking examples and sarcastic tone keep the reader's attention focused and help to educate him or her about the problem. When describing the *appropriate* message T-shirts that girls should wear, she explains that "a 'princess' would wear one of these scrawled across her chest: *Sweet Treats, Angel, Daddy's Girl, Official Cheer Bunny*." These slogans, which point to the way girlhood innocence is fetishized and linked to sexuality, might force readers to examine what is in their children's closets. Parents who have purchased their daughters Bratz dolls should realize that they are actually "a ratcheted-up male fantasy of what women should look like—big eyes, big lips, big breasts, an anorexic waistline and very long legs" (Linn qtd. in George, par. 25). The writer also uses several verbal examples and name brands throughout the essay, which are simultaneously humorous and horrifying: pictures of "six-year-olds in garters," "a line of Hasbro dolls aimed at six-year-olds," and a line of clothing for babies called Pimpfants (par. 28). These examples force the reader to stop and think about the harmful messages of girls' toys, which may have previously gone unnoticed.

And to appeal to the parents of a previous age and show how far this sexualization has progressed (or regressed), George recalls one of the most popular toys, Barbie, which was much derided by several 70s feminists: "We used to worry for Barbie, with her improbable proportions and dismal math skills. Now we long for Barbie. Not the new Bling Bling Barbie, but the old one with the job. At least she tried to do math" (par. 25). Barbie is remarkably tame next to the Bratz dolls, whose main activities of socializing and shopping set the bar pretty low for young girls. George makes the reader laugh and cry at the same time, wondering what can be done to stop this trend.

Although George's argument is, at times, meandering, and it is not clear whether the eroticization of girlhood is just another sartorial shift, an effect of marketing, the result of a backlash against feminism, or collateral damage connected to women's own sexual confusion, she makes one point very clear. If readers want their daughters to have a childhood, to experience the joys of imaginative play, to not be obsessed with image, to not accept limiting gender roles, they need to resist marketing and media trends and step in to help their kids make the right choices about clothing, toys, and role models. In helping their daughters, parents, especially women, will learn more about themselves and help produce a less narcissistic generation. And maybe they can drive the kiddie thong producers out of business too.

Work Cited

George, Lianne. "Why Are We Dressing Our Daughters Like This?" *Maclean's* 1 Jan. 2007: 36-40. Print.

Composing Research Papers

A **research paper** is an expository or persuasive essay in which your analysis or point of view is supported by facts and opinions from other sources. As you will see in the two sample research papers (Parts 11 and 12 in this chapter), the best secondary sources are usually published books and articles on the subject. Research material, however, can also include interviews, primary research, and other data.

The purpose of a research essay is to examine a subject in greater depth than would be possible using only your own knowledge. In many cases, you may not have any prior knowledge to draw upon. For example, how many of us, without using research material, could write an essay on the controversy over the trial of Louis Riel? Writing research essays, then, is one of the best ways to extend your knowledge of a subject. Though you will find that writing research essays is a lot of work, you should also find the process both useful and enjoyable.

In the world of work, research papers are written by specialists for other specialists. Citations and references allow these readers to evaluate both facts and opinions and to follow up possible lines of investigation. As a student writing a research paper, you too are learning to act like a specialist in a particular field. As such a specialist, you will present your material differently than you would for a general audience, using a more specific vocabulary, adopting a slightly more formal tone, and assuming your readers' general familiarity with the subject. Still, a research paper should not sound as though it had been compiled by a committee. The best research papers are those in which the style and tone reflect something of the writer: flashes of wit, clear thinking, depth of knowledge, sudden insights, and a genuine respect for language.

1. CHOOSING A TOPIC AND NARROWING YOUR FOCUS

Your first step is to choose a topic. Because you will be working on your research paper for a while, select a topic that fascinates and provokes a strong response in you.

Having a focused idea before you start to write and research will result in a better essay. Although instructors can ask pointed essay questions, many will give you a vague topic to explore, such as the effects of violent media. In this example, you know that you are expected to write an essay that explores effects, but your subject, violent media, is obviously too vague. To write a controlled, effective essay, you will have to narrow your topic. If you don't, your beginning idea will be too broad and the resulting essay too vague and unconvincing. Below are some pertinent questions you might ask about this topic:

- On what type of media do I want to focus? Video games? Movies? Graphic novels? Cartoons? Computer games?
- What effects do I want to consider? Psychological? Physical? Both?
- Do I want to consider effects on the individual? The populace?
- What particular group do I want to discuss? Adults? Teens? Teens with psycho-social problems? Children?

Because you have adult friends who regularly play violent video games, and because you believe the argument about the negative effects of violent media on children has been overused and exaggerated, you decide that in your causal analysis essay, you will concentrate on adults, arguing that violent video games, instead of being dangerous, actually have very few long-lasting negative effects and may actually be beneficial in solving problems, reducing stress, and so on.

2. FORMING YOUR OWN OPINION

A research paper, then, is not to be merely a compilation of other people's ideas or a summary of secondary sources. In the research paper, you begin with your own argument. Your goal is to integrate your secondary sources with your own opinions and knowledge. To make sure that you have your own opinion or some idea of your direction before researching, use brainstorming or discovery questions to gather some questions to answer in your paper.

For non-literary research papers, first sketch out your own opinion, even if it seems undeveloped. You may not know actual facts about violent video game use, but you have played them and have heard about their questionable negative effects. To clarify or broaden your own thinking, you might first write an outline or even a short draft.

If you are writing a literary research paper, consider jotting down a draft that contains your answer to the assigned question or your interpretation or analysis of the text, so that you can easily distinguish your ideas from those of your secondary sources. Writing this draft, then, will not only help you develop your argument but also protect you against plagiarism.

3. UNDERSTANDING BASIC TERMINOLOGY: PRIMARY AND SECONDARY SOURCES

Your instructor may ask you to use both **primary** and **secondary sources**, terms that confuse most students. According to *The Online Dictionary for Library and Information Science,* a primary source is "[a] document or record containing first-hand information or original data on a topic. . . ." Primary sources are works created at the time of an event or by a person who experienced the event. These sources also contain original research never before shared. Some examples of primary sources are interviews, diaries, letters, journals, speeches, autobiographies, government documents, and public records. They also include artifacts, original works of art, music, and literature.

For instance, a painting by Picasso is a primary source as is an interview with Picasso; however, an article analyzing Picasso's numerous romantic relationships and how they influenced his artistic subjects is a secondary source. If you are writing an essay on *Frankenstein,* the novel is your primary source, whereas critical interpretations of the novel, such as articles, are secondary sources.

That is, a secondary source is "any published or unpublished work that is one step removed from the original source, usually describing, summarizing, analyzing, evaluating, derived from, or based on primary source materials . . ." (*The Online Dictionary for Library and Information Science*). Secondary sources, therefore, comment, elaborate, and build upon primary sources.

The terms *primary* and *secondary,* though, are relative; that is, disciplines may designate primary and secondary sources differently. For instance, in the humanities, a peer-reviewed article is always a secondary source; an article written about *Frankenstein*, even if it does contain original research, is still considered a secondary source. In the sciences, a peer-reviewed article may be primary or secondary, depending on whether it contains new research or not. Thus, you will have to read a scientific periodical article very closely to determine whether its data is original, previously unpublished, and so on.

4. EXPLORING YOUR TOPIC BY RESEARCHING ON THE WEB

Online Encyclopedias

If your topic has been previously touched on or discussed in class, you might want to review your lecture notes, chat with your classmates, or meet with your instructor to toss around ideas. If the topic you have chosen is completely foreign to you, you will probably conduct some preliminary research.

At this point, you will probably turn to the Web, regardless of your familiarity with the topic. If you do so, remember that not all Web sources are created equal. Your first and safest step might be an investigation of respectable online dictionaries and encyclopedias, such as the following:

www.answers.com

www.bartleby.com

www.thecanadianencylopedia.com

www.reference.com

www.encylopedia.com

However, not all of these encyclopedias contain the same content or even the same search tools. For instance, encylopedia.com boasts that it has "more than 100 trusted sources," including other "encylopedias, dictionaries, and thesauruses." Imagine that your topic is health food in North America. You decide that you will argue that although health food is definitely more mainstream today, it is and always has been associated with a counterculture movement. At encyclopedia.com, you obtain more information on the beginning of the health food movement in North America. For instance, you type in "cornflakes," one of the original health foods, and are directed to the entries in other encyclopedias, such as the *Gale Encyclopedia of U.S. Economic History*, the *Encyclopedia of Food and History,* and the *Enclopedia of World Biography*. At encyclopedia.com, you discover that you can also narrow or broaden your search to include/not include dictionaries, thesauruses, etc.

However, in www.references.com, putting in the term "cornflakes" immediately brings up the patent and ingredients of this product whereas the left sidebar contains related searches, such as their history, inventor, and even recipes. And hitting on these related searches takes you to ads, articles, or books. Here lies the disadvantage of online encyclopedias and web-based sources: pop-up ads. These ads, which can appear anywhere in the article, are definitely distracting to the researcher.

The Trouble with Wikipedia

Though online encyclopedias are of varying worth, they are useful entry points to other reference sources. However, most instructors will prefer that you not rely on them too heavily. And several may disapprove of one particular online encyclopedia: Wikipedia.

Wikipedia is an online encyclopedia based on specialized wiki or collaborative software that allows users to add or edit content. This feature sounds ingenious, but is, in fact, a double-edged sword. Because Wikipedia employs no fact-checkers or editors, and because anyone with a Web browser can contribute to or edit its pages, its information can be unreliable or even wrong. For example, if the reader is an expert on Arthur Conan Doyle's fiction and he notices an error about Sherlock Holmes, he can amend the article, making it more accurate. However, if that user is a jokester and a disgruntled student forced to read *The Hound of the Baskervilles* against her will, she might choose to vandalize the entry, perhaps by changing the text's ravaging dog from a angry mastiff cross to a basset hound. Because it may take days or even *weeks* for this error to be discovered and fixed, this untruth could be read by thousands of people. Thus, misinformation, even if it appears minor or silly, is spread.

The creators of Wikipedia have attempted to make the site more credible, arguing that the more people who edit it, the more accurate the sources will be. This online resource, however admirable its intentions and however admittedly fun it is to browse, is still prone to vandalism and falsehoods. According to a 2006 piece by T. Chesney entitled "An

Empirical Examination of Wikipedia's Credibility," although the articles in Wikipedia are definitely more accurate than those written by non-experts in various fields, an average of 13 percent of the articles still contain mistakes (http://outreach.lib.uic.edu/www/issues/issue11_11/chesney/#c1).

Often, too, the referencing in Wikipedia is suspect; in those entries written by non-experts, there may be passages taken verbatim from other undocumented sources. Thus, citing an improperly referenced article from Wikipedia can lead to unintentional plagiarism.

Even if you shouldn't rely on Wikipedia, it can be useful for one thing: the list of references at the bottom of the page. Depending on the article, you may find that these entries are varied, scholarly, and credible. For instance, the page on Arthur Conan Doyle has a list of references that includes several books, peer-reviewed periodical articles, the Edinburgh Research Archive, and Project Gutenberg.

Web Search Engines

Search engines, in general, are computer programs that retrieve documents or data from a database. Web search engines are designed to search for information on the World Wide Web, displaying these results (which are called *hits*) in a list, usually from most to least relevant. A number of these Web search engines can be searches using Boolean operators; some cast a wider net, whereas others are better for answering factual or specific questions.

Currently, Google is the most popular search engine. According to the Nielsen MegaView search, Google had 65.1 percent of the share of searches in May 2010 (http://en-us.nielsen.com/content/nielsen/en_us/insights/rankings/internet.html). Still, there are several other choices if Google doesn't return the correct hits.

Some Reliable General Search Engines

www.altavista.com

www.bing.com

www.lycos.com

www.yahoo.com

www.msn.com

Some Reliable Fact-Based Search Engines

www.answers.com

www.ask.com

www.askjeeves.com

www.brainboost.com

Some Reliable Meta Search Engines

A meta search engine explores multiple search engines and places the answers on a single page. These search engines are most useful if your topic is obscure, new, or multidisciplinary. Some examples of meta search engines are

www.dogpile.com

www.excite.com

www.search.com

www.webcrawler.com

Websites

When doing preliminary research and even when looking for other non-print sources, you may decide to include websites, especially if your instructor has indicated you can use respectable and credible ones. Be especially sceptical, however, of the authenticity and credibility of information from general websites, listservs, and newsgroups. Also, familiarize yourself with the most popular suffixes so that you can recognize types of websites: com (businesses), ca (Canada), org (organization), edu (educational institutions in the US), and gov (American governments). For instance, www.utah.gov is the official site for Utah whereas www.canada.gc.ca is the official site for the Government of Canada.

Because the Internet is a place not only of education but also of commerce, you should be very sceptical about the reliability of information obtained from websites with the suffix .com. These sites are always trying to sell you something, usually an idea followed by its associated product. For instance, at www.ourhollowearth.com, you can learn about the "theory" that there is a tunnel stretching from the North to the South Pole, specifically located at 87.7 degrees North and South latitude, in which can be found "the original garden of Eden, the lost tribes of Israel, and the Lost Viking colonies of Greenland." And to further your discovery, which may include actually locating this tunnel yourself, you can order the e-book for only US$12.00.

Although people are rightly suspicious of .com sites, they are less wary of .org sites. Students, in particular, often think of organizations as professional, trustworthy entities, but not all organizations are respectable or offer truthful or unbiased information. For instance, the website www.theflatearthsociety.org, even though it has no marketing, is dedicated to the belief that the earth is not spherical, but flat. Other websites marked .org might also be promoting even more dangerous beliefs, such as racism and misogyny. For instance, the website www.martinlutherking.org, which Grant MacEwan University librarian Marge Gray regularly uses to teach students about evaluating websites, features a large picture of the civil rights leader on its home page. Although, on first glance, you might think this website is reputable, if you examine it closely, you will discover that it is actually hosted by Stormfront, a global white pride movement. Instead of celebrating the accomplishments of King, this website actually denigrates him and other African-Americans. Stormfront's website itself is www.stormfront.org.

Although your institution may have specific handouts on analyzing websites, several colleges and universities want you to apply the CRAP test to websites. The acronym CRAP stands for the following:

Currency—the last update of the website, its currency to your topic

Reliability—the credibility of the info, whether it is primarily opinion, balanced information, with or without references

Authority—the writer of the website, whether he or she is an educated expert in the field

Purpose and Point of View—why the website was put up (to sell an idea or a product), the domain extension, the intended audience

For a more extended version of the CRAP test, check out http://www.workliteracy.com/the-crap-test or see if your librarian has a more detailed information sheet. Furthermore, if you are unsure about the reliability of any other web-based sources, check with your instructor and your librarian, who might have lists of reputable web-based sources that are approved by your institution.

5. RESEARCHING YOUR TOPIC AT OR THROUGH THE LIBRARY

If in your Web search, you have had no luck with online encyclopedias and search engines, you might want to check out your library's reference desk, which offers general **reference materials**, such as encyclopedias and dictionaries, and more specialized ones, such as *The Guide to Literary Theory and Criticism, The Cambridge Dictionary of Human Biology and Evolution, The Animal Behaviour Desk Reference,* and *The Dictionary of Health Economics and Finance.* Your library probably has an impressive array of such books. General references, whether web-based or print-based, are especially useful if you must define essential terms or need ideas to narrow your search.

After completing your preliminary investigation, you are ready for more intensive research. Using your library's online catalogue, search for **books** by author, title, or subject. Subject searches, which are quite useful, allow you to locate dozens of potentially valuable items in seconds. They can also be frustrating if you have not chosen appropriate search terms or if you fail to limit your search sufficiently.

Your instructor will probably also ask you to find articles from **periodicals**, which are simply magazines and journals printed "periodically." These publications are divided into three main types: scholarly, which are written for a specialized discipline, and which usually have an extensive bibliography (*literature* or *medicine,* for example); trade journals, which are written for people in a particular industry or profession; and popular magazines, which are written for a general audience, contain plenty of pictures, and have no bibliographies. For most academic research essays, scholarly articles are ideal; however, your instructor may also allow articles from other periodicals, particularly if you are writing on a contemporary issue, a controversial subject, or a recently published literary work. For instance, if you were writing on the relatively new issue of cyberbullying, you might rely on newspaper and magazine articles for contemporary examples and commentary.

Periodicals, whatever their type, are located by using **article indexes**. If you happen to need an article published prior to 1980, it probably has not been transferred to an electronic database. To find an older article, you will have to search through the hard copies of these indexes. Consult a reference librarian for help using these resources. Before doing so, though, ascertain that your instructor allows older sources; most will prohibit articles more than five to ten years old. Most of your articles, however, will be found in **online periodical indexes**, otherwise known as electronic databases. Databases are either general (they carry periodicals covering a range of disciplines) or subject-based (they focus on one discipline or closely related fields). Three valuable general databases are *Academic OneFile* (book reviews and journal articles in humanities, education, science, and social science) and *MasterFILE Premier* (articles and pamphlets on numerous topics, including business, multiculturalism, and consumer health), and MLA International Bibliography, which is one of the pre-eminent indexes for researching literary works. These three databases contain full text and scholarly/peer-reviewed articles from more than a thousand journals and magazines. In some of these databases, you can also access dissertations.

Other useful **general databases** are CPIQ (Canadian Periodicals Index Quarterly), Canadian Literary Centre, Canadian Newstand/ Canadian Business and Current Affairs, Health Reference Center Academic, and ProQuest Science Journals. Some top subject databases are Biological and Agricultural Index, CINAHL (Cumulative Index to Nursing), and Communication and Mass Media Complete. For information on searching these databases, see section 6. Keep in mind that your learning institution chooses which databases to subscribe to based on its budget and its programs, so some of those listed above may be unavailable. Don't panic, for there *is* a wealth of information out there. Also, don't forget to consult with a librarian about the databases most useful to your research topic.

6. THE BASICS OF SEARCHING DATABASES

Electronic databases allow you to search for articles in several ways: by subject, keyword, peer-reviewed, full text, abstract, and so on. Electronic databases can be accessed from the library computer or from the comfort of your own home. To understand how to search in these databases, imagine that you are writing a psychology paper in which you are looking for sources on the effects of violent media.

To come up with some viable search terms, first do some brainstorming and get out your thesaurus. For media, for instance, you might come up with *movies, videos, video games, gaming, online games/gaming, television, cartoons, comics,* and so on. For effects, some of the possible terms are *aggression, desensitization, violence, violent behaviour,* and so on. Use these search terms for a **keyword search**, which locates the word in many different parts of the record. Keep in mind that most electronic databases are extremely literal about spelling. That is, if you put in *violet media,* instead of *violent media,* no sources will be returned.

You can narrow your keyword search by looking for only peer-reviewed or full-text articles, depending on your research project. You can also further refine your keyword search by using connectors from Boolean logic, a system of formulating precise questions, invented by nineteenth-century mathematician George Boole. The true/false nature of **Boolean logic**, compatible with the binary logic of digital computers, makes it ideal for searching indexes. Although you don't have to know *all* of Boolean logic, you should be familiar with some basic Boolean operators used to search within databases.

QUOTATION MARKS: Putting these around the phrase tells your computer to keep this phrase as is. Keywords *"violent media"* tell the computer to look for *violent media* together.

AND is the connector that *narrows* your search. Putting AND between your search terms indicates that those terms joined by AND must appear somewhere in the document, in any order and any distance apart. The more words connected by AND, the fewer documents you get. If you type in *violence* AND *media* in Academic Onefile, you will retrieve about 1,300 entries, but if you type in *violence* AND *media* AND *effects,* you will get 130 entries. And if you put in *violence* AND *media* AND *effects* AND *adults,* your list has a mere 3 entries. This connector is very useful when you are refining a heavily studied topic, such as *Hamlet* or heart disease.

OR is the connector that expands your search; it requires that just *one of the terms* appear in your document. That is, if you put in *violence* OR *media,* you will now get almost 95,000 sources! The OR connector, then, is most useful for small topics in which you want to cast a wide net. You might use the OR connector, for instance, if you are looking up sources on a recently published literary text, contemporary issue, or regional matter.

The ( ) symbol tells the computer to search for these terms *first.* You must use OR inside the parentheses if there is any other operator being used in the search. For instance, if you put in *violent media* AND *adult* AND *(effects* OR *aggression),* you would get the two first terms somewhere in the document and either *effects* or *aggression.*

Truncation tells the computer to search for forms of word. For instance, *adapt** would bring up *adaptation, adaptations,* and *adaptive* in your entries.

Keep in mind that various databases may also operate differently. Ask your librarian about other Boolean operators or useful search tools.

If possible, save your sources as pdf files to a memory key or send them to your university email account. A pdf file, which resembles a photocopy of the article, preserves the original pagination and is easy to work with. If the article is available only in html format, you can send it as well, but when you cite it, you may have to count the paragraphs and cite by paragraph number: (Adams, par. 4).

7. COMPILING A WORKING BIBLIOGRAPHY

Your next step is to compile a **working bibliography**, which will probably be at least twice as long as your final list of sources: a list of twelve to sixteen books, articles, and other material on your topic. This list should give you six to eight usable references, an adequate number for a research paper in an introductory course. (Students in advanced courses are generally expected to obtain more sources.) A longer list of references allows you to eliminate unavailable or irrelevant material and ensures that you do not depend too heavily on one or two sources. Also, if your material is too limited, you may get an inaccurate idea of the central issues or find it difficult to develop your own perspective.

There are a few key things to remember when compiling your working bibliography. Prepare it in a computer document so that you can cut and paste once you are ready to do the Works Cited or References page at the end of your essay. For each entry in your list of possible sources, include the call number or electronic address so you can easily locate the book or article. Remember that the database entries for your sources will probably not be cited in APA or MLA format and that you will have to reformat them accordingly. Some websites, as well, will use one particular format for their bibliographies. CPIQ, for instance, uses MLA style to reference its sources.

To get a jump-start on your References or Works Cited list, take the time to carefully format your sources at this point.

Compiling a working bibliography is a time-consuming process; don't expect to hammer out one the night before the essay is due. Also, don't expect that the sources you find will all be valuable or integrate neatly with your primary analysis. Still, you can prevent the panic that may lead to deliberate or unintentional plagiarism by allowing *at least* three weeks to brainstorm, compile a working bibliography, write a draft, and revise your research paper.

8. TAKING NOTES AND AVOIDING PLAGIARISM

Skim each item in your working bibliography, perhaps by reading the first and last paragraphs of your sources, and then select the six to eight most relevant ones. You are now ready to read these items and gather material from them. Making careful notes as you read will help you understand the source and figure out how to integrate it with your own ideas on the topic. Put these notes in the same document as your working bibliography, preferably immediately after the reference. An example of this system is shown below.

Source: Smith, Russell. "Go Ahead—Try to Use Some of These Beauties in a Sentence." *Globe & Mail* 17 June 2010: R1. *CPI.Q (Canadian Periodicals)*. Web. 17 June 2010

Summary of Article in Your Words:

In this article/opinion piece, Smith talks about a feature of the *New York Times* online, which allows readers to look up the meanings of complicated words found in the articles. Through this feature, the *Times* is able to analyze the words that its readers find most perplexing, if not incomprehensible. The author, a writer himself, uses this story to pose a deeper question about the difference between employing a varied and strong vocabulary that connects to readers and using difficult, elitist prose that alienates them. He also makes a connection between this online tool and the trends associated with language, asking both *how* and *why* certain words go in and out of fashion.

Possible Usable Quotes:

According to the author, "louche, saturnine, phlogiston and fungible were frequently looked up in 2009, but not in 2010" (par. 9). He also wonders what "any newspaper in 2009" is "doing discussing phlogiston (the essence of fire, a concept abandoned some 400 years ago)?" (par. 9).

"The fact that we can record these queries always raises the question among newspaper people about the level of vocabulary we should be striving for. It's fine to assume one's readers are not uneducated, say most editors, but merely showing off one's erudition is not in the service of communication. I would say that we can only learn and understand new words by encountering them, somewhere, for the first time, and that this is what many people read newspapers for" (par. 10).

Taking notes in this manner will also help you to avoid **plagiarism**, a serious academic offence that many students commit unintentionally. Plagiarism is the use of others' *words or ideas* without acknowledging the source. Although there is a clear moral difference between intentional and unintentional plagiarism, the consequences may be the same: penalties may range from a mark of zero on your paper to expulsion from your college or university.

Intentional plagiarism usually involves

- submitting a paper done wholly or in part by another person
- pasting together passages from one or more sources and using them without quotation marks and without properly acknowledging the source(s)

Unintentional plagiarism may include

- occasionally failing to use quotation marks to indicate quotations
- paraphrasing or summarizing in language that sounds too similar to that of the original source
- not carefully acknowledging where paraphrases begin or end
- omitting in-text references and/or a References or Works Cited page
- a discrepancy between the sources used in the essay and those on the References or Works Cited page

Whether you are **quoting**, **summarizing**, or **paraphrasing**, you must acknowledge the source of information and ideas immediately *in the text of your essay in a parenthetical citation* AND *in the list of sources* at the end of your essay.

Quoting

Quote sparingly in your preliminary notes so that you won't be tempted to copy long passages into your essay. Be sure to put quotation marks around any passage of three or more consecutive words taken directly from the source, and record the page (for printed texts) or paragraph number (for unpaginated electronic texts) where the passage can be found in the original, along with the author's name and the title. This information will allow you to keep track of your sources so that you can identify them appropriately in in-text citations and in your list of sources. The last thing you want is to be scrambling, at the eleventh hour, to locate a lost source.

Summarizing

You will probably need to condense most of the material in your research sources. Read the passage(s) until you can summarize, in your own words, the essence of the material. Record the author's name, a short version of the title, and page(s) or paragraph number(s).

Paraphrasing

If you have extremely complex, technical, or dry prose, you may prefer paraphrasing it, or putting it in your own words. When paraphrasing, you must change all of the original's sentence structure, phrasing, and wording. That is, the passage must be in *your* own style. To make sure that you are using your own style, put the original away and attempt to paraphrase from memory. Then, record the page(s) or paragraph number(s), the author's name (both MLA and APA), and date (APA).

Once you have a working bibliography and a full set of notes on the most relevant sources, you can begin the first draft of your research paper. As you write, carefully include author, title, and page or paragraph number for each quotation, summary, and paraphrase. It is better to be overly careful at this stage, for when you revise, you can then check that these references are in the appropriate format.

9. DOCUMENTING SOURCES

In North America, two main styles of documentation are used: MLA style, developed by the Modern Language Association, which is used primarily in the humanities; and APA (American Psychological Association) style, which is used in the social sciences. Determine which style you should use for your research essay.

Both styles require **in-text citations**, basic information (author and page number in MLA, and author, date, and page number in APA) identifying the source of your research material at the *exact* place you use it in your essay as well as a list of sources at the end of the paper that cross-references the information given in the in-text citations. Failing to include *both* of these necessary references constitutes **plagiarism**.

You need not fear accusations of plagiarism if you do your own work and completely and accurately document your sources. Do not attempt to mislead instructors; they are trained to recognize plagiarism. Also, your instructor, who knows your writing style, may immediately suspect dishonesty if the writing suddenly sounds different, more formal, stuffy, and so on.

Documenting Quoted Material

When you **quote** three or more words directly from a source, you must enclose these words in quotation marks. However, passages of **more than forty words** (APA) or **four or more typed lines** (MLA) are indented but not enclosed in quotation marks. Whenever you quote, you must state the author (and, in APA style, the date of publication), and the page or paragraph number locating the quoted passage in your source.

Imagine, for example, that you were writing a literary research paper entitled "*Tom Sawyer* and *Anne of Green Gables:* Two Models of Heroism." Because your instructor has allowed you to use older sources, you took out James L. Johnson's book *Mark Twain and the Limits of Power* (Knoxville: U of Tennessee, 1982). In it, you found the following paragraph stating that because Tom's village is not portrayed realistically, Tom is not changed by his seemingly serious experiences:

> Simply put, St. Petersburg is not a world in which children are easily turned into adults, for such a change requires that the child meet a real world and adjust himself, painfully but with more or less success, to its undesirable circumstances. Much of the idyllic quality of St. Petersburg is attributable to the fact that Twain has excluded from the novel a world in which experience produces consequent changes in character. Tom's world is one in which "adventure" replaces "experience"; his encounters with the alcoholic Muff Potter, the grave-robbing Dr. Robinson, the vengeful Injun Joe—encounters which should ordinarily produce some difference in his perception of the world—leave his character essentially untouched. (51)

If you were not careful to indicate quoted material and its source in your notes, your essay might contain a sentence like the one following:

Undocumented Quotation—Plagiarism

Tom Sawyer's adventures leave his character essentially untouched.

Documented Quotation

Tom Sawyer's adventures, as James L. Johnson argues, "leave his character essentially untouched" (51).

The revised sentence demonstrates one way to show the necessary information. For other examples, see the sample research papers at the end of this chapter.

Documenting Summarized or Paraphrased Material

Because integrating summarized and paraphrased ideas from your research sources is somewhat more complex than quoting directly, you may be tempted not to document. Let's suppose, for example, that you transferred your paraphrase of Johnson's passage from your notes to your essay without acknowledging the source.

Undocumented Ideas—Plagiarism

Tom's village, St. Petersburg, is not presented as a real world. A real world turns children into adults by forcing them to adjust to aspects of life they find undesirable. Twain presents St. Petersburg as idyllic (simple and charming) partly by excluding the kinds of experiences that would produce changes in character. In this idyllic world, Tom has adventures, such as his encounters with Muff Potter, Dr. Robinson, and Injun Joe, rather than experiences that would change his character or his perspective of the world.

How would you indicate that these are Johnson's ideas? If you merely added a citation at the end (Johnson 51), it would be unclear whether *all* the ideas in the paragraph were Johnson's, or merely the last point. Some instructors might even consider this faulty documentation to be plagiarism. To avoid this error, you can clearly distinguish your own thinking from the work of others by using a **signal phrase** to introduce the author's ideas and putting the appropriate citation at the end, as in this example.

Documented Paraphrase

James L. Johnson argues that Tom's village, St. Petersburg, is not presented as a real world. A real world turns children into adults by forcing them to adjust to aspects of life they find undesirable. Twain presents St. Petersburg as idyllic (simple and charming) partly by excluding the kinds of experiences that would produce changes in character. In this idyllic world, Tom has adventures, such as his encounters with Muff Potter, Dr. Robinson, and Injun Joe, rather than experiences that would change his character or his way of looking at the world (51).

In most cases, you should not rely so heavily on a single critic; you should rely on your own interpretation and examples from your primary source(s). Even so, this paragraph is an improvement because the reader knows whose ideas are being presented and exactly where the paraphrase begins and ends. If you carefully identify others' facts and opinions, your reader has more confidence that what remains is your own.

Creating a List of Sources

As stated earlier, for each source you have cited within the body of your essay, you must provide further information, so that a reader can locate the source. This information is compiled in a list of bibliographical entries on a separate page, which follows the end of your paper and which has a page number. There should be an exact match between the sources in the paper and the sources stated in your references list. If there isn't, your instructor might either dock marks and/or suspect an undocumented source (plagiarism) in the paper.

10. INTEGRATING RESEARCH MATERIAL

In your previous education, you may have written research papers in which you merely collected information on a subject and presented it in an orderly fashion. These assignments, though, were more akin to research reports or research summaries than to research essays.

In postsecondary courses, as noted before, research papers, like other kinds of essays, must have a thesis, a main point that the primary analysis and research material addresses. Your research material should relate to your thesis and your specific points. We will illustrate this process with two examples, one non-literary and one literary.

Non-Literary Example

Sample First Draft

Marleen C. Pugach of the University of Illinois has recommended these selection criteria for prospective Education students: (1) basic skills testing, consisting of entry-level tests in reading, mathematics, and written and oral communication; (2) a minimum grade point average; and (3) a structured interview to assess the applicant's personal qualities (161–63). At universities such as Oregon State and Northern Kentucky, students must successfully complete a two- to five-day full-responsibility teaching experience prior to being accepted into a teacher training program. The number of dropouts increased from approximately 5% to 25% (Edgar 96).

This draft paragraph serves the writer's need to gather information from a variety of sources. However, it does not serve the reader's need to state the significance of this information because the point of the paragraph gets lost among the examples.

Here is the material as it appeared in the student's final draft. With the added topic sentence, sentences explaining the relevance of each example, and a summarizing sentence to connect this material to the thesis, the original paragraph has become two.

Sample Final Draft

If teaching is to be regarded as the important job that it is, pride must first be generated within the profession itself.[1] One way to do this would be to have a more rigorous and effective set of criteria that applicants must meet before they are allowed into the profession.[2] Marleen C. Pugach of the University of Illinois has recommended a set of criteria that would function together to provide "entry-level hurdles to encourage self-selection, to serve as initial points in the process of continuous judgment of student progress, and to assist faculty members in making discriminations between applicants based on multifaceted data" (161). Pugach recommends these selection criteria: (1) basic skills testing, consisting of entry-level tests in

---

[1]This is the topic sentence.
[2]This is a statement supporting the topic sentence.

reading, mathematics, and written and oral communication; (2) a minimum grade point average; and (3) a structured interview to assess the applicant's personal qualities (161–63).[3]

Another criterion, used in universities such as Oregon State and Northern Kentucky, is also helpful in selecting suitable candidates.[4] Students must successfully complete a two- to five-day full-responsibility teaching experience prior to being accepted into a teacher training program. The number of dropouts increased from approximately 5% to 25% (Edgar 96).[5] Clearly, such intensive selection policies would attract applicants who seriously wish to pursue teaching, while deterring those who casually drift into teacher education. The sense of personal achievement that would come from gaining entrance to a faculty with such high entrance standards would contribute to a feeling of professionalism among candidates.[6]

—Carol Murray

Literary Example

Showing how your own interpretation of a literary text relates to other critics' opinions takes practice. We will look first at a draft paragraph on *The Adventures of Tom Sawyer* written before consulting the critics. Then we will discuss two ways of integrating other interpretations.

Sample Draft Paragraph: Student's Analysis

In *The Adventures of Tom Sawyer*, the adults are not presented as models of behaviour. They are often shown to be acting like children. When Tom tricks Aunt Polly at the beginning of the book, for instance, Aunt Polly has been attempting to trick him. Similarly, Tom shows off at Sunday School when Judge Thatcher visits, but the superintendent and the teachers are also described as "showing off." Even serious events in the adult world seem to parallel Tom's actions. The fight that ends with Injun Joe murdering Dr. Robinson has many of the same elements as Tom's fight with the new boy in town. It is no wonder then that even after his harrowing escape from the cave and his recovery of the treasure, Tom returns to playing at robbers. The adult world is not portrayed as different from the world of childhood, and so there is no reason for Tom to grow up.

Sample Draft Paragraph: Adding Support from Research Material

In this revised paragraph, the material from Johnson that we noted earlier is added to summarize and expand the point of the topic sentence.

The adults in *The Adventures of Tom Sawyer* are not presented as models of behaviour, but simply as older versions of Tom himself . . . [continue with examples from the original draft]. It is no wonder then that even after his harrowing escape from the cave and his recovery of the treasure, Tom returns to the boyhood world of playing at robbers, for the adult world offers no incentives for growing up. James L. Johnson argues that Tom's adventures "leave his character essentially untouched" because "such a change requires that the child meet a real world and adjust himself, painfully but with more or less success, to its undesirable circumstances" (51).

---

[3]These are examples of the criteria.
[4]Transitional statement that introduces another criterion.
[5]Another example.
[6]Commentary on the relevance of the examples, which connects the examples to the topic sentence.

But St. Petersburg, as Johnson points out, is an idyllic world, not a real world that would bring about change.

Sample Draft Paragraph: Synthesis of Student's Analysis and Research

In outstanding research papers, the writer does more than cite authorities for support: he or she synthesizes material from various sources by showing basic similarities and differences. This synthesis then provides a context for the writer's own interpretation. Note how the writer demonstrates her grasp of the debate about Tom Sawyer's relationship to the adult world in the following paragraph.

What, then, is the relation between Tom and his world? Robert Regan supports the view, originally put forward by Walter Blair, that the narrative strands of the novel "trace Tom's progress from childishness to maturity" (Regan 116). Several critics disagree. They argue that because the adults of St. Petersburg are essentially childish, there is no impetus for Tom to change (Fetterley 300; Johnson 51; Miller 73; Whitley 60). Numerous incidents in the book support this contention . . . [continue with examples from the original draft].

As you can see, crediting your sources, integrating research material, and synthesizing different points of view are not easy tasks, so do not leave them until the last minute.

11. SAMPLE NON-LITERARY RESEARCH PAPER (REFERENCES IN APA STYLE)

The paper below, which was written for an introductory college course, presents an answer to the following detailed question:

> Kathleen Berger's article "Bullies in School" presents some interesting and, perhaps, startling findings on the causes of both bullying and victimization. Although Berger mentions some of the general causes of bullying, she does not focus on the relatively new problem of cyberbullying. Write a 1,000- to 1,300-word persuasive causal analysis essay in which you explain the causes and effects of cyberbullying and what can be done to curtail this phenomenon. Make sure you support your analysis with at least three secondary sources.

Cyberbullying and the Internet

The convenience and speed of the Internet have definitely transformed how we communicate. To wish Grandma "Happy Birthday," you no longer have to pick up the phone and talk; you can use email, text messages, instant messenger, or Skype. But accompanying the Internet's expediency are new and significant challenges, such as questionable online communities and practices. Cyberbullying is one such recent dangerous online activity supported by the Web. Although there is no denying that bullying has been around much longer than the Internet, and that bullies have and will always find ways to manipulate and torment their targets, cyberbullying thrives because of the anonymity, accessibility, and abundance of available sources on the Internet.

Although the Internet's ease of communication has positive benefits, its convenience has also helped bullying evolve. T. Jacobs (2010) defined cyberbullying as the "use of electronic devices such as computers and cell phones to convey intimidating or harassing messages (i.e., text or IM messages, graphic harassment, and email)" (p. 175). Online bullying can consist of threatening remarks, embarrassing comments, or deliberate exclusions. Whereas cyberbullying is a relatively new issue, its prevalence has become substantial. A survey conducted by ERIN Research Inc. (2005) reported that 27% of Canadian students in Grades 7 to 11 have been bullied online (p. 9). Furthermore, Jacobs (2010) declared that 85% of American middle school students confess they've been victims of cyberbullying (p. 3). Admittedly, positive interactions do take place online; however, these statistics demonstrate how frequently the Internet is used to perform malicious acts.

There is a current lack of available data illustrating the possible effects of cyberbullying (Wright, Burnham, Inman, and Ogorchock, 2009, p. 35), but it is reasonable to expect that, like regular face-to-face bullying, online bullying can lead to severe emotional and social consequences. Arguably, cyberbullying often has even more lasting effects on victims because cruel comments or emails can be accessed indefinitely. Additionally, victims of online bullying may experience greater feelings of helplessness because there is no place for them to hide: they can be victimized anywhere and at all times. Because the Internet allows insults to be broadcast to vast audiences, the social consequences of this bullying are also extremely high. Reputations can be damaged quickly using the Web, because commentary can be shared with numerous people simultaneously. For instance, the messages that Billy is a bedwetter or Michelle's mom is an alcoholic can be immediately dispersed, resulting in much embarrassment and psychological harm. Online bullying, therefore, offers victimizers an easy means to relentlessly stalk or tease their prey.

Even though there are ways to cyberbully without using the Internet, the main sources of online bullying are through Internet applications. Some of these applications include Instant Messaging (IM), social networking sites, emailing, and online gaming. Buddenberg (2005), in fact, explained that Instant Messenger is a favourite tool of intimidators because of its immediate back-and-forth exchange (p. 52). Tormentors can engage in seemingly one-on-one conversations with their victims, but, in fact, have other kids with them who are secretly contributing to the harassment. Social networking sites, such as MySpace and Facebook, are also favourites of bullies. In fact, Wright et al. (2009) found that 53% of victims were cyberbullied through MySpace, and a further 70.6% of bullies confessed to using MySpace to conduct bullying (p. 39). In addition, troublesome emails can be sent to taunt victims, and can even be printed out and shared with others. Some online games also offer messenger services similar to IM; these group conversations can be used to send offensive notes to those who are singled out.

The anonymous aspect of the Internet likewise enables cyberbullying to thrive. When intimidating their victims, many online bullies hide behind secret or fake identities. Surprisingly, ERIN Research Inc. (2005) found that 59% of kids acknowledged they have assumed a fake identity online (p. 50). Among those children with artificial identities, 17% admitted they did so with cruel intentions (ERIN Research Inc., 2005, p. 51). Whereas traditional schoolyard bullies often use physical dominance to intimidate, online bullies do not rely on brute strength to gain power and control over their targets. Anyone can be a bully online, regardless of his or her size and power. Additionally, the anonymity of the Web may exacerbate bullying because there is less fear of repercussion. Online bullies may feel empowered to ridicule others because they aren't concerned that authorities will discover them. Using fake identities, cyberbullies take more risks, continuing or increasing their harassment. And the bullied may also feel powerless because there are no bystanders who can potentially intervene to stop a situation.

Furthermore, the accessibility of the Internet allows cyberbullying to flourish. The Internet revolution has shaped the way kids play, learn, and communicate: online technology has been integrated into many facets of daily life. Children use the Internet for recreation, education, and socializing. With 94% of students having Internet access at home (ERIN Research Inc., 2005, p. 4), the Web has quickly become a household necessity. Children are also becoming increasingly savvy with computer technology at younger ages: ERIN Research Inc. discovered that 62% of grade 4 students use the Internet to conduct research for school assignments (p. 53). This increase in Internet use has kids gravitating towards online communities for social and recreational purposes, setting a perfect stage for cyberbullying. Additionally, bullies are able to access the Internet in almost any location through a variety of methods: home computers, school computers, Internet cafes, laptops, cell phones, and even through some video game consoles. The Internet provides an advantageous environment for bullies to successfully implement their torments.

Cyberbullying is quickly becoming an effortless activity due to the combination of having nearly infinite amounts of targets available and a seemingly limitless audience. Bullies no longer need to meet people or even really know their targets. Children are using the Internet as a source to meet new people: ERIN Research Inc. (2005) reported that 66% of grade 11 students met new acquaintances online (p. 76). The Internet also provides bullies with a larger audience to humiliate their victims: Jacobs (2010) explained that "a photo, video, or conversation can be shared with a few people in an email or text . . . or broadcast to millions on a Web site" (p. 2). Cyberbullies may feel emboldened by having such a vast audience; therefore, their derision and abuse may increase.

In order to effectively minimize and control cyberbullying, students, parents, school authorities, law enforcement officials, and online servers must all work together. Belsey (2004) pointed out that though some cyberbullying incidents may fall under the Criminal Code of Canada, the Libel Law, or the Canadian Human Rights Act, it is very difficult to obtain the appropriate evidence needed to prosecute perpetrators (p. 2). There is a growing movement to establish more stringent laws, guidelines, and penalties for abusive and criminal activity conducted online. It is important that online servers bear some of the culpability for posted content, but school authorities and parents must also be responsible for developing and implementing guidelines that prohibit cyberbullying. Collectively, these groups can promote awareness about the damage caused by this act.

In conclusion, although there are numerous methods for and causes of bullying, it is obvious that cyberbullying is flourishing with the help of the Internet. Cyberbullying has quickly become a major issue that has caused a great deal of turmoil. Without the anonymity of the Web, bullies would not have the luxury of hiding behind fake identities. Cyberbullying is virtually effortless because online access is so available, there are numerous marks, and the audience is limitless. Jacobs (2004) confirmed that "the Internet is a modern wonder with unlimited potential . . . but if abused it can also wreak havoc on individuals, families, schools, and communities (p. 4).

—*Adapted from a paper written by Sarah Kennedy*

References

Belsey, B. (2004). Always on? Always aware! Retrieved June 14, 2010 from www.cyberbullying.ca

Buddenberg, L. (2005). Bullying in cyberspace. In J. Bolton and S. Graeve (Eds.), *No room for bullies* (pp. 51–60). Nebraska: Boystown Press.

ERIN Research Inc. (2005). *Young Canadians in a wired world: Phase II. Media awareness Network*. Retrieved from http://www.media-awareness.ca

Jacobs, T. (2010). *Teen cyberbullying investigated: Where do your rights end and consequences begin?* Minneapolis, MN: Free Spirit.

Wright, V. H., Burnham, J. J., Inman, C. T., & Ogorchock, H. N. (2009). Cyberbullying: Using virtual scenarios to educate and raise awareness. *Journal of Computing in Teacher Education 26*(1), 35–42. Retrieved from http://find.galegroup.com.ezproxy.macewan.ca

12. SAMPLE LITERARY RESEARCH PAPER

The essay below was written for an introductory English literature course. In the question, the student was asked to analyze *Frankenstein* as a tragedy while incorporating secondary sources. The student uses Aristotle's *Poetics* to frame her argument, whereas she integrates critical articles to support key points.

Frankenstein: Tragedy Exposed

A tragedy is a complex work of literature that is defined by Aristotle as "a mimesis of action—that is, it is [morally] serious and purposeful" and that "uses each of its resources . . . separately on the various sections [of the work]" to bring about through a process of pity and fear "the purification of those destructive or painful acts" (69). In Mary Shelley's *Frankenstein*, the protagonist, Victor Frankenstein, has a good life, yet still manages to commit a grave mistake leading to his fall. When the elements of Aristotle's *Poetics* (protagonist, *hamartia*, *peripety*, recognition, catastrophe, and catharsis) are applied to Mary Shelley's novel *Frankenstein*, the reader can see that the novel is, indeed, a tragedy.

Aristotle offers insight into the types of protagonists that should be included when he says that "tragedy stands in the same relation of difference to comedy, for the one [i.e., comedy] tends to take as subjects men worse [than the general run], and the other [i.e., tragedy] takes men better than we are" (53). Victor Frankenstein is one such man who conforms to Aristotle's formula for a tragic protagonist. He is given every opportunity to lead a morally upright life, as is seen in this description of his parents' love for him: "With this deep conscience of what they owed towards the being to which they had given life added to the active spirit of tenderness that animated both, . . . I received a lesson of patience, of charity and of self-control" (Shelley 35). That is, since birth, Victor was endowed with a model of how a parent should take care of a child; likewise, he was taught the essence of living a virtuous, moral life.

Aristotle also required that a protagonist be prone to error. Although Victor was given a good start and every advantage as a child, he did not use these to their full potential nor to his own good. Victor admits that "my temper was sometimes violent, and my passions vehement . . ." (Shelley 39). Frankenstein's parents were kind and gracious when raising their son, yet he received little of their empathy and was prone to violent tendencies. Victor also does not analyze his intentions, especially his overriding and blinding ambition, when creating the monster, and the novel shows him being of two minds; on one hand, he wants to improve human life, whereas on the other, he relishes the idea of being a sole creator. "He hopes to eliminate death, a seemingly noble goal given the suffering it causes" but is also "intent on acquiring a unique and far-reaching type of power; one that is tainted by the means by which it is to be attained and also by his illegitimate claim on it. In hindsight he recognizes his error, but initially Victor sought a high degree of omnipotence" (Allard pars. 13-14). Allard also confirms that "in attempting to discover the secret of life he does not carefully consider the various possible consequences of his actions" (par. 20). Frankenstein, then, despite his upbringing, his gifts, and his instruction in leading an honourable life, is prone to mistakes in his behaviour, his intentions, and his actions.

According to Aristotle, *hamartia* is "the change to bad fortune which [the hero] undergoes" that "is not due to any moral defect or depravity, but to an error of some kind" (21). From the Greek, the literal translation of the word means "missing the mark." There are several moments of *hamartia* in *Frankenstein*—instances in which Victor definitely misses the mark. The first debatable moment is Victor's creation of the monster itself (chapter five of the first volume). Victor himself believes the monster's birth to be his main error: "I must pursue and destroy the being to whom I gave existence; then, my lot on earth will be fulfilled and I may die" (Shelley 215). And because creating this monster is his main error, Victor believes he has every right to destroy it. Anne K. Mellor confirms, "Even on his death bed Frankenstein stubbornly believes he has acted correctly" (48). Unfortunately, by attempting to annihilate his daemon, Frankenstein unwittingly destroys the lives of others.

Whereas Frankenstein clings to the notion that the creation was a mistake that led to his catastrophic death, the monster contrarily believes that his creator's lack of presence and parenting led to his deranged mental state. Admittedly, the creature could not have become what it did, nor could it have caused the same destruction, had it never been created, but the monster makes a valid argument that Frankenstein's lack of parental concern was, in fact, the moment of *hamartia:* "Remember that I am thy creature; I ought to be thy Adam, but I am rather the fallen angel, whom thou drivest from joy for no misdeed. Everywhere I see bliss, from which I alone am irrevocably excluded. I was benevolent and good; misery made me a fiend!" (Shelley 103). The creature declares that when he was created, he was not a blank slate, but knew the basics of a righteous life, which Frankenstein denied him from leading. He argues that when every living being, including his creator, abandoned him, he became a monster.

Because of his upbringing, Victor had the capacity to love and teach the monster. Choosing to reject him could be his main error, which even Frankenstein admits, however briefly: "During these last days I have been occupied in examining my past conduct; nor do I find it blameable. In a fit of enthusiastic madness I created a rational creature, and was bound towards him to assure, as far as was in my power, his happiness and well-being" (Shelley 219). That is, the monster's happiness was indeed within the power of Frankenstein, who had the opportunity to shape his creation any way he wished, but chooses to abandon him and leaves him no companionship. Mellor adds that "Frankenstein's callous disregard of his responsibility as the sole parent of his only child is contrasted to the examples of two loving fathers: Alphonse Frankenstein and Father Delacey. Both [provide] . . . their motherless children . . . with loving homes and moral guidance" (49). When compared to these parental figures, Frankenstein fails miserably.

However, it is the presence and the role of these men which also support Frankenstein's claim that creating the daemon was the grave error. That is, although the daemon is unable to find a place in the world, the Delacey family shows him how to deal with misfortune. For instance, Felix had a promise broken, just as the daemon had, yet the former turns to a gentle and quiet life whereas the latter seeks vengeance on the man who harmed him. The daemon had some moral instruction, yet he is unable to control his desires. Therefore, the creature's malevolent actions, after being exposed to and learning from the Delacey family, support the idea that he has an inherently wicked nature.

The moment of hamartia gives life and motion to a story. Aristotle defines peripety as "a sudden change [over] of what is being done to the opposite . . ." (87). Once the mistake has been made, the consequences of the mistake follow, allowing the reader to experience pity and terror for the character's reversal of fortunes. Frankenstein's early life was one of advantage, rather than one of disadvantage. After he creates the monster, his life begins to fall apart. The moment of peripety may, then, be as early as Frankenstein's illness, for from this point onwards, he loses all the good in his life and all those whom he cherished, ending with his beloved Elizabeth.

Once his fortunes have been reversed, the protagonist is ready to recognize his error. The first awareness Victor has of his mistake coincides with the death of his brother. Victor recognizes that his creation is responsible for William's passing: "I had hitherto supposed him to be the murderer of my brother" (Shelley 104). Later, Victor again recognizes his role in the tragedy when Henry Clerval is killed by the daemon and he is arrested for the murder. Though he recognizes the daemon killed Henry, this time, the guilt and recognition turn into blame upon himself: "Have my murderous machinations deprived you, my dearest Henry, of life? . . . I called myself the murderer of William, of Justine, and of Clerval" (Shelley 181). Victor recognizes that by creating the being, he has helped to cause the deaths of his friends.

The murder to finish the daemon's list is Victor's own death. Catastrophe, one of Aristotle's elements, is fully realized when the creature outlives his creator. In the final conversations with Walton, Victor entreats him to destroy the monster so that the world can be restored to its natural state. "Miserable himself that he may render no other wretched, he ought to die. The task of his destruction was mine, but I have failed. When actuated by selfish and vicious motives I asked you to undertake my unfinished work; and I renew this request now, when I am only induced by reason and virtue" (Shelley 220). The final catastrophe in the novel, then, is that Victor dies before completing his task, but, technically, he really is slain by the monster: "Victor dies of exhaustion and heartbreak in a bunk aboard Watson's ice-trapped ship. Then after coming aboard the vessel to bid an emotional farewell to the corpse of a man who gave him life, who was his only father figure, the creature skulks away to immolate himself at the top of the world" (Thompson 84). Though the monster does, too, eventually die, neither Walton nor Victor witness its demise.

Catharsis, which Aristotle considers the final element of tragedy, can be defined in two ways: an emotional cleansing for the characters and reader; and eudemonia, which simply means human flourishing that is experienced and seen by the reader and the characters. "Now it is possible for an effect of pity and terror to come from the 'look' [of the actors] (opsis); but it can also come from the very structure of events, and this is nearer the heart of the matter and [the mark] of a better poet" (Aristotle 99). In the novel, both elements of catharsis are present. Because the book is organized as a chiasmus, more than one person perceives the suffering of another and then experiences emotional cleansing. At the centre and focal point of the novel, Victor experiences the emotional cleansing of pity and terror when confronted with the daemon's tale. Through Victor's tale, Walton also understands these emotions, but after meeting the monster, Walton knows more pity than fear. And the readers themselves, by seeing what happens to all three characters and witnessing the pathetic physical and emotional states of both Victor and the daemon, also experience catharsis.

Aristotle also argued that the structure of events could cause pity and terror. Critics have commented on how this novel's structure evokes sympathy for several of the characters:

Sympathy produces the novel's carefully structured pattern of three narratives framed by Walton's epistolary voice. . . . At the novel's outermost layers, Walton writes letters while he longs for a sympathetic friend; shortly thereafter, he pens a novel while such a friend speaks to him; finally, he resumes his letters as that friend approaches death. . . . the monster's tale begins when his creator feels reluctant sympathy for him; it ends with his request for a mate who will grant him the sympathy he has thus far been denied. (Britton 9)

Through this structure, readers not only see how the narratives connect, but also sympathize with and feel pity and terror for all the characters. Everyone in this novel is looking for consideration and human connection: Walton wants a friend, Frankenstein yearns for his lost loved ones, and the daemon desires a mate.

This quest for compassion and understanding, along with the need to rectify previous blunders, results in much story-telling. Seeing Walton as himself, and empathizing with him, Victor tells his narrative as a warning against ambition and pursuing science above all else: "Seek happiness in tranquility, and avoid ambition, even if it be only the apparent innocent one of distinguishing yourself in science and discoveries" (Shelley 220). Through the structure of his own life's events, Victor discourages Walton from making similar mistakes. This structure also allows the reader the necessary cathartic experience. In the letter marking the beginning of the book, Walton says, "This manuscript will no doubt afford you the greatest pleasure: but to me . . . . with what interest and sympathy shall I read it some future day" (Shelley 32). Walton writes the tale, hoping that someone will be able to learn from the lessons of Victor's story. Many years later, we read this novel and still receive instruction from it.

The formula of Aristotle's *Poetics*, which fits so well with *Frankenstein*, makes this novel a tragedy. Shelley provides the reader with a protagonist who has every benefit, yet is prone to failure because of his bad temper and irrational decisions; she includes several arguable moments of *hamartia*. Victor's life is a series of events demonstrating *peripety* or reversal of fortune, all of which lead to the recognition of his mistake and his catastrophe. Finally, Shelley places elements of catharsis throughout the narrative. Using Aristotle, then, the reader is able to discover the tragedy and subsequent lessons of *Frankenstein*.

—*Adapted from a composition by Jennifer Carbert*

Works Cited

Allard, Angie. "Moral Responsibility in Mary Shelley's *Frankenstein*." *Coastline Journal.* 15 Nov. 2009. Web. 2 July 2010.

Aristotle. *Poetics*. Trans. George Whalley. Ed. John Baxter. McGill-Queens University Press: Montreal, 1997. Print.

Britton, Jeanne. "Novelistic Sympathy in Mary Shelley's *Frankenstein*." *Studies in Romanticism* 48.1 (Spring 2009): 1-20. *Academic OneFile.* Web. 1 July 2010.

Mellor, Anne K. "Making a Monster." *Bloom's Modern Critical Interpretations: Mary Shelley's Frankenstein*. Ed. Harold Bloom. Chelsea House: New York, 2007. 43-60. Print.

Shelley, Mary. *Frankenstein*. Penguin Classics: New York, 2007. Print.

Thompson, Terry. "Shelley's *Frankenstein*." *Explicator* 64.2 Winter (2006): 81-84. *Academic Onefile.* Web. 1 July 2010.

Checklist: Research Essays

	OK	NEEDS WORK
1. In a research essay, have you included appropriate and correctly documented secondary sources?	☐	☐
2. Is all the secondary material relevant to your thesis?	☐	☐
3. Have you explained why you agree or disagree with this material?	☐	☐

Revising Your Essay: Structure

1. CHECKING YOUR PURPOSE AND YOUR AUDIENCE

Although you may have combined various rhetorical modes, and used various paragraph types within your essay, your essay will still probably have one main purpose: to narrate/describe/reflect on personal experience, to explain a subject or event, or to argue a main point. When revising, consider this main purpose as well as your audience. For instance, if you were writing an essay to a friend or a narrative for a blog, your audience is your peers, so you might include more personal details and use more casual language than you would for a personal essay for an English course.

2. CHECKING OVERALL ESSAY STRUCTURE

When revising your essay, ensure that your structure suits your purpose.

Expository and persuasive essays usually have deductive structures, with thesis statements in the introduction and topic sentences at the beginning of each paragraph. If you have chosen this structure, ensure that your thesis is at the end of your introduction and that each paragraph has a clearly stated and refined topic sentence *at or near* the beginning of each paragraph. Deductive essays, especially persuasive ones, often build to their strongest point; if your most important point is buried in the middle of your essay, you might need to reorganize your paragraphs.

Alternatively, if you have decided that your audience is unknowledgeable or hostile/resistant—you are explaining a very difficult process or arguing a controversial point, such as violent video games actually benefiting adults—you would probably use an inductive structure. To check the structure of your essay, get a friend to read it without the conclusion and get him or her to predict the thesis. If your reader grasps your main point, he or she has induced the thesis, and your content and organization are probably sound. However, if your reader is surprised or shocked by your thesis, you have not achieved your desired effect, and you may have to further develop or reorganize your argument.

In inductively structured personal essays, in which you are trying to create an effect or communicate an experience, remember that you still need a main point. You can similarly "test" the effectiveness of your essay by getting someone to read the essay, *sans* conclusion, and asking him or her about the relevance of the personal experience or event.

From *Forms of Writing: A Rhetoric and Handbook*, Sixth Edition, Kay L. Stewart, Marian Allen, Shelley Galliah.

3. CHECKING AND REVISING YOUR THESIS STATEMENT

In the process of writing your essay, you may have come up with new arguments or directions; thus, you may have to refine your thesis. Remember that your thesis, which predicts and controls your argument, is the most important sentence in your paper. Your thesis should match the structure and content of your finalized essay.

Recall that your thesis statement should contain an opinion with at least one reason to support it and that it should be neither too vague nor too detailed.

Below are some weak and revised thesis statements for various essay types:

WEAK   There are various steps to bathing your dog. (This thesis for an expository essay sounds too general and irrelevant. What can the reader gain from reading this essay?)

REVISED   *If you follow these three main steps to bathing your dog, both you and your dog will have a more pleasant experience.*

WEAK   Choosing a cancer treatment can be difficult. (This thesis for a persuasive essay contains an opinion, but a vague opinion, and no reasons to support it; additionally, this thesis does not indicate a clear basis of argument or structure.)

REVISED   *Because cancer treatments have various side effects, patients should thoroughly consult with their doctors about the treatment options that are best for managing their disease.*

Here are some additional pointers for refining the structure of your thesis:

- If your instructor has asked you to blueprint your thesis or indicate the main divisions of your essay, use tight parallel structures. In the example below, which is from a literary analysis essay, the three poetic elements are clearly listed as nouns.

  In "To His Importunate Mistress," Peter Devries uses speaker, structure, and prosody to reveal the inability of modern man to seize the day.

- If you are writing a persuasive essay, and you have to acknowledge a counter-argument, you might consider structuring your thesis as a *complex sentence.* That is, place the minor point or counter-argument in the dependent clause and your main point in the independent clause.

  Although video games are indeed becoming more violent, parents and educators should not scapegoat them or blame them for the deviant or violent behaviour of teens.

- If you are writing a personal essay, avoid the temptation to make your thesis too vague or oblique; make your thesis specific and meaningful to the reader.

  Training for a marathon taught me about pain, patience, and perseverance.

4. CHECKING PARAGRAPHS: LENGTH, DIVISION, AND TOPIC SENTENCES

Although paragraphs can vary in length, make sure that your paragraph length suits your essay's purpose. For instance, an expository essay on the steps to paint a room might require one long paragraph on choosing the colour, two short paragraphs on buying materials and prepping the room, two medium-length paragraphs on the processes and techniques of painting, and one short paragraph on cleaning up.

Alternatively, a comparison/contrast essay offering a balanced perspective on two health plans might require longer, equally developed paragraphs. And a persuasive essay on the dangers of violent media might place its most important point in TWO final longer paragraphs.

Some instructors may approve of short transitional paragraphs; most, however, approve of equally developed paragraphs. Check to see how your paragraphs look on the page; if you have really lengthy paragraphs— over a page long—look for a natural break to divide them. If you have several really short paragraphs, consider how to combine them under a single topic sentence.

If you see a weakness in your essay, your instructor will no doubt see it too.

Now is also the time to return to and revise your topic sentences, making sure that they are neither too vague nor too specific. Because topic sentences function as mini-thesis statements for the paragraph, they must match the content of the paragraph.

Examine the two topic sentences below for an essay on the dangers of blackouts.

> EXAMPLE 1   A blackout is an alcohol-induced memory loss.

Because this topic sentence simply defines blackouts, it is too specific for an expository essay on the causes and effects of blackouts.

> EXAMPLE 2   To understand the dangers of blackouts, we need to understand what they are and distinguish them from passing out and from drinking to the point of unconsciousness.

This topic sentence limits the discussion to defining blackouts and distinguishing them from other alcohol-related episodes.

5. CHECKING PARAGRAPH UNITY AND COHERENCE

Now that you are sure that your paragraphs are properly ordered and your topic sentences are sound, it's time to examine the internal structure of each paragraph. You need to check that your paragraphs are unified (they contain only information that develops the topic sentence) and coherent (their details are placed in the most effective order).

To check for unity, test every sentence against the topic sentence. Does each sentence support or develop the topic sentence's main point? If not, highlight, rather than delete, these extraneous sentences, for they may actually belong in other paragraphs. If you are crossing out a lot of unnecessary sentences, though, you might need to rethink the paragraph, either fleshing it out with more details or removing it entirely. If you don't have enough details to support your point, you might be accused of "jumping to conclusions," a serious logical flaw.

Next, verify the order of your details; a coherent paragraph is one in which the sentences are ordered effectively. This order, for instance, could be chronological, spatial, from least to most important, and so on, depending on what type of paragraph you are writing. See whether you need to reorder or remove sentences. Check to see that you are using ample and appropriate transitional words and sentences to enforce the existing relationships between ideas and to make your paragraph flow.

6. REVISING YOUR INTRODUCTION

Students often write their introductions and conclusions last, so these often get the least attention and revision. However, because these parts of your essay leave the first and the last impressions on your reader, they really merit your careful consideration.

Your main point gets clarified as you write, so your best statement of your thesis might actually be in your conclusion. If it is, relocate it to your introduction.

- Check the length of your introduction; it should neither be too terse (a few sentences long) nor too rambling (more than ⅓ to ½ a page). Your individual instructors may have specific guidelines about introductions; check with them if you are unsure.

- Check that you have not opened with a vague statement, such as "Since the beginning of time" or a truism, such as "Humans have always struggled with death." These are surefire ways to annoy your reader.

- Check that you have grabbed the reader's attention in a way that is appropriate to your purpose and audience. A persuasive essay on the need for handwashing might begin with a statistic about how many and what types of bacteria regularly reside on your hands, whereas a narrative essay on training for a marathon might open with a detail about hitting the notorious wall. Consider using description and narration in your introduction.

- Check that you have chosen *one* way to begin and that there is a clear bridge or segue between your opening material and your thesis statement.

- Below is an example of a strong introduction from a classification essay about television crime dramas. In the example, the segue has been <u>underlined</u> and the thesis **bolded**.

CSI, *Law and Order*, *Southland*, and *The Shield*. Bikinis, exotic locales, gritty interrogation rooms, political controversies, gory autopsies, fast cars, amoral characters, and straight shooters. Above are just a few examples of recent North American police/crime dramas and a partial list of their ingredients. Cop shows comprise a bewildering buffet indeed. <u>In order, then, for the viewer to choose the most satisfying bite of crime drama, he or she needs to become familiar with the cop show menu.</u> **Crime dramas can be divided into three major groups: location-driven shows, plot-driven shows, and character-driven shows**, each offering a different but satisfying entertainment experience.

This introduction, which uses a series of effective fragments, gives examples of the "ingredients" of crime shows before making a segue and then stating the thesis.

Below is an example of an introduction from a literary analysis essay. Why is it weak? How would you go about revising it?

Depression is a confusing, scary state, how can a person recover or at least be kept as comfortable as possible? Secluded from family and friends confined to an eerie, smouldering room covered in pale, smelly old wallpaper? Charlotte Perkins Gilman wrote this story in the nineteenth century, it was forgotten until feminists claimed it in the 60s. The story has an autobiographical connection, but the narrator is not Gilman, her name is Jane. Jane is a new mother struggling with postpartum depression. Although her husband is a well-known doctor, his techniques for helping his sick wife heal are somewhat questionable. He chooses a secluded house standing alone about three miles from the nearest village. "It makes me think English . . . there are hedges and wall and gates that lock, and lots of separate little houses for the gardeners and people" (83). Jane is placed in a nursery at the top of the house with bars on the windows. The walls are covered in old, smelly, faded paper. Mary is an author, although she is forced to hide her writing from her husband. I will talk about how the wallpaper symbolizes three different interpretations: how she felt suicidal, her confusion, and finally how she went completely insane.

7. REVISING YOUR CONCLUSION

Just as your introduction creates a first impression on your reader, your conclusion leaves a final impression. Your conclusion, then, should not be an afterthought but a decisive and powerful end to your essay.

Although you should summarize your main points in your conclusion, check that you have not restated your thesis verbatim and that your wording is substantially different in your introduction and conclusion. That is, don't simply cut your introductory material and paste it into your conclusion. After all, you have already explained a subject, narrated a personal experience, or argued a point—travelled from point A to point B, so to speak—so returning exactly to point A doesn't make much sense. After summarizing the main points, suggest the wider implications of your thesis or subject. In theory, then, a conclusion, which moves from specific (your thesis) to more general information, has the opposite structure of an introduction.

Below is an example of a conclusion from an essay about technology's effects on literacy; the summary of the writer's thesis is in bold font. Because this is a persuasive essay, she pushes her argument outwards by making suggestions for educators.

Andrea di Sessa optimistically suggests that "computers can be the technical foundation of a new and dramatically enhanced literacy" (4). **However, as this essay has shown, in the relatively short time that computer technology has been widely available to the public, literacy levels have not, in fact, increased, but actually plummeted.** Therefore, as technology continues to be integrated into and even take over classrooms, educators must be mindful of the absolute necessity of cultivating the basics: grammar and reading skills. This is a daunting undertaking for the education system; however, teachers cannot fail, for the readers produced by their schools, our children, will be the ones carrying the torch of literacy into the future.

In the conclusion from a literary analysis on Gilman's "The Yellow Wallpaper," the summation of the thesis is also bolded.

In Gilman's story "The Yellow Wallpaper," John symbolizes the patriarchal medical idea that women had to be protected from work and stimulation and the patriarchal male idea that women should be "seen and not heard," ideas that Mitchell also revisited and later refined. That is, after he read "The Yellow Wallpaper," Dr. S. Weir Mitchell changed both his Rest Cure treatment (Berman 237) and his thinking about appropriate treatments for women's ailments. Thus, Charlotte Perkins Gilman's "queer story" about one woman's depression not only changed the fate of women in her time but also changed the fate of women for all time.

8. CHECKING YOUR PRESENTATION AND ASSIGNMENT FORMAT

After you have checked the overall structure of your essay, you need to analyze how your essay looks. Keep in mind, though, that formatting your essay in the early stages will prevent you from obsessing over these details at the end, when you may be stressed and pressed for time.

First, examine the presentation of your essay, specifically your margins, spacing, font, and paragraph indentations. Make sure that you have followed any specific guidelines from your instructor. For instance, some instructors might ask you to underline your thesis, include certain information on your title page, or provide a word count.

Next, ensure that you have followed the requirements of your chosen format, specifically the format for title page, headers, parenthetical citations, and References/Works Cited page.

Instructors, especially in later assignments, generally expect you to make few formatting mistakes. They might even allot a significant portion of your grade—10 percent or more, for instance—to presentation and format.

Finally, after going over essay structure and format, remember to check the language and style of your paper and to proofread for editing, grammar, and punctuation mistakes.

Checklist: Revision

	OK	NEEDS WORK
1. Is your purpose clear?	☐	☐
2. Have you analyzed your audience?	☐	☐
3. Is the essay's organization/overall structure effective?	☐	☐
4. Is the thesis clearly stated at the essay's beginning or end?	☐	☐
5. Is the essay divided into the appropriate number of paragraphs?	☐	☐
6. Are the paragraphs effectively ordered?	☐	☐
7. Does each paragraph have a clear topic sentence or linking sentence?	☐	☐
8. Does each paragraph have enough details to support it?	☐	☐
9. Is each paragraph unified and coherent?	☐	☐
10. Does each paragraph use appropriate transitional words and expressions?	☐	☐
11. Does the essay have a powerful introduction?	☐	☐
12. Does the essay have a strong conclusion?	☐	☐
13. Are the style and language appropriate?	☐	☐
14. Is the format of the document correct?	☐	☐

Revising Your Essay: Checking for Appropriate Language and Style

1. CHECKING FOR APPROPRIATE LANGUAGE

Some writers use informal language in writing that actually requires more formal diction. Others adopt an overly formal vocabulary, so that their writing becomes stilted. Still others coast along, using words that are safe but dull. Paying attention to the words you use will help you remedy these problems and develop more lively and effective prose.

Understanding **levels of language** will help you choose words appropriate for your purpose and audience. Consider these words meaning *poor*:

Formal	Standard	Informal
impecunious, destitute	*poverty-stricken, poor*	*hard up, broke, busted*

These words illustrate levels of language, with "big words" such as *impecunious* and *destitute* at the formal end of the scale; colloquial and slang terms such as *hard up* and *busted* at the informal end; and the standard vocabulary of public writing and speaking in the middle (*poverty-stricken, poor*). Although you might use colloquial diction among friends, the words you use in writing for college or university should come from a standard vocabulary.

2. REVISING LANGUAGE: GUIDELINES FOR FORMAL WRITING

When you are writing academic essays, keep these suggestions about word choice in mind. Because students often can't recognize writing that is not formal enough and writing that is too formal, the first suggestions are for keeping your writing appropriately formal, whereas the latter suggestions are for keeping your writing lively yet concise.

1. **Avoid slang and colloquial expressions.**

   an acquaintance rather than *a guy I know*

2. **Avoid clichés.** Clichés serve a useful purpose in spoken language, but in formal writing, they may suggest that the writer is treating the subject superficially or vaguely.

   He was a straight shooter who always hit the nail on the head.

3. **Use contractions sparingly.** Some readers object to contractions in formal writing; others don't. If you use an occasional contraction, make sure you use the apostrophe correctly.

4. **Use *I* and *you* sparingly.** Don't distract your readers from your subject by constant references to yourself: *I think, I feel, I believe, it seems to me.* The reader knows you are expressing your opinion. However, when it is appropriate to use *I*, use it rather than *one* or *this writer*.

   NOT   It seems to me that this anthology is unsuitable for the high school curriculum.

   BUT   This anthology is unsuitable for the high school curriculum.

   OR   Although other reviewers consider this anthology suitable for the high school curriculum, I disagree.

   Similarly, avoid using *you* in formal writing to mean *people in general*.

   NOT   The university's marking system can be frustrating when all of your professors have their own scale within the scale.

   BUT   The university's marking system can be frustrating when professors have their own scale within the scale.

5. **Aim for a serious, knowledgeable, and businesslike tone, but avoid sounding stuffy or pompous.** In general, choose standard words rather than more formal terms (*need* rather than *necessity*). However, emphasize key points by selecting words from the slightly formal range (*poverty-stricken* or *destitute*, but not *impecunious*).

6. **Use specialized terms only when necessary.** Part of what you learn when you study psychology, sociology, and other academic disciplines is the language that specialists use when communicating with others in the same field. In an essay discussing Freud's theory of the unconscious, for example, you would use Freud's terms *id*, *ego*, and *superego*, for there are no adequate synonyms for these concepts.

   But when a specialized vocabulary is used inappropriately or out of context, it becomes *jargon*. Jargon obscures meaning instead of making it more precise. When jargon is combined with wordiness and an unnecessarily formal vocabulary, writing can become almost unintelligible, as in the examples below.

   NOT   As the precepts of individual psychology are ultimately reflected in social psychology, the psychic impairment experienced by the student as part of the educational process will be augmented within the context of the social environment.

   BUT   Because students carry their self-perceptions into the larger social world, any damage to their self-esteem becomes more severe when they leave school.

NOT   Management will access the input of all interested parties, prioritize their responses, and introduce modifications to the terms of the proposal accordingly.

BUT   The manager will ask all interested parties for their reactions to the proposal, review their responses, and make changes accordingly.

Exercise 1

Comment briefly on how jargon and big words affect the following paragraph, taken from a research paper on the back-to-basics movement in education. Then rewrite the paragraph in simpler, more concrete language.

The teacher I interviewed perceived her role as a socializing agent with a humanistic approach. She added that although students lacked skills to handle the grade five curriculum, her priority was to allow student-directed activities in a safe environment free of negative labelling. Correcting exams and clerical tasks presented a strain on her role. She felt psychology was the most beneficial course she had taken at university: she taught many children experiencing stress from broken families or families who did not share time.

Exercise 2

Underline inappropriate word choices in the following paragraph, adapted from a research paper on impaired driving. Then rewrite the paragraph so that the diction is more appropriate for the subject and audience.

Kathy Stechert's research on drunk driving (1984) has suggested some prevention techniques that you should consider when entertaining guests in your home: serve lots of food; provide non-alcoholic beverages; don't pressure guests to drink; water down drinks when guys are consuming too much alcohol. Don't let guests leave the house if they're tanked; ask them to wait until they've sobered up or to stay overnight. If they make a fuss and insist on leaving, drive them home. It is really amazing that many people don't think about what could happen after guests leave the party. It doesn't take a genius to see that these measures would help reduce drunk driving.

3. REVISING LANGUAGE: GUIDELINES FOR INFORMAL WRITING

For personal and persuasive writing intended for a general audience and for a non-academic audience, follow these guidelines:

1. **Try for the friendly, engaged tone of one person talking to another.** To create this tone, choose most of your words from the standard to slightly informal range (*poor, hard up*). Choose short, common words (those on the right) over longer synonyms.

   possess = own, have   automobile = car

   retain = keep   residence = home

   purchase = buy   difficulties = troubles

2. **Use more formal words to create suggestive images, humour or satire, and subtle shades of meaning.**

   the undulations of the wheat

   the writer was lionized in London, lampooned in LA

   serpentine streets

3. **Use concrete over abstract nouns and specific over general nouns. Abstract nouns** name qualities (*friendship, heroism*) or concepts (*the state, conservatism*). **Concrete nouns** name things we perceive through our senses (*your friend, the brain*). **General nouns** apply to classes of things (*adolescents, buildings*), while **specific nouns** refer to single, specific things (*the teenager who works at The Bay, the CN Tower*). Abstract and general nouns distance your reader.

4. **Use first- and second-person pronouns (*I, you*), where appropriate, to establish a personal relationship with your reader.**

5. **Use occasional contractions, colloquial expressions, or slang terms, if appropriate to your subject and audience.**

6. **Choose *active verbs* over *state-of-being verbs* and *verbs in the passive voice*.** By changing **state-of-being**, or **linking**, verbs (*is, seems, exists, has, contains, feels*) to active verbs, you can often transform a vague general statement into a precise, vivid image.

   NOT   She *has* short brown hair. Her face *is* round.

   BUT   Her short brown hair *cups* her round face.

   NOT   I *felt* angry.

   BUT   I *throbbed* with anger.

   OR   I *stalked* out of the room.

Note that verbs in the **passive voice** can take the energy out of your writing. In the two sentences below, the first focuses on the action whereas the second highlights the actor.

NOT   The winning goal was scored by me.

BUT   In the last few seconds of the game, I nailed the winning goal.

To see how changing the diction can improve a piece of writing, compare the following versions of a paragraph on the perils of sailing. In the first, the formal language makes the danger seem remote, even unreal.

Sample Draft Paragraph

Of course there are those who endure the elements as necessitated to earn a living. Traditionally they are the men of the sea. Sailors maintain many fears in terms of the elements. For instance, atmospheric electricity playing around the mast might cause a fire. To the sailor's peril, ice can cover the rigging, leaving the ship top-heavy and in danger of "turtling." Thrashing waves and Titanic swells can consume both craft and crew.

In the revised paragraph, the simpler language, active verbs, and concrete nouns create a vivid image of a ship in danger.

Sample Revised Paragraph

Sailors have traditionally earned their living by enduring the dangers of the elements. Sailors fear the blue haze of St. Elmo's fire encircling the mast, and its acrid smell of burning. They fear the surge that rises twelve metres above the mizzen and the waves that slam the hull from every direction. The wind, as it sings through the stays, charts a new course without aid of a compass, without earthly reason. But at no time is a sailor's job so perilous as when the wind chill plunges the mercury to minus thirty-five and droplets of mist condense on the supercooled rigging. Then layer upon layer of ice forms. When an ice-laden ship gets top-heavy, no amount of praying will keep it afloat. The captain's call goes out: "The gyros are toppling."

—*Chris Paterson*

Exercise 3

Underline word choices in the following paragraph that you find ineffective for a personal essay. Then rewrite the paragraph using more vivid language.

Chuck is, simply put, a mean person. One would not say that he is a sadist, exactly. He is not of the character to pull the wings off flies, albeit he does, on occasion, step on anthills. He merely loves practical jokes—mean-spirited practical jokes. One time a small, plastic-wrapped packet of cloves was left by Chuck on the desk of a fellow student named Ramona. Attached to the packet with tape was a note that read, "Cloves make an effective breath freshener." Ramona was, with justification, mortified and offended. On other occasions, sample bottles of deodorant and acne medication have been left on classmates' desks. One could say that these tactics work to undermine a person's self-confidence. Chuck also has an inconsiderate mouth. In the recent past, on the day we were being photographed for the yearbook, Jerry Johnson wore a new suit. Hiding behind his most sincere smile, Chuck told Jerry, "Jer, my man, that suit really suits you, ha, ha. I donated one just like it to the Sally Ann last week." I used to laugh at Chuck's peccadilloes, until this morning. As we were walking out of math class, the teacher directly behind us, that insensitive Chuck enunciated clearly, "Ken, I wish you would not say those things about Mr. Mueller. I think he is a fine teacher." I am planning how to asphyxiate Chuck in his sleep. The deed will definitely be done with malice aforethought.

4. BEING CONCISE AND AVOIDING WORDINESS

Whether your prose is formal, informal, or between the two, it is crucial that you avoid unnecessary wordiness.

There are several reasons students often submit wordy writing, but these are the most common: they need to meet the word count; they have written only one draft; they haven't clarified what they want to say; and they think that inflated diction makes them sound more intelligent. The first three reasons can be remedied by brainstorming and writing, whereas the latter can be fixed by thinking about writing in a new way.

Don't worry about sounding intelligent or authoritative; instead, worry about being clear. Understand that in good, clear writing, every word counts. Pruning the deadwood—unessential words, phrases, and sentences—clarifies your meaning and makes your writing easier to read. You want your reader to immediately grasp your meaning, rather than have to figure out what you are *trying to say.*

To make sure that every word counts, many writers set a goal of cutting their writing by 10 percent. If you tend to be wordy, you may need to set your goal even higher, perhaps 20 percent. Here are some practical suggestions for avoiding wordiness:

1. **Eliminate unnecessary repetition of words and ideas.**

REPETITIOUS PHRASE	Formerly, women's clothes were much more restrictive in the past.
REVISED	Women's clothes were much more restrictive in the past.
REPETITIOUS SENTENCES	Macbeth seems shaken by the witches' announcement that he will become king. He is uneasy when they tell him he is destined to gain the throne.
REVISED	Macbeth seems shaken by the witches' announcement that he will become king.

2. **Reduce or eliminate unnecessary phrases, clauses, and sentences.**

   Reduce phrases to single words (*in a short time = shortly*; *a lot of = many* or *much*; *at this point in time = now*).

   Reduce clauses beginning with *that, which*, or *who* to words or phrases.

   NOT   all employees who are interested

   BUT   all interested employees

   NOT   at the position that I was assigned

   BUT   at my position

   NOT   The current focus of the dental profession is reducing gingivitis.

   BUT   Dentistry currently focuses on reducing gingivitis.

3. **Remove any adjective or adverb that adds no new meaning to the sentence.**

   kind of, sort of, actually, basically, really, type of, generally, for all intents and purposes

   WORDY   The small, sporty-looking red car just left us in the dust.

   BETTER   The red sportscar left us in the dust.

4. **Eliminate unnecessary expletive constructions (those beginning with *it is, there are*, and so on).**

   NOT   It is a fact that the car has been stolen.

   BUT   The car has been stolen.

   NOT   It is obvious to everyone here that profits are down.

   BUT   Profits are down.

5. **Omit redundant word pairs.**

   When you use redundant word pairs, you are repeating yourself, revealing that you have either not edited or that you are not familiar with word meanings. Some annoying redundant word pairs are listed below:

   achieve success, true facts, free gift, end result, past history, future plans, unexpected surprise, horrible tragedy, final outcome, important essentials

6. **Replace roundabout expressions (circumlocutions) with shorter, direct expressions.**

INSTEAD OF	USE
the reason for, due to the fact that	BECAUSE
on the occasion that, in a situation in which	WHEN
as regards, in reference to, with regard to	ABOUT
it is crucial that, it is necessary that	MUST, SHOULD
is able to, has the opportunity to	CAN
it is possible that, there is a chance that	MAY, MIGHT, COULD

7. **Be careful with that most dangerous of beasts: the thesaurus.**

When you are revising, you may be tempted to go to your thesaurus to jazz up your vocabulary. If you do, make sure that you use the word nearest the top of the list, which is closest to the original's meaning. Normally, the words further down the list are more emotionally slanted and quite different in meaning from the original. For instance, one of the first synonyms for *like* is "feel partial to," but one of the last synonyms is "feel attracted to." Misusing synonyms, then, might be risky. Read your sentence out loud to make sure that you are not calling up a ridiculous image or using a word out of context.

ORIGINAL   I really like Martha Stewart.

NOT   I am really attracted to Martha Stewart.

BUT   I really think highly of Martha Stewart.

To see how being concise can clarify your meaning, consider these versions of a paragraph from an essay on the importance of options in the school curriculum.

Sample Draft Paragraph

There are a lot of other courses that are very important to children growing up today. Courses such as home economics, industrial education, accounting, and computer courses help children function better in the outside world—whether in the job market or in the home. These courses enable the children to be able to learn about a wide variety of things. Students today learn about health and nutrition, they learn about first aid, how to look after a home (boys as well as girls), they learn how to look after a vehicle, and even how to budget themselves and to do their own taxes. [103 words]

Sample Revised Paragraph

Many other courses are also important to today's adolescents, such as home economics, industrial education, accounting, and computer science. These courses help them function better in both the home and the job market. They also enable students to learn about health and nutrition, first aid, home maintenance, vehicle repair, budget balancing, and completing taxes. [60 words]

Exercise 4

In the following paragraph, underline all unnecessary words, phrases, and sentences. Then rewrite the paragraph in 200 words or fewer without omitting any necessary ideas.

At the base of the argument for an education based on facts lies a dangerous assumption: that a person with a good grasp of general knowledge has the will and the means to examine information critically to determine whether it is true and valid. Realistically, most people who get through school by memorizing information lack either the ability to think critically or the desire to think critically. A simple science fair project conducted by a junior high school student exposes people's failure to think critically and make reasoned judgments. At the Greater Idaho Falls Science Fair in April 1997, the student presented a presentation about the dangers of dihydrogen monoxide. The student asked people to sign a petition to have the chemical banned because of its harmful effects. The harmful effects included the statements that "accidental inhalation can cause death" and that dihydrogen monoxide "is a major component of acid rain." Of fifty people asked, forty-three supported elimination of the chemical, six people were undecided, and one person recognized that dihydrogen monoxide is the chemical term for H_2O. That is, dihydrogen monoxide is water. Clearly, these people did not analyze the situation effectively. The mental habits that enable people to make sound judgments are not inherent. Educators cannot expect that an individual will use his mind to reason, analyze, and make sound judgments simply because that person has a solid base of facts and knowledge. [235 words]

5. AVOIDING COMMONLY MISUSED WORDS

When you are checking your style, be on the lookout for words and expressions that many writers confuse or misuse. Here is a partial list. You will find others in the exercise below.

A Lot

A lot is an informal expression meaning *many, much,* or *a great deal of.* Although you should avoid *a lot* in most writing, when you use it, spell it as two words.

I have **a lot** of chores to do tonight.

All Right

All right should be spelled as two words. *Alright* is incorrect and should not be used.

"**All right**," the coach agreed reluctantly, "you can miss the practice Thursday afternoon."

Allude/Elude

Use *allude* when you mean *refer to,* as in an allusion to the Bible or to Shakespeare. Use *elude* when you mean *to avoid* or *escape.*

In his opening comments, the guest speaker **alluded** to Hamlet's indecision.

The wary old wolf managed to **elude** the hunter.

Among/Between

Use *between* when you are referring to two things. Use *among* when you are referring to more than two.

Divide the bill **between** Susan and Stacy.

Share the birthday cake **among** all the employees.

Amount/Number

Use *amount* to refer to things considered as a mass (*a large amount of work, a small amount of money*). Use *number* to refer to things that can be counted (*a large number of people, a small number* of desks).

A large **amount** of money is missing.

A large **number** of bills were stolen.

Bored with

Use *bored with* (never *bored of*) to mean *wearied with dullness*.

She is **bored with** her courses this year.

Hanged/Hung

Use *hanged* as the past tense of the verb *to hang* when you are referring to a person. Use *hung* when you are referring to objects.

The convict **was hanged** at dawn.

Her latest painting **was hung** in the city gallery.

Hopefully

Hopefully is an adverb meaning *full of hope*. It is used correctly in this sentence: *The sales representative knocked* **hopefully** *at the door.*

Do not use *hopefully* to mean *I hope* or *perhaps.*

NOT   **Hopefully**, we'll be able to meet next week.

BUT   Perhaps [Or: I hope] we'll be able to meet next week.

Lead/Led

The past tense of the verb *to lead* is *led*.

Yesterday he **led** the band in the Earth Day parade.

Less/Fewer

Use *less* with mass nouns (*less unemployment, less hunger*) and *fewer* with countable nouns (*fewer courses, fewer assignments*).

I'm having **fewer problems** this year.

I'm having **less difficulty** this year.

Lie/Lay

The principal parts of the verb *to lie* (to recline) are *lie, lay, lying,* and *lain*.

The principal parts of the verb *to lay* (to place) are *lay, laid, laying,* and *laid*.

Be careful not to confuse these verbs.

NOT   She **lays** on the deck all afternoon.

BUT   She **lies** on the deck all afternoon.

NOT   He **laid** in the sun for half an hour.

BUT   He **lay** in the sun for half an hour.

Like/As

Use *like* as a preposition. Use *as* to introduce a clause.

He danced **like** a maniac.

He danced, **as** he always danced, with gusto.

Loose/Lose

Loose is usually an adjective or adverb (*loose change, loose clothing, let loose*).

Occasionally *loose* is used as a verb meaning *to set free* (*He loosed the dog on the intruder*). Don't confuse *loose* with *lose* (to misplace).

He often **loses** his way when he is in a strange city.

I can give you only a **loose** translation of that phrase.

Take Part in/Partake of

To take part in something is *to join* or *to participate*. *To partake of* is *to have a share of something* (usually a meal).

Hamlet refused to **take part in** the wedding festivities.

Would you be willing to **partake of** our simple meal?

Exercise 5

For each word in the nine sets below, give a brief definition and then use the word in a sentence to distinguish it from the word(s) with which it is often confused. Use the entry for *take part in/partake of* (above) as a guide.

- affect/effect
- allusion/illusion
- cite/sight/site
- disinterested/uninterested
- elusive/illusory
- flaunt/flout
- principal/principle
- than/then
- thereby/therefore

Exercise 6

Correct all the usage errors in the following sentences. Some sentences have more than one error.

1. Although you have put on a few kilos, you still weigh considerably less then your father.

6. VARYING SENTENCE LENGTH

If you have proofed your writing for tone, wordiness, and word use, but your style still seems flat, you may want to vary your sentence length. If you want to create rhythm and emphasize important points, use a combination of short sentences (ten words or fewer), long sentences (thirty words or more), and medium-length sentences.

Short sentences are effective for rendering abrupt actions, giving directions, stating main points, making transitions, and creating emphasis.

ABRUPT ACTIONS	She stopped.
DIRECTIONS	First, stop the bleeding.
MAIN POINTS	One cause of high unemployment is government policy. [Essay topic sentence]
	Safety violations have increased 10 percent over last year. [Report topic sentence]
EMPHASIS	He loved no one.
	The war was over.

Long sentences are effective for expressing continuous action, giving a series of details or examples, and creating a sense of closure.

CONTINUOUS ACTION	After discovering Jack's country address, Algernon assumes his friend's secret identity and poses as wicked Ernest Worthing for his meeting with Cecily, Jack's sheltered young ward; but when they meet for the first time, the worldly, cynical Algernon is momentarily confounded by the sophisticated wit of "little" Cecily.
DETAILS	According to the criteria for student loans, students are considered to be financially independent only if they have no parent, guardian, or sponsor; are married or a single parent; have been out of secondary school for four years; or have been in the labour force for twenty-four months.

In the final analysis, the losers are not merely those who have been jailed for insider trading, nor the firms whose reputations have been sullied, nor the stockholders who have lost money; the losers are all those who have lost confidence in the integrity of the stock market.

Medium-length sentences, which will probably form the majority of your prose, are especially ideal for thesis statements and topic sentences.

THESIS STATEMENT   Although differing in their use of speaker, structure, and language, both Marge Piercy's "Barbie Doll" and Linda Pastan's "Marks" reveal the theme of stifling expectations for women.

7. ADDING INTEREST

If your instructor has told you that your writing is grammatical but that your writing lacks interest or panache, you might consider enlivening your prose by using quotations and other kinds of allusions, dialogue, and figurative language.

Quotations

Use familiar quotations—proverbs, lines from songs, advertising slogans, sayings of famous people, well-known bits of poetry and prose—to create an emotional appeal and a sense of shared experience. Remember to enclose these sayings in quotation marks, use a parenthetical reference (if the quote appears on a specific page), and provide complete bibliographical information at the end of your essay.

> When you are backpacking through Europe, your money will start to dwindle and you will feel moments of fear and desperation. As *The Hitchhiker's Guide to the Galaxy* so wisely advises, "Don't panic."
>
> —*Lori Yanish*

Allusions

An allusion is a casual reference to a figure, event, or document from history, literature, mythology, popular culture, or religion. Allusions not only help to establish your authority as a writer by indicating the breadth of your knowledge or experience but they also establish tone. Allusions can be used straight or ironically.

> Like Caesar, he came, he saw, he restored order where confusion reigned.
>
> —*Chris Carleton*
>
> Her hopes, like Miss Havisham's wedding cake, had been eaten away.
>
> —*Chris Carleton*

> I suspected life at Stephanie's house might be just like life at Dick and Jane's.
>
> —*Suzanne Cook*

Dialogue

Use dialogue for dramatic effect. Direct speech allows you to show what happened rather than merely telling. It also gives variety to your writing by introducing other voices.

> My parents were glued to a small black and white television in room #107. I wandered into the room and tugged on my mother's skirt until she lifted me into her lap. "Look, it's Neil Armstrong," she said as she directed my gaze to the small screen. "He's about to walk on the moon."
>
> —*Mario Trono*

Figurative Language

Figures of speech create vivid mental images for your readers. Use them to sharpen your descriptions and to convey your attitude toward your subject. Try your hand at the five types illustrated below: simile, metaphor, personification, hyperbole, and irony. As stated before, avoid clichés (*dead as a doornail*) and mixed metaphors (*flooded with an iron resolve*), which weaken your writing.

> The snow covered the ground like a thick comforting blanket. [simile]

> The sea dragged its heavy claws against the shore and roared. [personification]
>
> —*Shelley Galliah*

> We are nothing but a jar full of flour beetles, continually eating and reproducing. [metaphor]
>
> —*Cheryl Lewis*

> Those demonic savages, those cruel, sadistic, verminous beings, those bus drivers, have persisted in their heinous acts. [hyperbole]
>
> —*Amanda Thompson*

> Mr. Simpson would pretend to drive into Miss Merril's little BMW just to terrify her in a neighbourly way. [irony]
>
> —*Alex Cheung*

Parallelism

There are two ways to use parallelism in sentences.

- Join two or more closely related clauses with a coordinating conjunction or semicolon. (This pattern is also called a **balanced construction**.)

> You can allow your anxieties to rob you of sleep and satisfaction, or you can plan your time wisely and then enjoy your free time thoroughly.
>
> —*Wendy Amy*

- Arrange a series of words, phrases, or clauses in increasing importance.

Friends listen to you babble, tell you honest opinions when you prefer lies to the truth, tell you *I told you so* at annoying times, defend your reputation from others, and generally mother, father, grandparent, and sibling (brother or sister) you.

—*Amanda Thompson*

Rhetorical Questions

How many times have you waited in the rain or snow for a bus that is ten minutes late? How many times has a surly bus driver snapped an answer to your innocent question? How many times have you stood for half an hour in a bus crammed with people?

—*Cheryl Lewis*

Uncommon Constructions

Use paired conjunctions (*both/and*, *neither/nor*, *not only/but also*) to link ideas.

Neither fear of failure nor desire for glory drove her to practise that trumpet hour after hour.

Exercise 7

Rewrite a paragraph from one of your personal essays so that it includes two or more of the devices discussed in this section.

Exercise 8

Using the specific suggestions in this chapter as a guide, evaluate the stylistic strengths and weaknesses of the following paragraph:

As I returned home from interviewing my new client, I could not stop thinking about Jane. She had done nothing unusual during the interview. In fact, if I had not read her chart she would have appeared like the babysitter next door, except smarter. I felt that, for my own peace of mind and the safety of society, Jane should be wearing a tattoo on her forehead that said "psychopath." Inside I felt entirely unclean. The only emotion that came through clearly was fear. She was not someone who made me feel afraid for my personal safety, but she made me feel afraid for the world. She challenged the way I had categorized the world up until then. Jane was a woman with no mental illness, no deficits of intelligence or social skills, and apparently no conscience. She tortured and killed toddlers. She terrified me.

After proofreading for style, you can move on to the next step: editing for correct grammar, mechanics, and punctuation. Using any resources that your instructor has provided for you, read your essay carefully, focusing on your specific problem areas. For instance, if you struggle with comma use, circle and correct any unnecessary commas. If your instructor has previously commented on your use of fragments (incomplete ideas punctuated as sentences), zero in on these. It is this attention to detail that distinguishes a C from a B paper, or a B paper from an A one. Good luck (with your editing)!

Proofreading Strategies and Sentence Structure

Proofreading Strategies

After you have checked the structure, language, and style of your essay, you need to proofread. Proofreading involves looking for and correcting particular errors in sentence structure, grammar, punctuation, spelling, and format. Don't skip this last step, even if you are pressed for time or simply bored with a piece of writing. Poorly constructed sentences and slips in grammar can bring an A paper down to a B or lower, or a D paper down to an F. Spelling errors in a resumé or cover letter also make your documents look unprofessional; they might even prevent you from being asked for an interview. Assure the reader of your care and competence by giving your writing a final polish.

To locate the rough spots in your writing, try these strategies:

- Leave your paper for at least one day so you can better evaluate your writing.
- Use the Proofreading Checklist at the end of this chapter (before the Answer Key) to remind yourself of potential problems.
- Prepare a checklist of your common errors, which will focus your proofreading.
- Read your paper aloud either to yourself or to a friend. Revise awkward or unclear sentences.
- Read your paper backwards, sentence by sentence. This strategy is especially good for highlighting sentence fragments and spelling errors.
- Use the spell checker and other correction features provided by your word-processing software, but remember to customize the built-in dictionary to reflect Canadian spelling and usage.

Proofreading: Sentence Structure

Among other things, good writing is writing that "flows." Readers are quickly irritated by writing that doesn't flow because sentences are unvaried, incorrectly punctuated, or badly constructed. This section reviews some of the basics of sentence structure along with some of the most common sentence errors: comma splices, fused sentences, fragments, faulty parallelism, faulty subordination, and mixed constructions.

1. PHRASES

The foundations of sentences are phrases and clauses. A **phrase** is a group of grammatically linked words without either a subject or a verb; a **clause** is a group of grammatically linked words containing a subject and a verb. Phrases typically function as parts of speech in a sentence, acting as nouns, adjectives, and adverbs.

Types of Phrases

Verbal phrases consist of a verbal and any other objects and/or modifiers. The three main types of verbal phrases are **infinitive, participle**, and **gerund**.

Infinitive phrases include the infinitive form of the verb (*to* + verb) and the object of the infinitive and/or other related words. When infinitive phrases begin sentences, they must be logically connected to the main clause, or you will create a mistake called the dangling modifier.

> **To buy the music magazine** *Uncut*, you will need at least twelve dollars.

> If you want **to own a CD of rare music**, this magazine is worth your money.

Participle phrases include the present or past particle of the verb (formed by adding *ing* or *ed* to the present tense of the verb) along with the object of the participle and/or any other related words. Participle phrases function as adjectives within the sentence.

> **Jumping up and down**, Alicia shouted that she had won the Lotto 6/49. [*Jumping up and down* describes Alicia.]

> The astronaut **riding the space shuttle** is from Canada. (Which astronaut is from Canada? The one riding the space shuttle.)

> **Boxed in by other runners**, Rami was unable to make a break for the finish line.

When a participle phrase begins the sentence, as in the sentence above, it must be followed by the subject it is describing; if it isn't, the sentence will contain a dangling modifier.

Gerund phrases resemble participle phrases, but they function as nouns, acting as a subject, object, or subject complement.

> **Riding a bike without a light** is very dangerous. [subject] (What is very dangerous? Riding a bike without a light.)

> A behaviour parents often frown upon is **jumping on the furniture**. [subject complement] (What is a behaviour that parents often frown upon? Jumping on the furniture.)

> Adam avoided **working on his paper** while watching the soccer game. [object] (What did Adam avoid while watching the soccer game? Working on his paper.)

Absolute phrases resemble participle phrases that are preceded by a noun or a pronoun. However, absolute phrases have subjects; they can also modify a whole sentence.

Mike looked bloated, **his third dessert creeping up on him**.

Her arms and legs flailing madly, Sarah skated clumsily over the ice.

Prepositional phrases include a preposition, an object of the preposition, and/or any related words. Prepositional phrases can act as adjectives and adverbs. (Don't confuse prepositional phrases beginning with *to* with infinitive phrases.)

When we were camping, we awoke to a large noise **outside our tent**; it was a flying saucer hovering **above the lake**. Terrified, we ran **to the car** as quickly as possible.

Our newly elected mayor, known for attending strip clubs, was a man **of questionable morals**.

Appositives, which rename the subject, are usually placed after it.

We waited in the pub, **our favourite meeting place**.

Darcie, **my mixed-breed mutt**, is immensely spoiled.

Exercise 1

In the sentences below, identify the types of phrases indicated by the bolded words.

1. Although the practice is banned **in some countries**, cropping dogs' ears is still permissible **in the United States**.

2. However, several individual states oppose **performing the procedure**.

3. **Cropping ears, an unnecessary practice**, is controversial because some experts claim that dogs **with cropped ears** experience medical complications, such as infections, phantom pain, and even seizures.

4. Several dogs with this procedure have been known **to have behavioural problems**.

5. **Responding to the controversy**, the national clubs of some breeds have amended their standards **to include breeds with both cropped and non-cropped ears**.

6. Ear cropping is hopefully going out of fashion, **the practice not being taught in most respectable veterinary colleges**.

2. CLAUSES

A **clause** is a group of words containing at least a subject and a verb. An **independent (main) clause** expresses a complete idea and can stand on its own; a **dependent (subordinate) clause** does not express a complete idea.

> To get more exercise, Adam [subject] sometimes cycles to work [infinitive phrase + verb + prepositional phrase].

This subject-verb combination expresses a complete idea and is therefore an independent or main clause.

> After Adam and Darren [subject] run in Whitemud Creek [verb plus prepositional phrase].

Although we have a subject and a verb here, the sentence does not express a complete idea. What happens after these two run? Do they collapse? Stretch? Do yoga? This clause, therefore, is dependent because it needs a main clause to complete it.

> After Adam and Darren run in Whitemud Creek, they go immediately to Tim Hortons.

Types of Dependent Clauses

Dependent clauses can be identified according to their role in the sentence.

Noun clauses, which are the most difficult to recognize, do anything a noun can do; they can act as subject, object, or object of the preposition.

> **What Graham Bell knows about the comma** could fill an entire book. [subject]

> Mr. Boudreau finally revealed **what he had in mind for his staff**. [object]

Adverb clauses, which are the easiest to recognize, tell us something about the sentence's main verb: when, why, under what conditions. They begin with easily recognizable subordinate conjunctions, such as *as*, *because*, *before*, *since*, and *while*.

> **Before Eileen goes to bed tonight**, she has to do four sets of crunches.

> **Although the price of gas keeps increasing**, Albertans still drive large vehicles.

> **Whenever we go to Costco**, we always spend at least three hundred dollars.

Adjective clauses, just like adjectives, give more information about nouns and pronouns in the sentence. They begin with *who*, *which*, or *that*.

> Tim Berners-Lee, **who developed the World Wide Web**, might be shocked that his little invention is more of a marketplace than a library.

Adjective clauses are either **restrictive**, providing necessary information or **nonrestrictive**, giving extra but nonessential meaning.

Bob's Bird Emporium, **which is around the corner**, sells the healthiest parrots. [Because the pet store has already been identified by its name, the information about its location is nonessential. This is a nonrestrictive clause.]

The pet store **that is around the corner** sells the healthiest parrots. [Because we do not know which pet store is being referred to, this clause is restrictive.]

In formal writing, nonrestrictive clauses are introduced with *which* and set off with commas, whereas restrictive clauses are introduced with *that* and have no commas.

Exercise 2

Underline the main or independent clause(s) in each of the following sentences.

1. To prove your hypothesis, you must not falsify data or ignore contradictory evidence.

2. Clarence cut the questioning short with a caustic remark and a withering glance.

3. Furrowing her brow in concentration, Karen wound up for the pitch.

4. When he finished his project, Gavin admired his handiwork: a two-storey birdhouse with a railed porch and cedar roof.

5. Hans scrubbed at the large blue stain on his shirt front, but he couldn't get it out.

Exercise 3

Underline the subordinate (dependent) clauses in the sentences below. Above each subordinate clause, identify the type.

1. African dwarf frogs, or ADF's for short, are aquatic frogs that live submerged.

2. These frogs, which grow to only two inches long from snout to tail, are small enough for medium-sized aquariums.

3. Even though these frogs are tiny, you still need to provide at least 2.5 gallons of aquarium space per frog.

4. You also need to keep the water really clean by making frequent water changes and by using dechlorinators that remove heavy metals.

5. That they need variety in their diet is well known: bloodworms, beef heart, and tadpole pellets, which are all relatively cheap, are acceptable foods for ADF's.

6. Although they spend most of their time swimming, they also are known for their Zen-like behaviour, such as hanging upside down, standing on one leg, or floating.

7. Aquatic frogs, because they are easy to maintain and entertaining to watch, are ideal for people new to aquariums.

3. COMBINING CLAUSES INTO SENTENCES

Being able to distinguish phrases from clauses and understanding how clauses are connected within the larger structure of your sentence will help you to understand the basic types of sentences and help you to punctuate these sentences properly.

A sentence composed of only one independent clause is a **simple sentence**. Simple refers to the grammatical structure, not the content or length of the sentence.

A dragonfly is an insect. [This is a short simple sentence.]

Belonging to the order Odonata, the dragonfly has an elongated body, wide wings, and multifaceted eyes. [This sentence, though long and complicated, is still simple. It opens with a long phrase, but there is only one subject and verb relationship.]

A sentence consisting of two or more independent clauses is a **compound sentence**. Ideal for connecting related ideas, this sentence can be punctuated in three ways.

- **Independent clause + comma + coordinate conjunction (*for, and, nor, but, or, yet, so*) + independent clause**

Dragonflies may appear quite frightening, but they are harmless to humans.

- **Independent clause + semicolon + conjunctive adverb + independent clause (*or* clauses)**

Dragonflies may appear quite frightening; however, they are quite harmless to humans, and they are harmful only to mosquitoes, midges, and small insects.

- **Independent clause + semicolon + independent clause**

Be extremely careful when using a semicolon by itself. Make sure that your two sentences are either closely related and/or similar in structure.

Mosquitoes prey on humans; dragonflies prey on mosquitoes.

A sentence consisting of one independent clause and at least one dependent clause is a **complex sentence**. Complex sentences are ideal for establishing more intricate relationships between ideas. We will go over four ways to punctuate them.

- **Dependent clause + comma + independent clause**

  Although the size and wing span of dragonflies make them appear frightening, these bulky insects are actually harmless to humans.

- **Independent clause + dependent clause**

  A dragonfly will hover for several seconds while it is looking for its meal of mosquitoes.

- **First part of independent clause + comma + dependent clause + comma + second part of independent clause**

  The eyes of dragonflies, which consist of at least 30,000 facets, have 360-degree vision.

- **Dependent clause + comma + independent clause + comma + dependent clause**

  Although they look frightening, dragonflies are mostly enemies to mosquitoes, which they prey on mercilessly.

A special type of compound sentence is the **compound-complex sentence**, which is composed of two independent clauses and at least one dependent clause.

When I am running, I love to stop and watch the dragonflies manoeuvring like so many little coloured helicopters, for they remind of me of nature's ingenuity.

I would love for them to follow me home, so I could train them to clean up my backyard, which is infested with voracious mosquitoes.

Exercise 4

Identify whether the sentences below are simple, compound, complex, or compound-complex. Underline the dependent clauses.

1. According to a study published in *Neurology*, stressed people are more prone to age-related memory loss.

2. This study began with 1,265 people who had no cognitive impairment.

3. Over the course of twelve years, 482 people developed mild cognitive impairment.

4. When these 482 people were questioned about their stress levels, some interesting results were discovered, and they were subsequently analyzed.

5. The researchers found that 40 percent of the people with MCI complained of being frequently stressed, anxious, or angry at someone close to them.

6. This study supported the idea that chronic stressful experiences affect the part of the brain handling stress response, which is also the part regulating memory.

7. Stress plays an important role in the development of Alzheimer's; therefore, we should manage stress to avoid memory loss and to maintain brain health.

Exercise 5

The following paragraph sounds choppy because it is written almost entirely in short, simple sentences. Rewrite the paragraph to improve its sentence variety.

Being your own boss has its downside. I learned the hard way. One summer I decided to go into business for myself. I was tired of my usual part-time jobs. I was tired of the long hours and low pay at the fast-food restaurants and laundries I'd worked at in the past. I decided to strike out on my own. I started up the Domestic Bliss Home and Pet Care Service. It was a house-sitting service for clients away on vacation. I contracted to water plants, take in mail and newspapers, and feed pets. This last responsibility soon proved the most challenging. One of my charges was Baby. Baby was lonely. She was affectionate. She was untrained. She was a twenty-five-kilogram golden retriever who leapt into my arms with joy every time I stepped into her house. Another of my charges was the Queen of Sheba. She was an overstuffed Persian cat with surgical steel claws capable of slicing through even the thickest denim. Another of my charges was Jabberwocky, the parrot, who had apparently committed to memory *A Complete Dictionary of the Vulgar Tongue*. I spent a month cleaning up accidents and cleaning up litter boxes. I longed to be back in uniform behind a counter serving up chicken and fries. I completed the contracts with my current customers. I said farewell to all my furry and feathered friends. I closed the door on Domestic Bliss.

Exercise 6

If you are still having difficulty distinguishing the types of sentences, choose two subjects from this list: your favourite sport, your favourite musical artist, you favourite movie, your pet, or a room in your home. On each subject, write a simple, a compound, a complex, and a compound-complex sentence.

4. FRAGMENTS

Now that you have a basic understanding of the components and the punctuation of sentences, you are ready to recognize the sentence error called the fragment. A **fragment** is an incomplete idea punctuated as a sentence. In some contexts, such as informal letters, press releases, and ads, a fragment can catch your reader's attention.

A wonderful occasion for all of us.

The best buy ever!

A small step, but an important one.

If the rest of your sentences are grammatically complete, a fragment will stand out effectively for emphasis. On the other hand, if you mix several unintentional fragments with intentional fragments, you'll confuse your reader and lose your intended emphasis.

Remember, too, that fragments will make your writing seem less formal. Unless you want a casual tone, avoid fragments in reports, business letters, and essays. Also, ask your instructors how they feel about fragments. If you don't tell them that you are intentionally using fragments, they might mark them as wrong and think that you don't understand sentence structure.

Recognizing Sentence Fragments

- **Phrases or subordinate clauses punctuated as complete sentences**

Sometimes the fragment belongs with the complete sentence that comes before or after it in the passage.

FRAGMENT	Bill could balance a glass of water on his head. Without spilling a drop. [The second construction is a prepositional phrase and, like all phrases, lacks a subject and a verb.]
COMPLETE SENTENCE	Bill could balance a glass of water on his head without spilling a drop. [The phrase has been joined to the sentence before it.]
FRAGMENT	Because there had been two major rent increases in the last two years. Maureen decided to look for a new apartment. [The first construction is a subordinate clause, not a complete sentence.]
COMPLETE SENTENCE	Because there had been two major rent increases in the last two years, Maureen decided to look for a new apartment. [The subordinate clause has been joined to the following sentence to create a complex sentence.]

- **Sentences with missing verbs**

If you remember that verbs ending with *ing* must have an auxiliary or helping verb (such as *be*, *do*, or *have*) to be a complete verb, you'll be less likely to write this kind of fragment.

FRAGMENT	The child frantically searching for her mother.
COMPLETE SENTENCE	The child **was** frantically searching for her mother.

Be especially careful with *being*, which is a participle, not a verb. Avoid the phrase *the reason being*. Use *because* instead.

FRAGMENT The reason for her sore back being that she had fallen.

COMPLETE SENTENCE Her back was sore because she had fallen.

Exercise 7

Revise the following constructions to make them complete sentences.

1. Wendell driving around in circles, unable to find his date's house in the maze-like neighbourhood.

2. According to *The Hitchhiker's Guide to the Galaxy*, forty-two being the answer to the meaning of life, the universe, and everything.

3. After getting up to change channels himself because the remote control battery was dead. Brad sank back exhausted onto the couch.

4. Lydia, the last person I expected to quit school.

5. Angry at the parking attendant for writing up a ticket because the meter had expired.

Exercise 8

Revise the following constructions to make them complete sentences. If the sentence is correct, write **C**.

1. Always quick to judge others, but he bridled at even the mildest criticism.

2. Open your booklets and begin the exam.

3. The fans cheering wildly as the defenceman raced down the ice.

4. Turning his head for an instant to look at his program, Brendan missed the winning goal.

5. A woman with fierce pride and a determined spirit.

6. The reason for the fire being a pot of hot oil left burning on the stove.

7. Last year Donald was the grand prize winner in the Bulwer-Lytton bad writing contest.

8. Tearing open the envelope and nervously removing the transcript of her final grades.

9. Although I could detect movement inside, no one answering my knock.

10. Because he didn't phone in or show up for work.

Exercise 9

Restore the following paragraph to its original form by eliminating all inappropriate sentence fragments.

In life and in literature, people create alternate versions of reality. To avoid facing the unpleasant aspects of the lives they actually live. Or just to make their lives more exciting. In "Spy Story" by Filipino writer Jose Y. Dalisay, for example, Fred has convinced himself that he is a secret agent for the US Embassy. Thinking that everyone around him is a spy and up to no good. Fred creates some excitement in his otherwise boring job as a chauffeur. It's clear to most readers that Mr. Sparks, Fred's boss, is running a prostitution ring. Forcing Fred into the role of a pimp. But Fred imagines that Mr. Sparks is entertaining high-ranking American contacts to foil dangerous espionage activities. As well as commenting on our capacity for self-deception as individuals, "Spy Story," which has a significant political dimension. By setting his story in a seedy bar in the Philippines during the Cold War of the 1950s, Dalisay comments on the distortions of reality widely shared during this time of propaganda, spies, and secrets.

5. COMMA SPLICES

After you have checked your writing for variety in the length of sentences and in the type of sentences, you now have to make sure that you have punctuated these sentences correctly. A common error is the comma splice, which occurs when two **main (independent) clauses** are joined by only a comma (when compound sentences are not punctuated properly) or when **two complete sentences** are joined by only a comma.

COMMA SPLICE   She waved at the helicopter, she did not see the pilot wave back. [two independent clauses separated by only a comma]

COMMA SPLICE   The wind whipped up dead leaves in the yard, violent drops of rain beat against the ground, which looked pulverized. [an independent clause attached to a complex sentence by only a comma]

Comma splices, which indicate a lack of understanding of sentence structure, should be eliminated from your writing. You can do so by asking the following questions, which are derived from your previous reading about clauses:

Recognizing Comma Splices

1. Does my sentence consist of two or more clauses? (If *no*, you have a clause and a phrase; if *yes*, go to 2.)

    Looking grateful, she waved at the departing helicopter. [This is a participle phrase and clause separated by a comma. This is not a comma splice, but a well-constructed sentence.]

She waved at the departing helicopter, she was glad to see him leave. [There are two clauses here, so this could be a comma splice.]

2. Are both of the clauses in my sentence main clauses; that is, does each clause express a complete idea? (If *no*, you have a complex sentence; if *yes*, go to 3.)

She waved at the departing helicopter, she was glad to see him leave. [These are definitely main clauses; each can stand on its own as a sentence.]

3. Have I separated these two main clauses with only a comma? (If *yes*, you have a comma splice. Now that you have recognized it, you need to fix it!)

She waved at the departing helicopter, for she was glad to see him leave.

Exercise 10

Mark the following sentences **SPL** if they contain comma splices or **C** if they are correct.

1. When I worked as a cashier in a local supermarket, I dreaded the monthly special on quarter chicken legs.

2. The packages were poorly sealed, the three legs oozed raw chicken juices and blood.

3. The juices leaked all over the conveyor belt and all over my hands as I scanned and packed the chicken.

4. I was concerned about contamination, I sanitized the belt and my hands with antibacterial cleanser after each order.

5. Despite my best efforts to rid myself of the smell of chicken, my dog would practically knock me to the ground when I returned home.

6. FUSED SENTENCES

A **fused sentence**, sometimes called a **run-on sentence**, occurs when two main clauses or two complete sentences are joined with no punctuation between them. Like the term *simple*, the term *run-on* refers to the grammatical structure of the sentence and not the length or content; that is, a sentence can be quite long without being run-on.

CORRECT   Wendy stopped and glared angrily at the mischievous children as another snowball flew by, narrowly missing her head and crashing into the side of her house.

On the other hand, some fused sentences are quite short.

FUSED   Open the window I need some fresh air.

If you correct a fused sentence by adding only a comma, you will, unfortunately, turn this error into the dreaded comma splice discussed above. However, the good news is that the same techniques can be used for fixing both comma splices and fused sentences.

7. CORRECTING COMMA SPLICES AND FUSED SENTENCES

There are five ways to correct comma splices and fused sentences.

1. **Use a period to separate the two clauses.**

COMMA SPLICE	An enormous wave hit the boat, all those on deck were swept overboard.
REVISED	An enormous wave hit the boat. All those on deck were swept overboard.

2. **Use a comma and coordinating conjunction (*and, but, or, nor, yet, so, for*) to join the two clauses.** When you do so, you create a compound sentence.

FUSED SENTENCE	Peering through the darkness, they could see the lights of the settlement they struggled onward.
REVISED	Peering through the darkness, they could see the lights of the settlement, so they struggled onward. [compound sentence introduced by the participle phrase "Peering . . . darkness"]

3. **Use a semicolon and a conjunctive adverb, such as *however, therefore, thus,* or *then* to join the two clauses, creating another compound sentence.**

COMMA SPLICE	Sean drifted out of high school without a diploma, he now has the job of his dreams.
REVISED	Sean drifted out of high school without a diploma; however, he now has the job of his dreams.

4. **Use a semicolon to join the two clauses if they contain closely related ideas.**

FUSED SENTENCE	Fish stocks have declined in the last ten years fishing licences are now difficult to obtain.
REVISED	Fish stocks have declined in the last ten years; fishing licences are now difficult to obtain.

5. **Change one of the main clauses into a subordinate clause, creating a complex sentence.** Put a comma after the subordinate clause if it comes first in the sentence.

COMMA SPLICE	You need to get more rest, you will get sick.
REVISED	If you don't get more rest, you will get sick.

Exercise 11

First, identify whether the sentence contains a fused sentence or a comma splice; then, using a number of revision methods, revise the sentences to eliminate the errors. To get practice, try to revise the sentences in a variety of ways.

1. A loud crackling sound alerted Gerta to the fact that she had left the foil cover on the dish, both the meal and the microwave oven were ruined.

2. Alicia offered to replace my shift when I called to confirm the arrangement, however, she had changed her mind.

3. As we waited in line, we heard Jason's unmistakable braying laugh, we hoped he wouldn't see us before we could disappear into the darkened theatre.

4. Tina groaned in dismay at the error message she pulled out the massive user guide and started her search for help.

5. Neither team chose Maria, she took her ball and went home.

Exercise 12

Revise the following passage to eliminate all comma splices:

These days many people use their computers as both music stores and stereo systems, it's easy to access, buy, and download music online and then listen to it on a computer. In response, the major labels are experimenting with anti-piracy technology such as non-recordable CDs, they want to stop consumers from trading tunes on the Internet or burning recordable CDs. It's not clear how many non-recordable CDs have actually been released, however, the prospect has aroused considerable commentary. Some people say they have a right to burn their own CDs, the record companies are charging too much. Other people justify CD piracy by arguing that most of the money from sales goes to the companies, not the artists. In any case, it may not be possible to create a copy-proof CD that will still play in a computer. Trying to make one may annoy many consumers, the labels may decide it's not worth the risk.

Exercise 13

Revise the following paragraph to eliminate all fused sentences:

My final recommendation for becoming and staying a non-smoker is to eat Popsicles. Because you are taking on such a big commitment, you deserve a sweet treat now and then. Popsicles are low-calorie treats you will not gain weight. A Popsicle also gives you something to hold and put in your mouth just like a cigarette, but it is not a cigarette. You can choose any flavour you like when you have a really strong craving, you should not tear off the wrapper and plunge the Popsicle into your mouth because it will stick to your tongue and lips. If this happens to you, as it did to me, don't attempt to pull the Popsicle out it hurts. Have one of your support team come to your aid with warm water.

—Athena Greba

8. FAULTY PARALLELISM

The principle of **parallelism** is that similar ideas should be expressed in grammatically similar ways. Whenever you use a coordinating conjunction (*and, but, or, nor, yet, so, for*), be sure to join grammatically equal words, phrases, or clauses. Parallel structures enhance your ideas and logic and reveal that you care about your writing style.

Her New Year's resolutions were to **quit smoking, lose weight**, and **exercise regularly**.

Faulty parallelism occurs when ideas of equal value are not expressed in the same grammatical form.

Her New Year's resolutions were to quit smoking, lose weight, and she wanted to exercise regularly. [Two phrases and a clause create a faulty-parallelism error.]

Avoiding Faulty Parallelism

- **Use the same part of speech for each item in a series of words.**

NOT	The family has wealth, reputation, and **is powerful**. [noun, noun, adjective]
BUT	The family has wealth, reputation, and **power**. [three nouns]

- **Use the same construction for each phrase or clause in a series.**

Do not mix phrases and clauses, or even different kinds of phrases.

NOT	Maurice decided to complete his second year at college, look for a job, and **then he and Eva would get married**.
BUT	Maurice decided to complete his second year at college, look for a job, and **then marry Eva**.

- **Make sure that items in a bulleted or numbered list have the same grammatical form, especially when you are taking notes or writing resumés.**

  NOT   1. Open the packet.
             2. The contents should be poured into a bowl.
             3. Add one cup of water.

  BUT   1. Open the packet.
             2. Pour the contents into a bowl.
             3. Add one cup of water.

  [Note that each item in this list begins with a verb.]

- **Make sure that you include both elements in a comparison.** (Failing to do so creates a mistake known as a **faulty comparison**.)

  NOT   My paper is as long as **Bill**. (Huh? Your paper is the same length as Bill, the person?)

  BUT   My paper is as long as **Bill's** [paper].

  NOT   Sally wants to get married more than him.

  BUT   Sally wants to get married more than he [does].

- **Complete balanced constructions with grammatically similar sentence elements.**

  NOT   The more I work on this assignment, **I don't seem to accomplish much.**

  BUT   The more I work on this assignment, **the less I seem to accomplish.**

- **Read your sentences closely to make sure that correlative conjunctions (*either/or, neither/nor, not only/but also, whether/or, both/and*) join grammatically similar sentence elements.**

  NOT   **Not only** the curtains **but** the drapes were **also** on sale.

  BUT   **Not only** the curtains **but also** the drapes were on sale.

Exercise 14

Make elements in the following sentences parallel. If the sentence is correct, write **C**.

1. Robert can either work and save money for college, or he can take out a student loan.

2. The more I try to convince him otherwise, he is more determined to dye his hair green.

3. The Bennetts' house is smaller than their neighbour.

4. My car needs new paint, new tires, and the transmission is shot.

5. Not only did Marvin borrow my book without asking, but he also bent the cover and wrote in the margins.

6. The store went out of business because of inferior merchandise, their prices were high, and poor customer service.

7. Gina is both a skilled pianist and she is a talented baseball player.

8. Before becoming actors, some famous stars worked in other fields. For example, Harrison Ford was a master carpenter, and there is Michelle Pfeiffer, who was a cashier.

9. Some people keep repeating their mistakes; others keep making new ones.

10. • Graduated from Bishop Stratford High, 2004
    • Diploma in Automotive Repair, Mount Royal College, 2005
    • I took off to travel in Central and South America in 2006–2007
    • Completed my BS in Computing Science in 2010

Exercise 15

The errors in parallel sentence structure introduced into this passage make it wordy and confusing. Revise where necessary to make sentence elements parallel.

In an essay titled "The Pain of Animals," David Suzuki's subject is the pain humans inflict on animals by using them in scientific experiments, we hunt them, and some animals are kept in zoos. Suzuki's thesis is that we use animals for these purposes because their nervous systems are like ours and humans and animals have similar emotional responses. This similarity between humans and animals means, however, that animals feel fear and have pain feelings just as we do. Suzuki develops his essay by giving a series of examples of pain inflicted on animals in zoos and scientists perform experiments on them. He ends his essay with an account of his experience watching a film about the suffering endured by chimpanzees used for medical research. Their agony provides the strongest evidence for his argument that the similarities between chimpanzees and humans ought to make us more compassionate and we shouldn't be as exploitive in our treatment of animals.

9. FAULTY SUBORDINATION

Faulty subordination is both a logical and grammatical error that occurs when you fail to differentiate less important ideas from more important ideas OR when you use an inappropriate subordinate conjunction.

Avoiding Faulty Subordination

- **When you are writing a complex sentence, check that you have attached the subordinate conjunction to the appropriate clause.**

Some common subordinate conjunctions are *before, after, since, while, when, if, unless, until, because, although.* You can signal the connections among your ideas more accurately by putting the less important idea in the subordinate clause and by beginning the subordinate clause with the appropriate conjunction.

NOT   Because he could not go to the gym, he forgot his running shoes.

The subordinate conjunction *because* is in front of the wrong clause, thus making an illogical sentence. Certainly someone can't intentionally forget.

BUT   **Because** he forgot his running shoes, he could not go to the gym.

- **Avoid using subordinate conjunctions colloquially; use the most precise subordinating conjunction.**

Pay particular attention to your use of *since* and *as. Since* can mean *because,* but it can also mean *from the time that.* In some sentences, *since* is confusing. In these cases, it is best to rephrase the sentence.

CONFUSING   Since Sandy broke her leg, she hasn't been playing basketball.

CLEAR   Sandy hasn't played basketball since she broke her leg.

CLEAR   Because Sandy broke her leg, she hasn't been playing basketball.

As is another troublesome conjunction. In colloquial and informal writing, *as* is often used as *because,* but it's clearer to use *as* to mean *during the time that.*

CLEAR   As the rain poured down, we made our way to the deserted cabin.

CONFUSING   **As** she cycles to work, she never gets stuck in traffic.

CLEAR   **Because** she cycles to work, she never gets stuck in traffic.

Note: In your previous education, you may have been told not to begin a sentence with *because.* However, you can do so; just make sure to include a main clause in the sentence.

- **Limit the number of subordinate clauses in a single sentence.**

By piling subordinate clauses on top of each other, you can make it difficult for the reader to judge how your ideas are related. Your reader has to work at sorting out the clauses in order to understand your logic and meaning. Also, if you string too many subordinate clauses together, your sentences take on a monotonous rhythm.

Revise these troublesome sentences by rephrasing the sentence or by reducing some of the clauses to phrases or single words.

NOT	**Because the committee could not reach a decision**, the project was stalled **because no one knew what to do next**.
BUT	The **committee's failure to reach a decision** stalled the project because no one knew what to do next.
NOT	The party **that wins the election, which will be held on November 10**, will set economic policies **that will affect the country** for the next ten years.
BUT	The party **that wins the November 10 election** will set the **country's** economic policies for the next ten years.

Exercise 16

Revise the following sentences to correct faulty or excessive subordination.

1. Since their home was badly damaged by fire, the Wongs have been living in a rented house.

2. Although Gina used the proper amount of bromine, the pool sides were still covered with algae although she also shocked the pool regularly with chlorine.

3. The fireplace that is in the basement has a pilot light that frequently goes out when snow blocks the outside vent.

4. Todd forgot to include his charitable receipts in his income tax return because his refund was delayed.

5. If you want to buy a computer, the person whom you should call is Roman, who is an expert on what are the best buys.

6. Craig isn't doing well in physics although he doesn't seem particularly concerned.

7. When I entered the building, I knew I was late for class when I heard the final bell.

8. Marina hates the taste of ketchup even though she likes ketchup-flavoured potato chips.

9. As I couldn't hear what he was saying, I asked him to speak up.

10. Since the air conditioner broke down, everyone has been complaining about the heat.

10. MIXED CONSTRUCTIONS

In **mixed constructions**, incompatible grammatical units are mixed to produce sentences that seem awkward and illogical. Either the sentence's subject and verb don't go together, or the sentence begins with one grammatical structure and then switches to another. This mistake is often the result of last-minute sentence combining. You can avoid this error by proofreading carefully and by understanding basic sentence construction and punctuation.

For example, let's say you have these two sentences in mind:

June is exhausted because she has three small children.

The reason June is exhausted is that she has three small children.

If you are not paying attention, you might lose track of what you are writing and combine these sentences to produce a mixed construction:

MIXED   The reason June is exhausted is because she has three small children.

You can recognize awkward constructions by reading your work aloud to yourself or a classmate. Here are ways to avoid four common types of mixed constructions:

1. **Think of definitions and explanations as equations joined by the linking verb *is*.** When you use *is* in these equations, it must join two nouns. That is, avoid writing definitions and introducing examples with *is when*, *is where*, and *is because*.

   MIXED   True love is when you lose your mind.

   REVISED   True love is the state of losing one's mind.

   MIXED   A comma splice is where you join two independent clauses with a comma and no coordinating conjunction.

   REVISED   A comma splice occurs if you join two independent clauses with a comma and no coordinating conjunction.

   MIXED   **The reason** the brakes failed **is because** the brake fluid was removed.

   REVISED   The reason the brakes failed is **that the brake fluid was removed**.

   REVISED   The brakes **failed** because the brake fluid was removed.

2. **Make sure that when combining sentences, you don't have an adverbial subordinate clause acting as the subject.** In this error, the sentence starts out as complex one, but then turns into a simple one in which the subordinate clause inappropriately becomes the subject.

   MIXED   **Because he was always late** [subordinate clause] **was the reason** he was fired.

   REVISED   **His habitual lateness** was the reason he was fired.

   REVISED   Because he was always late, he **was fired**.

3. **Make sure you have a subject in the main clause.** Remember that a prepositional phrase is never the subject of a sentence.

MIXED   In the article "Anorexia and the Adolescent" [prepositional phrase] explains Lilian Donaldson's views on the connection between self-starvation and the adolescent's need for control.

REVISED In the article "Anorexia and the Adolescent," Lilian Donaldson [subject] explains the connection between self-starvation and the adolescent's need for control.

REVISED The writer of the article "Anorexia and the Adolescent" [subject] explains her views on the connection between self-starvation and the adolescent's need for control.

4. **Don't create confusion by combining questions and statements.**

MIXED   She wondered how long will it be until I see him again?

REVISED She wondered how long it would be until she saw him again.

REVISED She wondered, "How long will it be until I see him again?"

Exercise 17

Revise the following sentences to eliminate mixed constructions.

1. Geraldine asked her brother Ben how much longer will he be in the shower?

2. Because my dog ate my memory key is the reason my paper is late.

3. Portaging is when you carry a boat overland between navigable lakes or rivers.

4. In Darrin's letter explained why he resigned his position.

5. The reason we cut our vacation short is because it rained for a solid week.

6. Without more donations means that the shelter will have to close.

7. Looking at his bank statement, Dominic wondered how did he spend so much money in only a month?

8. An example of Mary's thoughtfulness is when she cuts the lawn for her elderly neighbours.

9. In the theatre program lists all the actors in the play.

10. The next day is when Frank finally thought of a snappy comeback to Vincent's insulting remark.

Checklist: Proofreading

	OK	NEEDS WORK
	✏	✏

1. Have you corrected errors in **sentence structure**?
  a. fragments, comma splices, fused sentences
  b. faulty parallelism, faulty subordination, mixed constructions
	☐	☐

2. Have you corrected errors in the use of **verbs**?
  a. verb forms
  b. subject-verb agreement
	☐	☐

3. Have you corrected errors in the use of **pronouns**?
  a. pronoun agreement
  b. pronoun form
  c. pronoun reference
	☐	☐

4. Have you corrected errors in the use of **modifiers**?
  a. misused adjectives and adverbs
  b. misplaced and dangling modifiers, split infinitives
	☐	☐

5. Have you corrected errors in **punctuation**?
  a. commas and semicolons
  b. quotation marks
  c. apostrophes
  d. other punctuation
	☐	☐

6. Have you corrected errors in the use **abbreviations**, **capitalization**, and **numbers**?	☐	☐

7. Have you corrected errors in **format**
  a. in MLA-style writing assignments
  b. in APA-style writing assignments
	☐	☐

8. Have you corrected errors in **spelling**?
  a. names, places, titles, other proper nouns
  b. homonyms, frequently misspelled words, typos
	☐	☐

ANSWER KEY

Exercise 1

1. prepositional phrase, prepositional phrase
2. gerund phrase
3. gerund phrase, appositive phrase, prepositional phrase
4. infinitive phrase
5. participle phrase, infinitive phrase
6. absolute phrase

Exercise 2

1. you must not falsify data or ignore contradictory evidence
2. Clarence cut the questioning short
3. Karen wound up for the pitch
4. Gavin admired his handiwork
5. Hans scrubbed at the large blue stain; he couldn't get it out

Exercise 3

1. that live submerged = adjective clause
2. which grow to only two inches long from snout to tail = adjective clause
3. Even though these frogs are tiny = adverb clause
4. that remove heavy metals = adjective clause
5. That they need variety in their diet = noun clause; which are all relatively cheap = adjective clause
6. Although they spend most of their time swimming = adverb clause
7. because they are easy to maintain and entertaining to watch = adverb clause

Exercise 4

1. simple
2. complex   <u>who had no cognitive impairment</u>
3. simple
4. compound-complex   <u>When these 482 people were . . . levels</u>
5. complex   <u>that 40 percent of the people . . . them</u>
6. complex   <u>that . . . response, which . . . memory</u>
7. compound

Exercise 5

Answers to this exercise will vary, but you should make sure that your paragraph has a variety of simple, compound, complex, and compound-complex sentences as well as a variety of short and long sentences.

Exercise 6

Answers for this exercise will vary.

Exercise 7

1. Wendell **drove** around in circles, unable to find his date's house in the maze-like neighbourhood.

2. According to *The Hitchhiker's Guide to the Galaxy*, forty-two **is** the answer to the meaning of life, the universe, and everything.

3. After getting up to change channels himself because the remote control battery was **dead**, **Brad** sank back exhausted onto the couch.

4. Lydia **is** the last person I expected to quit school.

5. **The driver was** angry at the parking attendant for writing up a ticket because the meter had expired.

Exercise 8

1. **He was** always quick to judge others, but he bridled at even the mildest criticism.

2. **C**

3. The fans **cheered** wildly as the defenceman raced down the ice.

4. **C**

5. **She is** a woman with fierce pride and a determined spirit.

6. The reason for the fire **was** a pot of hot oil left burning on the stove. [**Or:** The fire was caused by a pot of hot oil left burning on the stove.]

7. **C**

8. **She tore** open the envelope and nervously **removed** the transcript of her final grades.

9. Although I could detect movement inside, no one **answered** my knock.

10. Because he didn't phone in or show up for work, **Garry lost his job**.

Exercise 9

In life and in literature, people create alternate versions of reality to avoid facing the unpleasant aspects of the lives they actually live or just to make their lives more exciting. In "Spy Story" by Filipino writer Jose Y. Dalisay, for example, Fred has convinced himself that he is a secret agent for the US Embassy. **Thinking that everyone around him is a spy and up to no good, Fred creates some excitement in his otherwise boring job as a chauffeur.** It's clear to most readers that Mr. Sparks, Fred's boss, is running a prostitution ring **and forcing** Fred into the role of a pimp. But Fred imagines that Mr. Sparks is entertaining high-ranking American contacts to foil dangerous espionage activities. **As well as commenting on our capacity for self-deception as individuals, "Spy Story" has a significant political dimension.** By setting his story in a seedy bar in the Philippines during the Cold War of the 1950s, Dalisay comments on the distortions of reality widely shared during this time of propaganda, spies, and secrets.

Exercise 10

1. **C**

2. **SPL**

3. **C**

4. **SPL**

5. **C**

Exercise 11

Because sentences containing comma splices can be corrected in a number of ways, these sentences suggest only one of a number of possible revisions.

1. A loud crackling sound alerted Gerta to the fact that she had left the foil cover on the dish; both the meal and the microwave oven were ruined.

2. Alicia offered to replace my shift; however, when I called to confirm the arrangement, she had changed her mind.

3. As we waited in line, we heard Jason's unmistakable braying laugh. We hoped he wouldn't see us before we could disappear into the darkened theatre.

4. Tina groaned in dismay at the error message; then she pulled out the massive user guide and started her search for help.

5. Neither team chose Maria, so she took her ball and went home.

Exercise 12

These days many people use their computers as both music stores and stereo systems: **it's** easy to access, buy, and download music online and then listen to it on a computer. In response, the major labels are experimenting with anti-piracy technology such as non-recordable CDs **because** they want to stop consumers from trading tunes on the Internet or burning recordable CDs. It's not clear how many non-recordable CDs have actually been released; **however**, the prospect has aroused considerable commentary. Some people say they have a right to burn their own CDs **because [, for]** the record companies are charging too much. Other people justify CD piracy by arguing that most of the money from sales goes to the companies, not the artists. In any case, it may not be possible to create a copy-proof CD that will still play in a computer. Trying to make one may annoy many consumers, **and so** the labels may decide it's not worth the risk.

Exercise 13

My final recommendation for becoming and staying a non-smoker is to eat Popsicles. Because you are taking on such a big commitment, you deserve a sweet treat now and then. Popsicles are low-calorie treats, **so** you will not gain weight. A Popsicle also gives you something to hold and put in your mouth just like a cigarette, but it is not a cigarette. You can choose any flavour you like. **When** you have a really strong craving, you should not tear off the wrapper and plunge the Popsicle into your mouth because it will stick to your tongue and lips. If this happens to you, as it did to me, don't attempt to pull the Popsicle out. **It** hurts. Have one of your support team come to your aid with warm water.

Exercise 14

1. Robert can either work and save money for college or take out a student loan.

2. The more I try to convince him otherwise, the more determined he is to dye his hair green.

3. The Bennetts' house is smaller than their neighbour's.

4. My car needs new paint, new tires, and a new transmission.

5. Marvin not only borrowed my book but also bent the cover and wrote in the margins.

6. The store went out of business because of inferior merchandise, high prices, and poor customer service.

7. Gina is both a skilled pianist and a talented baseball player.

8. Before becoming actors, some famous stars worked in other fields. For example, Harrison Ford was a master carpenter, and Michelle Pfeiffer was a cashier.

9. **C**
10. • High school diploma, 2004
    • Diploma in Automotive Repair, 2005
    • Travel in Central and South America, 2006–2007
    • BS in Computing Science, 2010

Exercise 15

In an essay titled "The Pain of Animals," David Suzuki's subject is the pain humans inflict on animals by using them in scientific experiments, **hunting them, and keeping them in zoos**. Suzuki's thesis is that we use animals for these purposes because their nervous systems **and emotional responses** are like ours. This similarity between humans and animals means, however, that animals feel fear and **pain** just as we do. Suzuki develops his essay by giving a series of examples of pain inflicted on animals in zoos and **in scientific experiments**. He ends his essay with an account of his experience watching a film about the suffering endured by chimpanzees used for medical research. Their agony provides the strongest evidence for his argument that the similarities between chimpanzees and humans ought to make us more compassionate **and less exploitive** in our treatment of animals.

Exercise 16

1. Because their home was badly damaged by fire, the Wongs have been living in a rented house. [**Or:** The Wongs have been living in a rented house since their home was badly damaged by fire.]

2. Although Gina used the proper amount of bromine and shocked the pool regularly with chlorine, the pool sides were still covered with algae.

3. The pilot light in the basement fireplace frequently goes out when snow blocks the outside vent.

4. Because Todd forgot to include his charitable receipts in his income tax return, his refund was delayed.

5. If you want to buy a computer, call Roman, who is an expert on the best buys.

6. Although Craig isn't doing well in physics, he doesn't seem particularly concerned.

7. When I entered the building and heard the final bell, I knew I was late for class.

8. Even though Marina hates the taste of ketchup, she likes ketchup-flavoured potato chips.

9. Because I couldn't hear what he was saying, I asked him to speak up.

10. Everyone has been complaining about the heat since the air conditioner broke down.

Exercise 17

1. Geraldine asked her brother Ben how much longer he would be in the shower.

2. Because my dog ate my memory key, my paper is late.

3. Portaging is carrying a boat overland between navigable lakes or rivers.

4. In his letter, Darrin explained why he resigned his position.

5. We cut our vacation short because it rained for a solid week.

6. Without more donations, the shelter will have to close.

7. Looking at his bank statement, Dominic wondered how he had spent so much money in only a month.

8. Mary shows her thoughtfulness when she cuts the lawn for her elderly neighbours.

9. The theatre program lists all the actors in the play.

10. The next day Frank finally thought of a snappy comeback to Vincent's insulting remark.

Proofreading: Verbs

Because the most important components of sentences are subjects and verbs, it is important that we use the right tense and form of verbs and that we make our subjects and verbs agree. It is also crucial to use the right verb voice. These are not easy tasks, however. Because the English verb system is quite complex, it's easy to make errors involving both verb tenses and verb forms.

1. THE PRINCIPAL PARTS OF VERBS

Each verb has four principal parts, from which all its other forms are derived.

- The **infinitive** form (*to* + a verb) names the verb: *to walk, to run, to think*. The present tense is derived from the infinitive: *I **walk**, you **walk**, she **walks***.
- The **past tense**: *Yesterday I **walked** to school.*
- The **present participle**: *I **am walking** to school right now.*
- The **past participle**: *I **have walked** to school every day this week.*

Regular verbs form the past tense and the past participle by adding *ed* to the infinitive: *walked, have walked; visited, have visited.*

Irregular verbs form the past tense and the past participle in a variety of ways: *drank, have drunk; brought, have brought; ran, have run*, etc. If you are not sure of the principal parts of an irregular verb, check your dictionary, or search the Web for a list of irregular verbs in English.

2. AUXILIARY VERBS

A number of verb tenses are formed by combining a participle with one or more **auxiliary verbs**:

am, is, was, were	*can, could, may, might*
be, being, been	*shall, should, will, would*
have, has, had	*ought to, have to, used to*
do, does, did	*supposed to*

From *Forms of Writing: A Rhetoric and Handbook*, Sixth Edition, Kay L. Stewart, Marian Allen, Shelley Galliah. Copyright © 2012 by Pearson Canada Inc. All rights reserved.

3. COMMON ERRORS WITH VERBS

- ## Using the past participle instead of the past tense

  NOT   I **seen** [past participle] him yesterday.

  BUT   I **saw** [past tense] him yesterday.

- ## Using an auxiliary verb with the past tense

  NOT   Ahmed **had went** to visit his parents in Manitoba.

  BUT   Ahmed **went** to visit his parents in Manitoba.

  OR   Ahmed **had gone** to visit his parents in Manitoba.

- ## Using *being* as a main verb instead of *is* or *was*

  NOT   The reason **being** that I was already late.

  BUT   The reason **is** that I was already late.

- ## Using *of* to mean *have*

  NOT   He should **of** known better.

  BUT   He should **have** known better.

- ## Using too many *coulds* or *woulds* in *if/then* statements

  NOT   If you **would have asked** me, I would have helped.

  BUT   If you **had asked** me, I would have helped.

- ## Omitting verb endings

Be sure the verb ending agrees with the subject of the sentence and that the tenses are consistent.

    NOT   She **walk** to the video store.

    BUT   She **walks** to the video store. [simple present tense]

    NOT   After they **watched** the movie, they **walk** home.

    BUT   After they **watched** the movie, they **walked** home.

    [simple past tense]

- ## Misplacing prepositions that are part of phrasal verbs

If English is not your first language, you may find phrasal verbs (verb + preposition that functions as part of the verb, such as *figure out, look up, take care of*) confusing. If in doubt, keep the preposition with the verb.

    NOT   He **looked** his brother **after**.

    BUT   He **looked after** his brother.

Exercise 1

Revise the following sentences so that auxiliaries and principal parts are used correctly. If the sentence is correct, write **C**.

1. You should of did the dishes instead of playing computer games.

2. How could you have wore a hole in your new running shoes already?

3. Whenever Martin gets the urge to work, he lies until down he feels better.

4. If I would have known you were in town, I would have invited you to the party.

5. The reason being that they couldn't find a babysitter.

6. Yvette rung the doorbell and waited to be admitted.

7. Susan has not wrote to her parents in over two months.

8. If Tom had submitted the essay on time, he would not have lost marks.

9. I am positive that I seen Jocelyn at the concert, but she insists that she wasn't there.

10. Rosa has swum in that lake every summer since she was a child.

4. KEEPING VERB TENSES CONSISTENT

Once you have decided on the tense—present, past, or future—of a particular piece of writing, be consistent. Occasionally, you may have to shift tenses to clarify time relationships, but don't do so unnecessarily. Use the present tense when you are writing about literature.

Note the use of the present tense in the following paragraph analyzing Stacey MacAindra, who is the central character in Margaret Laurence's novel *The Fire Dwellers*.

Stacey's inability to communicate with her husband and children is a manifestation of the "tomb silences" of her own parents. Again we see Laurence's concern with the past as a source of isolation, for Stacey's background does not give her the means to be fully open with others. Moreover, she is a victim not only of her past but also of the past influences that shape her husband, Mac, who inherits his reticence and his tendency to misinterpret Stacey's remarks from a father who is himself often restrained and imperceptive. Because of their childhoods, both Stacey and Mac believe that "nice" people do not talk about fear or pain. Stacey understands the limitations of this belief, but her inability to free herself from its influence leads her to remark that everyone in her family is one-dimensional. This image conveys Stacey's feelings of dissociation from her husband and children.

Exercise 2

Revise the following paragraph to eliminate unnecessary tense shifts. Use the present tense. The paragraph deals with Thomas Hardy's novel *The Mayor of Casterbridge*.

It's important to see that Michael Henchard in Thomas Hardy's novel *The Mayor of Casterbridge* is a kind of Everyman figure. Like most of us, he is motivated by psychological forces that he did not recognize or understand. For example, he never seems to understand why he sells his wife and then remarried her. Henchard was also affected by external forces over which he, like the rest of us, has no control. During the 1840s when the novel was set, long-established agricultural practices were being modernized by machines, and business practices are now much more complex. In addition to the forces of industrialization, Henchard, as a wheat trader, is especially vulnerable to natural forces such as the weather. After all, he made his living by predicting the harvest yields. Finally, Henchard is affected by chance and coincidence. It just happens that Farfrae, the man with exactly the skills Henchard needed, showed up when he is looking for an assistant manager.

5. MAKING SUBJECTS AND VERBS AGREE

Along with keeping your verb tenses consistent, you also need to make sure that your subjects and verbs agree.

The principle of **subject-verb agreement** is that singular subjects take singular verbs and plural subjects take plural verbs. This principle can be a bit confusing to non-native speakers because in the English language, singular subjects have no *s* whereas singular verbs do; on the other hand, plural subjects have an *s* whereas plural verbs do not.

My **dog Darcie bolts** when **she sees** a squirrel. [singular]

The **dogs bolt** when they see a squirrel. [plural]

Darcie and Bandit often **chase** balls. [plural]

Here are the most common causes of errors in subject-verb agreement:

- **The indefinite pronouns *everyone*, *no one*, or *each* as the subject**

Remember that the indefinite pronouns *everyone*, *no one*, and *each* as subjects are *always* singular.

Everyone is going to be at the party tonight.

No one leaves until I say so.

- **Pronouns *either* or *neither* as the subject**

When *either* and *neither* appear alone (without their sidekicks *or* and *nor*), they are singular.

Neither of these menus **appears** to be satisfactory.

Either movie **is** fine with me.

- **Subjects linked by paired conjunctions: *either/or*, *neither/nor*, *not only/but also***

However, in sentences with the paired conjunctions above, the subject closest to the verb makes the verb singular or plural.

Neither Reuben nor **his cousins were prepared** to kiss the bride.

Not only the students but also the **teacher was delighted** by the unexpected holiday.

- **A prepositional phrase separating subject and verb**

The subject and verb may be separated by a prepositional phrase (*of the workers, between the houses, across the field, including all team members, along with all his supporters*). Remember to disregard these words and concentrate on matching the verb to the actual subject.

One of the workers **has filed** a complaint with the grievance committee.

Mrs. Murphy, along with her five noisy children, **attends** mass regularly.

- **Sentences beginning with *there* or *here***

There or *here* may be the first word of the sentence, but neither will be the subject of the sentence. Look for the genuine subject, which comes after the verb.

There **are** only five **bananas**, not enough for everyone.

Here **come** the **Jackson twins**, just in time for dinner.

- **Subjects that may be singular or plural**

The verb accompanying pronouns such as *all, none,* or *some* as well as fractional expressions will be determined by whether what follows can or cannot be counted.

None of the cake **is** left.

None of the cookies **are** left.

Some of the students **are** going.

Some of the student body **is** here.

Half of the grain **has** been damaged. (cannot really count the grain)

Two-fifths of the students **were** convinced that there would be no final exams.

Collective nouns, such as *team, group,* and *committee,* are considered singular when they refer to people or things acting as a unit.

Our **team is** on a five-day road trip.

The **herd has settled down** for the night.

However, collective nouns are considered plural when they refer to people or things in the group acting individually or not as a unit.

The **team do** not **agree** about the need for a new manager.

The **herd have scattered** in every direction.

Collective nouns of quantity (*number, majority, percentage*) are singular when preceded by *the,* plural when preceded by *a.*

The number of unemployed people **is increasing**.

A number of unemployed people **are** still **looking** for jobs.

Words joined by *and* are considered singular when they refer to a single unit or to the same person.

Bread and butter makes a fine basis for a sandwich.

My **neighbour and best friend has moved** to another city.

Exercise 3

Make subjects and verbs agree in the sentences below. If the sentence is correct, write **C**.

1. Neither Stephanie nor her sisters is available to help at the bazaar on Saturday.

2. The team have won the championship fours years in a row.

3. Neither of the applicants are willing to relocate to a branch office.

4. There goes the Pied Piper, along with all the children of Hamelin.

5. Fear of falling and of loud noises are instinctive.

6. Either the love birds or the goldfish make a suitable pet for an apartment resident.

7. The number of hamburgers sold has increased significantly this quarter.

8. The jury have been sequestered for three days.

9. Each of the committee members have made a different selection for Citizen of the Year.

10. Nothing I've seen in the last three clothing stores seem suitable for graduation.

6. UNDERSTANDING AND USING THE ACTIVE AND PASSIVE VOICE

English verbs have two voices: the **active** and the **passive**. In an active construction, the subject performs the action of the verb and the sentence is set up as subject + verb in the active voice + object. In a passive construction, the subject is acted upon and the sentence is set up as object + verb in passive voice + subject. In the passive voice, the subject may be present and preceded by the preposition *by*, or the subject may be absent.

Edward made the announcement. [active]

The announcement was made by Edward. [passive]

The announcement was made. [passive]

When to Use the Active Voice

In most writing situations, it's best to use the active voice. Active constructions are usually more concise and more forceful than passive constructions.

PASSIVE   The homeowners were informed by the city that the weeds would have to be cleared from their lots immediately.

ACTIVE   The city informed the homeowners that they would have to clear the weeds from their lots immediately.

When to Use the Passive Voice

However, there are certain circumstances in which you should use the passive voice.

- **When you don't know the person or agent that/who performed the action**

  My bike was stolen last night.

  The streets of prairie cities are typically laid out in a grid pattern.

- **When you want to emphasize the person, place, or object acted upon rather than the agent performing the action**

  Janna's sister was run over by a drunk driver.

- When you want to avoid blaming, giving credit, or accepting responsibility

  Jeremy's two front teeth were knocked out.

  The lowest bid was submitted by Megaproject Developments.

  My ring was lost.

- **When you want to sound objective, as in scientific, technical, and legal writing**

  The experiment was repeated with four groups of subjects.

  All construction work must be completed by November 15.

  The defendant was found guilty and sentenced to five years in prison.

Note: Passive constructions distance you and your reader from your material. Don't use them merely to sound more formal; use them carefully, making sure you follow the above guidelines. Your writing will be more lively, engaging, and concise if you use the active voice whenever possible.

Being Consistent

Avoid mixing active and passive constructions in the same sentence.

NOT   A letter was written by the homeowners saying the weeds would be cleared when they (the homeowners) were good and ready.

BUT   The homeowners wrote a letter saying they would clear the weeds when they were good and ready.

Exercise 4

Change passive constructions to active constructions where appropriate. If the passive voice is preferable, write **C**. Be prepared to defend your choices.

1. The light changed to amber before the intersection was reached by Oliver.

2. The municipal swimming pool was opened for the summer last week.

3. My directions were completely misunderstood by Burt.

4. After much lengthy debate, the meeting was finally adjourned.

5. The milk, eggs, butter, and cream were mixed by Marietta.

6. The building site has been shut down until all safety hazards have been eliminated.

7. Marcia was hurt by Sarah's careless remark.

8. Three trials of the experiment were performed by the researchers.

9. Before setting out to write my exam, I searched for my good luck pen, but it couldn't be found anywhere.

10. The newspaper was delivered late again this morning.

Weblinks

- Online English Grammar, which has useful information on grammar and writing topics.

   www.edufind.com/english/grammar/index.cfm

- a handy list of irregular verbs provided by Purdue University's Online Writing Lab (OWL).

   owl.english.purdue.edu/handouts/esl/eslirrverb.html

- OWL's explanation of verb tenses

   owl.english.purdue.edu/handouts/esl/esltensverb.html

- exercises on subject-verb agreement from *Grammar Bytes*

   www.chompchomp.com/exercises.htm#Subject-Verb_Agreement

- an explanation of subject-verb agreement and link to interactive exercises

   grammar.ccc.commnet.edu/grammar/sv_agr.htm

ANSWER KEY

Exercise 1

1. should have done

2. have worn

3. **C**

4. had known

5. The reason is

6. rang

7. has not written

8. **C**

9. saw

10. **C**

Exercise 2

It's important to see that Michael Henchard in Thomas Hardy's novel *The Mayor of Casterbridge* is a kind of Everyman figure. Like most of us, he is motivated by psychological forces that he **does** not recognize or understand. For example, he never seems to understand why he sells his wife and then **remarries** her. Henchard **is** also affected by external forces over which he, like the rest of us, has no control. During the 1840s when the novel **is** set, long-established agricultural practices were being modernized by machines and business practices **were becoming** much more complex. In addition to the forces of industrialization, Henchard, as a wheat trader, is especially vulnerable to natural forces such as the weather. After all, he **makes** his living by predicting the harvest yields. Finally, Henchard is affected by chance and coincidence. It just happens that Farfrae, the man with exactly the skills Henchard **needs**, **shows** up when he is looking for an assistant manager.

Exercise 3

1. sisters/are

2. team/has

3. Neither/is

4. **C**

5. Fear/is

6. goldfish/makes

7. **C**

8. jury/has

9. Each/has

10. Nothing/seems

Exercise 4

1. The light changed to amber before Oliver reached the intersection.

2. **C** [The agent opening the pool is unknown or unimportant.]

3. Burt completely misunderstood my directions.

4. **C** [The agent adjourning the meeting is unimportant.]

5. Marietta mixed the milk, eggs, butter, and cream.

6. **C** [The agents shutting down the site and eliminating the safety hazards are unknown.]

7. **C** [if you want to emphasize Marcia's feelings]

8. The researchers performed three trials of the experiment.

9. Before setting out to write my exam, I searched for my good luck pen, but I couldn't find it anywhere.

10. **C** [The sentence emphasizes the late delivery.]

Proofreading: Pronouns

Pronouns substitute for nouns or other pronouns. The word to which a pronoun refers is called its **antecedent**.

My **grandmother** goes bowling every Wednesday. Then **she** eats lunch at **her** fitness club. [**Grandmother** is the antecedent of **she** and **her**.]

We will discuss the five most common types of pronoun problems:

- pronoun shifts
- pronoun case errors
- possessive pronoun errors
- pronoun agreement errors
- pronoun reference errors

1. PRONOUNS OF ADDRESS

Just as you must choose what verb tense to use in writing a composition, you must choose what pronoun of address to use and then stick with it. You establish your relationship to the reader by the **pronouns of address** you use (or don't use) in your first paragraph.

If you want readers to focus on you—your ideas, your experiences—use first-person pronouns (*I, me, my, mine*). If you want readers to consider how your subject relates to them directly (as in sermons, advertisements, directions), use second-person pronouns (*you, your, yours*). If you use only nouns and third-person pronouns (*he, she, it, they*), you will encourage readers to focus on your subject.

These sentences illustrate the different relationships you might establish with your readers in an article about word processors.

FIRST PERSON	When I first began to use a computer, I lost several files.
SECOND PERSON	When you first begin to use a computer, you may lose a few files.
THIRD PERSON	When most people first begin to use computers, they lose a few files.

Once you have established the basic pronouns of address for a piece of writing, do not shift abruptly and without reason to another set of pronouns.

From *Forms of Writing: A Rhetoric and Handbook*, Sixth Edition, Kay L. Stewart, Marian Allen, Shelley Galliah.

NOT	When **you** first begin to use a word processor, **one** may lose a few files. [shift from second person to third person]
NOT	When **most people** begin to use a word processor, **you** may lose a few files. [shift from third person to second person]

Confusing pronoun shifts may occur *between* as well as *within* sentences.

NOT	When **I** began to use a word processor, **I** lost several files. **You** find it hard at first to master the sequence of commands. [shift from first person to second person]

These shifts disrupt your relationship with the reader and make your writing hard to follow.

Correcting Pronoun Shifts

In the following example, the perspective shifts from the third person, *Conrad* (*his*), to the second person, *you.*

Conrad has invested **his** money wisely because, as an oil rig worker, **you** always face the possibility of seasonal unemployment.

There are two ways to correct this error.

- **Replace *you* with *he*.**

  Conrad has invested **his** money wisely because, as an oil rig worker, **he** always faces the possibility of seasonal unemployment.

- **Rephrase the sentence to eliminate the use of the pronoun.**

  Conrad has invested his money wisely because oil rig workers always face the possibility of seasonal unemployment.

Exercise 1

Revise the following sentences to eliminate pronoun shifts. Where there are several possibilities, be prepared to explain your choice. If the sentence is correct, write **C**.

1. I dislike asking Pauline for help because you never know whether she will keep her promise.

2. Even when you are knowledgeable and competent, many sales associates find dealing with a difficult customer to be an unnerving experience.

3. When you see Simon, you will be surprised at the changes in his appearance.

4. The owners claim that you can hear their ancestor's ghost on his nightly tour of the old mansion.

5. Colin has agreed to have a root canal rather than an extraction because you don't want to lose a tooth that can be saved.

Exercise 2

Revise the following paragraph to eliminate all pronoun shifts:

Participants will get a more effective workout in your next fitness class if you follow this advice. Novices should position themselves near the instructor so you can see and hear clearly. The participant near the front is also less likely to be distracted by other participants. We should give the class our full attention, so don't spend your time worrying about whether other people are watching you or whether you put enough change in the parking meter. Although one might be tempted to compensate for lack of ability with expensive exercise clothes, don't spend a fortune on exercise accessories. All participants really need is a T-shirt, shorts, running shoes, and a willingness to devote an hour to their own good health.

2. PRONOUN CASE

The **subject pronouns** (*I, we, you, he, she, it, they*, and *who*) are used as the subject of a sentence or a clause—who or what is performing the action. The **object pronouns** (*me, us, you, him, her, it, them*, and *whom*) are used as the object of a verb or a preposition—who or what is receiving the verb's action, either directly or indirectly. The most common error in pronoun case is confusing the subject and object pronouns.

Subject Pronouns

Use subject pronouns in the subject position in the sentence. Don't be confused when the pronoun is part of a compound subject.

NOT   Frances and **me** went to the Farmers' Market on Saturday to buy vegetables.

BUT   Frances and **I** went to the Farmers' Market on Saturday to buy vegetables.

Don't be confused when the subject pronoun is followed by an explanatory noun (*we home owners, we students, we smokers*). The pronoun is still in the subject position.

NOT   **Us** residents are presenting a petition to city council.

BUT   **We** residents are presenting a petition to city council.

Use subject pronouns after comparisons using *than* or *as*.

NOT   Peter is as tall as **me**.

BUT   Peter is as tall as **I (am tall)**.

NOT   No one was more surprised than **her**.

BUT   No one was more surprised than **she (was)**.

Use a subject pronoun as the subject of an embedded subordinate clause. Be especially careful with *that* clauses.

NOT   Ramesh said that **him** and his wife would be glad to help.

BUT   Ramesh said that **he** and his wife would be glad to help.

If you are confused, seek out the verb in the clause and match it with the pronoun. For instance, in the above examples, you wouldn't write *him would be glad to help*; you would write *he would be glad to help*.

Object Pronouns

Use object pronouns as the direct or indirect object of a verb. A direct object answers *what* whereas an indirect object answers *to whom* or *for whom*.

NOT   The manager assigned Loretta and **she** a double shift.

BUT   The manager assigned Loretta and **her** [indirect object] a double shift [direct object].

NOT   Please let your mother or **I** know when you will be home.

BUT   Please let your mother or **me** know when you will be home.

Use object pronouns in prepositional phrases.

NOT   Between you and **I**, there is something strange about our new neighbour's nocturnal digging.

BUT   Between you and **me**, there is something strange about our new neighbour's nocturnal digging.

NOT   The city replied to **we** homeowners.

BUT   The city replied to **us** homeowners.

Note: Don't use a **reflexive pronoun** (a pronoun ending in *self/selves*) as a substitute for a subject or object pronoun. Some students mistakenly think that reflexive pronouns make their writing more formal. However, a reflexive pronoun must reflect on the subject or complete the meaning of the verb; it can be used only when there is a subject pronoun in the sentence.

OK   She asked **herself** if she was ready to go on stage.

OK   He allowed **himself** a third trip to the buffet table.

NOT   My family and **myself** will be going to Nova Scotia for a camping holiday.

BUT   My family and **I** will be going to Nova Scotia for a camping holiday.

NOT   Ms. Chang asked that all inquiries be directed to **herself** rather than to Mr. Morgan.

> **BUT**   Ms. Chang asked that all inquiries be directed to **her** rather than to
> Mr. Morgan.

Who and Whom

Who is a subject pronoun. Use it to refer to a subject noun or pronoun.

> Helen is the candidate. She is sure to win.

> Helen is the candidate **who** is sure to win. [*Who* replaces *she*.]

Whom is an object pronoun. Use it after prepositions and to refer to an object noun or pronoun.

> **To whom** do you wish to speak?

> He is a lawyer. We can trust him.

> He is a lawyer **whom** we can trust. [*Whom* replaces *him*.]

Exercise 3

In these sentences, correct all pronoun case errors. Mark **C** for the correct sentences.

1. Us workers must stand firm in our demand for safer conditions.

2. Him and me agree on hardly anything.

3. Todd is no more likely to know the answer than her.

4. Can you tell me who to contact about this insurance claim?

5. Please let Mrs. Wallace or I know your vacation plans.

6. James said that you can get additional copies of the newsletter from Serena or he.

7. Adrilla and myself share the same birthday.

8. Michael, Stephen, and him will be working for the same tree-planting company this summer.

9. Olga told me that her and her sister haven't seen each other in years.

10. She is the kind of person who isn't afraid to express an unpopular opinion.

3. POSSESSIVE PRONOUNS

Use **possessive pronouns** (*my*, *mine*, *our/ours*, *your/yours*, *his*, *her/hers*, *its*, *their/theirs*, *whose*) to show ownership or possession. Pay especially close attention to the following points.

- **Don't confuse the possessive pronoun *its* with the contraction *it's* (*it is*).**

  POSSESSIVE   The committee has tabled **its** report.

  CONTRACTION   Don't call me unless **it's** an emergency.

- **Don't confuse the possessive pronoun *your* with the contraction *you're* (*you are*).**

  POSSESSIVE   Did you bring **your** books?

  CONTRACTION   **You're** late.

- **Don't confuse the possessive pronoun *whose* with the contraction *who's* (*who is*).**

  POSSESSIVE   I didn't hear **whose** name was announced as the winner.

  CONTRACTION   I don't know **who's** calling.

- **Don't confuse the possessive pronoun *their* with the contraction *they're* (*they are*) or the adverb *there*.**

  POSSESSIVE   The Séguins are attending **their** family reunion in Regina.

  CONTRACTION   **They're** staying with Cousin Denis and his family for two weeks.

  ADVERB   They hope to see the whole family **there**.

- **Do not use apostrophes with *hers*, *its*, *ours*, *yours*, and *theirs*.**

  The battered canoe tied to the dock is **theirs**.

  This sweater must be **yours**.

- **Add *'s* to indefinite pronouns.**

  Everyone's assignments have been returned.

  Someone's keys were turned in to the receptionist.

Exercise 4

Correct all errors in the use of possessive pronouns in the following sentences:

1. It is anyones guess why Greg didn't show up for the interview.

2. Who's piece of chocolate cake is on the table?

3. I know that the suitcases are identical, but I'm certain this one is your's.

4. There's is the most beautiful garden in the neighbourhood.

5. The dog bared it's teeth and growled menacingly.

Exercise 5 Review of Pronoun Case and Possessive Pronouns

Correct all errors in pronoun case and possessive pronouns. If the sentence is correct, write **C**.

1. Please tell Nigel or myself if you need a ride on Saturday.

2. Dale promised that him and his brothers would vacuum the pool before the barbecue.

3. No one is happier than me that you and her have won the scholarships.

4. The Vachons sold most of there furniture and moved into a condominium.

5. Do you know who's limousine is stopped at the light?

6. Justine claims that the idea was entirely her's.

7. Between you and I, she is not giving Ian his share of the credit.

8. Put everything back in its proper place.

9. The earliest that Dave and me can be there is noon.

10. Evangeline hopes that her boyfriend and herself are accepted by the same university.

Exercise 6 Review of Pronoun Case and Possessive Pronouns

Correct all errors in pronoun case and the use of possessive pronouns in the following passage:

Last February Peter and me decided to get married. We wanted to get married in June, so their were four months to plan the wedding. Although our wedding cost only $2,000, it turned out beautifully. Here's how we did it.

First we made a list of everything we could do ourself. Me and my sister spent two weeks shopping every chance we got in Value Village stores and all the second-hand vintage clothing shops. Luckily, I found the perfect dress for just under $50 and my sister found a gorgeous bridesmaid's dress for $100. I didn't mind that her's cost twice as much as mine because she said that her and her boyfriend might get married theirselves and she would wear that dress to the wedding. Peter was able to borrow his dad's dark suit, which his dad said looked better on Peter than it did on he. Peter's brother Tom had just gotten married, so he had a dark suit he could wear as best man.

Having dealt with the clothing issue, we went to a pawnshop and bought two gold rings for $50 each.

Now we had to find a place to get married. We have a friend who's parents own a cottage near a local lake. They agreed to lend us there place for the weekend. For $200 we could rent canopies and tables to put on the lawn. Then I persuaded my mother to let Peter and myself raid her garden for lilacs, tulips, and daisies. They made lovely bouquets for all the tables.

Peter's Uncle Ted said that him and his friend, an amateur photographer, would take all the photographs. If we supplied the film, which cost about $100, he would print the photos with his own computer.

Now we had to find someone to marry us. We contacted a local marriage commissioner and discovered that the usual gratuity is $50. We had to give her another $50 to cover her travelling expenses. The marriage licence cost $50. So far, we had spent $700.

Its probably not surprising that food and liquor were our biggest expense. Because so many of our guests had allergies or were on special diets, we decided on a simple meal of chili, homemade cornbread, and huge salads, with beer and wine. For dessert, we had soy ice cream and a vegan wedding cake made by my father and I. Buying the food and liquor, and renting cutlery, glasses, and dishes cost about $700.

Of course, what's a wedding without music and dancing? No one knows more about the local music scene than Peter and myself, so we hired a band for $300. We didn't need to provide any of the sound equipment because the band said they would bring their's. Naturally, there were a few more miscellaneous expenses, but the total cost of our wedding was well under $2,000. Between you and I, the wedding couldn't have suited we thrifty folks better if it had cost $20,000.

4. PRONOUN AGREEMENT

Errors in pronoun agreement, just like errors in subject-verb agreement, occur when writers don't match a singular pronoun with a singular noun or a plural pronoun with a plural noun. Pronoun agreement errors occur most frequently in the following situations:

Agreement with Singular Nouns

Pronoun agreement errors often involve using a plural pronoun, most commonly *their*, to refer to a singular noun. Most often, the noun names a type of person (the alcoholic, the mature student, the typical worker) rather than an individual, as in the following example:

ERROR   The **alcoholic** may blame **their** drinking problem on unsympathetic family members.

There are four ways to avoid this kind of agreement error.

1. **Use a singular possessive pronoun.**

   The alcoholic may blame **his** drinking problem on unsympathetic family members.

   Although this version is grammatically correct, the use of *his* is unappealing because it implies that all alcoholics are men.

2. **Use the phrase *his or her*.**

   The alcoholic may blame **his or her** drinking problem on unsympathetic family members.

   This correction works well in single sentences but becomes cumbersome when repeated frequently. Avoid using *he/she, s/he,* or *him/her* in any piece of writing.

3. **Make the noun plural.** Pluralizing is often the simplest and most effective way to ensure pronoun agreement, especially in longer pieces of writing.

   Alcoholics may blame **their** drinking problems on unsympathetic family members.

4. **Alternate masculine and feminine pronouns.** If you were writing about types of people, such as the teacher and his or her students or the doctor and his or her patients, you could alternate masculine and feminine pronouns by referring to the teacher or doctor as *he* in one paragraph and as *she* in the next paragraph. Alternating masculine and feminine pronouns paragraph by paragraph is much less confusing and distracting than alternating them within a single paragraph.

Exercise 7

Revise the following sentences to make antecedents and pronouns agree:

1. Every manager has been asked their opinion of the merger.

2. A new immigrant generally suffers from culture shock, no matter how well they have prepared for the move.

3. A daycare worker must ensure that their qualifications in basic first aid are current.

4. It is not unusual for even an experienced actor to suffer from stage fright before they begin a performance.

5. A customer service representative needs to remain calm and polite in their dealings with the public.

Agreement with Collective Nouns

Collective nouns are words such as *jury, team, band, audience, group, family, committee, congregation, herd,* and *flock* that refer to people or things taken together.

When a collective noun refers to people or things acting as a single unit, the collective noun takes singular verbs and singular pronouns.

The **jury was** unanimous in **its** verdict.

The **band was** doomed without **its** leader.

When a collective noun refers to people or things acting as individuals or not as a unit, the collective noun takes plural verbs and plural pronouns.

The **jury were divided** in **their** judgment of the defendant.

The **band were arguing** over **their** next number.

When a collective noun is followed by a prepositional phrase, be careful to match the pronoun with the collective noun and not with the noun inside the prepositional phrase.

A small **group** of hecklers made **its** impact on the meeting.

The stranded **herd** of horses lost **its** way.

Agreement with Indefinite Pronouns

Singular Indefinite Pronouns

The following indefinite pronouns are always singular. They take singular verbs, and any pronouns referring to them should also be singular.

everyone	*anyone*	*no one, one*	*someone*	*either*
everybody	*anybody*	*nobody*	*somebody*	*neither*
everything	*anything*	*nothing*	*something*	*each*

Here is a typical example of an agreement error with an indefinite pronoun:

Everyone in the office had put in **their** request for time off at Christmas.

Here *everyone,* which is singular, and *their,* which is plural, do not agree.

You could correct this error by using the strategies suggested above for singular nouns. Alternatively, you could rephrase the sentence and eliminate the pronoun altogether.

Everyone in the office had requested time off at Christmas.

Don't be misled by prepositional phrases. If a singular indefinite pronoun is followed by a prepositional phrase ending with a plural noun (*of the children, in the houses, under the benches*) the verb and any pronouns referring to the subject are still singular.

Neither of the drivers has contacted **her** insurance agent.

In this sentence, the antecedent of *her* is *neither*. Because *neither* is singular, the pronoun referring to it must also be singular.

Plural Indefinite Pronouns

(many, few, several, both)

The indefinite pronouns *many*, *few*, *several*, and *both* take plural pronouns.

Both of the drivers filed claims with **their** insurance companies.

Singular or Plural Indefinite Pronouns

(all, none, some)

The indefinite pronouns *all*, *none*, and *some* are matched with singular pronouns when they are followed by a prepositional phrase that contains a singular noun.

None of the furniture has been moved from **its** original position for years.

These pronouns are matched with plural pronouns when they are followed by a prepositional phrase containing a plural noun.

None of the chairs have been moved from **their** original positions for years.

Exercise 8

Revise the following sentences where necessary to make antecedents and pronouns agree. If the sentence is correct, write **C**.

1. Everyone purchasing these selected products is eligible to submit their name for the grand prize in the draw.

2. None of the witnesses on shore were prepared to risk their own safety to rescue the drowning man.

3. Each of the crafters is selling their best creations at the fall fair.

4. Neither of the men left their names when they called this morning.

5. Anyone interested in joining the canoe trip should send his or her payment to Harriet by the end of the month.

Agreement with *Either/Or*, *Neither/Nor*, *Or*, *Nor*

Singular nouns joined by *either/or*, *neither/nor*, *or*, and *nor* are matched with singular pronouns.

Neither Farida nor Barbara has contacted **her** lawyer.

Either Mark or Craig will lend you **his** truck for the move.

Plural nouns joined by these conjunctions take plural pronouns.

Neither the students nor the teachers had time to collect **their** belongings when the fire alarm sounded.

When singular and plural nouns are joined by these conjunctions, place the plural noun last and use a plural pronoun.

NOT   Neither the dancers nor the lead singer **has** been fitted for **her** costume.

BUT   Neither the lead singer nor **the dancers** have been fitted for **their** costumes.

Exercise 9

Revise the following sentences where necessary to make antecedents and pronouns agree. If the sentence is correct, write **C**.

1. Neither the employees nor the supervisor believed that their position was wrong.

2. Either Sheryl or Jennifer will lend you her bicycle for the outing.

3. The herd of cattle left their grazing area and wended their way home.

4. Next week the safety committee will publish the results of their investigation.

5. If you need help with opening night at your restaurant, either Matt or Richard will offer their services.

6. The municipal government has issued their recommendations on property tax increases.

7. The weary group of tourists finally arrived at their hotel.

8. The class were packing their books in anticipation of the bell.

9. A family of bats has made their home in our attic.

10. I know you are curious, but neither Pierre nor Antoine wants me to tell you their plans for the weekend.

Exercise 10 Pronoun Agreement Review

Revise the following sentences where necessary to make antecedents and pronouns agree. If the sentence is correct, write **C**.

1. An experienced writer considers their readers' needs.

2. Neither of the suspects has confessed their involvement in the embezzlement.

3. The congregation is unanimous in its support of the new minister.

4. No one in the office has submitted their ideas on the proposal.

5. Some of the passengers stowed their baggage in the overhead bins.

6. After dissecting a frog in biology class, neither Stacey nor Veronica could eat their lunch.

7. A gambling addict may go deeply into debt to finance their habit.

8. All of the stolen money has been returned to its rightful owner.

9. An army marches on their stomach.

10. Everyone is expected to be on their best behaviour.

11. The band began its Canadian tour in Halifax.

12. Either Sandra or Brianne will give their oral presentation on Friday.

13. Neither of the two lost little boys knew their home address.

14. Every winner will have their picture in the newspaper.

15. Mr. Warden is a man who does their work without complaint.

Exercise 11 Pronoun Agreement Review

Revise the following paragraph to eliminate all errors in pronoun agreement:

A PowerPoint presenter arranges words and pictures into a series of pages that they project from a laptop computer onto a screen. Each of the screens typically has their heading followed by bullet points: six or seven words a line, six or seven lines a slide. Paragraphs and even sentences have too many words for a PowerPoint presentation, so the presenter must reduce their most complex ideas to little phrases. Of course, the bullet points eliminate the need for transitions, such as *because* or *on the other hand,* that might help a viewer understand connections among these phrases. The typical presenter hasn't noticed the absence of transitions. They have been so caught up in the technical features of PowerPoint that they have concentrated on the appearance of the text and the accompanying graphics. Never mind, if there are enough snappy visual aids, neither the viewers nor the presenter may notice that their presentation has the intellectual substance of a kindergarten show and tell.

5. PRONOUN REFERENCE

When you are speaking, you can usually make your meaning understood even if your pronoun use is vague. When you are writing, however, you don't have the opportunity to point to things or to explain vague ideas to your reader; thus, you need to make the connections between pronouns and nouns very clear. When this connection is confusing, you have made an error in pronoun reference.

Here are some of the most common errors in pronoun reference:

Confusing Pronoun References

This problem is most likely to occur in sentences containing indirect speech.

VAGUE	When Kevin told Ali that **he** was being laid off, **he** was very upset.
CLEAR	Kevin was very upset when **he** told Ali, "I'm being laid off."
CLEAR	Kevin told Ali, "You are being laid off." Ali was very upset.

Vague Use of *They* and *It*

Avoid using *they* if it doesn't refer to a specific noun in your writing.

VAGUE	**They** say that a number of Western democracies are shifting politically to the right.
CLEAR	**Respected commentators** say that a number of Western democracies are shifting politically to the right.

You can see a similar problem with *it* in this sentence:

VAGUE	I spent hours working out a detailed budget, but **it** didn't solve my financial problems.

This sentence leaves your reader wondering what didn't help and what, exactly, *it* refers to: the time you spent working on your budget? Or the budget itself?

CLEAR	I spent hours working out a detailed budget, but **this effort** did not solve my financial problems.
OR	I spent hours working out a detailed budget, but **the budget itself** did not solve my financial problems.

Vague Use of *That, Which,* and *This*

In vague sentences, *that, which,* or *this* can refer to several different ideas.

VAGUE	The cousins fought on different sides in the war, **which** tore their family apart.

What tore their family apart—the fact that they fought on different sides? The exploits? The war? A clearer version might read like this.

CLEAR	The family was torn apart by the cousins' **decision** to fight on different sides in the war.

The pronoun most often used vaguely is *this*. Although students frequently use it to indicate the content of the previous sentence, *this* needs to refer to a particular antecedent. If your instructor has pointed out that you use pronouns vaguely, you may want to use the find-and-replace function to seek out and correct vague or confusing uses of *this*, *that*, and *which*.

Exercise 12

Revise the following sentences to clarify vague pronoun references:

1. They say that nightmares are caused by anxiety.

2. Why do you tease your sister and call her names when you know it upsets her?

3. Natalie was disappointed when Nicole told her that she didn't get the job.

4. I rested and drank plenty of fluids, but it didn't make me feel better.

5. Maxine wanted to subscribe to the newspaper, but they said that home delivery was not available in her neighbourhood.

6. The cash register stopped working because a customer's child had turned off the main switch, but at the time Giselle didn't know it.

7. Raul added too much water to the dough and beat it mercilessly, which is why the pie crust is tough.

8. Rex is lazy, immature, and irresponsible, but that doesn't bother his friends.

9. I heard that Candace left her husband and children and ran away to Tahiti to paint. This greatly surprised me.

10. Mr. Carlson applied too much weed killer and overwatered the grass, which ruined the lawn.

Exercise 13

Revise the following paragraph to eliminate all vague and ambiguous pronoun references:

Vegans do not eat any animal products. This means that many of the foods most people enjoy, such as ice cream, mayonnaise, bacon and eggs, even toast with honey, are off limits. Because most prepared foods contain some animal products, eating out can be a real challenge, which is why many vegans cook at home and bring food with them when they go out. Of course, vegan cooking presents its own difficulties. When I became a vegan, I bought a cookbook with lots of delicious-looking recipes, but it didn't help. They put so many exotic ingredients in each recipe that I had to dash to the health food store before I could begin. Despite these obstacles, I'm glad to be a vegan. Now that they talk about so many diseases carried by cows, fish, and birds, who would want to eat meat even if they were killed more humanely?

Weblinks

- more explanations of pronouns from Charles Darling

   grammar.ccc.commnet.edu/grammar/pronouns1.htm

- a convenient handout on pronoun case from Purdue University's Online Writing Lab (OWL)

   owl.english.purdue.edu/handouts/grammar/g_proncase.html

- pronoun-agreement and reference exercises from *Grammar Bytes*

   www.chompchomp.com/exercises.htm#Pronoun_Agreement

ANSWER KEY

Exercise 1

1. because I never know

2. Even when they are knowledgeable and competent,

3. **C**

4. The owners claim that they can hear [**Or:** visitors can hear]

5. because he doesn't want to lose a tooth that can be saved.

Exercise 2

You can write this paragraph in either the third person (*participants/ they*) or the second person (*you*). Both versions are shown below.

You will get a more effective workout in your next fitness class if you follow this advice. **If you are new**, position **yourself** near the instructor so you can see and hear clearly. **If you are near the front**, **you** are also less likely to be distracted by other participants.

You should give the class **your** full attention, so don't spend your time worrying about whether other people are watching you or whether you put enough change in the parking meter. Although **you** might be tempted to compensate for **your** lack of ability with expensive exercise clothes, don't spend a fortune on exercise accessories. All **you** really need is a T-shirt, shorts, running shoes, and a willingness to devote an hour to **your** own good health.

Participants will get a more effective workout in **their** next fitness class if **they** follow this advice. **Novices** should position themselves near the instructor so **they** can see and hear clearly. **Those** near the front **are** also less likely to be distracted by **others**. **All participants** should give the class **their** full attention **rather than** worrying about whether other people are watching **them** or whether **they** put enough change in the parking meter. Although **some people** might be tempted to compensate for lack of ability with expensive exercise clothes, **no one needs to** spend a fortune on exercise accessories. All participants really need is a T-shirt, shorts, running shoes, and a willingness to devote an hour to their own good health.

Exercise 3

1. We workers
2. He and I
3. than she
4. whom to contact
5. Mrs. Wallace or me
6. Serena or him
7. Adrilla and I
8. Michael, Stephen, and he
9. that she and her sister
10. **C**

Exercise 4

1. anyone's
2. Whose
3. yours

4. Theirs

5. its

Exercise 5

1. Nigel or me

2. he and his brothers

3. than I that you and she

4. their furniture

5. whose limousine

6. hers

7. Between you and me

8. **C**

9. Dave and I

10. she and her boyfriend

Exercise 6

Last February, Peter and **I** decided to get married. We wanted to get married in June, so **there** were four months to plan the wedding. Although our wedding cost only $2000, it turned out beautifully. Here's how we did it.

First we made a list of everything we could do **ourselves. My sister and I** spent two weeks shopping every chance we got in Value Village stores and all the second-hand vintage clothing shops. Luckily, I found the perfect dress for just under $50 and my sister found a gorgeous bridesmaid's dress for $100. I didn't mind that **hers** cost twice as much as mine because she said that **she** and her boyfriend might get married **themselves** and she would wear that dress to the wedding. Peter was able to borrow his dad's dark suit, which his dad said looked better on Peter than it did on **him**. Peter's brother Tom had just gotten married, so he had a dark suit he could wear as best man. Having dealt with the clothing issue, we went to a pawnshop and bought two gold rings for $50 each.

Now we had to find a place to get married. We have a friend **whose** parents own a cottage near a local lake. They agreed to lend us **their** place for the weekend. For $200 we could rent canopies and tables to put on the lawn. Then I persuaded my mother to let Peter and **me** raid her garden for lilacs, tulips, and daisies. They made lovely bouquets for all the tables.

Peter's Uncle Ted said that **he** and his friend, an amateur photographer, would take all the photographs. If we supplied the film, which cost about $100, he would print the photos with his own computer.

Now we had to find someone to marry us. We contacted a local marriage commissioner and discovered that the usual gratuity is $50. We had to give her another $50 to cover her travelling expenses. The marriage licence cost $50. So far, we had spent $700.

It's probably not surprising that food and liquor were our biggest expense. Because so many of our guests had allergies or were on special diets, we decided on a simple meal of chili, homemade cornbread, and huge salads, with beer and wine. For dessert, we had soy ice cream and a vegan wedding cake made by my father and **me**. Buying the food and liquor, and renting cutlery, glasses, and dishes cost about $700.

Of course, what's a wedding without music and dancing? No one knows more about the local music scene than Peter and **I**, so we hired a band for $300. We didn't need to provide any of the sound equipment because the band said they would bring **theirs**.

Naturally, there were a few more miscellaneous expenses, but the total cost of our wedding was well under $2,000. Between you and **me**, the wedding couldn't have suited **us** thrifty folks better if it had cost $20,000.

Exercise 7

1. manager/his or her [**Or:** all managers/their]

2. immigrant/he or she [**Or:** new immigrants/they]

3. daycare worker/his or her [**Or:** daycare workers/their]

4. actor/he or she [**Or:** actors/they]

5. customer service representative/his or her [**Or:** customer service representatives/their]

Exercise 8

1. Everyone/his or her

2. **C**

3. Each/his or her

4. Neither/his/he

5. **C**

Exercise 9

1. supervisor/his **or** supervisor/her [**Better:** Neither the supervisor nor the employees/their]

2. **C**

3. herd/its/its

4. committee/its

5. Matt/Richard/his

6. government/its

7. group/its [**Or:** the hotel]

8. **C** [class acting as individuals]

9. family/its [family acting as unit]

10. Pierre/Antoine/his

Exercise 10

1. writer/his or her [**Or:** writers/their]

2. Neither/his

3. **C**

4. No one/his or her

5. **C**

6. Stacey/Veronica/her

7. addict/his or her [**Or:** addicts/their]

8. **C**

9. army/its

10. Everyone/his or her

11. **C**

Exercise 11

PowerPoint presenters arrange words and pictures into a series of pages that they project from a laptop computer onto a screen. Each **screen** typically has **a** heading followed by bullet points: six or seven words a line, six or seven lines a slide. Paragraphs and even sentences have too many words for a PowerPoint presentation, so **presenters** must reduce their most complex ideas to little phrases. Of course, the bullet points eliminate the need for transitions, such as *because* or *on the other hand*, that might help a viewer understand connections among these phrases. **Typically, presenters haven't** noticed the absence of transitions. They have been so caught up in the technical features of PowerPoint that they have concentrated on the appearance of the text and the accompanying graphics. Never mind, if there are enough snappy visual aids, neither the viewers nor the presenter may notice that **the** presentation has the intellectual substance of a kindergarten show and tell.

Exercise 12

1. Experts say

2. when you know your behaviour upsets her?

3. when Nicole told her, "You [or I] didn't get the job."

4. but my efforts

5. the customer service representative said

6. but at the time Giselle didn't know what had caused the problem.

7. The pie crust is tough because Raul added too much water to the dough and beat it mercilessly.

8. but these characteristics don't bother his friends.

9. Her actions greatly surprised me.

10. Mr. Carlson ruined the lawn by applying too much weed killer and overwatering the grass. [**Or:** By applying too much weed killer and overwatering the grass, Mr. Carlson ruined the lawn.]

Exercise 13

Vegans do not eat any animal products. This **dietary limitation** means that many of the foods most people enjoy, such as ice cream, mayonnaise, bacon and eggs, even toast with honey, are off-limits. Because most prepared foods contain some animal products, eating out can be a real challenge, **so** many vegans cook at home and bring food with them when they go out. Of course, vegan cooking presents its own difficulties. When I became a vegan, I bought a cookbook with lots of delicious-looking recipes, but **these recipes** didn't help. **Each recipe contained so many exotic ingredients** that I had to dash to the health food store before I could begin. Despite these obstacles, I'm glad to be a vegan. Now that **stories about so many diseases carried by cows, fish, and birds are in the news,** who would want to eat meat even if **animals** were killed more humanely?

Proofreading: Troublesome Adjectives and Adverbs

1. KEY TERMS TO KNOW

Adjectives modify nouns and pronouns (that is, they describe the physical, mental, and emotional qualities of the people, places, and things named by nouns and pronouns). Words that end with *ful, ish, less, like* (*thankful, foolish, helpless, childlike*) are usually adjectives.

> The quick brown fox jumped over the lazy dog. [*Quick* and *brown* modify *fox*; *lazy* modifies *dog*.]

Adverbs modify verbs, adjectives, and other adverbs; they describe the manner or degree of the actions or qualities named by verbs, adjectives, and other adverbs. Many descriptive adverbs end in *ly* (a few adjectives, such as *friendly* and *lovely*, also end in *ly*). Some common adverbs, such as *very, always, not, well*, and *often*, do not end in *ly*.

> The cat stretched lazily in the sun. [*Lazily* modifies the verb *stretched*.]

> Dr. Lucas' lecture on the shortage of clean water in Ghana was extremely interesting. [*Extremely* modifies the adjective *interesting*.]

> The car went by too quickly for me to see the driver. [*Too* modifies the adverb *quickly*.]

2. COMPARATIVE FORMS OF ADJECTIVES AND ADVERBS

Most adjectives and adverbs have degrees of comparison (*pretty, prettier, prettiest; interesting, more interesting, most interesting*). If you are not sure of the comparative form of a particular adjective or adverb (should it be *clearer* or *more clear*?), consult your dictionary. Avoid using double comparisons, such as *more happier* or *most fastest*.

Some adjectives (such as *unique, perfect, empty*) express absolute concepts. One piece of pottery cannot be *more unique* than the rest, one math test cannot be the *most perfect* in the class, and one glass cannot be *more empty* than another.

3. TROUBLESOME ADJECTIVES AND ADVERBS

- ### *Good, well*

Good is an adjective.

> I haven't seen a **good** movie for ages.

Well is usually an adverb.

> NOT   Declan **ran good** in the last race.
>
> **BUT**   Declan **ran well** in the last race.

Well in reference to health is an adjective.

> Jane hasn't been **well** since her bout of mononucleosis.

- ### *Bad/badly, real/really*

Bad and *real* are adjectives.

> This is a **bad** photograph of me.
>
> The huge boulder looks **real**, but it is actually made of papier-mâché.

Badly and *really* are adverbs.

> NOT   The roof was damaged **bad** in the hailstorm.
>
> **BUT**   The roof was **badly** damaged in the hailstorm.
>
> NOT   Ben is **real** eager to begin his new job on Monday.
>
> **BUT**   Ben is **really** eager to begin his new job on Monday.

- ### *Less* and *fewer*

Though they are both adjectives, *less* and *fewer* are used differently. *Less* (the comparative of *little*) is an adjective used with items that cannot be considered as separate objects: *less* food, *less* kindness, *less* snow. *Fewer* (the comparative of *few*) is an adjective used with things that can be counted individually: *fewer* students, *fewer* courses, *fewer* responsibilities.

> NOT   **Less** students have enrolled than we expected.
>
> **BUT**   **Fewer** students have enrolled than we expected.

- ### Adjectives ending with *ing* and *ed*

If your first language is not English, you may find it confusing to decide on the correct meaning and appropriate ending for adjectives formed with an *ing* ending (present participle) or an *ed* ending (past participle of a regular verb).

> She is **exciting**. [meaning that she causes others to feel excitement; *exciting* is an adjective]
>
> She is **excited**. [meaning that she herself feels excitement; in form, *excited* is a past participle of the verb *excite*, but *excited* functions as an adjective here]

A good dictionary should help you decide on the correct ending.

- **Articles (*a, an, the*)**

Many languages do not have articles, so learners of English often find this aspect of the language difficult. These guidelines may help:

1. Use the article *a* (or *an* before vowels) to indicate a noun in general terms (*a* meal, *an* orange).

2. Most proper nouns do not use an article. *The* is used with some plural proper nouns to indicate specific people (*the* Smiths) and geographical designations (*the* Rockies). *The* is also used with collective proper nouns referring to countries or groups (*the* United States of America, *the* United Kingdom, *the* NHL).

3. Use *the* to indicate a particular noun or one that has been mentioned earlier. (*The* photograph of *the* moon that I referred to is on page 10.)

Exercise 1

Revise the following sentences so that adjectives and adverbs are used correctly:

1. He looked at me serious and began to speak.

2. The engine still runs good, but the body is badly rusted.

3. Less players have registered for hockey camp this summer.

4. The supervisor is real interested in your opinion of the proposal.

5. Clarence gets good grades in physical education, but he doesn't do so good in chemistry.

Exercise 2

Revise the following sentences so that adjectives and adverbs are used correctly. If the sentence is correct, write **C**.

1. Lynette is the most liveliest member of my aerobics class.

2. You will feel considerable better after you have taken this medication.

3. The play went good in rehearsal, but opening night was a disaster.

4. Since landing a full-time job, Satpal has been able to afford more dressy clothes, but she has less social occasions on which to wear them.

5. The milk bottle in the refrigerator is completely empty.

6. Of the two reports, which is the more informative?

7. Eric answered all of the questions as honest as he could.

8. Although the hikers were real tiring, they decided to press on.

9. The door opened more easily after Jack adjusted the hinges.

10. Max is less happier living on his own than he was living at home.

4. MISPLACED MODIFIERS

One morning, I shot an elephant in my pajamas. How he got into my pajamas, I'll never know.

—*Groucho Marx*, Animal Crackers

As the above example suggests, comedians have long known the humour of the misplaced modifier, the grammatical error in which a modifier (adjective, adverb, or phrase or clause acting as one of these) is in the wrong location in the sentence. The misplaced modifier can create a *confusing* and unintentionally *amusing* sentence. Often students create this error by tacking on inappropriate phrases at the end of their sentences.

Mr. Kowalski saw a horse by the side of the road on his way home from work.

Because Mr. Kowalski is more likely to be on his way home from work than a horse is, the prepositional phrase *on his way home from work* should be placed closer to *Mr. Kowalski* in the sentence.

On his way home from work, Mr. Kowalski saw a horse by the side of the road.

A misplaced modifier, such as that in the sentence below, often calls up a ridiculous image in the reader's mind.

Hanging from the ceiling, I noticed a large chandelier.

In this sentence, the participial phrase (*Hanging . . . ceiling*) modifies the "I" of the sentence. But because it is unlikely that the speaker is hanging from the ceiling, the phrase should be in a different location so that it modifies the noun *chandelier*.

I noticed a large chandelier hanging from the ceiling.

Limiting adverbs such as *only*, *hardly*, *barely*, *nearly*, and *almost* are especially troublesome because they can easily be misplaced. Be especially carefully when using these words with adjectives expressing absolutes.

NOT   She was **almost pregnant** every year.

BUT   She was pregnant **almost every year**.

NOT	He was **only perfect** at this audition.
BUT	He was perfect **only at this audition**.
NOT	I **only want** a minute of your time.
BUT	I want **only a minute** of your time.

Note: Do not use *hardly* and *barely* with *not*.

NOT	I **can't hardly** hear you.
BUT	I **can hardly** hear you.
NOT	She **couldn't barely** hear the faint sound coming from the basket on the front steps.
BUT	She **could barely** hear the faint sound coming from the basket on the front steps.

5. SPLIT INFINITIVES

An **infinitive** is *to* + a verb: *to think, to walk, to breathe*. A **split infinitive** occurs when a modifier (usually an adverb) is misplaced between *to* and the verb (*to quickly run*). It is best to avoid splitting an infinitive, especially when the resulting construction is awkward. You can correct a split infinitive by rephrasing the sentence.

SPLIT INFINITIVE	Marjorie needed time to **mentally prepare** for the exam.
REVISED	Marjorie needed time to **prepare mentally** for the exam.

Sometimes, however, a split infinitive sounds less awkward than the revision.

The diners asked the man at the next table **to please stop** smoking his cigar. [Putting *please* anywhere else in the sentence would be clumsy.]

Exercise 3

Revise the following sentences to avoid split infinitives and to fix misplaced modifiers.

1. Soak the shirt in cold water with the spaghetti sauce stain.

2. Sonia could almost run ten full circuits around the field.

3. Preserved in formaldehyde, the students examined the jar of tapeworms.

4. I promise not to unfairly judge you.

5. I had difficulty hearing the conversation standing by the band.

Exercise 4

Revise the following sentences to avoid split infinitives and to fix misplaced modifiers. If the sentence is correct, write **C**.

1. The singer's fans couldn't hardly wait for the concert tickets to go on sale.

2. Properly cooked, you can eat hamburger without fear of food poisoning.

3. I want to thoroughly consider all my options before making a decision.

4. Greg has only enough money to cover this month's rent.

5. Seeing the accident ahead, the car pulled to the side of the road, and Tran got out to investigate.

6. We enjoyed the beautiful lawn and gardens eating our lunch on the patio.

7. You must be ill; you only ate half the pizza.

8. Jim heard the phone ring with his mouth full of toothpaste.

9. There is a family picture of our trip to Nassau on the hall table.

10. I asked him one final time to please stop pestering me.

6. DANGLING MODIFIERS

Participial and infinitive phrases at the beginning of a sentence normally modify the subject of the main clause. **Participial phrases** are formed with the present or past participle of a verb.

Twisting in the wind, the kite rose higher.

Driven from their homes, the villagers set up camp in the hills.

Sometimes the introductory phrase suggests a participial form rather than stating it directly.

While [travelling] **in France**, we visited many wineries.

Infinitive phrases are formed with an infinitive (*to* + verb).

To swim well, you need to coordinate your stroke with your breathing.

To mend the tire, she had to find the leak.

Recognizing Dangling Modifiers

An introductory phrase that does not modify the subject of the following clause or that has no logical subject to modify is called a **dangling modifier**. This error most commonly occurs with dangling infinitive and participial phrases.

DANGLING   **Driving down the mountain**, three bears were seen.

DANGLING   **To run a marathon**, endurance must be built up gradually.

Notice that if you expand these phrases into clauses, the subject is different in both sentences: *We* were driving down the mountain. *Three bears* were seen.

Notice too that the verbs in the main clause are in the passive voice: *were seen*, *must be built up*. Introductory phrases are more likely to dangle when the verb in the main clause is in the passive voice.

NOT   After discussing the case for days, a verdict **was** finally **reached** by the jury.

BUT   After discussing the case for days, the jury finally **reached** a verdict.

When you put the verb into the active voice, the phrase no longer dangles because the subjects are now the same (*the jury*).

Exercise 5

Underline the dangling modifiers below. If the sentence is correct, write **C**.

1. Before signing a contract, a lawyer should go over it with you.

2. In the middle of the night, we were awakened by police sirens screaming down the street.

3. To reduce conflicts with their children, better listening skills are needed.

4. When in Rome, the social customs of the Romans should be followed.

5. Because they arrived early, the Chans had good seats for the concert.

Correcting Dangling Modifiers

When an introductory phrase dangles, you can revise the sentence in one of two ways. You can either expand the dangling phrase to a subordinate clause or revise the main clause so that the introductory phrase has a logical subject to modify.

NOT	Intending to finish the report by the end of the day, my plan was to work through lunch and coffee breaks.
BUT	Because I intended to finish the report by the end of the day, my plan was to work through lunch and coffee breaks.
OR	Intending to finish the report by the end of the day, I planned to work through lunch and coffee breaks.

You could correct the dangling modifier in the next sentence by changing the prepositional phrase to a clause, with the subject clearly stated.

NOT	After being honoured by sports writers and fellow athletes, the retired hockey star's name was inscribed in the Hall of Fame.
BUT	After the retired hockey star was honoured by sports writers and fellow athletes, his name was inscribed in the Hall of Fame.

Sometimes, however, it is necessary to revise a sentence extensively to eliminate the dangling modifier.

NOT	Upon learning about the budget cutbacks, it was difficult for Ruth to hide her concern that her position would be abolished.
BUT	When Ruth learned about the budget cutbacks, she found it difficult to hide her concern that her position would be abolished.

Exercise 6

Correct each dangling modifier. If the sentence is correct, mark **C**.

1. Walking into the room, a strange sight caught my eye.

2. While in high school, George's father was promoted and the family moved to Vancouver.

3. Exhausted by a heavy work schedule, a complete rest was recommended by the doctor.

4. To make a perfect omelette, the freshest ingredients are required.

5. After pleading earnestly, the curfew was extended to midnight.

6. Hoping to catch the final inning of the baseball game on television, Michael left the office early.

7. Driven by arrogance and greed, Joe's friends were soon alienated from him.

8. After working so hard on the committee, our gratitude is definitely deserved.

9. To extend your cable service, you may call any time during office hours.

10. While reading Stephen King's *Cujo,* my dog began barking in the backyard.

11. Driving on the highway, Hank's car engine suddenly seized.

12. Staring intently at the small print, spots began to swim before my eyes.

Exercise 7

The following paragraph contains errors in the use of modifiers. Revise the passage to correct these errors.

Nineteenth-century workers couldn't hardly survive without spending long hours at demanding jobs. Farm workers and outside workers in the summer toiled from sunrise to sunset. Working shorter hours in the winter, less money was made. Shop employees were treated equally bad. To effectively meet the needs of their customers, shops stayed open very long hours, with employees working fourteen- to sixteen-hour shifts. The most dreadfulest conditions were found in the factories. Treated as part of the machinery and forced to work at the pace of the machine, there was no time to talk or joke with other workers. Children as young as seven worked twelve-hour shifts and slept in factory dormitories. In England by the middle of the nineteenth century it was illegal to employ children under the age of nine in textile factories, but most children were working full time by the time they were thirteen or fourteen in 1900.

Weblinks

- a useful page is from the University of Ottawa's writing centre

  www.uottawa.ca/academic/arts/writcent/hypergrammar/ modifier.html

- Charles Darling's page on modifier placement and associated online exercises

  grammar.ccc.commnet.edu/grammar/modifiers.htm

- OWL'S *very* useful handout on understanding and fixing dangling modifiers

  owl.english.purdue.edu/handouts/grammar/g_dangmod.html

ANSWER KEY

Exercise 1

1. seriously
2. runs well
3. fewer players
4. really interested
5. do so well in chemistry

Exercise 2

1. the liveliest
2. considerably better
3. went well
4. fewer social occasions
5. is empty
6. **C**
7. as honestly
8. really tired
9. **C**
10. less happy

Exercise 3

1. Soak the shirt with the spaghetti sauce stain in cold water.
2. Sonia could run almost ten full circuits around the field.
3. The students examined the jar of tapeworms preserved in formaldehyde.
4. I promise not to judge you unfairly.
5. Standing by the band, I had difficulty hearing the conversation.

Exercise 4

1. The singer's fans could hardly wait . . .
2. You can eat properly cooked hamburger . . .

3. I want to consider all my options thoroughly . . .

4. **C**

5. Seeing the accident ahead, Tran pulled the car to the side of the road and got out to investigate.

6. Eating our lunch on the patio, we enjoyed the beautiful lawns and gardens.

7. . . . you ate only half the pizza.

8. With his mouth full of toothpaste, Jim heard . . .

9. On the hall table there is a family picture . . .

10. **C**

Exercise 5

1. Before you sign a contract

2. **C**

3. To reduce conflicts with their children

4. When in Rome

5. **C**

Exercise 6

1. Walking into the room, I saw a strange sight. [**Or:** When I walked into the room, a strange sight caught my eye.]

2. While George was in high school, his father was promoted and the family moved to Vancouver.

3. Because Maurice was exhausted by a heavy work schedule, the doctor recommended a complete rest.

4. To make a perfect omelette, you require the freshest ingredients.

5. After Theresa pleaded earnestly, her parents extended her curfew to midnight.

6. **C**

7. Driven by arrogance and greed, Joe soon alienated his friends.

8. After working so hard on the committee, Bernard definitely deserves our gratitude.

9. **C**

10. While I was reading Stephen King's *Cujo*, my dog began barking in the backyard.

11. While Hank was driving on the highway, his car engine suddenly seized.

12. As I stared intently at the small print, spots began to swim before my eyes.

Exercise 7

Nineteenth-century workers **could hardly** survive without spending long hours at demanding jobs. **In the summer**, farm workers and outside workers toiled from sunrise to sunset. Working shorter hours in the winter, **they made less money**. Shop employees were treated equally **badly**. **To meet the needs of their customers effectively**, shops stayed open very long hours, with employees often working fourteen- to sixteen-hour shifts. The most **dreadful** conditions were found in the factories. Treated as part of the machinery and forced to work at the pace of the machine, **factory workers** had no time to talk or joke with their mates. Children as young as seven worked twelve-hour shifts and slept in factory dormitories. **By the middle of the nineteenth century it was illegal in England** to employ children under the age of nine in textile factories, **but in 1900** most children were working full time by the time they were thirteen or fourteen.

Proofreading: Punctuation and Mechanics

1. COMMAS

When you are proofreading for comma errors, remember the following two principles:

- **Single commas** are used to separate the items in a series of words, phrases, or clauses and to set off elements at the beginning or end of the sentence.
- **Pairs of commas** are used to enclose parts of a sentence.

Key Terms to Know

A **series** consists of three or more similar grammatical constructions, whether they be words, phrases, or clauses.

> To complete grade twelve, Petra needs **English, chemistry**, and **physics**. [a series of nouns]

> Before leaving for the lake, Simon needs to **buy groceries, pack the camper**, and **pick up his children**. [a series of phrases]

> **If you can meet the entrance requirements, if you can find a sponsor**, and **if you can arrange your own transportation**, you can run in this year's marathon. [a series of three dependent clauses]

A **phrase** is a group of words without a subject and a verb (*around the corner, looking out the window, to finish the test on time*).

A **clause** is a group of words with a subject and a verb.

A **main clause** can stand on its own as a sentence (*Bob walked his ferret*).

A **subordinate or dependent clause** cannot stand alone as a sentence (*After Bob walked his ferret*).

Using Commas to Separate

Separating Items in a Series

Use a comma to separate words, phrases, or clauses in a series. Although usage varies, we recommend putting a comma before the *and* or other conjunction that joins the last two items in the series, both to provide emphasis and to prevent misreading:

- **Words in a series**

  I forgot to buy **orange juice, milk, bread, peanut butter**, and **jam**.

Note 1: Without the comma, the sentence would read ". . . peanut butter and jam." Because you can actually buy peanut butter and jam mixed together, you need this comma between the last two items to clarify whether you are buying one item or two.

Note 2: However, do **not** put a comma between pairs of items considered a single unit.

> The prime minister said that full employment, regional development, and **law and order** are the chief priorities.

- **Phrases in a series**

> The frightened puppy raced **through the door**, **down the hall**, and **under the bed**.

- **Clauses in a series**

> **Mohammed handles the budget**, **Judy handles customer complaints**, and **Philip handles the advertising**.

Setting Off Main Clauses

Use a comma before the coordinating conjunctions *and, but, or, nor, for, yet,* and *so* when they join main clauses.

> Retired racing greyhounds make lovely pets, **yet** thousands of them are euthanized every year.

> The greyhound can run at least 40 mph, **but** it prefers to rest on the couch.

However, the comma is often omitted before *and* and *or* if the clauses are short.

> You stand in line **and** I'll find a table.

To prevent misreading, always use a comma before *for*, *so*, and *yet* when they are used as coordinating conjunctions, because these words also have other uses.

> The dog limped, **for** it was old. [coordinating conjunction]

> The dog limped **for** the door. [preposition]

Setting Off Introductory Subordinate Clauses

Use commas after introductory subordinate clauses that begin with subordinating conjunctions, such as *although, because, after, when, before, since,* and *while.*

> **Before anyone could stop the baby**, she had grabbed the edge of the tablecloth and pulled the dishes to the floor.

> **Because there has been so much rain**, the mosquitoes have been bad this year.

Add all necessary commas to the following sentences:

1. Lorraine packed two suitcases called a cab and headed for the airport.

2. The secret ingredients in my stew are eye of newt toe of frog wool of bat and tongue of dog.

3. We have agreed to put the armoire in the master bedroom the console in the hall and the pine desk in the study.

4. We'll need bread cheese cold cuts fruit and sodas for the picnic.

5. The diner complained that the meat was underdone the vegetables were soggy and the wine was sour.

6. We must go now for our ferry leaves exactly at noon.

7. Freida knocked down the wall and David hauled away the rubble.

8. Liam is a painstaking editor yet a few small errors escaped even his sharp eye.

9. The Richardsons knew that they must replace the worn linoleum and repaint the walls a neutral colour or the house would never sell.

10. When Fiona first began working as a cashier she thought that she would never remember the PLU's for produce but she had soon memorized dozens of codes.

Setting Off Other Introductory Elements

- **After introductory phrases of more than five words**

  Sitting patiently beside my neighbour's woodpile, Brutus stood vigilant guard over escaping field mice.

- **After introductory transitional words and phrases**

The usual practice is to put a comma after transitional phrases such as *for example, on the other hand, in contrast*. Also, put a comma after conjunctive adverbs of more than two syllables: after *nevertheless*, but not after *thus*.

On the other hand, many prairie grain farmers are in desperate straits.

Nevertheless, people were optimistic that the economy would improve.

Thus we need to work out a new system to deal with rural bankruptcies.

Note: Do **not** confuse subordinate conjunctions with introductory transitional words; do not put a comma after subordinate conjunctions but after the entire clause.

NOT **Although**, she wanted to leave the party, she was afraid of being rude.

BUT **Although** she wanted to leave the party, she was afraid of being rude.

- ### After introductory interjections

Use a comma after mild interjections (*oh, well, my goodness, my*), and after *yes* and *no*.

My, what an ugly baby.

- ### After any introductory element to prevent misreading

In the evening, darkness settled over the town.

Setting Off Elements at the End of a Sentence

Use a comma to set off a word, phrase, or clause at the end of a sentence that qualifies, contrasts, or questions what comes before. Don't, however, put a comma in front of all subordinate clauses.

A puppy is a perfect pet, **if you have lots of patience**. [qualifying clause]

I ordered the chicken, **not the squid**. [contrasting element]

You'll give me a hand, **won't you**? [question]

Exercise 2

Add all necessary commas to the following sentences:

1. For example pizza has ingredients from all four food groups but it can also be high in fat.

2. During his years at university in Calgary Louis never took the opportunity to visit Banff or Lake Louise.

3. When Bret dropped the iron skillet on the tile floor he heard a sharp crack.

4. High above the planes flew in precise formation.

5. No I don't remember your lending me ten dollars.

6. It's best to feed a cold and starve a fever isn't it?

7. Time and tide wait for no man if you catch my drift.

8. Music has charms to soothe the savage breast not the savage beast.

Using Pairs of Commas to Enclose

Enclosing Interruptions in the Sentence

Use a pair of commas to enclose words, phrases, or clauses that slightly interrupt the flow of the sentence but add no essential meaning. Such expressions include parenthetical remarks (*of course, indeed, for example*), transitions (*however, therefore*), interjections (*well, oh*), and nouns of direct address (*Henry, Mother*).

> I will, **as I have already told you**, investigate the matter fully.

> The events described in this story are true. The names, **however**, have been changed to protect the innocent.

> I'd say he weighs about, **oh**, 80 kg.

> This decision, **Kevin**, is for you to make.

Enclosing Nonrestrictive Phrases and Clauses

Use a pair of commas to enclose a nonrestrictive phrase or clause. These phrases and clauses function as adjectives, but they are unessential; they supply additional information and can be removed without changing the sentence's meaning. These clauses and phrases usually modify **proper nouns**—nouns that name a person, place, or thing.

NONRESTRICTIVE PHRASE	Bob Edward, publisher of *The Calgary Eye-Opener*, was an influential and controversial figure until his death in 1922.
NONRESTRICTIVE CLAUSE	Clarence's Uncle David, who is an accomplished seaman, is planning to sail around the world.

In formal writing, clauses beginning with *which* are nonrestrictive; clauses beginning with *that* are restrictive.

NONRESTRICTIVE CLAUSE	In "The Lottery," which is about a seemingly ordinary village lottery, the horrifying nature of the prize is not revealed until the draw is made.
RESTRICTIVE CLAUSE	I've lost the book that I intended to lend you.

Note: Do **not** use commas to enclose a restrictive phrase or clause that provides essential information in the sentence.

RESTRICTIVE	All customers who install a smoke detector are eligible for a discount on insurance premiums. · [Only customers who install a smoke detector are eligible.]
INCORRECT	All customers, who install a smoke detector, are eligible . . . [If you write the sentence this way, you are technically saying that all customers are eligible.]

Exercise 3

Add all the necessary commas below. If the sentence is correct, write **C**.

1. Thank you Mr. Sutherland for booking your vacation trip through our travel agency.

2. The people who live next door are covering their entire backyard in artificial grass.

3. Punch Dickins who won the Distinguished Flying Cross in World War I gained fame as a bush pilot in the 1920s.

4. Monty's python which hasn't eaten in a month has escaped from its cage.

5. Monty promised us however that we had nothing to fear.

Using Commas in Conventional Places

- **Use a comma to set off direct speech and quotations from the rest of the sentence.**

  Alice remarked, "The lights are on, but no one seems to be home."

  We see Hamlet's growing awareness of the burdens placed upon him when he says, "The time is out of joint. O cursed spite / That ever I was born to set it right!"

Note: Do *not* use a comma when a quotation is introduced with *that*.

  We see Hamlet's hostility when he says that Claudius is "A little more than kin and less than kind."

- **Use a comma to separate the day of the month from the year.**

  Canada celebrated its centennial on July 1, 1967.

Note: Do **not** use a comma when only the month and year are given.

  Canada celebrated its centennial in July 1967.

- **Use a comma to separate the elements in geographic names and addresses.**

  Architect Douglas Cardinal designed the Museum of Civilization in Hull, Quebec.

  Bill and Audrey were married at St. Joseph's Basilica, 10044 113 Street, Edmonton, Alberta.

- **Use a comma after the salutation in personal or informal letters and after the closing in all letters.**

  Dear Aunt Margaret,

  Yours truly,

  Sincerely yours,

Exercise 4 Comma Review

Add all necessary commas and delete unnecessary commas in the following sentences. If the sentence is correct, write **C**.

1. However I always counter "Look before you leap."

2. After Christmas the family ate turkey sandwiches turkey casserole and turkey croquettes for a week.

3. Repairing the defective component after the warranty has expired Mr. Fortino is not our responsibility.

4. When the signal on the microwave sounded Ted poured the wine and called his guests to the table.

5. The Sandersons are the only people who did not contribute money to the Victoria Day fireworks display.

6. Whenever we go camping Father always says "If you don't fish where the fish are you'll be having hot dogs for supper."

7. Albert opened the window took a deep breath and composed his thoughts.

8. The one novel that I didn't read, was the basis for the essay question on the English exam.

9. Lucy Maud Montgomery the author of *Anne of Green Gables* was born in Clifton Prince Edward Island on November 30 1874.

10. Well you have certainly chosen a deep subject for your research paper.

11. To put the matter into its proper perspective I want you to consider the following factors.

12. Yes we do have that shoe style in your size.

13. I decided that Howard would bring the food Cliff would bring the drinks and you would bring the music.

14. The snow blockaded the door in deep drifts and icicles hung like spears from the roof.

15. Here is my estimate of the cost of paving your driveway. Taxes of course are not included.

16. Even during the day light could not penetrate the canopy of leaves.

17. Mr. Ramondo said "We're a few bricks short of a load but I think we have enough to build the firepit."

18. Anyone who is caught stealing money will be fired immediately.

19. On a dark stormy night I like nothing better, than to curl up with a good novel.

20. Cynthia went back to university to study engineering, because she discovered, that her BA in linguistics was not highly marketable.

2. SEMICOLONS

If the comma and period were to marry and mate, their child would be the semicolon. The semicolon creates a pause that is stronger than a comma, but it is usually used after a complete sentence, like a period.

Use a semicolon in the following ways:

- **By itself to join two clauses that are closely related or grammatically balanced**

  The storm struck with a destructive fury; the ship was broken by the violent wind and waves.

- **With a conjunctive adverb** (*nevertheless, however, otherwise, consequently, thus, therefore, then, meanwhile, moreover, furthermore*) or **with a transitional phrase** (*in addition, as a result, for example*) to join the main clauses

  The advertisement states that applicants with a degree in a related area are preferred; **nevertheless**, applicants with a diploma and relevant experience will be considered.

- **With a coordinating conjunction** (*and, but, or, nor, for, yet, so*) when the main clauses contain internal commas. Use this rule carefully and sparingly.

  Already late for work, I dressed hurriedly, ran out of the house, and jumped into the car; **but** when I turned the key, I heard only the ominous clicking sound of a dying battery.

- **Instead of a comma** between items in a series when the items themselves have internal punctuation

  The lottery prize includes the dream home, custom-built by a leading home builder; custom-made draperies, professional interior decorating, and exclusive furnishings; and free cleaning for one year.

Note: Semicolons are special punctuation marks that should not be abused. They should be used sparingly, sprinkled not like salt but like a fine spice that adds flavour and flair to your writing. If you're becoming addicted to the semicolon, you're probably relying too heavily on coordination to join your ideas, or you may be using this punctuation mark improperly, as in the examples below.

Unnecessary Semicolons

Note 1: Never use a semicolon to join a subordinate clause to a main clause.

> NOT   Although it had snowed heavily during the day; the roads were clear by midnight.

> BUT   Although it had snowed heavily during the day, the roads were clear by midnight.

Note 2: Avoid using a semicolon as a kind of big comma for emphasis.

> NOT   Horrified, Nelson watched the tidal wave approach; knowing that his tiny boat could never withstand its force.

> BUT   Horrified, Nelson watched the tidal wave approach, knowing that his tiny boat could never withstand its force.

Exercise 5

In the following sentences, add any necessary semicolons and replace any unnecessary ones with the correct punctuation. If the sentence is correct, mark **C**.

1. Emilio wanted to be a famous astronaut he ended up operating the Ferris wheel at the amusement park.

2. When John graduated from university, he was fortunate to get a junior management position with an accounting firm; he then began setting aside money to repay his student loan.

3. The variety show will feature Vox Populi, a well-known local band, the Crazy Bones, a hilarious comedy act, and the Tumbling Turners, an acrobatic troupe.

4. Zack thought that he had enough money in his account to pay for the new jeans however, his direct debit payment was not approved.

5. When the smoke had cleared from the oven, Lucas was afraid to open the door but, fortunately, a quick glance showed that the roast still looked edible.

6. Ashley is going camping with her family Erica has therefore agreed to take over the paper route for a week.

7. Even though the skater was disappointed with the poor marks for artistic interpretation; he was pleased with the high marks for technical merit.

8. There was a heavy frost in the night as a result, farmers are concerned about the peach crop.

3. APOSTROPHES

Because plurals, possessives, and contractions that end in *s* sound the same, your ear is not a reliable guide for when and how to use an **apostrophe**. Instead, you need to pay close attention to these forms so that you can use the apostrophe appropriately. Remember, too, that if you're unsure of how to use an apostrophe, you are as likely to put it in the wrong place as to omit it in the right place. The apostrophe, because it is so abused and misused in our culture (check out the signs in your neighbourhood) might take you a while to figure out. But if you return regularly to this section, you can use the apostrophe properly and not contribute to its widespread misuse.

- A **plural noun**, which is usually formed by adding *s* or *es*, indicates that you are discussing more than one person, place, or thing. Do not add apostrophes to plurals that are not possessive. Be especially careful with proper nouns.

  PLURAL   All the **Joneses** congratulate you on keeping up with them. [The plural of *Jones* is formed by adding *es*.]

  POSSESSIVE   The **Joneses'** car is in the garage. [The apostrophe indicates that the car belongs to the Joneses.]

- A **contraction** indicates the omission of one or more letters. The sense of the sentence will indicate whether the apostrophe signals possession or a contraction.

  CONTRACTION   Your **report's** already three weeks late. [report's = report is]

  POSSESSIVE   Your **report's** recommendations are out of line with current department policy. [The apostrophe indicates that the recommendations belong to the report.]

- **Possessive pronouns** (*yours, hers, its, ours, theirs*) do not take apostrophes. Only nouns and indefinite pronouns (*someone, something, somebody, everyone, everything, everybody, no one, nothing, nobody, anything, anybody*) take an apostrophe to show possession.

  NOT   These problems are **their's** to solve.

  BUT   These problems are **theirs** to solve.

- *Its* is a possessive; *it's* is a contraction.

  POSSESSIVE   The dog buried **its** bone in the garden.

  CONTRACTION   **It's** a serious problem.

Making Nouns and Indefinite Pronouns Possessive

- **To make an indefinite pronoun possessive, add 's.**

  This is **nobody's** business.

  Everyone's assignments have been marked.

- **To make a singular noun that does not end with _s_ possessive, add _'s_.**

  The **child's** bike lay abandoned on the driveway.

  The **horse's** saddle is hanging on a nail in the barn.

- **To make a singular noun that ends with _s_ or _ss_ possessive, add _'s_ if the word is one syllable. Add only an apostrophe if the noun is more than one syllable.**

  James's gloves are lying on the hall table.

  The **boss's** instructions are on her desk.

  The next **witness'** testimony is crucial to the defence.

  The **actress'** hopes were raised by the screen test.

- **To make a plural noun that ends with _s_ possessive, add only an apostrophe.**

  All **students'** marks will be posted by the main office.

  There will be a meeting of the **girls'** hockey team on Wednesday.

- **To make a plural noun that does not end with _s_ possessive, add _'s_.**

  Men's suits are on sale this week.

  The **children's** story hour has been cancelled.

- **To make a compound noun possessive, add _'s_ to the last word.**

  Mario borrowed his **father-in-law's** lawn mower over the weekend.

- **To indicate that two or more people own one thing (joint possession), add _'s_ to the last name.**

  Carmen and Roberta's restaurant opened last month.

- **To indicate that two or more people own things separately (separate possession), make all the names possessive.**

  Ralph's and **Howard's** cars are in for repairs.

Note: Possessive nouns do not always refer to people. They can also refer to animals or objects.

  The **sun's** rays are very strong today.

  Today's news is better.

  This **society's** children have special needs.

Other Uses of the Apostrophe

- **To form the plural of letters, add _'s_.** Italicize or underline the letter but not the _s_.

  Pay particular attention to the long **_o_'s** in this poem.

- **To form the plural of words referred to as words, add _'s_.** Italicize or underline the word but not the _s_.

  There are five **_a lot_'s** in this one paragraph.

- **To form the plural of abbreviations, add _'s_.**

  She has two **MA's**, one in English and one in history.

- **You have a choice in forming the plural of numerals and dates. Add _'s_ or _s_ alone.**

  His family emigrated from Scotland in the **1920's [Or:1920s]**.

  What are the chances of rolling nothing but **2's [Or: 2s]** in a dice game?

Exercise 6

Add all necessary apostrophes to the following sentences:

1. Helens and Stephanies projects both won honourable mentions at this years science fair.

2. Several patrons cars were vandalized in the mall parking lot.

3. Nobodys pecan pie is as good as yours.

4. For some reason, I can never remember that _vacuum_ has two _us_ and only one _c_.

5. Its important to respond to your hostess invitation promptly and courteously.

6. Lester and Marys puppy chewed up three pairs of shoes in less than a week.

7. Justins parents cottage is badly in need of a new roof.

8. I need to buy some apples and bananas for the childrens lunches.

9. Short pauses in your oral presentation are perfectly acceptable. Dont fill the space with _ums_ and _uhs_.

10. Wont you have more tea and another of Grandmother Mildreds ginger snap cookies?

---

4. COLONS AND DASHES

The **colon** and the **dash** can both be used to introduce a phrase or clause that explains or illustrates what precedes it. Whereas a colon is more formal, a dash is less formal.

After the tenth day without food, the subject began to exhibit psychological debilitation: he had trouble concentrating and slept much of the time.

I still love listening to the Beatles—they remind me of the sixties.

A pair of dashes can also be used to enclose parenthetical comments that slightly disrupt the flow of the sentence. By using dashes rather than commas or parentheses, you can set off these comments more emphatically from the rest of the sentence.

> The relationship between father and son—never very good—worsened as the son began to assert his independence.

Be careful not to overuse the colon and the dash. Too many sentences containing colons will make your writing too formal and stilted, and, as Lewis Thomas says, make your reader feel like he or she is being ordered around. On the other hand, too many sentences containing dashes will make your writing look too choppy and informal.

Colons

Use a colon in the following situations:

- **To introduce a list or series preceded by a complete main clause**

  You will need the following equipment: a small tent, a sleeping bag, and a camp stove.

- **In a sentence introducing a list of items**, you can use a colon after a verb when *as follows* or *the following* is **strongly implied**, as in this example:

  Our report includes:

  1. background information about the problem

  2. an analysis of its causes

  3. recommendations for solutions

  4. a detailed budget

Note: Do **not** use a colon with *such as* or *for example*.

> NOT   The Robinsons brought back a number of souvenirs, such as: a red plush cushion with "Visit Niagara Falls" emblazoned on it, a slightly pornographic calendar, and two incredibly ugly beer mugs.
>
> BUT   The Robinsons brought back a number of souvenirs, such as a red plush . . .

- **To introduce a concluding explanatory phrase**

  She dedicated her research to one goal: finding the link between Einstein's theory of relativity and the theory of quantum mechanics.

- **To join main clauses when the second clause restates, explains, summarizes, or emphasizes the first**

  The movie was a complete waste of time: the plot dragged, the characters were boring, and the special effects were silly.

- **To introduce a formal quotation.** Both the sentence introducing the quotation and the quotation itself must be grammatically complete.

  In Alice Munro's short story "Boys and Girls," the narrator gradually becomes aware of the full implications of being a girl: "A girl was not, as I had supposed, simply what I was; it was what I had to become. It was a definition, always touched with emphasis, with reproach and disappoint-ment. Also it was a joke on me."

Note: Do **not** use a colon when the sentence introducing the quotation ends with *that* or is otherwise incomplete.

NOT   Hamlet shows a new acceptance of death when he says that: "There is a special providence in the fall of a sparrow."

BUT   Hamlet shows a new acceptance of death when he says that "There is a special providence in the fall of a sparrow."

- **In biblical references** (John 3:16)
- **In time references** (9:45, 12:05)
- **Between the title and the subtitle of an article or a book**

  (*A Harvest Yet to Reap: A History of Prairie Women*)
- **After the salutation in a business letter**

  Dear Business Manager:

  Dear Editor:

  Dear Ms. Bennett:

Dashes

Use a dash in the following situations:

- **To indicate a sudden interruption or change of thought**

  I left my briefcase—I remember it distinctly—right here by the front entrance.

  And then she said—but I see you've already heard the story.
- **To emphasize parenthetical remarks**

  Antonia worked hard—perhaps too hard—in spite of her illness.
- **After a series at the beginning of a sentence**

  Sports figures, entertainers, politicians—all have been invited to the wedding.
- **To set off a series that comes in the middle of a sentence**

  It had everything—power, grace, beauty—that Chantal wanted in a car.
- **To emphasize an expression that explains or illustrates**

  Philip worked tirelessly toward his goal—an A in English.

Exercise 7

Add colons and dashes where appropriate to the following sentences. Where either is possible, be prepared to explain your choice. If the sentence is correct, write **C**.

1. Mae West offers an interesting perspective on making moral choices "When choosing between two evils, I always like to try the one I've never tried before."

2. I have registered in the following courses for the winter term Basic Calculus, Fluid Dynamics, and Introductory Drafting.

3. I am convinced I say this without reservation that Brad and Jennifer will never get back together.

4. None of the suspects Winken, Blinken, or Nod knew that they were under surveillance for stealing the sleeping pills.

5. My cat Puck is an excellent companion he is intelligent, affectionate and infinitely patient.

6. He had no means of escape all of the exits were blocked.

7. When Herb boasted that he was a "self-made man," Vernon replied, "That's the trouble with cheap labour."

8. Weaving and willow furniture all will be for sale at the spring craft show.

5. PARENTHESES AND BRACKETS

Both **parentheses** and **brackets** serve to set apart certain information in a sentence or a paragraph, but they are used in different circumstances.

Parentheses

Use parentheses in the following situations:

- **To set off supplementary material that interrupts the flow of the sentence**

  The council finally agreed (but only after a heated debate) to the proposed amendments.

Note 1: Parentheses, dashes, and commas can all be used to set off nonessential information. When you enclose material in parentheses, you signal to your reader that it is relatively unimportant. Dashes tend to emphasize its importance, whereas commas will give it approximately equal weight.

Note 2: Do *not* use parentheses to enclose important information. In the example below, the parentheses are misleading because they suggest that essential information is incidental.

  Although he was only fifteen, Victor was sentenced to nine months in a juvenile detention centre. (This sentence was the result of his fifth conviction for theft over $1,000 in two years.)

- **To enclose explanatory material, such as bibliographical citations, brief definitions, and pieces of historical information**

  The Celsius (centigrade) thermometer was invented by the Swedish astronomer Anders Celsius (1701–1744).

- **To enclose letters or numerals in a list of items**

  Each oral presentation will be graded on (1) delivery, (2) voice, (3) content, and (4) language.

Resist the temptation to use parentheses too often. Information enclosed in parentheses interrupts the flow and meaning of a sentence. Too many of these interruptions will make your writing sound haphazard and your ideas irrelevant, as in this example:

Headhunting (often called an executive search) is the practice of seeking out (sometimes through advertising, sometimes through more direct approaches to individuals) senior, specialized employees (when no one with sufficient expertise is available within an organization) for business.

Rewritten with only one pair of parentheses, the paragraph reads much more smoothly.

Headhunting (as executive searches are often called) is the practice of seeking out specialized senior employees for business firms when no one with sufficient expertise is available within an organization. Headhunters may advertise these positions or approach prospective candidates directly.

Using Other Punctuation with Parentheses

- If the parenthetical remark is a **sentence within another sentence**, the parenthetical sentence does not begin with a capital or end with a period.

  The baby was sleeping (at least his eyes were closed) when I peeked into the room.

- If the parenthetical remark is a **complete separate sentence**, capitalize the first word and put the end punctuation inside the closing parenthesis.

  After weeks of dull, cloudy weather, the first snowflakes began to fall on Christmas Eve. (The children had been convinced that Christmas wouldn't be Christmas without snow.)

- If the parenthetical construction within a sentence **requires a question mark or exclamation mark**, that punctuation goes inside the closing parenthesis.

  It is important for students to learn how to think (who can deny that necessity?), but they also need facts and information to think about.

Brackets

Use brackets in the following ways:

- **To enclose explanatory material inserted into a quotation.** These square brackets tell your reader that the material was not part of the original quotation.

  In the essay "Grace before Meat," Charles Lamb says, "I hate a man who swallows it [his food], affecting not to know what he is eating. I suspect his taste in higher matters."

Note: The punctuation of the original sentence (the comma after *it*) goes outside the material enclosed in brackets.

- **To show that you have changed a word** (usually a verb or a pronoun) in a direct quotation so that it will fit grammatically with your sentence

  Old King Cole [is] a merry old soul / And a merry old soul [is] he.

- **With the word *sic* (Latin for *thus*)** to indicate that an error in spelling, grammar, or fact is part of the original quotation

  The reporter stated, "Affects [*sic*] of cutbacks [are] not yet known."

6. QUOTATION MARKS

The main purpose of **quotation marks** is to acknowledge that you have used someone else's words. Use quotation marks in the following situations:

- Whenever you **quote** from any printed material

  According to Vince Raley, many primatologists and psychologists believe that "chimpanzees have the capacity for self-awareness, self-consciousness, and self-knowledge" (126).

- When you **include comments** made by someone you have interviewed

  According to Sharon Bush, records clerk in the registrar's office, "The completion rate for this course averages about 30 percent."

- When you **include dialogue** in a personal narrative or a short story. Indent the words of each speaker as you would indent separate paragraphs.

  "Do you have any plans to publish your autobiography?" the critic asked the novelist.

  "Actually, I was saving the best till last," remarked the author. "I might even arrange to have it published posthumously."

  "The sooner, the better," replied the critic.

Note: Remember that quotation marks set off direct speech. Don't use them with indirect speech.

DIRECT SPEECH	The clerk asked the customer, "Will you pay cash, or shall I charge this purchase to your account?"
INDIRECT SPEECH	The clerk asked the customer whether she wanted to pay cash or charge the purchase to her account.

- Use single quotation marks to indicate a **quotation within a quotation**.

  The witness testified, "I was present when the accused said, 'She'll pay for what she did to me!'"

Other Uses of Quotation Marks

- Put quotation marks around the titles of short works that have not been published separately, such as titles of chapters, short stories, articles, and most poems.

    His favourite Poe story is "The Fall of the House of Usher."

- When you want to **draw your reader's attention to a word used in a special way**, you can either underline/italicize the word or put quotation marks around it.

    It's quite acceptable to begin a sentence with *because*.

    It's quite acceptable to begin a sentence with "because."

- Do **not** use quotation marks or italics merely to draw attention to slang or irony or to disown words or clichés that you don't want responsibility for.

    NOT   My sister has become a real "couch potato."

    NOT   Our "paperboy" is at least fifty years old.

    NOT   We need "to think outside the box" to solve this problem.

Exercise 8

Use quotation marks appropriately in the following sentences. If the sentence is correct, write **C**.

1. Two negatives make a positive, explained Ludwig. However, two positives don't make a negative.

2. Yeah, right! replied Noam.

3. Heather said that she would pick Katie up from work and save Mother the trip.

4. According to an old Russian proverb, When money talks, the truth keeps silent.

5. I wish you would stop saying like and basically in every sentence. That habit drives me crazy, you know.

6. Virginia Woolf's essay The Death of the Moth is a thoughtful meditation on the nature of the life force.

Using Other Punctuation with Quotation Marks

When you close a quotation, you may be uncertain whether the end punctuation goes inside or outside the quotation marks. Follow these guidelines:

- **As a general rule, commas and periods go inside quotation marks; colons and semicolons go outside of them.**

Staring in disgust at the cans of escargots in the specialty section of the grocery store, Mr. Johnson remarked to his wife, "Let's can all the snails from the garden. We'll make a fortune." [The period is inside the quotation marks.]

Facing Mr. Waters squarely, William replied, "That, sir, is not your concern"; he then walked resolutely out of the room. [The semicolon is outside the quotation marks.]

- **When a quotation is a question or an exclamation, the question or exclamation mark goes inside the quotation marks.**

"Where are the snows of yesteryear?" she asked pensively.

"Get out of my way!" the enraged customer bellowed as he pushed through the crowd.

- **When the entire sentence containing the quotation is a question or an exclamation, the question or exclamation mark goes outside the quotation marks.**

What does it mean to say, "A stitch in time saves nine"?

The Great China Circus is now truly "the greatest show on Earth"!

- **When a quotation ends a sentence, whatever punctuation is inside the quotation mark also ends the entire sentence. Don't add any other punctuation.**

Jane listened with growing horror as the voice from the attic screamed, "Please let me out!"

When you have a parenthetical citation, however, the end punctuation goes after the citation. The sentence is not grammatically complete without this citation.

In *The Jazzonians*, Graff writes, "Ballroom dancing is art set to music" (103).

Exercise 9

Use quotation marks and other punctuation appropriately in the following sentences. If the sentence is correct, write **C**.

1. No, I won't move my car shouted the irate driver

2. Aunt Eva is fond of saying that no one is responsible for making another person happy

3. Was it Archimedes who said Give me a firm place to stand, and I will move the earth

4. The term portmanteau word refers to a word combining the sounds and meanings of two other words. For example, the word smog is a blending of the words smoke and fog

5. In today's English class we explored the attitudes to war expressed in Wilfred Owen's poem Dulce et Decorum Est and Randall Jarrell's poem The Death of the Ball Turret Gunner

6. What did Mother mean when she said The acorn never falls far from the oak tree

7. If fifty million people say a foolish thing noted Anatole France it is still a foolish thing

8. Hearing the familiar bell, the children ran into the street yelling We all scream for ice cream

9. The words chimpanzee, gorilla, and zebra all came into English from African languages

10. Sitting alone in the darkened room, Steve morosely hummed the tune to Sam Cooke's Sad Mood

7. ITALICS AND UNDERLINING

Use **italic** script in typeset and word-processed material, or **underlining** in handwritten or typewritten material, **for each of the following cases**:

- For the **titles** of books, newspapers, magazines, pamphlets, plays, films, television and radio series, works of art, albums, or long musical compositions

The city library has purchased two sets of *The Canadian Encyclopedia*.

The police drama *Southland,* though loved by critics, was dropped by NBC.

- For the **names** of airplanes, ships, trains, and spacecraft

Very Important: Do not italicize or underline *the* or abbreviations that come before a name.

Captain James Cook commanded the H.M.S. *Resolution* on his second Pacific voyage.

- For **foreign words and phrases** that have not been accepted as English terms

Examples of these expressions include the following:

bon vivant (a person who enjoys food and drink)

casus belli (an event that brings about war)

carpe diem (seize the day)

Weltanschauung (a comprehensive concept of the universe and the relationship of humans to it)

- **For words referred to as words, letters referred to as letters, and numerals referred to as numerals**

The one word on the test that I couldn't define was *dipsomaniac*.

Don't forget to cross your *t*'s.

Is this an *8* or a *3*?

- **For emphasis and clarity**

  I asked *who* you are, not *how* you are.

  Late papers will *not* be accepted.

Note: Be cautious whenever you are tempted to use italics for emphasis. Like exclamation marks, italics lose their effectiveness if overused.

8. HYPHENS

Hyphens are used as part of some compound words (*father-in-law*, *trade-in*). Other compound words are written as one word (*hairbrush*, *stepmother*) or as two words (*lawn bowling*, *token payment*). Because there is no pattern for forming compound words, and because compound words are constantly changing, your best source of current information is an up-to-date dictionary.

You may even find that dictionaries disagree on compound forms. For instance, the term *cyberbullying* is also written as *cyber bullying* and *cyber-bullying*. If dictionaries disagree, choose one spelling of your term and use it consistently throughout your piece of writing.

Use a hyphen in the following ways:

- With **two-word numbers** from twenty-one to ninety-nine

  There are **ninety-nine** bottles of beer on the wall.

- With **numbers used as adjectives**

  Is the tank **three-quarters** full?

  Atsuko, a **thirty-four-year-old** musician, made her television debut last night.

- With the **prefixes** *self* (*self-satisfied*), *ex* (*ex-husband*), and *all* (*all-purpose*); with **prefixes that come before proper nouns** (*anti-Catholic*); and with the **suffix** *elect* (*minister-elect*).

- To **avoid an awkward combination** of letters or to **prevent misunderstanding**: *re-cover* (cover again)

- To indicate that **two or more prefixes or words share a common root**

  Both **pre-** and **post-natal** classes are available.

  This course covers **eighteenth-** and **nineteenth-century** drama.

- To **join two or more words that function as a single adjective** conveying a single concept: Liza's *well-written essay* won the award; David's *reddish-brown hair* is the envy of many.

Note 1: However, if these constructions come after the noun, they are **not** hyphenated.

  The essay is well written.

  Her hair is reddish brown.

Note 2: If the group of words contains an *ly* adverb, do **not** hyphenate: *poorly conceived plan, frequently used reference book.*

Hyphenating Words at the End of Lines

It's best to avoid dividing words at the end of a line if possible. Occasionally, however, you may not be able to squeeze all the letters onto the line you are writing. Here are the guidelines to follow:

- **Always hyphenate a word between syllables.** The first part of the word must contain at least three letters. Try to divide the word in two approximately equal parts that convey the sense of the whole word (*butter-fly* not *but-terfly*).

- **Include a single-letter syllable with the first part of the word** (*regu-late* not *reg-ulate*).

- If the root word ends in a double consonant, **divide between the root word and the suffix** (*bill-ing* not *bil-ling*).

- Do **not** hyphenate **one-syllable words or words of five or fewer letters** (regardless of the number of syllables). If possible, avoid hyphenating words of six letters.

- Do **not** hyphenate **figures** ($21.36, 123,000), dates (Dec. 10, 1926), **abbreviations** (UNICEF), or **proper names** (Albert Einstein, Calgary).

- Do **not** hyphenate the **last word of more than two consecutive lines**.

- Do **not** hyphenate the **last word in a paragraph or the last word on a page**.

Exercise 10

Add, change, or take out hyphens as necessary in the following sentences:

1. This neutral carpet can serve as an allpurpose floor-covering in any room.

2. You are looking particularly selfsatisfied after winning the job over twenty three equally-qualified candidates.

3. If you want to use gender neutral terms, use "workers" rather than "work-men" and "humanity" rather than "man-kind."

4. The ninety year old woman made her first parachute jump on the week-end.

5. Julia's ex boyfriend returned all the compact-disks she had given him as presents.

Exercise 11

How would you hyphenate each of the following words if it appeared at the end of a line? If the word should not be hyphenated, write **C**.

1. iconoclast
2. crybaby
3. wrapping
4. faded
5. CUSO

6. railroad
7. thrilling
8. jimjams
9. memorize
10. radio

9. ABBREVIATIONS

Abbreviations are appropriate in scientific and technical writing and in footnotes and bibliographies. In most other kinds of writing, though, use abbreviations sparingly. If you wish to abbreviate a term that you intend to use repeatedly, write the term out completely the first time you use it, and then use the abbreviation.

American Sign Language (ASL) is the first language of many deaf children. Because ASL has a different grammatical structure from English, deaf children who use ASL must learn English as a second language.

The following guidelines cover the appropriate uses of abbreviations in nontechnical writing.

Names of Dates and Times

- **Write out the names of months and holidays.**

    Hanukkah comes in the darkest part of December.

- Use *a.m.* (*ante meridiem*) to refer to exact times before noon and *p.m.* (*post meridiem*) to refer to exact times after noon. Note that these abbreviations are not capitalized.

    The meeting began at 9:07 a.m. and concluded at 5:31 p.m.

- **Use *BC* (Before Christ) to refer to dates before the birth of Christ.** Put *BC* after the date. **Use *AD* (*Anno Domini*) to refer to dates after the birth of Christ.** Put *AD* before the date. Stop using *AD* when you can assume that your reader knows that the event did not take place before the birth of Christ, usually for any date after AD 500.

    Julius Caesar, who unified the Roman Empire under his dictatorship, was assassinated in **44 BC**.

    Hadrian's Wall, completed in **AD 123**, was constructed to prevent northern tribes from invading Roman Britain.

    If you prefer, use *BCE* (Before the Common Era) and *CE* (Common Era). Both of these abbreviations follow the year.

Units of Measurement

Write out metric words such as *gram, metre*, and *kilometre* when you use them without numerals.

Speed limits are now given in **kilometres** per hour.

Abbreviate these words when you use them with a numeral. Don't put a period after the abbreviation.

Combine **100 g** flour with **1 L** milk.

Scientific and Technical Terms

Some commonly known scientific and technical terms are usually abbreviated.

DNA (deoxyribonucleic acid)

DDT (dichlorodiphenyltrichloroethane)

AIDS (acquired immune deficiency syndrome)

Common Latin Terms

Although it's useful to know the following Latin abbreviations, it's usually better to omit them or replace them with English equivalents. If you use them, note the periods.

e.g.   *exempli gratia* (for example)

i.e.   *id est* (that is)

etc.   *et cetera* (and so forth)

Be especially careful with *etc*. Using it at the end of a list suggests that you have run out of ideas. Instead, end the list with an inclusive phrase like "and other. . . ." or begin the list with the phrase *such as* or an equivalent expression.

NOT   The Niagara region grows apples, peaches, pears, **etc**.

BUT   The Niagara region grows apple, peaches, pears, **and other fruits**.

OR   The Niagara region grows fruits **such as** apples, peaches, and pears.

The Ampersand (&)

Never use this symbol in general writing. Use the ampersand only when you are copying the name of an organization or following APA documentation style.

He works the night shift at the local **A&W**.

Maccoby, E. E., **&** Jacklin, C. N. (1974) . . .

10. CAPITALIZATION

All proper nouns are capitalized. A proper noun names a specific person, place, or thing.

> Meet me at the main entrance of **The Bay**.

Use capitalization in the following way:

- For kinship terms such as mother, father, brother, sister when they are part of a name (as in *Mother Teresa, Grandfather McGregor*) or when they are used as a substitute for the proper name. Do not capitalize kinship terms preceded by a possessive adjective (*my, our, your, her, his, their*).

  Is **Baba Kostash** going to the dance?

  Is **Grandfather** going to the dance?

  We are going with our father and mother.

- **For titles used as part of a person's name**

  I have a meeting with **Professor Qureshi** this afternoon.

  I get along well with two of my **professors** this term.

- **For the names of directions** (*north, south, east, west*) when they are part of a proper name or refer to a region

  It has always been his ambition to travel to the **North**. [a region]

  The house faces **north**. [a direction]

- **For the names of planets, stars, and other heavenly bodies.** Do not capitalize *sun* and *moon*. Do not capitalize *earth* when it is modified by *the*.

  The astronauts saw **Earth** from their spaceship.

  Unless we act now, all the waters of **the earth** will be polluted.

- **For the names of institutions, organizations, political parties, and branches of government.** Do not capitalize words such as *party, college,* or *university* unless you are using the term as a shortened version of the full name.

  Faryl has a **university** degree in biology.

  Tim will complete his final year at **Capilano College** this spring.

- **For nationalities, languages, religious groups, religions, sacred and religious names**

  Canadian, Cree, Protestant, Taoism, the Qur'an, the Bible

- **For days of the week, the months, holidays, events.** Do not capitalize the names of seasons.

  Monday, January, New Year's Eve, the Middle Ages, summer, winter, spring, fall

- **For the names of specific courses.** Do not capitalize the names of general subjects, except languages.

Psychology 101, **Chemistry** 400

I studied **English, French, drama, math**, and **sociology** in my first year of university.

Other Occasions for Capitalization

- **Capitalize the first word in a quotation if the quotation is a complete sentence.** If the quotation is not a complete sentence, do not capitalize the first word.

  The instructor turned to me and said, "Please give me your views on the opening scene in *Macbeth.*"

  Susan remarked that she would rather be "poor and healthy" than "rich and sick."

- **When using MLA style, capitalize *all* words in the titles** of books, short stories, plays, poems, articles, newspapers, magazines, movies, and musical compositions *except* articles, conjunctions and prepositions of fewer than four letters. However, you must capitalize *any* word that immediately follows a period, colon, or dash or is the first or last word in a title.

"Back in the USSR"	*River of the Brokenhearted*
"To an Athlete Dying Young"	*The American*

11. NUMBERS

Numerals are appropriate and preferred in scientific and technical writing. In general writing, however, certain conventions determine the use of numerals or words to express numbers.

Numerals

Use numerals in nontechnical writing in the following cases:

- **To provide a series of numbers**

  In 1986, **250** children were involved in the school lunch program. By 1987, the number had increased to **300** children. Last year, **350** children were eating lunch at school.

- **To express a number that would take more than two words to spell out**

  Last year the shelter for battered women helped **259** women and their children.

- **To express exact times of the day and with *a.m.* and *p.m.***

  We'll begin the meeting at **9:15 a.m.** sharp.

  The plane from Toronto will arrive at **8:03 p.m.**

- **To express exact sums of money**

  This wonderful car can be yours for only **$14,999.99**.

- **To express dates.** Years are always expressed in numerals; centuries should be written out.

The events between **1939** and **1945** affected the rest of the **twentieth century**.

You can use *st, nd, rd, th* with numerals in dates if you do not give the year, but these abbreviations are not essential.

The concert is scheduled for August 20th [**Or:** August 20].

- **To express addresses**

  2939 107 Street; #976, 10098 Elm Street; P.O. Box 12

- **To express percentages and decimals**

  29%, 87 percent, 3.9 cm

- **To express page, line, verse, act, and scene numbers in literary works.**

  Act 3, Scene 2, lines 23–38 [**Or:** 3.2.23–28]

  John 1:1–5; 1 and 2 Corinthians

Words

Use words in place of numerals in these instances:

- **For numbers that can be spelled out in one or two words**

  At least **fifty** people were invited to the party.

- **To express approximate numbers used with money, times of day, and measurements.** In these cases, the whole of the round number should be expressed in words. If the number is *very* large, a combination of numerals and words can be used.

  When Grandpa Koehler was a child, he could buy a huge bag of candy for less than **ten cents**.

  Every day she gets up at around **five o'clock** to do her homework.

  By the end of this century, **10 billion** people will compete for the earth's resources.

- **When a sentence begins with a number**

  Thirty percent of first-year students need some form of financial assistance.

Note: Use a combination of words and numerals as necessary to prevent confusion.

NOT   He ordered **2 10 cm** pieces of wood.

BUT   He ordered **two 10 cm** pieces of wood.

Exercise 12

Correct all errors in the use of numerals or words to express numbers in the following sentences. If the sentence is correct, write **C**.

1. He bought 4 250-page packages of binder paper at the beginning of the term.

2. 15 percent of those polled responded that they were still undecided about how they would vote in the election.

3. At least 20 customers have returned the sheets because they were labelled the wrong size.

4. Including the sales tax, the chocolate bar costs $1.14.

5. Some sports analysts say that Wayne Gretzky was at his peak playing with the Edmonton Oilers in the nineteen eighties. Gretzky retired from professional hockey in nineteen ninety-nine.

Weblinks

- Guide to Grammar & Writing, Capital Community College—links to word- and sentence-level topics, among others; includes interactive quizzes

  grammar.ccc.commnet.edu/grammar/

- UBC Writing Centre Online Resources—links to Purdue University On-Line Writing Lab; The Rensselaer Writing Center; University of Victoria Writer's Guide; Rutgers University Guide to Grammar and Style

  www.writingcentre.ubc.ca/online_resources.html

- UBC Writing Centre's Writers' Workshop—links to dictionaries, grammar and composition resources, general writing references

  www.writingcentre.ubc.ca/workshop/reference.htm

- Maine Writing Project—links to grammar and mechanics guide, writing resources, dictionaries, thesauruses, foreign language dictionaries, citation format guides, ESL resources, composition and rhetoric resources

  mainewritingproject.org/mwp/

- Hypergrammar, University of Ottawa Writing Centre—online grammar handbook

  www.uottawa.ca/academic/arts/writcent/hypergrammar/

- Advice on Academic Writing, University of Toronto—links to style and editing resources, grammar and punctuation resources, ESL answers, among others

  www.writing.utoronto.ca/advice

- University of Wisconsin-Madison Writing Center, Writer's Handbook—links to resources on grammar and punctuation, improving your writing style, among others

www.wisc.edu/writing/Handbook/index.html

General Writing Resources

If you log on to **www.altavista.com** and type "online writing" in the SEARCH box, you will find dozens of sites for online writing resources.

ANSWER KEY

Exercise 1

1. two suitcases, called a cab, and headed for the airport.

2. eye of newt, toe of frog, wool of bat, and tongue of dog.

3. to put the armoire in the master bedroom, the console in the hall, and the pine desk in the study.

4. bread, cheese, cold cuts, fruit, and sodas

5. the meat was underdone, the vegetables were soggy, and the wine was sour.

6. We must go now, for our ferry leaves exactly at noon.

7. Freida knocked down the wall, and David hauled away the rubble.

8. Liam is a painstaking editor, yet a few small errors escaped even his sharp eye.

9. The Richardsons knew that they must replace the worn linoleum and repaint the walls a neutral colour, or the house would never sell.

10. When Fiona first began working as a cashier, she thought that she would never remember the PLU's for produce, but she had soon memorized dozens of codes.

Exercise 2

1. For example, pizza/food groups, but

2. in Calgary, Louis

3. on the tile floor, he

4. High above, the planes

5. No, I don't remember

6. fever, isn't it?

7. no man, if you catch my drift.

8. the savage breast, not the savage beast.

Exercise 3

1. Thank you, Mr. Sutherland,

2. **C**

3. Punch Dickins, who won the Distinguished Flying Cross in World War I,

4. python, which hasn't eaten in a month,

5. promised us, however, that

Exercise 4

1. However, I always counter, "Look

2. turkey sandwiches, turkey casserole, and turkey croquettes

3. has expired, Mr. Fortino, is not

4. microwave sounded, Ted

5. **C** [no commas]

6. Whenever we go camping, Father always says, "If you don't fish where the fish are, you'll be having hot dogs for supper."

7. opened the window, took a deep breath, and composed

8. The one novel that I didn't read was the basis for the essay question on the English exam. [no commas]

9. Lucy Maud Montgomery, the author of *Anne of Green Gables*, was born in Clifton, Prince Edward Island, on November 30, 1874.

10. Well, you

11. perspective, I

12. Yes, we do

13. Howard would bring the food, Cliff would bring the drinks, and you

14. deep drifts, and icicles

15. Taxes, of course, are

16. Even during the day, light

17. Mr. Ramondo said, "We're a few bricks short of a load, but I

18. **C** [no commas]

19. dark, stormy night, I like nothing better than to

20. to study engineering because she discovered that

Exercise 5

1. astronaut; he

2. **C**

3. The variety show will feature Vox Populi, a well-known local band; the Crazy Bones, a hilarious comedy act; and the Tumbling Turners, an acrobatic troupe.

4. pay for the new jeans; however, his

5. open the door; but, fortunately, a quick glance

6. family; Erica has therefore agreed (**Or:** has, therefore, agreed)

7. interpretation, he was pleased

8. night; as a result, farmers are

Exercise 6

1. Helen's/Stephanie's/year's

2. patrons' cars

3. Nobody's

4. *u*'s

5. It's/hostess'

6. Lester and Mary's

7. Justin's/parents'

8. children's

9. Don't/*um*'s/*uh*'s.

10. Won't/Mildred's

Exercise 7

1. choices: "When choosing

2. term: Basic Calculus, Fluid Dynamics, and Introductory Drafting

3. convinced—I say this without reservation—that Brad and

4. suspects—Winken, Blinken, or Nod—knew

5. companion: he

6. escape: all [**Or:** escape—all]

7. **C**

8. furniture—all

Exercise 8

1. "Two negatives make a positive," explained Ludwig. "However, two positives don't make a negative."

2. "Yeah, right!" replied Noam.

3. **C**

4. proverb, "When money talks, the truth keeps silent."

5. "like" and "basically" [**Or:** *like* and *basically*]

6. essay "The Death of the Moth"

Exercise 9

1. "No, I won't move my car!" shouted the irate driver.

2. **C**

3. said, "Give me a firm place to stand, and I will move the earth"?

4. The term "portmanteau word" refers to a word combining the sounds and meanings of two other words. For example, the word "smog" is a blending of the words "smoke" and "fog." [period goes inside the quotation marks] [**Or:** *portmanteau word/smog/ smoke/fog.*]

5. poem "Dulce et Decorum Est" and Randall Jarrell's poem "The Death of the Ball Turret Gunner." [period goes inside the quotation marks]

6. said, "The acorn never falls far from the oak tree"?

7. "If fifty million people say a foolish thing," noted Anatole France, "it is still a foolish thing."

8. yelling, "We all scream for ice cream!"

9. "chimpanzee"/"gorilla"/"zebra" [**Or:** *chimpanzee/gorilla/zebra*]

10. Sam Cooke's "Sad Mood."

Exercise 10

1. all-purpose floor covering

2. self-satisfied/twenty-three/equally qualified

3. "workmen"/"mankind"

4. ninety-year-old/weekend

5. ex-boyfriend/compact disks

Exercise 11

1. icono-clast

2. cry-baby

3. wrap-ping

4. **C** [no hyphen]

5. **C** [no hyphen]

6. rail-road

7. thrill-ing

8. jim-jams

9. memo-rize

10. **C** [no hyphen]

Exercise 12

1. four 250-page

2. Fifteen percent

3. twenty

4. **C**

5. 1980s **or** 1980's/1999

APPENDIX

ESSAY AND CITATION FORMAT

FORMAT CONVENTIONS

A1 FORMATTING: WRITING ASSIGNMENTS

The presentation of any written assignment not only creates a first impression but also ensures that your ideas are clearly communicated. Therefore, take time to proofread and format your paper properly, using the following guidelines.

■ *Typing*

Strive to produce a clean, professional-looking paper. Most instructors prefer papers to be typed and some insist on it. (Publishers accept only typed material.) If you are allowed to submit handwritten papers, use blue or black ink.

Make sure you have chosen an acceptable font, such as Times New Roman or Arial. Avoid fonts and typographical devices—especially on the title page and in the header—that create a cluttered look. Avoid last-minute problems by testing your printer well before the essay is due.

Proofread your final hard copy and, if necessary, make neat corrections in ink.

■ *Paper*

Use standard white computer paper that is 216 mm × 279 mm or 8½ × 11 in. Use only one side of the page.

■ *Computer settings and functions*

Become familiar with your computer's default settings and particularly those functions that change paragraph format (indenting, spacing), insert automatic page numbers, sort and format works cited or reference entries, and so forth.

■ *Spacing*

Always type double spaced to allow room for comments. Many readers also prefer handwritten work, such as exams, to be double spaced for the same reason.

■ *Margins*

The default margins on most word-processing programs are adequate. If you need to set margins, leave 2.5 cm (1 in.) margins all around the page. Left-justify your margins.

■ *Title*

The title should clarify your paper's main point to the reader. An essay's title is often a short form of the thesis. Don't use labels such as "Essay #1" or "Personal Essay." A better title would be "Animalizing and Displacing the Poor in Swift's 'A Modest Proposal.'"

■ *Title page*

Determine the documentation style you will use throughout your essay. Then see Section B (MLA) or Section C (APA) for title-page guidelines and sample title pages.

■ *Pagination*

In both the MLA and APA documentation styles, all pages are numbered at the top right corner. See Sections B and C to see how these right headers differ.

■ *Bibliography*

If your instructor requests it, end your paper with a bibliography, which is a reference list (in APA documentation style) or works cited (in MLA documentation style). Be sure to number these pages.

■ *Fastening*

Use a staple or paper clip to fasten the pages. (Some instructors and editors object to staples; all object to straight pins and other hazardous devices.)

■ *Copies*

Make at least two backup copies: one on your hard drive and one on a disk or memory key. Set your computer's backup function to ten minutes or less, and overwrite revisions as necessary.

■ *Compatibility*

Be aware of possible incompatibilities between the program you use at home and those of other computers you use to print or submit your work. If your computer lab doesn't allow disks or memory keys to be brought in from the outside because they might spread viruses, consider emailing your essay to yourself to print at school. If you submit work electronically, through a course tool such as Blackboard or by email attachment, ensure that your instructor will be able to open and convert your documents. For instance, don't send zipped files unless specifically requested to do so.

A2 DOCUMENTATION: GENERAL GUIDELINES

Whenever you use quotations, facts, or ideas from other sources, whether in a research paper or any other kind of writing, you must clearly indicate what you have borrowed, and you must do so in **two separate places**. That is, you must use parenthetical references (called *in-text citations*) to acknowledge your sources **within your paper** and also include a list of those sources **at the end of your paper**. The sources within the paper direct the reader to your reference list or works cited list at the end, which provides more complete bibliographical information.

Documenting your sources is important for several reasons. First, it enables your reader to check statements that you have made or to look up more information on your subject. Second, it ensures that you do not take credit for information that is not your own. For these reasons, knowing *what* to document is just as important as knowing *how* to do it.

- You **don't** need to document the source of commonly known pieces of information, such as the fact that the earth is the third planet from the sun, or the source of familiar quotations, such as Homer Simpson's infamous "D'Oh!"
- You **do** need to document quotations and paraphrases from primary and secondary sources.
- You **do** need to document the source of all facts, ideas, and opinions that are taken from other sources *whether or not* you have quoted directly or paraphrased (put these ideas in your own words). Be especially careful to acknowledge the source of statistics.

When paraphrasing, don't make the mistake of thinking that you can avoid acknowledging the source of your information by simply changing the wording slightly. Failure to cite your references in this situation is still **plagiarism**.

There are two main systems of documentation. The Modern Language Association of America (MLA) is the accepted authority for documentation in the humanities (for example, English, film studies, or philosophy). The American Psychological Association (APA) is the accepted authority for documentation in education, the social sciences (for example, psychology, sociology, or anthropology), and many fields in the physical sciences. See Sections B and C, respectively, for an introduction to these documentation styles.

A3 QUOTATIONS: GENERAL GUIDELINES

Although you need to acknowledge all your sources of information, you don't always need to quote. In fact, in non-literary essays, avoid quoting unless the exact wording seems particularly important. Better alternatives are paraphrasing and summarizing. However, when you analyze works of literature, such as essays and poems, you will probably use several short quotations to support each point you make.

It takes skill and practice to use direct quotations effectively. Here are some general points to remember.

■ *Use brief quotations to support points.*

When you are writing, make all the major points in your own words and then use brief quotations to support them. That is, do not rely on the quotation to speak for you or make your point; your reader's interpretation may be quite different from yours. Also, don't let quoted material dominate your paper. That is, try to shorten a passage by expressing most of it in your own words and quoting only the crucial part.

■ *Use quotations in context.*

Do not take quotations out of context and use them to mean something other than what the writer originally intended, as in this example, which is fairly typical of movie reviews.

Original Text

"The movie was entertaining, but it wasn't true to the characters and complexities of the novel."

Misleading Extract

"The movie was entertaining . . . true to the characters and complexities of the novel."

■ *Clarify the context for quotations.*

Introduce each quotation with a sentence clarifying its context. Identify the speaker and the circumstances of the comment. Don't string several quotations together. Make sure that the quotation fits grammatically with the sentence introducing it.

Weak Example
(Quotation not introduced)

"It is a truth universally acknowledged, that a single man in possession of a good fortune must be in want of a wife" (1). This quotation is a good example of Jane Austen's irony because in her time, it was single women who needed to marry, not single men.

Weak Example
(Quotation introduced but not commented on)

The opening sentence of *Pride and Prejudice* is ironic because "It is a truth universally acknowledged, that a single man in possession of a good fortune must be in want of a wife" (1).

Strong Example

The ironic opening sentence of Jane Austen's *Pride and Prejudice* introduces the novel's central concern—the economic necessity for women to marry: "It is a truth universally acknowledged, that a single man in possession of a good fortune must be in want of a wife" (1). In Austen's time, it was single women, not single men, who needed to marry to preserve their livelihoods and guarantee their futures.

■ *Punctuate quotations appropriately.*

Pay close attention to punctuation before the quotation. If the introductory material ends with *that* and you are integrating the quote grammatically into your sentence, you do not need to punctuate or capitalize the first word of the quotation, unless it is a proper noun.

> The writer of the editorial states **that** "the Gulf oil spill might be the one thing that sticks to President Obama" (Wellstead B9).

When you formally introduce a quotation with words such as *states, says, argues, remarks,* and so forth, use a comma. Capitalize the first word of the quotation.

In this morning's editorial, the writer states, "The Gulf oil spill might be the one thing that sticks to President Obama" (Wellstead B9).

Finally, use a colon after a sentence that introduces a long and grammatically complete quotation.

The editorial in this morning's paper captures how the recent environmental disaster may tarnish the reputation of Barack Obama: "The Gulf oil spill might be the one thing that sticks to [the president]" (Wellstead B9).

Notice that the end punctuation always follows the parenthetical citation, for the sentence is not grammatically complete without this reference. In the last example, note also how square brackets are used to indicate the change from "President Obama" to "the president."

These rules for introducing and punctuating quotations apply to all documentation styles; however, MLA and APA format differ when it comes to the names of the authors, the content of the parenthetical citations, and the treatment of page numbers.

B

DOCUMENTATION: MLA SYSTEM

As previously mentioned, the main system of documentation in the humanities is the one developed by the Modern Language Association of America. The material in this section is only a summary of the most common types of MLA documentation. Your college or university library may also have printed and electronic summaries; as well, numerous websites post style sheets for MLA users. For more advanced work, consult the explanations and examples in the 7th edition of the *MLA Handbook for Writers of Research Papers* or check the updates at <http://www.mla.org>.

Please note that your instructors may have specific preferences or additional guidelines for you to follow. Be sure to consult with them if you have any questions about MLA format.

B1 FORMATTING YOUR ESSAY

The First Page of Your Essay

The formatting guidelines in the previous section apply to essays in MLA style. Unless your instructor asks for a separate title page, prepare the first page of your paper as follows:

- Create a header that includes your last name and an automatically inserted page number. In Word 2010, create this header by going to the top Insert tab, and clicking "Page Number." From the two options (Top or Bottom), select Top, then make your selection for the page style. Next, type your last name in front of the page number, making sure to leave one space before it. For instance, if your last name is Raley and you follow this process, this header will appear on all pages of the essay as Raley 1, Raley 2, Raley 3, etc.

- Beginning on the first available line and flush with the left margin, type your name.

- On the next and subsequent double-spaced lines, type your instructor's name, your course number, and the date.

- On the next line, centre the title of your essay.

- Immediately below the title, begin your essay text. Indent the first line of all paragraphs 1.25 cm (1/2 inch) or one tab.

Here is a scaled-down example of the first page of an essay in the MLA style:

Raley 1

Carol Raley

Professor Pavic

English 111 (54X)

9 October 2010

Animalizing and Displacing the Poor in Swift's "A Modest Proposal"

   Jonathan Swift's classic essay "A Modest Proposal" is written from the perspective of a humble, mild-mannered economist who, after careful consideration, believes he has the solution to Ireland's dire poverty problem. Though the speaker builds a strong logical appeal through his clever causal analysis structure and his careful use of authorities and sources, his most potent persuasive tool is his pathos, particularly his word choice and imagery. His depictions of poverty as a mere mathematical problem and the poor as both criminals and animals are what truly make his case and convince his reader to accept his not-so-modest plan.

The Second and Subsequent Pages of Your Essay

- Consistently double space your entire paper (write on every second line). Do not insert extra spaces between paragraphs. If your computer automatically includes these spaces, you will have to turn off this feature. For instance, in the Home tab of Word 2010, select Paragraph, "Indents and Spacing," and check the box that says, "Don't add space between paragraphs of the same style."
- Indent the first word of all paragraphs 1.25 cm (1/2 inch) or one tab.
- Insert one space after a comma, period, colon, semicolon, and closing quotation mark.
- Do not insert a space between an opening punctuation mark and the first letter of a sentence OR a period (or comma) and the closing punctuation mark.

Treatment of Titles in Your Paper

- Italicize the title of independently published works such as books, plays, magazines, journals, websites, films, television shows, CDs, etc. For instance, the title of K-OS's third album, *Atlantis: Hymns for Disco,* is italicized.

- Put double quotation marks around shorter works inside longer or independently published works, such as poems, songs, stories, essays, articles in magazines or journals, and chapters of books. For instance, the title of "Sunday Morning," a song in *Atlantis: Hymns for Disco*, is placed inside double quotation marks.

- Capitalize the first, last, and all principal words (not articles and prepositions) of titles, regardless of whether these titles appear in the essay body or in the works cited list. For instance, in "Mirror in the Sky," a song from K-OS's third album, note how the preposition **in** and the article **the** are not capitalized.

B2 IN-TEXT CITATIONS

In-text citations provide enough information for your reader to locate full bibliographical references in your works cited list; they give page numbers (or, for some electronic sources, paragraph numbers) for quoted, paraphrased, and summarized material.

- The basic format consists of putting the last name of the author(s) and the page or paragraph number(s) in parentheses immediately after the quoted material and as close as possible to the paraphrased material.

  In Raymond Carver's short stories, characters are often limited by their silence and inarticulateness (Nolan 24).

- MLA format avoids repetition. Therefore, if you have included the name of the author(s) in your introduction to the quotation or paraphrase, which is often referred to as a signal phrase, provide only the page or paragraph number(s) in parentheses.

  Nolan argues that in Carver's fictional world, people are often limited by their inability to communicate (24).

- If you refer to more than one work by the same author, however, include a shortened version of the title in the parenthetical citation.

  In a recent article, Nolan explains how the setting of "Hopelessville" is central to Carver's fiction ("Nowhere to Go" 178).

- For works with two or three authors, write the last names in the order they appear on the title page. For works with more than three authors, either list all the authors or give only the first author's last name and add *et al.* (meaning "and others").

  The development of the bourgeois family can be traced in the novels of the nineteenth century (Seligman and Urbanowitz 112-13).

  The editors of this anthology provide helpful comments on prosody (Kennedy et al. 2330).

- For works without an author, use the first word of *or* a shortened version of the longer title that appears in the list of works cited.

> A *Daily Express News* editorial calls the film "a gross distortion of history" ("Crusade" A8).

Sample In-Text Citations

In the following entries, pay special attention to the punctuation surrounding the passage and the location of the in-text citations.

Quotations

■ *Short quotations of prose (author not previously identified)*

If the quotation is four typed lines or less, incorporate it into the body of your essay. Do not change the capitalization. If the quotation is obviously incomplete, do not put an ellipsis (three spaced periods) before or after it. Put the in-text citation after the quotation, followed by the end punctuation for the sentence.

> Elizabeth's pride in her own intelligence is obvious in her remark that she would "never ridicule what is wise and good" (Austen 50).

■ *Short quotations of poetry (author previously identified)*

Incorporate three lines or less of poetry into your sentence. Punctuate exactly as in the original. Use a slash, with a space before and after it, to indicate line divisions. Put the line reference in parentheses after the quotation. If you are quoting from a play with act, scene, and line numbers, give these in your reference.

> Claudius realizes that Hamlet is neither lovesick nor mad: "Love! His affections do not that way tend, / Nor what he spake, though it lacked form a little, / Was not like madness" (3.1.156-58).

■ *Long quotations of prose or poetry*

For quotations that are five typed lines or more, start on the next available line, double space, and indent the whole quotation 2.5 cm (1 inch) from the left margin. Do not use quotation marks unless the passage includes dialogue. Put the parenthetical citation **after** the final punctuation at the end of the long quotation. Because long quotations break up your text and require a lot of explanation, avoid using them unless you will be making very detailed commentary on the passage.

> John Donne begins "The Sun Rising" by complaining that the sun has awakened him and his beloved:
>
>> Busy old fool, unruly sun,
>> Why dost thou thus,
>> Through windows, and through curtains, call on us?
>> Must to thy motions lovers' seasons run? (1-4)

■ *Quoted words inside secondary sources*

In this example, notice the single quotation marks around two words that, in the original passage, were emphasized by double quotation marks:

> Andrew Nolan points out that "Carver's world of 'Hopelessville' is primarily populated by alcoholics, loners, misanthropes, and voyeurs" (51).

■ *Indirect source*

An indirect source is a source cited by one of the authors you are using. To be honest, you first cite the original source and then the one you actually have consulted. For instance, in the example below, the student is directly citing the words of one source (Singer) that were found in another secondary source written by Holmes. Because she does not have the original Singer source, her reference is written as the following:

> According to Singer, "In its rates of obesity, Canada is definitely catching up to America" (qtd. in Holmes 299).

Or:

> "In its rates of obesity, Canada is definitely catching up to America" (Singer, qtd. in Holmes 299).

Paraphrased or Summarized Material

■ *Paraphrase or summary from primary source (author not previously identified)*

Because the excerpt below is from an essay that refers to more than one work by Margaret Atwood, the parenthetical citation must also include the title.

> A severe thunderstorm passing directly overhead reminds Iris of the advice that Reenie would give the girls: every piece a dire warning calculated to instill fear (Atwood, *Blind Assassin* 135).

■ *Paraphrase or summary from secondary source (author not previously identified)*

> Tom is not changed by his encounters with Muff Potter, Dr. Robinson, and Injun Joe, even though encounters such as these would ordinarily affect how a person sees the world (Johnson 51).

B3 LIST OF WORKS CITED

At the end of your paper, on a separate sheet entitled "Works Cited," present a list of sources. Your list of works cited should include only the works you have actually cited in your paper. If you consulted a reference but did not cite it, do not include it on the list.

When using parenthetical citations and a final list of sources, you must be very careful, for there are two situations that constitute careless documentation and might lead to unintentional plagiarism: The first situation arises when there are more in-text citations than there are end references; in this case, you need to add entries to your works cited list. A second possible instance occurs when the entries in the works cited list do not match the parenthetical citations in the paper's body; in this case, you need to reread the paper carefully, making sure you have not forgotten to document any paraphrases or quotations.

The works cited list, then, is very important, for it gives you credibility, protects you against plagiarism, and allows your readers to find and further explore your sources.

- Place the works cited page at the end of the paper, in the same document, and number it sequentially.

- Centre the words "Works Cited" in plain, regular font (the same font and size used in your essay).

- Consistently double space the entire page; that is, double space within the entry and between entries. The first line of each entry should start at the left-hand margin. Use the hanging indent function on your computer to indent the subsequent lines of each entry by 1.25 cm (1/2 inch).

- List the entries alphabetically according to the author's last name. If a work has more than one author, keep the names in the order they are given and alphabetize according to the first name in the list.

- If the author is not given, alphabetize according to the first word in the title (do not count the articles *The, A,* or *An*).

- *Do not* number the entries.

- Make sure every reference is in a form your readers can find. For instance, if you have cited an essay in an edited collection by its author, the works cited entry should appear under the name of the author of the essay, not under the name of the editor.

- Include the medium of publication, otherwise known as the provenance of your source (Web, Print, Film, Transcript, DVD, CD, Performance.) This last rule was introduced in the 7th edition of the *MLA Handbook for Writers of Research Papers.*

In the following examples, note both the order of information and the punctuation.

Sample Works Cited Entries

Print Sources

■ *Article from a scholarly journal*

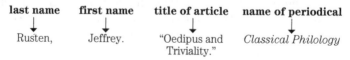

last name	first name	title of article	name of periodical
↓	↓	↓	↓
Rusten,	Jeffrey.	"Oedipus and Triviality."	*Classical Philology*

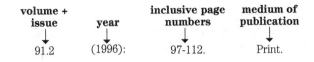

volume + issue	year	inclusive page numbers	medium of publication
↓	↓	↓	↓
91.2	(1996):	97-112.	Print.

■ *Book*

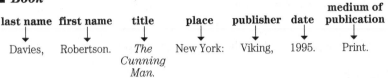

last name	first name	title	place	publisher	date	medium of publication
↓	↓	↓	↓	↓	↓	↓
Davies,	Robertson.	*The Cunning Man.*	New York:	Viking,	1995.	Print.

Note 1: If the city of publication is not well known or could be confused with another city of the same name, add the abbreviation for the province, state, or country (Paris, TX). If several places are listed, give only the first.

Note 2: Give only a short form of the publisher's name (McClelland, not McClelland & Stewart Ltd.).

■ *Chapter or article in an edited book*

Put the editor's name (if applicable) after the title and the inclusive page numbers of the part you are citing at the end.

> Atwood, Margaret. "Uglypuss." *Bluebeard's Egg.* Toronto: Seal, 1984. 67-93. Print.

> Cohen, Leonard. "Suzanne Takes You Down." *The HBJ Anthology of Literature.* Ed. Jon C. Stott, Raymond E. Jones, and Rick Bowers. Toronto: Harcourt, 1993. 632-33. Print.

> Drohan, Christopher M. "A Timely Encounter: Dr. Manhatten and Henri Bergson." *Watchmen and Philosophy.* Ed. Mark D. White. Hoboken: Wiley, 2009. 115-24. Print.

■ *Subsequent work by the same author*

Type three hyphens in place of the author's name. Continue as for the appropriate entry.

> ---. "Unearthing Suite." *Bluebeard's Egg.* Toronto: Seal, 1984. 240-58. Print.

■ *Multiple authors or editors*

Invert the order of the first name only.

> Barnet, Sylvan, and Hugo Bedau. *Critical Thinking, Reading, and Writing: A Brief Guide to Argument.* 4th ed. New York: Bedford, 2002. Print.

When there are more than three names, either list them all or use only the first name and *et al.*, following the same pattern you use for the in-text citation.

> Beaty, Jerome, et al., eds. *The Norton Introduction to Literature.* 8th ed. New York: Norton, 2002. Print.

■ Reference books

If the article is signed, the author's name comes first; if not, the title of the article comes first. If the reference work, such as an encyclopedia, is well known, omit the place of publication and the publisher, but include the edition (if given) and the year. If entries in the work are arranged alphabetically, omit the volume number and the page number.

"Biological Effects of Radiation." *Encyclopaedia Britannica.* 2008 ed. Print.

Electronic Sources

The format for citing material accessed through a portable electronic database, through an online database, or through the Internet does not differ much from other citations. Include everything you would give for the print version of the source, along with the following additional information:

1. *The date of the electronic publication*—Indicate both the date of the publication and the date you viewed it, for material online may be changed or updated frequently.

2. *The specific type of publication medium* (provenance)

Please note that unless you cannot locate the source without it, URLs are no longer required for Web publication entries.

You may not be able to find all of the required information. Cite what is available.

■ Books on CD-ROM

Cite these publications as you would the print version, but add the medium of publication.

medium
↓

The Oxford English Dictionary. 2nd ed. New York: Oxford UP, 1992. CD-ROM.

■ Article from an online database (pdf)

Several electronic databases are available online (Academic Search Premier, CPIQ, Eric) and by subscription through your college or university library. Provide all the information you would for the appropriate print version. Then add the name of the database (in italics) and the date you accessed the material.

Although according to MLA format the provenance and the website of your academic institution are no longer necessary, your instructor might still require them.

Strommen, Linda Ternan, and Barbara Fowles Mates. "Learning to Love Reading: Interviews with Older Children and Teens." *Journal of Adolescent & Adult Literacy* 48.3 (2007): 188-200. *Academic Search Premier.* Web. 24 May 2009.

↑   ↑

date accessed   **database**

Be sure to check with your instructor at your educational institution about preferences for citing online databases.

■ *Nonperiodical publications on the Web*

When you obtain research materials directly through your favourite search engine, include, in the order below, as much information as is available. Use periods to separate the items, except the website's publisher (or sponsor), which is followed by a comma.

- Name of the author, editor, etc.
- Title of the work, either in italics (if a major work) or in quotation marks (if part of a major work)
- Name of the website
- Version or edition used
- Website's publisher (or sponsor)
- Date of publication
- Provenance (Web)
- Date the website was accessed
- A URL if the website is difficult to find without it

■ *Article in an online magazine or newspaper*

Lewis, Leo. "Crime Student Charged with Murder after Death of Prostitutes." *Times Online.* Times Newspapers Ltd., 28 May 2010. Web. 23 June 2010.

Schachter, Lauren. "My Opera Monarch." *The Maynard.* 8 Feb. 2008. Web. 24 June 2010.

■ *Online article with no author*

"How to Make Vegetarian Chili." *eHow.com.* eHow, 10 May 2006. Web. 28 June 2010.

■ *E-mail message*

Smith, Graeme. "Re: Transgenics." Message to Brian Caplan. 2 June 2007. E-mail.

Other Sources

■ *Television program or radio broadcast*

"Episode 154." Host George Stroumboulopoulus. Perf. Jake Gyllenhaal, General Walter Natynczyk, and the Novaks. *The Hour.* CBC. 25 May 2010. Television.

■ *Film or video recordings*

Include the title, the director, the distributor, and the release date. Add any other information that is relevant to the discussion (such as the names of principal actors) just before the distributor and the release date. For videocassettes and similar recordings, give the original release date. Put the medium (DVD, Film) at the end of the entry.

Taken. Dir. Pierre Morel. Perf. Liam Neeson, Maggie Grace, and Leland Orser. Europa, 2009. Film.

If, instead of the film itself, you are citing the work of a director, actor, or screenwriter, begin your entry with that person's name.

■ *Interview*

Give the name of the person interviewed, the type of interview (personal, telephone, email), and the date.

Donahue, Bill. Personal interview. 24 May 2010.

DOCUMENTATION: APA SYSTEM

The system of documentation developed by the American Psychological Association (APA) is the accepted authority for research papers in education, health care, the social sciences (psychology, sociology, anthropology, and so forth), and many fields in the physical sciences. Students in a wide range of disciplines use this system of documentation for their papers.

The material in this section is only a summary of the most common types of APA documentation. Your college or university library may also have printed and electronic summaries; as well, numerous websites post style sheets for APA users. For more advanced work, consult the explanations and examples in the 6th edition of the *Publication Manual of the American Psychological Association*. For updates to APA style (especially electronic sources), consult http://www.apastyle.org.

Please note that your instructors may have specific preferences or additional guidelines for you to follow. Be sure to consult with them if you have any questions about APA format.

C1 FORMATTING YOUR RESEARCH PAPER

The general guidelines for formatting (Section A) also apply to student papers using the APA system of documentation. However, more rigorous formatting and stylistic requirements apply to papers published in professional journals. That is, for more formal papers, there are specific requirements for headings and sub-headings.

- Whereas the previous editions of APA asked for a right header on all pages of a manuscript, and a running head on the first available line of text, the current 6th edition asks for a combination of the running head and the page number, both of which are placed in the header portion. This running head and page number will appear on the title page and on all subsequent pages of your paper, including the references section.

  Although there are several ways to create the running head–page number combination in Word 2010, this is the easiest method: Go to the top Insert tab and select "Page Number." At the left margin, type an abbreviated version of your title in ALL uppercase letters. The running head, which must be no more than fifty characters, is followed by the page number. Cursor over until the page number is on the far right. If you follow this procedure, the running head and page number will appear on all pages of your text.

- Centre the rest of the information on the title page horizontally (Centre Align) and place it in the top half of the page (use Print Preview to judge). The official APA format calls only for the author's affiliation, followed by information about him or her, but most student papers usually include course information, as in our sample below. Present this information in double-space format:
  - the title of your paper
  - your name
  - the course and section number
  - the instructor's name
  - the date

Here is a scaled-down title page for the sample APA research essay:

MALE INVOLVEMENT IN VOLUNTEER PROGRAMS   1

Male Involvement in Social Services and

Healthcare Volunteer Programs

Sharon Cornelius

ENGL 108 Section 999

Jane Professor

April 18, 2011

C2 IN-TEXT CITATIONS

The basic information to be documented is the last name(s) of the author(s), the date, the page, or, for unpaginated electronic sources, the paragraph number.

- Place parenthetical references to your sources immediately after quoted or paraphrased material.

    When you are paraphrasing an idea, provide the author's last name, the year of publication, and the page or paragraph number.

    A recent study (Wu, 2002) suggests that although depression and substance abuse are associated, "it is not necessarily the depression that comes first" (p. 198).

- However, many instructors prefer that the author's name and the publication date be included in the sentence introducing the reference, which is then followed by the page number. Setting up your paraphrase this way clearly distinguishes your ideas from those of your sources and protects you from any charges of unintentional plagiarism.

In another study, Wu (2002) reports that although depression and substance abuse are associated, it is not necessarily the depression that comes first (p. 198).

- When quoting, you may either divide up the citation information or put it all immediately after the quotation.

Bauerlein (2008) explains, "The Dumbest Generation cares little for history books, civic principles, foreign affairs, comparative religions, and serious media and art, and it knows less" (p. 234).

"The Dumbest Generation cares little for history books, civic principles, foreign affairs, comparative religions, and serious media and art, and it knows less" (Bauerlein, 2008, p. 234).

If your source has no pagination, such as an html document or a website, you can cite by paragraph, using the abbreviation *para.* (Please note that in previous editions of APA style, the paragraph symbol [¶] was used.)

According to A. Cross (2010), "Canadian researchers say they've learned some bottled water in Canada contains more bacteria than what comes out of the tap—although they won't reveal which brands are the culprits" (para. 1).

- If you cite a work that is actually discussed in another work, first name the author of the original work in the text; then cite the source you consulted and give the date for that source.

Fraser's study (as cited in Johnston, 2009, p. 198) . . .

- If you have named the author of a work in the narrative and you repeat the same source in the same paragraph, and it is clear that you are doing so, you can give the author's name in the text without adding the year: see the second sentence of the example below. (In a parenthetical citation, you must include the year.)

James Hoggan (2009) traces the theory of the greenhouse effect from its first mention in 1824 to the late 1960s, when American oceanographer Roger Revelle explained it to Al Gore at Harvard (p. 138). Hoggan goes on to describe the growing concern among scientists.

- If you refer to more than one work written in the same year by the same person, use the year of publication and a lowercase letter that identifies the order of the work in the references.

Gibaldi (2009b)

- If the work has two authors, cite both names every time you refer to the work.

Gibaldi and Davis (2008)

If the work has three to five authors, cite all the authors in your **first** in-text citation; in subsequent references, include only the surname of the first author, followed by *et al.* and the year. (In the reference list, however, include the names of all the authors.)

Hornbrook et al. (2007)

If the work has six or more authors, in the first and subsequent citations, cite only the surname of the first author followed by *et al.* and the year.

- If the author of the work is not identified, give a short version of the title in your in-text citation.

("No Fear," p. 86).

- Spell out the name of corporate authors in every in-text citation.

(National Film Board, 1996)

- If a source has no date, use the abbreviation *n.d.* in place of the date.

(Martin, n.d., p. 89).

You can find more detailed information on parenthetical references in the most recent (6th) edition of the APA style manual; also, check to see if your library provides a summary of APA style.

Sample In-Text Citations

The following examples demonstrate various ways of integrating common materials into your APA-style paper.

Quotations

■ *Short quotations*

If a quotation is short (fewer than forty words), use regular (double) quotation marks and incorporate the quotation into the text of your paper. Put the final punctuation for the sentence *after* the parenthetical citation. This example also uses ellipses to indicate words omitted, and square brackets to indicate changes. The original passage includes a quoted portion; in the example, these words are enclosed in single quotation marks.

> A research question may be difficult or easy to answer directly; an example of a research question with a "final, definitive answer . . . [is] 'How does penicillin destroy bacteria?'" (Troyka, 2004, p. 131).

■ *Long quotations*

Use a long quotation (forty or more words) only when the original passage contains ideas or statistics that cannot be paraphrased easily. Set off the text as a block quotation and do not enclose it in quotation marks. Indent the quotation one tab from the left margin and double space it. Put the final punctuation *before* the parenthetical citation. Don't forget to introduce the quotation appropriately, as in the following example:

> F. C. Donders, a Dutch physiologist (1818–1889), invented mental chronometry, a method of measuring mental processes. Early psychologists eagerly adopted this new technique:

Precisely because it was a quantitative method, [mental chronometry] helped to ensure the scientific stature of experimental psychology as apart from somewhat questionable and highly debatable qualitative philosophical psychology. It took the mind out of the armchair and into the laboratory. (Leahey, 2000, p. 225)

■ *Quotation from a professional article*

This quotation is taken from a full-text article retrieved online. The document was saved as a pdf file, preserving the original pagination.

Lonsdale (2002) reminds us that a 1943 experiment found that "marginal thiamine deficiency produced bad behavior that would be traditionally thought of as psychological in character if it occurred spontaneously" (p. 86).

■ *Indirect quotation or citation*

When you refer to an author cited in another author's work, be careful to indicate both writers clearly. Give the page number from the source you have (in this example, Leahey's book) and list it in your references.

Ulric Neisser (as cited in Leahey, 2000) considered computer models of cognition as "simplistic" and not "satisfactory from the psychological point of view" (p. 505).

Paraphrased or Summarized Material

■ *Paraphrase or summary*

Often it is preferable to paraphrase a writer's ideas or shorten a passage. Name the author (with date) to make it clear that the paraphrased or summarized material reflects another writer's, and not your own, ideas. The examples below are, respectively, an appropriate paraphrase and a summary of quotations above.

Paraphrase

F. C. Donders (1818–1889), a Dutch physiologist, invented mental chronometry, a method of measuring mental processes. As Leahey (2000) explains, early psychologists were keen to use Donders' technique because it allowed mathematical, empirical inquiry and thus gave them the status of scientists rather than philosophers (p. 225).

Summary (shortened paraphrase)

Lonsdale (2002) explains that prior to the results of a 1943 experiment that attributed bad behaviour to a slight thiamine deficiency, sudden, unexplained bad behaviour was related to a psychological problem (p. 86).

■ *Personal communications*

In APA documentation, personal communications such as personal interviews, telephone conversations, and emails are cited in text and not included in the reference list. To cite personal communications, provide the initials and surname of the communicator, followed by "personal communication" and the date of the communication.

B. Donahue (personal communication, May 24, 2010)

C3 REFERENCE LIST

At the end of your paper, on a separate sheet entitled "References," present a list of all the works you have cited. There should be a direct match between the sources used in your paper and those cited at the end.

You need to use and check your sources carefully so you can avoid the two situations that might constitute careless documentation and even result in unintentional plagiarism. First, if there are more in-text citations than there are entries in the reference list, you need to add the extra citations in the paper's body to your reference list. Second, if the entries in the reference list do not match the parenthetical citations in the paper's body, you need to reread the paper carefully, making sure you have not forgotten to document any paraphrases or quotations.

This reference list, then, is very important, for it gives you credibility, protects you against plagiarism, and allows your readers to find and explore your sources.

- Place the reference list at the end of the paper, in the same document, and numbered sequentially.

- Centre the word "References" in plain, regular font (the same font and size used in your essay).

- Consistently double space the entire reference list; that is, double space within the entry and between entries. The first line of each entry should start at the left-hand margin. Use the hanging indent function on your computer to indent subsequent lines by 1.25 cm (1/2 inch). Do not number bibliographical entries.

- List the entries alphabetically according to the last name of the principal author (the one that appears first on the title page). Alphabetize government and corporate publications by the name of the government department, institution, or business where they originated, such as Statistics Canada, Royal Ontario Museum, or BC Hydro. For publications in which no author is named, such as unsigned newspaper pieces and encyclopedia entries, alphabetize by title, disregarding *A, An,* and *The.*

- Make sure every reference is in a form your readers can find. For instance, if you have cited an essay in an edited collection by its author, the references entry should appear under the name of the author of the essay, not under the name of the editor.

- Font style: Use plain font for the titles of sources not published separately and italics for the titles of books, periodicals, and other separately published works.

- Capitalization: Capitalize the first letter of every important word in periodical titles. Italicize periodical titles. For other titles, such as those of books, articles, or webpages, capitalize only the first word of the title and of the subtitle (the word following the colon) and proper nouns.

- Quotation marks: Do not put quotation marks around the titles of articles.

- When referencing a webpage, provide the full URL. However, if the webpage is within a site and can easily be found from the home page, provide the home page URL only.
- Because URLs can change over time, APA prefers the use of the DOI System. According to the APA style website, "A digital object identifier (DOI) is a unique alphanumeric string assigned by a registration agency (the International DOI Foundation) to identify content and provide a persistent link to its location on the Internet. The publisher assigns a DOI when your article is published and made available electronically." This site further explains that all "DOI numbers begin with a *10* and contain a prefix and a suffix separated by a slash." If an online article or book is assigned a DOI, you must also provide it in your reference. Usually, only scholarly journal articles and some online books include a DOI, which is the last piece of information you need to cite in an entry.

Sample Reference Entries

Print Sources

■ *Print article*

Do not use *p.* or *pp.* for page numbers of journal or magazine articles, but do use them for newspaper articles. Include the issue number only when each issue of the volume starts at page 1.

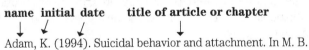

name   initial   date   title of article

Baumeister, R.   (1990).   Suicide as an escape from the self.

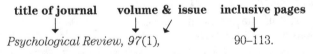

title of journal   volume & issue   inclusive pages

Psychological Review, 97(1),   90–113.

■ *Book with a single author*

name initial date   title   place of publication   publisher

Katz, J. (1991). *Seductions of crime.* New York, NY: Basic Books.

■ *Article or chapter in an edited book*

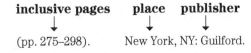

name initial date   title of article or chapter

Adam, K. (1994). Suicidal behavior and attachment. In M. B.

editor(s)   title of book

Sperling & W. H. Berman (Eds.), *Attachment in adults*

inclusive pages   place   publisher

(pp. 275–298).   New York, NY: Guilford.

■ Government documents and reports

The basic elements are similar to other APA reference entries. If a government catalogue, report, or publication number is given, put it in parentheses after the title. Always cite a government department from the most general to the most specific (department>agency>division>committee>subcommittee).

Individual Writer Given

Day, D. M. (1995). *School-based violence prevention in Canada: Results of a national survey of policies and programs* (Catalogue No. JS4-1/1994-2E). Ottawa: Solicitor General Canada, Ministry Secretariat.

Department as Author and Publisher

Statistics Canada, Environment Accounts and Statistics Division, System of National Accounts. (2002). *Human activity and the environment, annual statistics.* Ottawa: Author.

■ Subsequent work by the same author

If you have used more than one source by the same author, arrange the works by year of publication, starting with the earliest. Arrange two or more works by the same author in the same year alphabetically by the title (disregard *A, An,* or *The*). Add lowercase letters beside the year, within the parentheses.

Bowlby, J. (1977). The making and breaking of affectional bonds. *British Journal of Psychiatry, 130*, 201–210.

Bowlby, J. (1980). Attachment and loss. *Loss, sadness, and depression* (Vol. 3). New York, NY: Basic Books.

Freud, S. (1963a). *An autobiographical study* (J. Strachey, Trans.). New York, NY: Norton. (Original work published 1925)

Freud, S. (1963b). *A general introduction to psycho-analysis* (J. Riviere, Trans.). New York, NY: Simon & Schuster. (Original work published 1920)

■ Book with two authors

Provide last names followed by initials for all authors, in the exact order they appear in the publication. Use a comma and an ampersand to join the last two authors in the entry.

Wharf, B., & McKenzie, B. (1998). *Connecting policy to practice in the human services.* Toronto, ON: Oxford.

■ Reference books

If no author is given, begin with the title of the entry.

Dinosaurs. (1993). *Collier's Encyclopedia.* New York, NY: Collier.

Electronic Sources

■ *Journal article with DOI (one author)*

In your reference, provide the following information, in this order: author, date, article title, journal title, volume, issue number, pages, and DOI.

> Slater, W. (2008). Defining adult literacy: The pitfalls and the challenges. *Public Advocacy Journal, 14*(5), 167–178. doi:10.297/0004-9852.43.2.997

■ *Journal article without DOI (two to seven authors)*

In your reference, provide the following information, in this order: author, date, article title, journal title, volume, issue number, and pages. The next piece of information should be the home page of the journal (not the database name, even if you retrieved the article from a database), preceded by "Retrieved from." When a work has two to five authors, cite all of the authors' names in the reference entry.

> Amber, J., & Grant, W. (2008). Cyberbullying: The new swarming. *Parenting, 15*(3), 74–85. Retrieved from http://jop.org

■ *Journal article without DOI (eight or more authors)*

When a work has eight or more authors, list only the first six, followed by ellipsis points and then the last author's name, in the reference entry.

> Jones, A., Ryerson, B., Alma, C., Smithers, Y., Simpson, H., George, H., . . . Miller, D. (2006). Peer review: Fun or torture? *Writing across the Curriculum, 31*(13), 451–65. Retrieved from http://wac.colostate.edu/journal

■ *Daily newspaper article, electronic version*

> Waters, M. (2007, August 6). Doting doggie parents converge on Calgary. *Calgary Herald.* Retrieved from http://www.canada.com/calgaryherald

■ *Document created by a private organization*

> MADD Canada. (2003, April 23). *Checklist shows little done to fight impaired driving.* Retrieved from http://madd.ca/news

■ *Section in an Internet document*

> Statistics Canada. (2006, July 6). Overview of Canadians' eating habits. *The Daily.* Retrieved from http://www.statcan.ca/Daily/English/060706/d060706b.htm

Other Sources

■ *Audiovisual media*

Audiovisual media include films, television or audio broadcasts (including podcasts), maps, works of art, and photographs. Name the originator or primary contributors as the authors, and give their titles in parentheses; follow with the title of the work, the medium of publication in square brackets, the location, and the studio or record label, etc., as the publisher.

originator   and/or primary contributors

$\downarrow$ $\downarrow$

Kilbourne, J. (Writer), & Lazarus, M. (Producer/Director).

medium

$\downarrow$

(1987). *Still killing us softly: Advertising's image of women* [DVD]. Cambridge, MA: Cambridge Documentary Films.

See the current APA *Publications Manual* for sample citations of other types of audiovisual media.

Glossary of Grammatical Terms

Adjective
A word modifying a noun or a pronoun. An adjective can express quality (*red* balloon, *large* house, *young* child) or quantity (*one* apple, *many* peaches, *few* pears). Other words, phrases, and clauses can also function as adjectives, including present and past participles (*skating* party, *torn* shirt), phrases (Memphis is the dog *in the red coat*), and subordinate clauses (the woman *who is chairing the meeting*).

Adjectives change form to show degrees of comparison—positive, comparative, superlative (*dirty, dirtier, dirtiest*).

Adverb
A word that modifies or describes a verb (run *quickly*), an adjective (*extremely* heavy), or another adverb (eat *very* slowly). Adverbs usually answer the questions *how, when, where*, or *why*. (They whispered *quietly*. How did they whisper?)

Phrases (He walked *into a room*. Where did he walk?) and clauses (He couldn't speak *because he was angry*. Why couldn't he speak?) can also function as adverbs.

Adverbs also change form to show degrees of comparison—positive, comparative, superlative (*quickly, more quickly, most quickly*).

Antecedent
The noun to which a pronoun refers. It usually, but not always, precedes the pronoun.

The **dancers** [antecedent] are rehearsing **their** [pronoun] routine.

Appositive
An explanatory word or phrase that follows a noun or pronoun, further describing it.

Martha, **my closest friend,** is visiting from Halifax.

Auxiliary Verb
A verb that helps to form the tense or voice of another verb (*have been* practising, *should have* phoned, *was* consulted).

Case
The form of a noun or pronoun that shows its relationship to other words in a sentence.

Possessive case [nouns and indefinite pronouns]: **Bill's** car, **nobody's** business.

Subject case [personal pronouns]: **She** and I left early.

Object case [personal pronouns]: Give the message to **him** or **me**.

Clause

A group of words containing a subject and a verb. **Main clauses**, also called **independent clauses**, can stand on their own as grammatically complete sentences.

He didn't finish dinner.

Subordinate clauses, sometimes called **dependent clauses**, often begin with subordinating conjunctions such as *because, although, while, since, as, when*. These function as adverbs, answering *why, how, when*, or *where*.

Because he was in a hurry, he didn't finish dinner. (Why didn't he finish dinner?)

Other subordinate clauses begin with relative pronouns, such as *who, which*, and *that*. These subordinate clauses function as adjectives or nouns, answering who or what.

The man **who didn't finish dinner** is in a bad mood. [adjective clause] (Which man is in a bad mood?)

She wished **that the ordeal would end.** [noun clause] (What did she wish?)

Comma Splice

A sentence structure error in which main clauses have been joined by a comma alone, or by a comma and a conjunctive adverb.

The party is over, everyone has gone home.

The party is over, **therefore** everyone must go home.

Complex Sentence

A sentence containing one main clause and one or more subordinate clauses. See *Clause*.

If we can't fit everyone in the car, and if we rent a truck, we'll have to take the bus.

Compound Sentence

A sentence containing two or more main clauses. See *Clause*.

We can't fit everyone in the car, so we'll take the bus.

Compound-Complex Sentence

A sentence containing two or more main clauses and one or more subordinate clauses.

Before the storm broke, Mary put away the lawn chairs and Shistri closed the windows.

Conjunction

A word or phrase that joins words, phrases, or clauses. See *Conjunctive Adverb, Coordinating Conjunction, Correlative (Paired) Conjunctions*, and *Subordinating Conjunction*.

Conjunctive Adverb

An adverb used with a semicolon to join main clauses in a compound or compound-complex sentence. Some common conjunctive adverbs are *therefore, however, nevertheless, otherwise, thus, furthermore, moreover*.

I must hurry; **otherwise**, I'll be late for class.

Coordinating Conjunction

A word used to join ideas of equal importance that are expressed in the same grammatical form. The coordinating conjunctions are *and, but, or, nor, for, yet, so*.

He was down **but** not out.

The weather was good, **but** the facilities were terrible.

Coordination

The stylistic technique of using coordinating and correlative conjunctions to join ideas of equal importance. See *Coordinating Conjunction* and *Correlative (Paired) Conjunctions*.

The battery is dead **and** all four tires are flat.

Neither the fridge **nor** the stove is working.

Correlative (Paired) Conjunctions

A pair of conjunctions used to join ideas of equal importance expressed in the same grammatical form. The correlative conjunctions are *either/or, neither/nor, both/and, not only/but also*.

These apples are **not only** expensive **but also** tasteless.

These apples are **both** expensive **and** tasteless.

Dangling Modifier

A modifying phrase that is not logically connected to any other word in the sentence.

Turning green, the pedestrians crossed the street.

Driving down the highway, the moose ran in front of our car.

Definite Article

The word *the*, which specifies the noun it is describing: *the* book, *the* baby, *the* opportunity of a lifetime.

Fragment

A phrase or subordinate clause punctuated as if it were a complete sentence.

> And last but not least. [fragment caused by phrase (no subject and no verb) punctuated as a sentence]

> Although it seemed like a good idea at the time. [fragment caused by subordinate clause punctuated as a sentence]

Fused Sentence (also called *Run-on Sentence*)

An error in which two main clauses are joined without punctuation.

> It's cold today my ears are freezing.

Indefinite Article

The words *a* and *an,* which do not specify the nouns they describe: *a* book, *a* breakthrough, *an* amazing feat.

Infinitive

To + a verb: *to run, to walk, to think.* See *Split Infinitive.*

Interjection

A word or phrase thrown into a sentence to express emotion or to add style.

> **"Oh great**, we're going on a picnic!"

Some interjections can stand on their own as complete sentences.

> "Wow!" "Ouch!" "Hurray!" "D'oh!"

Misplaced Modifier

A mistake caused when a modifying word, phrase, or clause is placed in the wrong location in the sentence.

> The children saw ten squirrels **on their way home from school**.

Mixed Construction (also called an *Awkward Sentence*)

An error in which a sentence begins with one grammatical structure but switches to another. It often results from combining two sentences improperly or changing direction midway in a sentence.

> **An example of this is when** she daydreams constantly.

> The more he learns, **he doesn't seem to remember much**.

Modifier

A word, phrase, or clause changing or qualifying a noun, pronoun, or verb.

Restrictive modifiers provide essential information and are not enclosed in commas.

Teenagers **who take drugs** need help.

Nonrestrictive modifiers provide additional information and are enclosed with commas. They can be removed from the sentence.

Susan, **who has been taking drugs for several years**, needs help.

Mood
The form of the verb showing whether the speaker is stating a fact (indicative mood: He *wants* some food), giving a command or making a request (imperative mood: *Give* him some food), or suggesting a possibility or condition (subjunctive mood: If he *were* hungry, we *would give* him some food).

Noun
A word that names a person, place, thing, quality, idea, or activity. A **common noun** is not capitalized and refers to any one of a class: *woman, cat, city, school*. A **proper noun** is capitalized and refers to a particular person, animal, place, thing: *Linda, Fluffy, Guelph, Westlane Elementary School*. A **collective noun**, such as *herd, flock, family, community, band, tribe*, is considered singular when the group is acting as a unit and plural when the group members are acting as individuals.

The **band is** on an extended trip.

The **band are** unpacking their instruments.

Object
A word, phrase, or clause that receives the action of the verb or that is governed by a preposition.

Stephen lent **me** his **pen**. [*Pen* is the direct object (what is being lent) whereas *me* is the indirect object (who will eventually receive the pen).]

She has already left for **work**. [*Work* is the object of the preposition *for*.]

Parallel Structure
A construction in which ideas of equal importance are expressed in the same grammatical form.

His analysis is **precise, thorough**, and **perceptive**. [parallel adjectives]

What he says and **what he means** are completely different. [parallel clauses]

Participle
A verb form that can function as a verb or as an adjective. Present participles are formed by adding *ing* to the present tense. Past participles of regular verbs are formed by adding *ed* to the present tense.

When combined with an auxiliary verb, participles become the main verb in a verb phrase (*is laughing, has been dancing, could have finished*).

As adjectives, participles can modify nouns and pronouns (*smiling* face, *running* water, *chipped* tooth, *sworn* testimony; *frowning*, he addressed the assembly).

Parts of Speech
Types of words, such as nouns, verbs, and adverbs. See *Adjective, Adverb, Conjunction, Interjection, Noun, Preposition, Pronoun, Verb*.

Preposition
Prepositions include such words as *by, between, beside, to, of,* and *with*. A preposition, its object (usually a noun or a pronoun), and any words that describe the object make up a prepositional phrase (*toward the deserted beach*). These phrases can function as adjectives (the man *with the red beard*) or adverbs (walked *down the road*).

Pronoun
A word that substitutes for a noun.

Indefinite pronouns *everybody, everyone, everything, somebody, someone, something, nobody, no one, one, nothing, anybody, anyone, anything, either, neither, each, both, few, several, all*

Personal subject pronouns *I, we, you, he, she, it, they*

Personal object pronouns *me, us, you, him, her, it, them*

Possessive pronouns *my, mine, our, ours, your, yours, his, her, hers, its, their, theirs*

Reflexive/Intensive pronouns *myself, ourselves, yourself, yourselves, himself, herself, itself, themselves*

Relative pronouns *who, whom, which, that, what, whoever, whomever, whichever*

Pronoun Agreement
The principle of matching singular pronouns with singular nouns and pronouns, and plural pronouns with plural nouns and pronouns.

The **committee** forwarded **its** recommendations.

Everyone has made **his or her** views known to the nominating committee.

Pronoun Reference
The principle that every pronoun must clearly refer to a specific noun. See *Antecedent*.

Tom told Hussein that **he** had won the scholarship. [pronoun reference unclear]

Tom told Hussein, "**You** won the scholarship." [pronoun reference clear]

Pronoun Shift
The error of shifting abruptly and with no logical reason between personal pronouns.

> I didn't like working in the complaints department because **you** were always dealing with dissatisfied customers.

Split Infinitive
A form of misplaced modifier in which an adverb is placed between *to* and the verb.

> to **quickly** run

Subject
The word or group of words interacting with a verb to establish the basic meaning of a sentence or clause. Subjects are nouns, pronouns, or constructions acting as nouns.

> **Costs** are rising.

> **To argue with him** is a waste of time.

> **Cleaning the garage** is not my idea of a pleasant way to spend the weekend.

Subject-Verb Agreement
The principle of matching singular subjects with singular verbs and plural subjects with plural verbs.

> **He has** his work cut out for him.

> **They have** their work cut out for them.

Subordinating Conjunction
A word used to begin a subordinate clause—a clause that expresses an idea of subordinate or secondary importance. Subordinating conjunctions include words such as *although, because, before, since, while, when, if, until*. See *Clause*.

Subordination
The expression of less important ideas in subordinate clauses and phrases.

> **Although I am angry with you**, I am still willing to listen to your side of the story.

Tense
The form of the verb that shows its time (past, present, future).

Tense Shift
The error of shifting abruptly and with no obvious reason between verb tenses.

> Hamlet **was** angry when he **confronts** his mother.

Verb

A word that indicates action (*run, jump, breathe*), sensation (*feel, taste, smell*), possession (*have, own*), or existence (*are, were, seem, become*). A verb phrase consists of a main verb (a past or present participle) and one or more auxiliary verbs. For more information on verb phrases, see *Participle* and *Auxiliary Verb.* For more information on verbs, see *Tense, Mood, Verb Voice,* and *Subject-Verb Agreement.*

Verb Voice

Verb voice can be active or passive:

Active voice: A construction in which the subject performs the action of the verb.

Lightning **struck** the enormous tree. [subject + active verb + object]

Passive voice: In the passive voice, the **true subject** is receiving the action of the verb.

The enormous tree **was struck** by lightning. [object + passive verb + subject]

Index

Note: Page references in *italics* are glossary entries.

A

Checklists
    essays, 49–50, 161
    paragraphs, 35
    proofreading, 206
    purpose/audience, 8
    revision, 168
    writing process, 19–20
Circumlocutions, 175
Class definitions, 71
Classification (in expository writing)
    example, 99–101
    guidelines, 97–98
    overview, 96–97
Clauses, dependent (subordinate)
    adjective clauses, 188–189
    adverb clauses, 188, 204
    in complex sentences, 190–191, 197
    in compound-complex sentences, 191
    definition, 258, *318*
    faulty subordination, 202–203
    nonrestrictive adjective clauses, 188–189, 262
    noun clauses, 188
    punctuating element at end of sentence, 261
    punctuation of introductory clauses,
        259, 261
    restrictive adjective clauses, 188–189
Clauses, independent (main)
    comma splices, 195–196
    in complex sentences, 190–191
    in compound-complex sentences, 191
    in compound sentences, 190
    definition, 258, *318*
    description, 188
    fused sentences, 196–197
    mixed constructions, 205
    punctuation, 259, 265, 270
    in simple sentences, 190
Clichés, 169
Coherence, paragraph, 27–28, 164–165
Collective nouns
    definition, *321*
    pronoun agreement, 233
    subject-verb agreement, 218–219
Colloquial expressions, 169, 172
Colons, 269–271
Commas
    in addresses, 263
    in combining clauses, 190–191
    in conventional places, 263
    correcting sentence errors, 197
    with direct speech/quotations, 263
    items in a series and, 258–259
    nonrestrictive phrases/clauses, 189, 262
    pairs of, 258, 262
    salutations and closings, 263
    setting off elements, 259–261
    use of single, 258–261
Comma splices, 195–196, 197, *318*
Common nouns, *321*

formal writing, 169–171
informal writing, 172–173
interviewing, 64–65
letters to the editor, 123
narrative essays, 59–60
passive voice, use of, 220
punctuation with quotation marks, 275–276
reviews (brief), 121–122
thesis formulation, 37–38

H

Hanged vs. *hung*, 178
Headers, 297–298, 307–308
Hopefully, 178
Hostile audiences, 120
Hyperbole, 182
Hyphens
   in compound words, 278–279
   at end of lines, 279

I

Imagery
   adding interest with, 182
   in literary analysis, 111, 112–113, 115
   in personal narratives, 52
Indefinite articles (*a, an*), 248, *320*
Indefinite pronouns
   definition, *322*
   possessive, 267–268
   pronoun agreement, 233–234
   subject-verb agreement, 217
Independent clauses. *See* Clauses,
      independent (main)
Inductive essays, 47–49, 63–64
Inductive paragraphs, 26–27, 53, 77
Infinitive phrases, 186, 251–252
Infinitives
   split, 250, *323*
   of verbs, 214, *320*
Informal writing, 172–173, 220
Interjection, 261, *320*
Internet sources, citing, 304–305, 313, 315
Interviews
   citing, 306, 311
   in personal writing, 64–66
In-text citations, 149–150, 299–301, 308–311
Introductions
   in essays, 44–45, 47, 48, 109
   revising, 165–166
Irony, 182
Irregular verbs, 214
Italics, 277–278

J

Jargon, 170
Journalling, 11–12

K

Keyword searches, 146

L

M

N

Note taking, 147–149
Noun clauses, 188
Nouns
  capitalization, 282–283
  collective, and pronoun agreement, 233
  collective, and subject-verb agreement, 218–219
  definition, *321*
  in informal writing, 172
  plural, 267–268
  possessive, 267–268
  pronoun agreement, 231–235
Novels (summaries of), 107
Numbers
  numerals, 283–284
  written out, 278, 284
Number vs. *amount*, 178

O

Object
  active *vs.* passive constructions, 219–220
  definition, *321*
  object pronouns, 227–228, *322*
Online encyclopedias, 140–142
Online periodical indexes, 145
Opinion pieces, 124–130
Opinions (in research papers), 139
Organization
  block method, 45, 89–90, 92–93
  descriptive essays, 62
  expository essays, 81–82
  literary analysis, 109
  persuasive writing, 120–121, 131, 135
  point-by-point method, 90–91, 93–94
Outlines
  formal, 17–19
  preliminary, 16
  revising, 16–17

P

Paired conjunctions, 183, 217–218, *319*
Paragraphs
  body, 24–26
  checklist, 35
  coherence, 164–165
  conclusion, 46–47, 49, 166–167
  introductory, 44–45, 47, 48, 109, 165–166
  length/divisions, 33–34, 164
  middle, 45–47, 48
  revising, 164–165
  structure (deductive *vs.* inductive), 26–27
  topic sentences, 21–24, 164
  transitions (*see* Transition words and phrases)
  unity/coherence, 27–28, 164–165
Parallelism
  definition, *321*
  faulty, 199–200
  in paragraphs, 31–32
  principle of, 199
  in sentences, 182–183

Punctuation (*Continued*)
  hyphens, 278–279
  parentheses, 272–273
  periods, 197, 275–276
  question mark, 273
  quotation marks, 274–276
  semicolons, 190, 197, 265–266
Purpose of writing
  essays, 162
  explaining, 2, 67
  persuading, 2–3
  sharing personal experience, 1–2

Q

Questions
  discovery, 12–13, 110–111
  evaluating appeals, 132–133
  for interviews, 64–65
  for reader profiles, 5–7
  rhetorical, 183
Quotation marks
  with closing punctuation, 275–276
  for emphasis, 275
  with quoted material, 274
  with titles of short works, 275
Quotations
  adding interest with, 181
  capitalization, 283
  general guidelines, 294–296
  in-text citations, 300–301, 310–311
  punctuation of, 263, 270–271
  research papers and, 149

R

Reader profiles, 5–6
Real vs. *really*, 247
Reference, pronoun, 236–238, *322*
Reference materials, 144–145
References (for research papers). *See* APA style;
    Documentation of sources; MLA style
Reflexive pronouns, 227–228, *322*
Regular verbs, 214
Repetition
  as transitions, 30
  unnecessary, 174
Research papers
  checklist, 161
  database research techniques, 145–147
  documentation (*see* APA style; Documentation of sources;
    MLA style)
  formatting, 307–308
  forming opinions, 139
  integrating research material, 152–154
  library research sources, 144–145
  note taking/plagiarism, 147–149
  online research sources, 140–144
  paraphrasing, 149, 151
  primary/secondary sources, 139–140
  quotations, 149, 150